THE NEW NATURALIST LIBRARY

A SURVEY OF BRITISH NATURAL HISTORY

THE MARCHES

CW00819991

THE NEW NATURALIST LIBRARY

THE MARCHES

ANDREW ALLOTT

Andrew Allott

Collins

This edition published in 2011 by Collins,
an imprint of HarperCollins Publishers

HarperCollins Publishers
77–85 Fulham Palace Road
London W6 8JB
www.collins.co.uk

First published 2011

A CIP catalogue record for this book is available
from the British Library.

Set in FF Nexus

Edited and designed by
D & N Publishing
Baydon, Wiltshire

Printed in Hong Kong by Printing Express

Hardback
ISBN 978-0-00-724816-2

Paperback
ISBN 978-0-00-724817-9

Contents

Editors' Preface

In 2008 we welcomed George Peterken's volume, *Wye Valley*, as the fourth of our regional titles to deal with an area of outstanding natural beauty and one of the best-known landscapes in lowland Britain. The volume covered that part of the English–Welsh borderlands from Hereford southwards to the junction of the Wye and the Severn at Chepstow. It is with great pleasure that we now introduce Andrew Allott's volume that extends the story of the English–Welsh borderlands northwards from Hereford to cover that part of England that borders on Wales, known historically as the Marches.

The author has chosen to define the western boundary of his area by Offa's Dyke, possibly the most famous earthwork in Britain. The area is one of astonishing geological and topographic diversity with a long history of geological research, starting with James Hutton's seminal visit in the 18th century. In particular it is famous for the richness of its fossil deposits, including the first record of the earliest type of trilobite in the British Isles. It is, therefore, a happy coincidence that fossils are one of Andrew's particular interests and readers will find a separate chapter on the fossils of the area, the first of its kind in a New Naturalist volume. The ice ages have also left their imprint on the landscape of the Marches, especially in the mires and meres that have long attracted the attention of naturalists, whilst throughout the length of the Marches England's longest river, the Severn, flows as a continuous co-ordinating theme.

Andrew Allott is especially well qualified to author this particular volume. Although a relative newcomer to the Marches he has developed a detailed knowledge and appreciation of its landscape and natural history as Head of Biology at Shrewsbury School. After graduating in Botany at Oxford, he embarked upon a career as a schoolmaster, whilst at the same time widening his interests in natural history and geology and his involvement in conservation. As well as his first interest in plants, he is now prepared to confess to a particular interest in spiders! Charles Darwin attended Shrewsbury as a boarder from 1817 to 1825, and as Andrew Allott has written in his biographical note on the most famous Old Salopian, the landscape and natural history of the Marches must have been hugely influential in the development of his interests, certainly more so than the Latin verses that the then classical education demanded and which he found so irksome. It is singularly appropriate that the school that spawned the young Darwin has now produced the definitive account of the countryside that inspired him.

Author's Foreword and Acknowledgements

This addition to the New Naturalist series was originally intended by the author to appear in 2009, as a contribution to the celebration of two anniversaries: 200 years since Charles Darwin's birth in Shrewsbury and 150 years since the publication of the Origin of Species. Perhaps appropriately, given the long gestation period of Darwin's great work, these anniversaries passed before the book was completed. Nonetheless, Darwin's birth and boyhood in the Marches will be of continuing interest.

Born in 1809, Darwin was a pupil at Shrewsbury School from 1817 to 1825. In his spare time he was allowed to roam freely in the countryside, where he collected insects and other specimens. Inspired by Gilbert White's account of the natural history of Selborne, Darwin observed the habits of birds, wondering why every gentleman did not become an ornithologist. In his brief autobiographical notes he wrote that: 'In 1822 a vivid delight in scenery was first awakened in my mind, during a riding tour on the borders of Wales, and this has lasted longer than any other aesthetic pleasure.' Darwin became interested in the rocks of the area, including erratic boulders and their possible origin. If it is true that the boy is father of the man, then the landscape and natural history of the Marches must have been hugely influential in the development of his interests and approach to science. One phrase written in his diary at the end of his voyage aboard the Beagle is especially appropriate to this book: 'As a number of isolated facts soon becomes uninteresting, the habit of comparison leads to generalisation.' The Marches is a region where comparison is almost unavoidable, because of the many transitions: between upland and lowland Britain, between hard Palaeozoic rocks and softer Mesozoic ones, between areas covered by ice during the last glaciation and those that were not and between parts that have been transformed by human activity and others that have remained almost pristine.

The author's aim has been to explore themes, rather than to catalogue isolated or inconsequential facts. Each chapter takes one theme and considers its relevance across much or all of the Marches. The hope is that the Marches will be seen as somewhere and everywhere, rather than just as somewhere.

The writing of this book has been a collaborative venture and many individuals have been extremely generous with their help. It should immediately be added that any mistakes are the sole responsibility of the author. I am most grateful to my wife Alison and son William for supporting me throughout, and to my mother Edrey for her unwavering encouragement. I am indebted to my former colleague Joe Williams for scrutinising the whole text and for suggesting many improvements. I also wish to pay tribute to the many naturalists, both amateur and professional, who have shared their knowledge of the area with me: Bill Allmark, Norman Allott, John Arnfield, Chris Bainger, Simon Barker, Danny Beath, Amanda Bevan, Sarah Bierley, John Bingham, Mick Blythe, Pete Boardman, John Box, Chris Bradley, Jenny Britnell, Paul Bromley, Shaun Burkey, Richard Callow, Malcolm Calvert, Peter Cann, Peter Carty, Ian Cheeseborough, Stewart Clarke, Jonathan Clatworthy, Tim Coleshaw, Joan Daniels, Paul Day, Iain Diack, Richard Dibble, Tim Dixon, Ian Dormer, Mark Duffell, Dianne Edwards, Sian Edwards, Matthew Ellis, Brian Formstone, Sarah Gaskell, Martin Godfrey, Fiona Gomersall, Harry Green, Jean Green, Joan Green, Francesca Griffiths, Bill Hankers, Victoria Harley, John Hawkins, Brian Hickes, Ian Hickman, Alistair Hotchkiss, Rob Ireson, Andrew Jenkinson, Nigel Jones, William Jones, Jenny Joy, Mike Kelly, Peter Lambert, Julian Langford, Mark Lawley, James Lawson, Robert Lee, Stephen Lewis, Geoff Locke, Daniel Lockett, Alex Lockton, John Mackintosh, Robin Mager, Jane Mainwaring, Jacqui Malpas, Peta Marshall, Carmen Mayo, Jan McKelvey, Dennis Moir, Malcolm Monie, Richard Morgan, Brian Moss, Jason Orme, Ben Osborne, Robert Owens, David Pannett, George Pearce, George Peterken, Donald Piggott, Cath Price, Alan Reid, Joy Rickets, Raymond Roberts, Michael Rosenbaum, Russell Rowley, Phil Rudlin, Janet Simkin, David Siviter, Derek Siviter, David Smith, Edward Tate, Geoffrey Thomas, John Thompson, Peter Thompson, Stephanie Thomson, Kate Thorne, Catherine Tobin, Peter Toghill, Hugh Torrens, Sue Townsend, Jackie Tweddle, Mark Twells, Caroline Uff, John Voysey, Chris Walker, Tom Wall, Penny Ward, Sarah Warrener, Brett Westwood, Anne Wheeler, Sarah Whild, Robert Williams, Rosemary Winnall, Mike Worsfield, Dan Wrench and Colin Wright.

CHAPTER 1

Borderlands

THE WELSH MARCHES ARE THE PARTS of England that border on to Wales. To the south of Hereford, the name Welsh Marches is not now much used but to the north it is still, though almost always abbreviated to the Marches. This book will describe the natural history of such areas to the north of Hereford and for brevity these areas will be referred to as the Marches or simply as 'here'.

Marches are borderlands. They are tracts of country near an inland frontier and so usually have a turbulent history of territorial claim and counterclaim. For the last few hundred years the Welsh Marches have been a quiet and peaceful region but conflict and strife had been common in earlier times. Earthwork dykes consisting of a ditch and an embankment were constructed at various times and in various positions to help in the demarcation and defence of boundaries. Before and immediately after Roman rule the conflicts were between the Celtic tribes that inhabited Britain. Wat's Dyke, which stretches from the Dee estuary near Flint to a tributary of the Vyrnwy south of Oswestry, was built between AD 410–560 to mark the boundary between two Celtic tribes.[1] The Celts typically lived in small farmsteads and constructed hill forts to control and protect territory or livestock. Almost every hilltop in the Marches has the remains of fortifications, constructed between 800 and 400 BC (Fig. 1). Indeed, the concentration of these so-called Iron Age hill forts in south Shropshire and north Herefordshire is the highest in Britain. When Roman military power reached the Marches in AD 52, the hill forts were abandoned or over-run, but the pattern of settlement in much of the Marches, especially the hill country, continues to be based on isolated farmsteads, often with a country road passing directly through.[2]

During the 7th century there was a large migration of Anglo Saxons westwards into the Marches. They spoke a different language and brought very different cultural traditions. It is not certain to what extent the Celtic inhabitants were displaced but this was no more than partial if it occurred at all. Walton and Walcot are common place names here, derived from *walh*, a derogatory Anglo-Saxon term for Celts.[3] The Anglo Saxons, conquerors or immigrants, established nucleated hamlets, which subsequently grew into villages and these therefore have Anglo Saxon rather than Celtic placenames. However, their main settlements such as Shrewsbury and Much Wenlock had both English and Welsh names and up to the 18th century Welsh was widely spoken as far east as Shrewsbury and Bewdley, suggesting Celtic rather than Anglo-Saxon ancestry for much of the population. Celtic resistance certainly limited Anglo-Saxon advances into the

FIG 1. Caer Caradoc hill fort, near Clun. (Clwyd Powys Archaeological Trust)

hill country in the west but there was also a trend for Celtic recolonisation eastwards into the lowlands. This had happened when Offa became King of Mercia in AD 757. Offa reconquered territory in the early years of his reign. In around AD 893 Bishop Asser wrote:

> 'There was in Mercia in fairly recent times a certain vigorous king called Offa, who terrified all the neighbouring kings and provinces around him, and who had a great dyke built between Wales and Mercia from sea to sea.' (Fig. 2)

In the second half of the 9th century Mercian dominance over other Anglo-Saxon kingdoms weakened and Danish raids increased, but apart from areas between Chester and the Irish Sea there is little evidence for Danish invasion and settlement in the Marches. Instead, the conflicts between Celtic kingdoms and Anglo Saxons continued into the 11th century.

In 1066 the Norman conquest of England brought few new inhabitants to the Marches, but led to the establishment of marcher lordships, not only in what later became the English counties of Herefordshire, Shropshire and Cheshire, but also parts of central Wales, which was then considered to be part of the March. The marcher lordships were given special privileges that amounted to partial independence, in return for their insulating the rest of England from attacks. Interestingly, place-name evidence suggests a spread of Welsh speakers to the east of Offa's Dyke after 1066.[4] Between 1272 and 1284, King Edward I conquered the

FIG 2. Offa's Dyke, looking south from Spoad Hill, near Clun. (Robin Jukes-Hughes)

last of the Welsh principalities and gained control over the whole of Wales. The power of the marcher lordships diminished from then onwards, as their role in defending against Welsh princes had largely ended.

In 1485 Henry Tudor, who came from an Anglesey family that claimed ancestry from princes of Gwynedd, won the battle of Bosworth, ending the Wars of the

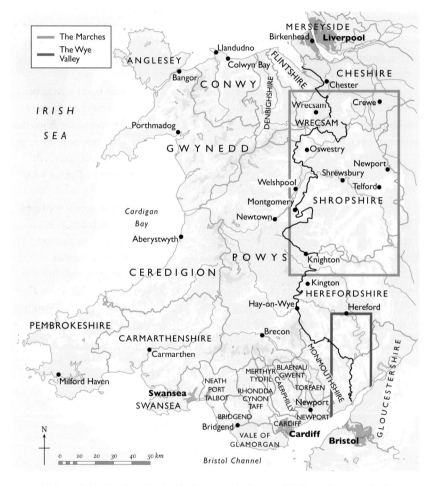

FIG 3. Wales and the Marches. The border between England and Wales is shown in black and modern county boundaries in red. The part of the southern Welsh Marches described by George Peterken in *New Naturalist Wye Valley* is indicated by the blue rectangle. The part of the central and northern Welsh Marches described in this volume is shown approximately by the orange rectangle. The boundaries of the area are described more precisely later in the chapter.

Roses and placing Henry on the English throne. In 1536 the Act of Union created one kingdom out of England and Wales and the administration throughout became organised following the English pattern of counties. The marcher lordships were made part of English or Welsh counties in a way that now seems rather arbitrary and peremptory, with petty political expediency the driving force, rather than any obligation to establish a rational national boundary, based on language or culture. The result is an English–Welsh boundary that makes far less sense in terms of population, topography and natural history than Offa's Dyke. The assignment of districts to England or Wales was probably not expected to be very significant as all counties were now part of one kingdom[5] (Fig. 3).

The problem in fixing a Welsh–English border is of course that there is no abrupt boundary between English and Welsh populations and culture: there is instead a gradual transition or merging. In a way that those who live far from the border do not always appreciate, both English and Welsh contributions to life in the Marches are appreciated. As a mark of this, both 'God Save the Queen' and 'Mae hen wlad fy'n nhadau' are sung during closing ceremonies of a great local event, the Shrewsbury Flower Show.

The historical events that have been briefly mentioned here were not played out on a featureless field: they happened within the context of a landscape. To a large extent, this region became a political borderland because of its natural features, with landscape and history interrelated in a highly complex way. Landscape and natural history are also intertwined and the purpose of this book is to disentangle, as far as possible, the natural history of the Marches. The themes that we shall return to repeatedly are transitions and edges. The Marches were on the edge of the area covered by ice sheets in the last glaciation. There are many transitions from upland to lowland Britain in the characteristics of rock, soil, geomorphology, climate and ecology. This results in there being many edges in the distributions of species of plant and animal. These edges, it should be stressed, are rarely fixed like the Welsh–English border, but can shift endlessly in response to environmental changes.

DEFINING THE MARCHES

To establish the scope of this book, a judgement has to be made about the extent of the Marches. The Welsh–English border, as established by the Tudors, starts at the confluence of the Wye and the Severn in the south and winds its way to the mouth of the Dee in the north. Marcher country can be taken to extend up to 50 km eastwards, but a strip of this width up the whole Welsh–English border would be too large and heterogeneous for description in a single 'New Naturalist'. George Peterken has already described the southern parts in his 'New Naturalist', *Wye Valley*.[6] This book will therefore describe an area to the north of the Wye

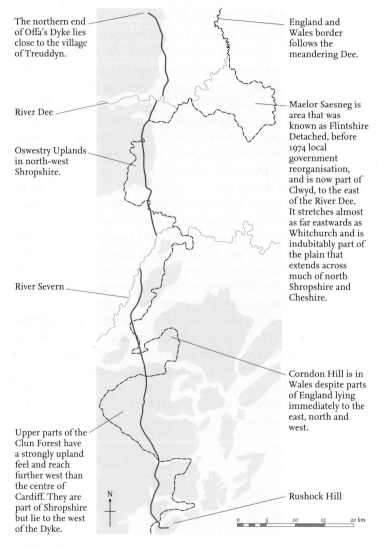

The northern end of Offa's Dyke lies close to the village of Treuddyn.

England and Wales border follows the meandering Dee.

River Dee

Oswestry Uplands in north-west Shropshire.

Maelor Saesneg is area that was known as Flintshire Detached, before 1974 local government reorganisation, and is now part of Clwyd, to the east of the River Dee. It stretches almost as far eastwards as Whitchurch and is indubitably part of the plain that extends across much of north Shropshire and Cheshire.

River Severn

Corndon Hill is in Wales despite parts of England lying immediately to the east, north and west.

Upper parts of the Clun Forest have a strongly upland feel and reach further west than the centre of Cardiff. They are part of Shropshire but lie to the west of the Dyke.

Rushock Hill

N

0   5   10   15   20 km

FIG 4. Offa's Dyke (shown as a red line) was constructed in the 8th century and follows a much more natural line than the English–Welsh border established in the 16th century (dashed black line).

Valley. The Welsh–English border zigzags east and west, mostly ignoring natural features, so anomalous areas would be excluded or included if it were used to define the western limit of the area (Fig. 4).

Though obsolete as a political boundary, Offa's Dyke makes a much more convincing natural one and it will therefore be used to establish the western limit of the Marches in this book. Despite Bishop Asser's assertion, archaeological evidence suggests that Offa's Dyke did not reach either the Irish Sea in the north or Bristol Channel in the south. This fits with its original role in defining the boundary between Mercia and Powys, rather than between the whole of England and Wales. Ignoring a 16-km section of dyke in the lower Wye Valley and three fragments on the Herefordshire plain totalling 5.5 km that are sometimes included but probably have different origins, Offa's Dyke starts in the south on Rushock Hill, north of Kington[7]. There are views from here across the Herefordshire Plain to the Wye above Hereford. The start of Offa's Dyke will therefore be taken as the southern limit of the Marches. The Dyke extends northwards for about 100 km, with minor diversions to the east or west that allow natural boundaries to be followed, often the west-facing sides of hills. The northern end of Offa's Dyke is at Treuddyn, near Mold. Further north the influence of the sea starts to be felt, adding elements to the natural history for which there is not space in this book, so the end of the Dyke at Treuddyn will be taken as the northern limit of the Marches here. To complete a strip about 50 km wide, a line that broadly follows the eastern boundaries of the marcher counties of Cheshire and north Shropshire will be used and then the Severn from Bridgnorth southwards. The overall area can be defined as *the borderlands to the east of Offa's Dyke*. There is a clear rationale for the extent of this area but it does not conform to any administrative districts and includes parts of the English counties of Herefordshire, Worcestershire, Shropshire, Cheshire, and the Welsh counties of Clwyd and Powys. Most, but not all of the Shropshire Hills Area of Outstanding Natural Beauty, or AONB, is included.

A TOPOGRAPHIC INTRODUCTION

The Marches as defined earlier lie almost entirely to the northwest of the Tees–Exe Line, so according to this division they are part of upland Britain. The surface rocks are therefore expected to be Palaeozoic – older than Triassic. In fact there are also large areas of younger Mesozoic rocks. The border between the rocks of these two eras is just as tortuous as the Welsh-English border and paradoxically, the Palaeozoic are mostly to the south and the Mesozoic to the north. We do not

Legend:
- Lugg Valley
- Northwest Herefordshire Uplands and Clun Forest
- Vale of Montgomery
- Shropshire and Montgomeryshire Hills
- Oswestry and Wrecsam Uplands
- North Shropshire and Cheshire Plain
- Severn Valley
- Teme Valley

FIG 5. This map of the Marches shows the areas that are described in the topographical introduction and names of settlements that are used throughout the book to provide locations.

therefore find simple north–south transitional belts – the geology and therefore the topography is much more complex. Overall we can divide the area very roughly in two: the southern part with older harder rocks, which mostly form hill country, and the northern part with younger, softer rocks that have mostly eroded to leave a low-lying plain. The Marches were also on the borders during the last glaciation, with ice sheets from the north and west reaching the area but not spreading beyond. These acted like a huge conveyer belt, with the Marches at its end, depositing immense quantities of debris over thousands of years. These materials have had major effects on landscape and ecology, particularly in the lower lying northern areas. We can again make a broad north–south division, but this is of course a huge oversimplification and these two parts each contain distinctively different areas. Many readers will know this area well. For those that are less familiar, a brief description will now be given, starting and ending in north Herefordshire and following a clockwise itinerary (Fig. 5).

Lugg Valley

Our tour begins north of Leominster, at the margins of the area described by George Peterken in his 'New Naturalist' on the Wye Valley. There are two broad valleys between Leominster and the uplands to the northwest. One runs almost exactly northwards towards Ludlow and contains only small streams. It is the former valley of the Teme, diverted during the last ice age. The other, which runs northwestwards, contains the middle reaches of the Lugg, which meanders its way down the valley, fringed by alder woods in many places (Fig. 6). This is farming country, with rich alluvial soils and gentle gradients. Just before the

FIG 6. Lugg Valley below Mortimer's Cross, with meandering river, pollarded willows and alder woodland.

uplands are reached there is a belt of hummocky moraines and kettle holes left
by the Welsh ice sheet, stretching from Staunton on Arrow to Orleton.

Northwest Herefordshire uplands and Clun Forest

This is the area to the east of the southernmost part of Offa's Dyke. A small part
lies in Radnorshire, but most of it is in Herefordshire and Shropshire. Like the
Yorkshire Dales, it consists of a series of river valleys, separated by higher ground.
To the west of Offa's Dyke the river valleys stretch further up into the hills, which
rise higher and higher, eventually reaching the upper parts of the Clun Forest
and the Radnor Forest. These extensive upland areas are beyond the scope of
this book. The principal rivers, from the south to the north, are the Arrow, Lugg,
Teme and furthest north, the Clun with its tributaries, the rivers Redlake and Unk
(Fig. 7). The narrow, steep-sided valleys through which they flow are unspoilt and
beautiful. The hills rising up between the valleys are rounded, with many of the
tops covered with conifer plantations. The soils are moderately fertile and even
to the hilltops the land is enclosed by fences or other field boundaries. Grassland
prevails but there is some arable farming even on the higher ground. Both the
Kerry Hill and Clun Forest breeds of sheep were developed in this area. This is
quiet country, where the transition from lowland to upland is at its most gradual.
Maybe not the greatest of verses, A. E. Housman's description of villages in the
Clun valley is still memorable:[8]

FIG 7. River Redlake valley, a tributary of the Teme, looking northwest from Bucknell, with
coniferised hilltops. (Shropshire Council)

Clunton and Clunbury,
Clungunford and Clun,
Are the quietest places,
Under the sun.

A hundred years after Housman wrote this, a survey carried out by the Council for the Protection of Rural England in the 1990s found the Marches to be one of the three most tranquil areas in England, if not under the sun. An ancient drovers' road, the Kerry Ridgeway, begins in the small town of Bishop's Castle and runs along the northernmost ridge, offering fine views to the Vale of Montgomery with the Shropshire and Montgomeryshire hills beyond.

Vale of Montgomery

To the north of the Kerry Ridgeway is an area of low-lying country. On the east side there is a broad and remarkably flat-bottomed valley, through which the River Camlad flows. West of this is the gently undulating agricultural land of the Vale of Montgomery, with hills rising to more than 300 m encircling it (Fig. 8). Offa's Dyke crosses the western side of the vale, with the small and very quiet town of Montgomery on rising ground to the west of the Dyke. Marrington Dingle is a dramatically deep and wooded valley on the eastern edge of the Vale, through which the middle section of the River Camlad flows, before flowing across the north of the vale to reach its confluence with the Severn. The Vale of Montgomery is listed on the Register of Landscapes of Outstanding Historic Interest in Wales.

FIG 8. Vale of Montgomery: a typical view of a former glacial lake, now a historic farm landscape, with hills beyond.

Shropshire and Montgomeryshire Hills

This is a large area containing the best-known hills of the Marches, with great diversity both in terms of landscape and natural history. Separating the hills are dales, again each with its own character. The Clee Hills are at the southeastern extreme of this area, between Ludlow and Bridgnorth. Two prominent hills rise above a wide undulating plateau. Brown Clee, to the north, is the highest hill south of the Pennines in England, apart from parts of the Black Mountains in Herefordshire and the northeast part of Dartmoor. Titterstone Clee to the south has particularly fine views across Worcestershire and Herefordshire. The Clee Hills have wild and rather sombre summits, scarred in places by industry. Corvedale, which is broad and agricultural, lies to the northwest. Beyond it are two parallel scarps with Hopedale between them. Much Wenlock lies at the northeastern end of Hopedale. The first of the two scarps is the higher, but the second, more northwesterly one is better known. This is Wenlock Edge, which runs in an unbroken line for 30 km between Ironbridge Gorge and Craven Arms. Its scarp faces Apedale to the northwest and is continuously wooded, so is a prominent feature over a wide area.

Moving northwestward again, we reach some of the best known and most frequently walked hills in the Marches: Caer Caradoc, the Lawley, Helmeth, Hazler and Ragleth hills are collectively known as the Stretton Hills (Fig. 9). Further to the northeast, but part of the same formation, are the Wrekin and the

FIG 9. From left to right: the Stretton valley, Caer Caradoc, Helmeth Hill with woods and in the far distance the Wrekin. (Gareth Thomas).

FIG 10. Corndon Hill formed by volcanic intrusion, with block fields and scree on its eastern flanks. (Andrew Jenkinson)

Ercall. All of these hills are steep sided, with shapes that are often described as whalebacks. Nowhere in the Marches are there large natural crags, but these hills have some moderately sized rocky outcrops.

The Stretton valley, to the northwest of the Stretton Hills, has a broad but far from flat bottom. On its northwest side is the Long Mynd, the largest but not the highest hill in the Marches. It has an extensive summit plateau that has been managed as a grouse moor in the past. Deep valleys incise the plateau on the eastern side, whereas much of the west side is an unbroken escarpment that follows the line of a geological fault. Much of the Long Mynd is common land, owned by the National Trust, and it has been the site of considerable efforts, to some extent experimental, to reduce the intensity of grazing. To the northwest again is the Stiperstones, a National Nature Reserve and another former grouse moor. It has distinctive rocky tors along its ridge and other features that are periglacial in origin. The Stiperstones is just part of an area of hills that extends westwards to the Vale of Montgomery. These hills contain veins of metalliferous ores, which have been worked from Roman times onwards. Corndon Hill lies within this area but its shape, which from some directions appears elegantly conical, is distinctively different from the surrounding uplands (Fig. 10). This is still not a good enough reason for the diversions of the Welsh–English border that were needed to place Corndon Hill in Montgomeryshire!

To the north of the Stiperstones and its fellows is the broad Marton valley, stretching from Chirbury to Pontesbury, and beyond this is the Long Mountain. It is the gentlest of mountains, with a broad and level summit ridge that stretches for 5 km. The English–Welsh border zigzags in its usual haphazard fashion across the eastern side of the Long Mountain, with Offa's Dyke running along the western face. The part of the Severn that is to the west of the Long Mountain and beyond it the town of Welshpool and the Powis Castle estate are therefore just outside the scope of this book. To the north of the Long Mountain is another broad valley, containing the villages of Middletown and Trewern. Beyond it are the Breidden Hills, the final group in the magnificent sequence of hills that stretches for over 40 km from the Clees. The Breiddens are steep sided and dramatically shaped, but unfortunately composed of rock that is ideal for road building, hence the large working quarry disfiguring the western side. Offa's Dyke passes west of the Breidden hills, where it meets the Severn and probably ran along its eastern bank.

Oswestry and Wrecsam uplands

Although most of the northern half of the Marches is a low-lying plain, some hills on the western side of the plain are also included (Fig. 11). This is because they lie east of Offa's Dyke, which follows a route a little way into the hill country rather than across the plain. These hills have a long history of industrial exploitation and much of the landscape is scarred and urbanised, but there is still surprisingly rich natural history. There has been extensive quarrying of limestone in the area to the west of Oswestry and this continues at Llynclys. In the hills around Wrecsam there was both coal mining and steel making. Most of the industry has now ended and the sites are being cleared and reused, or are being allowed to return to semi-natural conditions.

FIG 11. Oswestry Uplands, viewed from the ramparts of Oswestry Old Fort.

North Shropshire and Cheshire Plain

This is an extensive area that covers south and central Cheshire, most of
north Shropshire and also Maelor Saesneg. It will be referred to as the North
Shropshire–Cheshire Plain in this book, despite parts of it lying in Wales
(Fig. 12). The plain is low lying, mostly between 15 and 100 m above sea level.
The term 'plain' is something of a misnomer, as many parts of it are far from
level. It is also not uniform in its topography and has some very distinctive
features. Its landscape interest is subtler than that of the hill country to the south
and its natural history can also take some searching out, but those prepared to do
this are amply rewarded.

The ice sheets of the last glaciation covered the entire North Shropshire–
Cheshire Plain and left deposits of sand, silt and clay over most of it. These
deposits are distributed evenly in some areas, with a small number of surviving
heaths on areas of sand or gravel deposits. In other parts of the plain there are
moraine fields with a dizzying topography of ridges, hummocks and hollows.
There are also kettle holes formed by the melting of ice blocks at the end of the
glaciation. Many of the hollows and kettle holes are now filled either with meres
or mosses, which are the names used locally for lakes and bogs.

The meres and mosses are one of the most distinctive features of this area.
This was acknowledged when English Nature chose to call the North Shropshire-

FIG 12. North Shropshire–Cheshire Plain, with Fenn's and Whixall Mosses in the middle
distance. (Shropshire Council)

Cheshire Plain the Meres and Mosses area, when defining natural areas across England. Aqualate Mere and Wybunbury Moss are National Nature Reserves. The Fenn's complex of mosses is one of the largest areas of raised mire in England and Wales and is also a National Nature Reserve. In yet another example of the inanity of the Welsh–English border, it crosses Fenn's Complex following the line of a drain for over 3 km!

Scattered across the North Shropshire–Cheshire Plain are sandstone hills, which are visible over long distances. They appear especially prominent from the south, as many of these hills have sandstone cliffs facing in that direction, some natural and some the result of quarrying. On the northern part of the plain are some distinctive small valleys, which are mostly tributaries of the Dee. They were formed when streams or small rivers cut down through soft glacial deposits. Damp woodlands clothe the steep valley sides. Elsewhere on the plain there is little woodland and the land is devoted to agriculture, mostly livestock, but some arable farming. There has been some removal of field boundaries in arable areas but livestock farming and a landscape of relatively small fields enclosed in hedges still predominates. Maelor Saesneg is included on the Register of Landscapes of Outstanding Historic Interest in Wales, largely because of the survival of its traditional agricultural landscape. There are huge numbers of ponds on farmland in both Maelor Saesneg and south Cheshire, with almost every field having one or more. Most of them are former marl pits, with the calcareous marl having been dug out and spread over fields to enrich the soil.

The rivers that flow on the plain are mostly small and some areas have few natural watercourses, underlying glacial sands and gravels allowing drainage of groundwater. Gradients in streams and rivers are typically shallow, especially as glacial deposits invariably prevent direct routes being taken from source to sea. Flow rates are therefore often slow and some rivers suffer from silt deposition as a result of soil erosion from agricultural land. The principal rivers flow across the margins of the plain. The Severn passes from Welshpool to Ironbridge around the southern edge. The Dee emerges from the Vale of Llangollen and then follows a meandering path northwards towards Chester. Both of these rivers have created a series of river terraces, which are level areas of deposited silt. The lowest terraces are the current flood plains, which are often inundated in winter and occasionally during other seasons. The main section of the Shropshire Union Canal runs from north to south on the eastern side of the plain and the Llangollen branch crosses the plain from east to west. There are also some disused sections of canal with greater natural history interest; the Prees Branch Canal along with parts of the Montgomery Canal and Newport Canal all have SSSI status.

Severn Valley

The Severn rises on Pumlomon Fawr in mid-Wales and reaches the Marches near Welshpool. It then flows across the southern edge of the North Shropshire–Cheshire Plain. At Buildwas it passes between the Wrekin and Wenlock Edge and enters Ironbridge Gorge. This is where the Severn Valley is considered to begin. It continues below the Gorge to Bridgnorth, Bewdley and Stourport on Severn. The river flows in a deep channel, but still sometimes rises sufficiently to flood surrounding land. River terraces at various sites show the level at which flooding took place in former periods.

Together with the side valley of Coalbrookdale, Ironbridge Gorge is often regarded as the cradle of the Industrial Revolution. A large area of intense industry eventually developed both north and south of the Gorge, including Broseley, Dawley, Hadley and Donnington. This is the Coalbrookdale coalfield and it extended over 60 km². The rocks of the coalfield contain ironstone and high quality clays, as well as the rather thin seams of coal. All were worked from mines in the area. Limestone required for iron making was mined in Ironbridge Gorge. Extensive spoil heaps were created and aerial photos of the coalfield at the end of the industrial period show a devastated lunar-like landscape (Fig. 13). This has since been transformed, with large areas reclaimed and used for the construction of the new town of Telford. Other areas have been allowed to regenerate naturally. The steep sides of the Ironbridge Gorge

FIG 13. Coalbrookdale Coalfield, looking southwest from Lilleshall Company Priorslee Furnaces, with Old Park beyond. (Ironbridge Gorge Museums Trust)

FIG 14. Wyre Forest. An aerial photograph from Longdon on Dowles, looking southwards down Park Brook valley. Only a small part of the forest is seen in this view. (Forestry Commission)

and adjacent areas to the west now have some of the finest stands of limestone woodland in the Marches.

The ice sheets of the last glaciation did not extend eastwards as far as the Severn Valley or very far southwards beyond the Ironbridge Gorge. There is a part of Shropshire to the east of the river, but the Severn is taken as the eastern edge of the Marches from Bridgnorth southwards. To the west of the Severn Valley the Mor, Borle, Dowles, Gladder and Dick brooks have cut deep valleys in soft rock and the steep valley sides are mostly wooded. There are also more extensive areas of woodland that were formerly coppiced to provide fuel for the iron industry before Abraham Derby developed the use of coke for smelting. The largest area of such woodland is Wyre Forest, northwest of Bewdley (Fig. 14). All but a small portion of Wyre is to the west of the Severn and so is within the area defined as being the Marches. Naturalists from Worcestershire might contest this, but the natural history of Wyre has more in common with western oakwoods than those of the Midlands to the east, including the characteristic avifauna of redstart, pied flycatcher and wood warbler. Wyre is the third largest

FIG 15. Teme valley near Shelsley Walsh looking northwestwards, with the wooded scarp facing northeast.

area of ancient woodland in England and a large part of it is a National Nature Reserve, so it is in any case too good an area to exclude! To the south of Wyre are Ribbesford Woods, where research on dormouse *Muscardinus avellanarius* ecology has been carried out, and Shrawley Wood, with remarkable stands of small-leaved limes *Tilia cordata*.

Teme valley

To the west of the Severn Valley, between Bewdley and Shrawley is an area of gentle hills, part in Herefordshire and part in Worcestershire, that completes our clockwise tour of the Marches. The underlying rocks are Devonian, mostly Old Red Sandstones, which give rise to fertile red soils. The middle reaches of the Teme flow through from the northwest to the southeast. On the southwest side of the Teme valley, harder cornstones form a mainly wooded escarpment (Fig. 15). The main tributaries of the Teme are the River Rea and Mill Brook, joining from the north, and the Kyre Brook from the south. There are also many narrow wooded valleys, known as dingles, through which smaller tributaries flow. Ice sheets moved southwards and eastwards through much of the Marches during the last glaciation but did not reach these hills and valleys, which helps to explain the differences in the landscape that tell us that we are here on the edge of the borderlands.

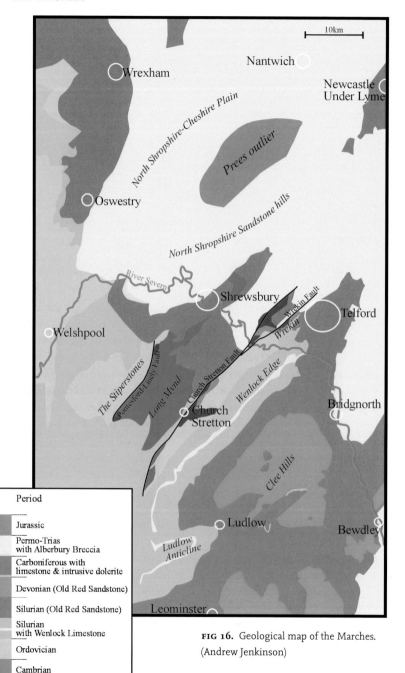

FIG 16. Geological map of the Marches.
(Andrew Jenkinson)

Date (Millions of years ago)	Period
145	Jurassic
199	Permo-Trias with Alberbury Breccia
299	Carboniferous with limestone & intrusive dolerite
359	Devonian (Old Red Sandstone)
416	Silurian (Old Red Sandstone)
443	Silurian with Wenlock Limestone
488	Ordovician
542	Cambrian
	Longmyndian
	Uriconian

CHAPTER 2

Rocks

THE ROCKS OF THE MARCHES form an intriguing and extremely complicated three-dimensional puzzle, the detail of which can be left to geologists (Fig. 16). However, the broader aspects are relevant to this book. The legacy of rocks is the dominant influence on landscape and natural history in many parts of the Marches. This is most obvious in the uplands of south Shropshire and north Herefordshire, but is also true on the scattered hills further north. The rocks of low-lying parts of the Marches are almost everywhere covered by glacial or alluvial deposits, so have less direct influence. Twelve groups of hills will be defined in this chapter, with frontiers that may not be initially obvious, but which are clearly definable (Figs 17 and 18). A chronological sequence will be followed, from the Precambrian to the Jurassic. These groups of hills are extraordinarily varied and are one of the principal glories of the Marches.

WHALEBACKS AND CONES – URICONIAN VOLCANICS (GROUP 1)

At the end of the M54, thankfully the only motorway in the Marches, is a cutting through Overley Hill. From here there is a wonderful panorama of Marches hills. The pink coloured rock that is exposed in the cutting is rhyolite, one of the three main types of fine-grained igneous rocks that are formed by cooling of lava, the others being basalt and andesite. All three occur in the Uriconian Volcanics – the rocks that form the first group of hills. Rhyolite's high silica content makes it an acidic rock, with nutrient-poor and acidic soils developing on it. Basalt is much lower in silica than rhyolite. Geologists regard it as a basic rock, though it does not give rise to alkaline soils, rather to soils that are slightly

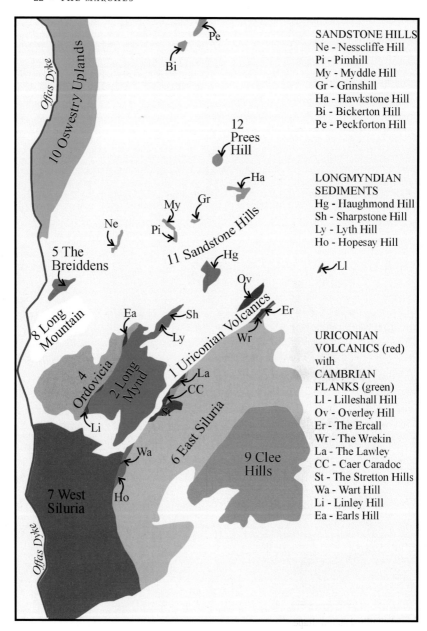

FIG 17. Map of the 12 areas of hills defined in this chapter. Areas 1, 2 and 11 are fragmented, so individual hills are named.

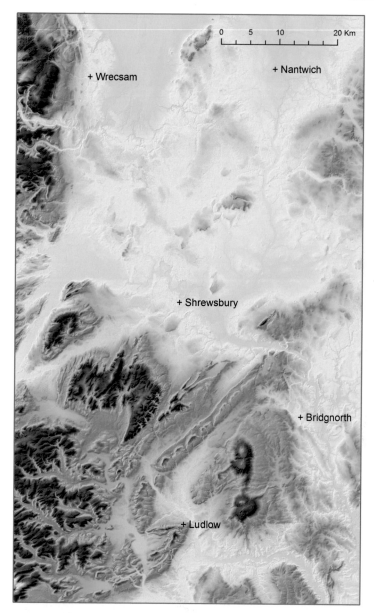

FIG 18. Altitudinal colour drape of the Marches overlain by hillshading from the northwest at an elevation of 25°. (Map constructed by Geoff Thomas using data kindly provided by Intermap Technologies)

less acidic, with higher concentrations of bases such as calcium and magnesium. The silica content of andesite is between that of rhyolite and basalt and so it is an intermediate fine-grained igneous rock. Two types of medium-grained rock, formed by intrusion of magma into previously hardened rocks, are also found in these hills. Granophyre is a pink acidic rock and gives rise to similar soils to those on rhyolite, whereas dolerite is basic.

Two lines of hills running from northeast to southwest through the centre of Shropshire are made of Uriconian Volcanics. These rocks were formed between 570 and 560 million years ago, at the end of the Precambrian. The endurance of the hills is testament to the hardness of the Uriconian Volcanics, but is also due to repeated upfaulting of these rocks among newer, softer ones that have since been eroded away. The characteristic shapes of the hills are whalebacks and cones, but each one is distinctive. Typically steep-sided, with slopes of up to 35° in places, they are however mostly not broken by natural crags and are thus rounded in appearance. The hills lie on the southeast sides of two geological faults, the Church Stretton Fault and the Pontesford–Linley Fault, and are known respectively as the Eastern and Western Uriconian outcrops respectively (Fig. 19).

A tour of the Eastern outcrops from northeast to southwest begins near Newport, with Lilleshall Hill, a modest eminence rising to just 132 m above sea level. The first substantial hills are the Ercall and the Wrekin, to the south of Wellington. Both are largely composed of andesite and rhyolite. Dolerite and basalt cut into these rocks and cover them in places, as a result of intrusions and flows of magma or lava. The whole of the Ercall is covered in woodland,

FIG 19. Uriconian volcanic whalebacks viewed from the Long Mynd, from right to left: Caer Caradoc, the Lawley and in the distance to the north east, the Wrekin.

whereas the Wrekin is wooded on its lower slopes but the summit ridge is upland grassland. The Ercall and the Wrekin lie on a branch of the Church Stretton fault. The outcrops on the other branch, slightly to the northwest, form a series of low hills: Wrockwardine, Overley and Charlton hills.

Moving to the southwest again, there is a distance of 15 km with only a few very small exposures of Uriconian rocks before the next extensive group of outcrops. These form a series of strikingly beautiful hills along the main Church Stretton fault: the Lawley, Caer Caradoc and the other Stretton hills. The Lawley is a narrow steep-sided ridge, nearly 3 km long. It is chiefly made of andesites and basic tuffs, with some rhyolite and a band of dolerite north of the summit. Caer Caradoc's ridge is mostly similar in height to the Lawley but there is a conical main summit that rises much higher (Fig. 20). Again there is a variety of rock types: rhyolite forms the summit, with basalt and dolerite along the ridge to the north and andesite, dolerite and rhyolitic tuffs to the south. Hazler Hill is composed mainly of basalt and Ragleth Hill of a salmon-pink rhyolitic tuff and basic tuffs. Although there have not yet been detailed surveys, differences in rock can be correlated with the composition of upland grassland on these hills. For example, carline thistle *Carlina vulgaris* occurs where there are is an outcrop of basic rock at Three Fingers Rock on Caer Caradoc, but not in the surrounding areas of more acidic soil.

To the east of the Stretton hills lies about 8 km² of Uriconian Volcanics, including Hope Bowdler, Willstone and Cardington hills. Andesites, rhyolites and tuffs are all represented. There are crags of rhyolite, including the Battlestones and Gaerstone, but neither these nor the crags on the eastern

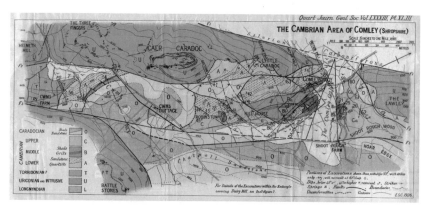

FIG 20. Geological map of the Caer Caradoc area, drawn by local geologist Edgar Cobbold in the 1920s. (Geological Society of London)

FIG 21. Earl's Hill in centre view with north Shropshire in the distance beyond. Lawn Hill, which is composed of Longmyndian sediments, is nearer and to the right. (Mark Twells)

side of Caer Caradoc's summit are large enough to attract peregrine falcons *Falco peregrinus* or other specialists of rocky outcrops. Our tour of the Eastern Uriconian outcrops ends in a small outcrop of basalts and andesites at Wart Hill near Hopesay.

The Western Uriconian outcrops extend intermittently from Linley in the southwest to Pontesford and Plealey in the northeast. Earl's Hill is the most impressive feature (Fig. 21). It is made of rhyolites, basalts and dolerite. On the east side are crags with screes below, but otherwise there is mostly acid grassland, as on most of the hills made of Uriconian Volcanics. Pontesford Hill lies immediately to the north and is currently covered with woodland of various types, including conifer plantations. Conservationists would prefer to see the woodland removed and grassland re-established. An added advantage would be to restore the leonine shape of the hill that was familiar to past naturalists.[1]

SCARPS AND PLATEAUX – LONGMYNDIAN SEDIMENTS (GROUP 2)

The hills in the next group are very different in appearance, although their rocks were formed at about the same time as the Uriconian Volcanics. The most northwesterly is Haughmond Hill. Moving southwestwards, after a gap cut through by the Severn at Shrewsbury, there is a series of hills of modest but increasing height. These are Sharpstones Hill, Lyth Hill, Broom Hill, Lawn Hill, Paulith Bank, Gatten, Linley Hill and to the southeast, Hopesay Hill.

To the east of Gatten and Linley Hill is the Long Mynd (Fig. 22). This is larger by far than any of the other hills, being 12 km long and up to 8 km wide. It is unique in its geology, landscape and natural history, giving its name to the rocks of which the hills in this group are composed: the Longmyndian Supergroup. The rocks are chiefly sandstones, shales and conglomerates, with a few discrete volcanic dykes. The entire sequence of Longmyndian rocks can be traced from the Stretton Shale Formation to the Bridges Formation by walking up Cardingmill valley to the plateau and on westwards to Bridges. The same strata then outcrop beyond Bridges in reverse order. This is a classic geological excursion used to educate students and interested amateurs alike. The strata are steeply dipping, with those that disappear in the east and the west

FIG 22. The Long Mynd, viewed across the Chrurch Stretton valley from Caer Caradoc, with the level summit plateau and many narrow valleys or batches visible. (Andy Pritchard)

presumed to meet underground – a famous example of a syncline. This is the
result of deformation that occurred between 555 and 550 million years ago. The
Longmyndian rocks became hardened and resistant to erosion at this time, when
there was mild metamorphism due to tectonic pressures, with deep burial and
concomitant hot diagenesis, or transformation of the rocks. A good example
of the hardness of such rocks is the conglomeratic greywacke that is quarried
at both Sharpstones Hill and Haughmond Hill. It is always in demand as the
finest and most hardwearing of roadstones, giving grip to the tyres of countless
speeding motorists.

Many of the hills composed of Longmyndian rocks have a summit plateau
with steep scarps at the edge, rather than sloping up continuously to a narrow
ridge. This is seen on a small scale at Lyth Hill and Haughmond Hill near
Shrewsbury and also at Hopesay Hill. The Long Mynd has a very extensive
undulating summit plateau, with scarps on both the west and east side, much
favoured by geostationary kestrels *Falco tinnunculus*. The western side is
particularly prominent and, as in many such cases, movement at a geological
fault is the origin of the scarp. The usual origin of plateaux is horizontal or nearly
horizontal stratification, with the most resistant strata uppermost forming a
capping which protects softer strata beneath from erosion. The Spanish word
'mesa' is sometimes used for hills that form in this way, but it is not appropriate
here. The Longmyndian strata are far from horizontal, typically dipping very
steeply (Fig. 23). Narrow hills called hog's backs are often found where there are

FIG 23. Steeply
inclined strata in
Townbrook Valley
on the Long Mynd,
with corresponding
distribution of gorse
and other plants.

steeply dipping strata of sedimentary rock, and where some strata are more resistant to erosion than others. The 7,000 m thickness of rocks on the Long Mynd is obviously too great for them to form a narrow hog's back ridge. The strata do vary in hardness and some sign of this might be expected in surface topography, with the hardest strata outcropping more prominently. This is occasionally seen in the valleys on the Long Mynd, as in Lightspout Hollow, where a layer of hard sandstone forms the lip over which a waterfall plunges. On the summit plateau there is remarkably little sign of the differences in erosion rate. The probable explanation is that Longmyndian rocks were previously worn down to form an extensive and low-lying erosional surface or peneplain, on which other rocks were repeatedly deposited and then eroded away to re-expose the peneplain. The probable periods of exposure were during the late Ordovician before Silurian rocks were deposited, during the Middle Devonian before the deposition of Carboniferous limestone, during the middle Carboniferous before the deposition of the Coal Measures and yet again during the Permian and Triassic. There is evidence for these periods of exposure and erosion from sites where later deposits of rock lie unconformably on so-called red beds. The red colour is the result of oxidation of iron salts.

These red beds also show signs of deep tropical weathering processes, where rainwater sometimes laced with acid from plant deposition, penetrates the rock and leaches out soluble minerals, even silica. Given the long periods of erosion and leaching to which the rocks on the summit plateaux of the Long Mynd and the higher hills in this group have been subjected, it is not surprising that the soils that are now found there are infertile. There is a resemblance to parts of Australia where leaching over a billion years and a lack of nutrient inputs from alluvium, glacial deposits or vulcanicity has left soils very infertile and particularly deficient in phosphate. The soils that have developed on the summit plateaux are free-draining stony podzols and acid brown earths.

Cardingmill Valley, mentioned earlier, is just one of many deep, steep-sided and repeatedly branched valleys, known locally as batches, beaches or hollows, which dissect the summit plateau of the Long Mynd on its eastern side, and to a lesser extent on the western side. They are a puzzling geomorphological feature, as they cut eastwards though hard and soft strata, rather than following softer strata northwards or southwards. They are considered to be young valleys, yet are surprisingly deep. The streams currently flowing in them are relatively small, yet there are large alluvial fans of eroded sand and gravel at the ends of the batches. The origin of the batches is probably due partly to tropical weathering long ago and partly to events during and after the last glaciation that are described in Chapter 5.

CAMBRIAN FLANKS AND FRAGMENTS (GROUP 3)

The small and scattered outcrops of Cambrian rock in the Marches were all deposited unconformably on Uriconian Volcanics, so they form part of the hills composed of such rocks or lie close to them.[2] There is Cambrian quartzite and sandstone on the southeast flanks of the Wrekin and the Ercall. These rocks also form parts of the southeast sides of Sharpstones near Cardington and of the Lawley and Caer Caradoc. Shallow stony or sandy podzolised soils have developed where there are Cambrian quartzites, usually with acid grassland or, as on the southeast face of the Ercall, scrubby downy birch *Betula pubescens* woodland. Acid brown earths typically develop on Cambrian sandstones, supporting acid grassland or stands of bracken *Pteridium aquilinum*.

RIDGES, DOMES AND TORS – ORDOVICIAN VARIETY (GROUP 4)

Between the Long Mynd and the Vale of Montgomery is another upland area with a wonderfully varied tumble of hills (Fig. 24). Murchison[3] described it as a 'picturesque hilly tract' and included the rocks in his Silurian system, but Lapworth[4] reassigned them to the Ordovician system. The rocks here were formed between 495 and 450 million years ago. They extend for about 10 km westwards from the Pontesford–Linley fault, gradually decreasing in altitude but with crest after crest giving a rugged feel to the whole area. The England–Wales border in this area plunges erratically to and fro and is best ignored. As there are clear natural boundaries, the land deserves its own name. Murchison had it as part of his *Siluria*, so it will here be renamed *Ordovicia*, although geologists have already given it the more prosaic name of the Shelve Inlier. Whatever name we use, the area is splendidly scruffy and disreputable but also wild and romantic. There are former squatter cottages with small patches of enclosed land from which a poor living was scratched, the abandoned lead mines adding an air of desolation. Stiperstones is the best-known hill, but there are others of great character, with fine views and few visitors.

The topography of *Ordovicia* is complicated, because there are both hard and soft marine sediments and also extensive intrusion of volcanic rocks. The oldest rocks outcrop in the east and the youngest in the west, but there are geological faults, a syncline and an anticline to complicate the sequence of rocks. The Stiperstones is the easternmost of the hills, topped by extremely hard quartz arenite, which, though not a true quartzite, is known as Stiperstones Quartzite.

FIG 24. Hills of *Ordovicia*: on the skyline, from left to right: Lan Fawr, Corndon Hill and Stiperstones.

This forms a series of distinctive rocky outcrops along the crest of the ridge. One of these, Manstone Rock, is higher than any point in the Marches except Brown Clee. The Stiperstones is a National Nature Reserve, managed to encourage the heather *Calluna vulgaris* moorland along its ridge.

The western side of the ridge and its deep, steep-sided valleys are made of siltstones and sandstones, known as Mytton Flags. Extensive mineralisation of these rocks occurred in the Carboniferous period, creating the veins of lead, zinc and barytes that were once mined. To the west of the Stiperstones is an undulating plateau of shales and mudstones, at an altitude of 300–350 m. Steep-sided hills rise up from this plateau, composed of rocks formed by volcanic activity during the Ordovician period. Heath Mynd and Cefn Gunthly are rounded hills composed of acid tuffs called Hyssington Volcanics. To the west, Corndon Hill is a strikingly shaped cone of dolerite. It has been interpreted as a phacolith – a mushroom-shaped intrusion into a pre-existing fold of rocks. Moving west again, there is a line of hills that are outcrops of Stapeley Volcanics. From south to north these are Todleth Hill, Roundton Hill (Fig. 25), Lan Fawr and Stapeley Hill. These hills are varied in shape, with some craggy outcrops. They are rarely visited despite offering splendid westward views into Wales. Stapeley Volcanics also outcrop at Bromlow Callow, a hill that features in Mary Webb's *Gone to Earth*.[5] It has the local nickname of Caterpillar Hill because of the prominent circle of conifers on the summit. Stapeley Volcanics are quite varied and include basic and intermediate tuffs, andesite and basalt, with corresponding variation in soils and a fascinating range of grassland communities. Roundton Hill is a Montgomeryshire Wildlife Trust reserve.

FIG 25. The southwestern outposts of *Ordovicia*: Roundton Hill (left) and Lan Fawr (right). The Kerry Ridgeway climbs westwards into Wales on the ridge in the distance. (Mark Twells)

To the west of the Stapeley Volcanics is an outcrop about 800 m wide of Weston Flags. This formation includes beds of sandstone, siltstone and shale, with more persistent sandstones forming high ground at Priest Weston, The Rowls and Rorrington Hill. The *Ecological Flora of the Shropshire Region*[6] describes maiden pink *Dianthus deltoides* growing on these rocks at Priest Weston 'with unmaidenly abandon'. To the west of these hills there is a series of shale and sandstone deposits, where the land drops down steeply before rising briefly to a ridge formed from Hagley Volcanics. Beyond this ridge there are softer shales and a further drop down to the well-concealed depths of Marrington Dingle. The eastern side of this valley is particularly steep and is composed of Whittery Volcanics. More shales outcrop to the west at the end of the Ordovician sequence. Beyond are the younger and softer Silurian rocks that underlie the Vale of Montgomery.

THE BREIDDENS (GROUP 5)

Ordovician rocks outcrop again about 15 km northwest of *Ordovicia* to form
the striking Breidden hills. As in *Ordovicia*, there are both sedimentary rocks,
including shales and mudstones, and volcanics. The three main eminences are
all volcanic. Breidden Hill itself with the ludicrously priapic Rodney's Pillar on
its summit is composed of Criggion dolerite. The north side of this hill is very
steeply sloping, with crags and areas of natural scree. The soils formed from
the dolerite are as base rich as those on many limestones and the associated
flora is distinctive and nationally important, with calcicole and calcifuge species
growing in close proximity. To the southwest, Moel y Golfa is composed of
andesite and, except for a small area around its summit, is wooded. From
here, a ridge that is mainly composed of conglomerate runs northeastwards
to Middletown Hill. This conglomerate has been called Bomb Rock because
it consists of large andesitic boulders erupted from nearby volcanoes during
latter parts of the Ordovician. There is unenclosed grassland on the steep
slopes of this ridge.

SCARPS AND VALES – ORDOVICIAN AND SILURIAN SHELF SEQUENCES (GROUP 6)

Southeast of the line of Uriconian Volcanic hills that stretches from the Wrekin
to Ragleth Hill is a classic scarp and vale landscape. This landscape is the
consequence of successive strata of harder and softer rock, with a uniform dip
to the southeast (Fig. 26). The base of this sequence is a band of Ordovician
rocks about 30 km long and up to 3 km wide that outcrops in the northwest.
The oldest of these rocks are the Shineton Shales, formed in the first epoch of
the Ordovician. Near the Wrekin these are the only Ordovician deposits, but
near the Stretton hills there are also deposits from the fourth and penultimate
epoch, the Caradoc. The most complete sequence of Ordovician scarp and vale
is found to the southeast of the Lawley. Soft Sheinton Shales occur in the first
vale. The first scarp is Hoar Edge, capped by Hoar Edge Grit, followed by a
vale where the rocks are the much softer Harnage Shale. Yell Bank is the next
scarp, composed of Chatwall Sandstone and Alternata Limestone, with a vale of
sandstones and mudstones beyond. These were the last Ordovician rocks to be
deposited here.

The next strata are Silurian and rest unconformably on the Ordovician. The
first scarp is composed of Kenley Grit, with softer shales forming Apedale to the

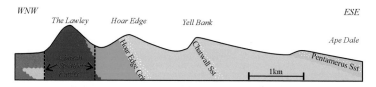

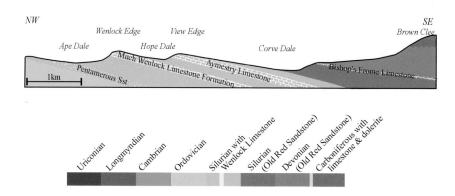

FIG 26. Geological section of *East Siluria*, from the Lawley to Brown Clee, showing scarps and vales, and inclined strata of Silurian rock. (Andrew Jenkinson)

southeast. Wenlock Edge follows, stretching unbroken for 30 km from Ironbridge Gorge to Craven Arms. The scarp face is composed of calcareous mudstones, capped by harder Much Wenlock Limestone. Wenlock Edge is the most famous scarp of all, forming a very strong feature in the landscape of the Marches, celebrated in the poetry of Housman and the music of Vaughan Williams.

Moving southeast from The Edge, as it is locally known, first are softer shales and then a scarp capped by Aymestry Limestone that rises higher than Wenlock Edge. Between the two limestone scarps, where springs rise, there is a series of six settlements in funnel-shaped hollows. These settlements all have the suffix *-hope*, meaning secluded place, in their name, for example Westhope. Collectively this area is known as Hopedale (Fig. 27). Rather than a single stream draining the whole of Hopedale, the streams rising at each spring flows southeastwards in a valley cut through the Aymestry Limestone. The scarp therefore consists of a series of arc-shaped sections. Callow Hill is the highest point along this scarp and is topped by Flounder's Folly, a tower that is occasionally open to the public and from which there are fine views. Siltstones, limestones and then sandstone form the dip slope that leads down into the broad valley of Corvedale. The rocks that underlie Corvedale are Old Red Sandstone, deposited during the final part of the

FIG 27. Wenlock Edge, looking northwestwards along its wooded scarp face, with Hopedale and the similarly wooded scarp face of Aymestry Limestone beyond. (Robin Jukes-Hughes)

Silurian period. These rocks, which were laid down in terrestrial conditions, are easily eroded and give rise to fertile red-brown soils, as in much of Herefordshire. Lower lying areas near the Corve are enriched with alluvium and are prime agricultural land.

In the scarp and vale country the steep scarp faces are almost all wooded, partly by semi-natural mixed broadleaved woodland and partly by conifer plantations. Wenlock Edge is tree clad from end to end, and at 30 km it must one of the longest continuous stretches of woodland in England. The dip slopes are enclosed farmland, with mostly fertile, well-drained soils. There are some areas of unimproved grassland, including calcicolous meadow, but improved pasture and arable land predominates even to the tops of the dip slopes.

Although the scarps of Wenlock and Aymestry Limestone appear to end in the southwest at Craven Arms, they are merely interrupted by the Onny valley and continue beyond. After heading south for about 7 km, between the valleys of the Clun and the Onny, the two scarps turn east and then curve round to the west again, forming a giant amphitheatre about 5 km in diameter, with

Marlbrook Hall at its centre. This is part of the famous Ludlow anticline
(Fig. 28). It was formed towards the end of the Silurian period when two
continental plates collided, uniting the rocks of England and Wales with
those of Scotland. The impact caused the tilting of strata to the southwest that
established the scarp and vale landscape. It also created a fold in the Ludlow
area, which is the anticline. The upper parts of the fold have eroded away,
leaving scarps of the more resistant rocks. The outer rim of the amphitheatre is
Aymestry Limestone and is mostly coniferised. The largest of the plantations is
the Mortimer Forest, southwest of Ludlow.

The highest point on the Aymestry Limestone is the easternmost,
appropriately called High Vinnals, which offers splendid views now that
conifers have been removed from the summit. An inner and lower scarp in the
amphitheatre is Much Wenlock Limestone, and large parts of it support oak
woodland, especially on the south side. It is cut in several places by small valleys
with streams draining towards the middle of the amphitheatre. This area looks
superficially like a broad river valley, but rather than there being a river draining
down the middle, there is a gentle ridge, with separate streams draining the areas
to the north and south of the ridge.

FIG 28. The Ludlow anticline viewed from Wigmore Rolls to the west. The dome of limestone
linking outcrops on the left and right has been eroded away since the Silurian. (John Voysey)

FOOTHILLS OF MID-WALES – SILURIAN BASIN SEQUENCES (GROUP 7)

The outcrops of Wenlock and Aymestry Limestone end a few kilometres to the south of the Ludlow anticline, to the west of the River Lugg at Aymestrey. Silurian rocks continue to the west but they are different in origin and character from those of the scarp and vale country, so forming a separate area, in which limestone is no longer a prominent component. The rocks of the scarp and vale country were laid down in shallow seas over a continental shelf: the Midland Shelf. At the same time, there were deeper seas to the west: the Welsh Basin. In this basin, greater thicknesses of siltstones, mudstones and shales were being deposited. The rocks formed in these two areas are known as the shelf sequence and the basin sequence. The rocks of the basin sequence outcrop in a large area to the west of the Ludlow anticline. They extend from the valleys of the Arrow and the Lugg in the south to the valley of the rivers Caebitra and Camlad in the north. If we think of the Shelve Inlier as *Ordovicia*, then the scarp and vale country is *East Siluria*, and the area of basin sequence rocks is *West Siluria*. However, the boundary between east and west is not a sharp one. Instead, the outcrops of limestone gradually become thinner and are replaced by calcareous mudstones and siltstones. Rocks of the basin sequence extend on into Mid-Wales, with the lime content continuing to decrease and associated soils becoming thinner and less fertile.

In some parts of this area the upper deposits were formed in the last epoch of the Silurian, when the sea had retreated and there was terrestrial deposition. This transition from marine to terrestrial conditions can be seen in the rocks. Moving up through the sequence there are increasing amounts of sandstone and less mudstone. Green or grey coloration gives way to red as iron becomes oxidised rather than reduced. These upper Silurian deposits, called Old Red Sandstone, outcrop in an area around Clun and also to the northwest of Presteigne. Because of the gradation in the rocks, there are no sharp transitions in the landscape or natural history; indeed, this whole area of Silurian rocks has a rather homogeneous character. Whereas in other parts of the Marches it is the hills that are the dominant landscape feature, in this area it is the river valleys. Each has its own character and is worthy of exploration. The Teme is a Site of Special Scientific Interest along its whole length, including the upper reaches in this area, but the other rivers also have considerable natural history interest. Between the river valleys there are undulating ridges. Individual hills rise above these ridges in places, but they tend not to be prominent and are mostly rounded rather than craggy. These ridges and hills are more extensively planted with conifers than other parts of the Marches.

THE LONG MOUNTAIN (GROUP 8)

Between the Shelve Inlier, or *Ordovicia*, and the Breidden Hills there is another distinctive member of the diverse company of Marches hills. It presents a remarkably level skyline from both north and south, which is probably the reason for its name: the Long Mountain (Fig. 29). The underlying rocks were formed during the 30 million years of the Silurian period. They survive between two areas of Ordovician rocks because the compression of the Earth's crust that caused the upward folding of the Ludlow anticline caused downward folding in the area of the Long Mountain. This has allowed younger rocks to survive cycles of erosion that removed Silurian rocks to the north and south. So, climbing up to the summit ridge from the valleys both to the northwest and the southeast, a sequence of younger and younger Silurian rocks is encountered. The rocks are basin sequences that were deposited in deeper seas: shales, mudstones and siltstones, some of which are calcareous. The Long Mountain is asymmetrical, with steeper northwestern slopes. These are mostly wooded, with conifer plantations predominating. Streams on the more gently sloping southeastern side have cut a series of steep-sided dingles, again mainly wooded, making it easiest to negotiate the Long Mountain by the Roman road on the summit ridge.

FIG 29. Long Mountain with its level summit and wooded dingles, viewed from Arddleen to the northwest, across the flood plain of the Severn.

Both the summit ridge and slopes are enclosed, with a mixture of pasture and arable farming. The Long Mountain must have one of the lowest population densities in the Marches, with no villages and few farmsteads: another area of blissfully quiet country.

PLATEAUX AND SILLS – THE CLEE HILLS (GROUP 9)

Devonian rocks outcrop in the triangular tract of country between Ludlow, Bridgnorth and Cleobury Mortimer. This area is sometimes described as a plateau as it is raised up from the adjacent river valleys and the strata are relatively level, but it is undulating country. Many small brooks have cut valleys down through the relatively soft Devonian strata, which are collectively known as Old Red Sandstone. Carboniferous rocks once covered this entire area but they now survive only where protected from erosion by dolerite sills on the summits of the Clee Hills. These hills rise up steeply from the plateau, so are easily seen and identified from many parts of the Marches. Radio masts adorn the twin summits of Brown Clee and the tilted summit plateau of Titterstone Clee has a white, spherical radar dome. Geologists have found it difficult to define the base of the Devonian rocks in the Marches, as deposition of Old Red Sandstone in terrestrial conditions had already begun in the late Silurian. The current understanding is that the lowest and therefore oldest Devonian strata are the deposits of cornstone, interspersed with softer siltstones and marls that are collectively known as Bishop's Frome Limestone. The cornstones are resistant enough to form the prominent escarpment that extends for about 25 km from just north of Ludlow, along the southeast side of Corvedale northeastwards almost as far as Morville.

Above the escarpment of Bishop Frome Limestone is a plateau composed of a complex and repeating sequence of sandstones, marls, cornstones and cornstone conglomerates, with marls forming about three-quarters of the sequence. The soils on the plateau are red-brown silty or sandy loams and allow arable cultivation, particularly cereals, in much of the area. There is also livestock farming, especially where the soils are gleyed and the drainage is poor.

Brown Clee Hill rises up from the middle of the plateau (Fig. 30). The rocks that outcrop on its lower slopes are still from the Lower Devonian but they are mainly sandstones, with much less marl and cornstone. Above these, two areas of Carboniferous rock form the twin domes of Abdon Burf and Clee Burf. Coal Measures form the bulk of each dome, with dolerite forming the summits. The outcrops of dolerite are the remains of a sill, mostly now eroded, that

FIG 30. A distant view of Brown Clee Hill from the Long Mynd, with the Stretton Hills in the middle ground and the wooded Aymestry Limestone scarp face beyond.

was intruded into the rocks of the Coal Measures late in the Carboniferous. Titterstone Clee Hill lies on the southern edge of the Old Red Sandstone plateau. Although the summit is 7 m lower than Abdon Burf, the area of high ground around it is much larger than that of Brown Clee Hill, with a broad ridge extending for 10 km from Knowbury in the southwest to Oreton in the northeast. Titterstone Clee itself lies in the southeastern half of this ridge and Catherton Common, recently acquired as a nature reserve by Shropshire Wildlife Trust, in the northeastern half. Carboniferous limestone forms narrow outcrops at north and south ends of the ridge.

A thick deposit of Carboniferous sandstone, equivalent to the Millstone Grit of the Pennines, lies on the limestone, with the varied rocks of the Coal Measures lying on this. As with Brown Clee Hill, the summit of Titterstone Clee Hill has a capping of dolerite, intruded into the Coal Measures during the late Carboniferous. This rock is known locally as dhustone. Both Brown Clee Hill and Titterstone Clee Hill could be regarded as mesas, but the capping of dolerite on Brown Clee Hill is not really extensive enough, and the strata forming the summit of Titterstone Clee Hill slope gently, making it a tilted plateau, rather than a true mesa (Fig. 31).

FIG 31. Titterstone Clee Hill with inclined summit, viewed from Wenlock Edge, with Corvedale in the middle ground and beyond it an undulating plateau of Devonian rock. (Robin Jukes-Hughes)

The summits of the Clee Hills offer fine views, but are not areas of unspoilt beauty. Wherever rocks of the Carboniferous period occur in the Marches, they have been plundered. Coal and ironstone were mined for hundreds of years. The extremely tough dolerite or dhustone has been extensively quarried for roadstone, paving and stone sets. The pattern of land use is interesting, with land enclosure, where it has occurred, being partly planned and partly due to the activities of squatters. On the unenclosed parts of the Clee Hills semi-natural communities are still found. Soils are varied, with areas of shallow sandy loam that are heavily leached and podzolised, now mostly unenclosed dry heather moorland, and also poorly drained areas on clay, where the soils are gleyed and peat has accumulated to a much greater degree than is usual in the Marches. These are either rush pasture or wet heath. There are extensive blockfields on Titterstone Clee, which have probably changed little since their formation during the last glaciation.

LIMESTONE COUNTRY – FOOTHILLS OF BERWYN (GROUP 10)

To the west of Oswestry is an area of hills formed from Carboniferous limestone and sandstone. The sandstone outcrops on the east-facing slopes of these hills, from Trefonen northwards. The soils here are shallow, acidic, free-draining brown earths. Livestock farming predominates, with small fields and hedges. The limestone was deposited soon after that of Titterstone Clee Hill, this outcrop beginning at Llanymynech and continuing northwards in a series of hills to Selattyn and beyond. The prominent cliffs on Llanymynech Hill, which are visible from far to the east, might be mistaken for a rocky scarp, but are actually the result of quarrying (Fig. 32). As the limestone strata dip to the east, the natural escarpment is on the opposite side of the hill and faces west into Wales. Offa's Dyke follows this escarpment, wherever possible, as far north as the lovely Ceiriog valley, beyond which the outcrops of limestone become intermittent and then head west of the Dyke.

FIG 32. Llanymynech Hill, visited by Darwin while a student at Cambridge. He measured the strike of the rocks using a newly acquired clinometer.

The hills in the limestone area are relatively flat topped and steep sided. The soils are mostly alkaline clay loams on the hilltops, and there are some glacial deposits. Shallower rendzina soils are found on the slopes, many of which are wooded. The limestone hills occupy a relatively small total area, but they have considerable natural history interest and are important outposts for a number of scarce species. Shropshire Wildlife Trust has a cluster of nature reserves here to protect calcicolous grasslands, woodlands and one rare example of fen. Prominent quarries scar the hills, with active working still at Llynclys, but most are abandoned and in some cases now support rare species.

To the west of this limestone country and west of Offa's Dyke is a large area of Ordovician rocks, rising up to the mountains of Berwyn. The Carboniferous limestone and sandstone hills east of the dyke can be regarded as the first foothills of Berwyn. Given that they are contiguous with a large tract of Welsh uplands, it is not surprising that they have a Welsh feel themselves, in terms of the landscape, pattern of farming and place names. The rocks further east are softer Permo-Triassic sandstones and Carboniferous Coal Measures that have been eroded away to form the North Shropshire–Cheshire Plain.

PERMIAN AND TRIASSIC SANDSTONE HILLS (GROUP 11)

Drift deposits cover most of the North Shropshire–Cheshire Plain. These deposits are deep enough to prevent the underlying Permian and Triassic rocks from having any significant influence on the soils or natural communities. However, scattered across the plain are escarpments where the harder sandstones outcrop. Most of these face south or southwest in north Shropshire, as the strata dip gently northwards. The most prominent ones are part of the same geological formation that has subsequently been divided into three sections by geological faulting. The western section is from Ruyton to Nesscliffe. Further east is the section of escarpment between Myddle and Grinshill, with part of it including Pimhill displaced southwards by faulting. The easternmost section consists of two main escarpments, from Lee Brockhurst to Hopton (Fig. 33) and from Hawkstone to Hodnet. The rocks that form these escarpments extend northwards into Cheshire. There they form a line of hills that splits the Cheshire Plain in two, with Bickerton and Peckforton hills the southernmost. The strata here dip to the east, so the escarpment faces west.

The surrounding low-lying country makes these sandstone scarp faces very prominent, despite their modest height. In places, there are natural cliffs of sandstone, but there are also many former quarries with vertical and in some

FIG 33. Sandstone cliffs in the escarpment between Lee Brockhurst and Hopton; above is the Iron Age hill fort of Bury Walls.

cases flat faces. The stone that is quarried is variable in quality; some erodes extremely quickly, but other strata have yielded large freestone blocks that are among the finest in Britain. The colour varies from a bright red, seen at Nesscliffe and Myddle, to a pale cream in some of the best Grinshill stone.[7]

These sandstone hills are rather disappointing in their natural history. This may be because they are relatively small in area and surrounded by farmland or habitations, with too many people living close by for them to remain unadulterated. The hilltops have thin acid soils overlying the sandstone and most are wooded. A few have semi-natural communities. There is sessile oak woodland on both the dip and scarp slopes of Peckforton Hill, with a ground flora that is characteristic of acid sandy soils. This site has Site of Special Scientific Interest, or SSSI, status because of the scarcity of semi-natural woodland on the sandstone hills. In the past both sessile *Quercus petraea* and pedunculate *Quercus robur* oaks were recorded growing apparently naturally on Nesscliffe Hill.[8] A diverse mixture of tree species grows there now, including the southern beeches *Nothofagus obliqua* and *N. nervosa*, Douglas fir, western hemlock, Scots pine and Wellingtonia. On most of the sandstone hills there are conifers, either planted or self-sown. Scots pines *Pinus sylvestris* seem to thrive especially well. Rhododendrons *Rhododenron ponticum* have spread widely on Nesscliffe and other hills, to the detriment of the natural shrub and ground flora. There are few ledges on either natural cliffs or quarry faces, so little opportunity exists for birds that choose such nest sites. We should perhaps value these sandstone hills for their contribution to the landscape, rather than their natural history. At Hawkstone Hill they formed the inspiration for a famous landscape garden with grottos and follies, created in the 18th century but still visitable. Modest outcrops of Permian and Triassic sandstones continue along all the east borders of Shropshire, often with vertical cliffs in box-valleys of incised misfit streams, for example Badger Dingle northeast of Bridgnorth.

THE YOUNGEST ROCKS – PREES HILL (GROUP 12)

The last of the 12 hill areas is the smallest and perhaps least important for its natural history, but it is included here for reasons of geological completeness. At Prees, to the northeast of Wem, there is a gently contoured and smoothly rounded hill (Fig. 34). Its summit is a mere 122 m above sea level, but it is nonetheless the highest ground for some distance around. The rock of Prees Hill is Jurassic Middle Lias. It is not certain how far it extends because of the covering of drift deposits. Murchison showed the town of Wem positioned over

FIG 34. Prees Hill from the south, at sunset in December.

Triassic rock in his geological maps, but the Jurassic Lower Lias may extend up to Wem or beyond. This is still uncertain more than 150 years after Murchison's conjectural mapping. A recent finding is an additional outlier of Lower Lias to the east of that already described; outcrops have been found near Adderly, beyond the mapped Wem fault.[9]

Apart from a basalt dyke of Tertiary rock at Grinshill, the Jurassic of Prees Hill is the youngest solid rock in the Marches. Any later rocks that were deposited have been eroded away. Even without these youngest strata, the presence in an area of the size of the Marches of rocks from all geological periods from the Precambrian to the Jurassic can scarcely be matched anywhere in the world. The next chapter will explain what the fossils and other evidence in these rocks reveal about how they came to be juxtaposed.

CHAPTER 3

Fossils

T HE FOSSILS OF THE MARCHES ARE ABUNDANT and diverse. They form a record of past life that has fascinated palaeontologists for over two hundred years. Leading palaeontologists continue to be attracted to sites here and some of the most exciting discoveries have been made only very recently. New techniques are allowing far more to be learned from fossil specimens than was possible in the past, so despite dealing with ancient subjects, this is a very active research field. Fossils are used to define geological periods and some of the pioneering work to establish these periods was carried out in the Marches, with local place names such as Ludlow, Wenlock and Caradoc now used internationally for particular epochs. Each fossil can provide evidence of characteristics of the ancient ecosystem in which the original organism lived. These ecosystems were very diverse: tropical and temperate, marine and terrestrial, desert and rainforest. This is because of an extraordinary journey that the rocks of the Marches have taken, from 65° south of the equator in the Precambrian period, to 53° north today.

The abundance of fossils from many geological periods can be attributed to the presence nearby of a continental tectonic plate margin during most of the past 600 million years. For much of this time, shallow seas covered the area, and material deposited in these seas, including the remains of organisms, became sedimentary rocks. The Marches have been borderlands in another respect – two major faults, which can be regarded as geological frontiers, cross the area: the Pontesford-Linley fault and the Church Stretton fault. Lateral movement along both of these brought together rocks of different origins. Vertical movements changed the position of the coastline and the depth of the seas and deposition of sediments differed on opposite sides of one or other of the faults for long periods. Geological maps show the complex juxtapositions that have resulted from the processes of deposition and erosion, uplift and subsidence, faulting and deformation (see Fig. 16). The variation in the ages of Marches rocks, ranging from 670 to 190 million years, and including all nine geological periods from the Precambrian to the Jurassic, is extraordinary. The details of the rock formation can mostly be left to geologists but are too interesting to neglect entirely, as are the fossils within the rocks.[1] This chapter will therefore give a brief summary.

PRECAMBRIAN (MORE THAN 544 MYA) – PUTATIVE LIFE IN SOUTHERN SEAS

James Hutton, father of modern geology, visited Shropshire in 1774 and climbed the Wrekin. He could see that its rocks were crystalline and therefore 'primitive' in origin: what we now call igneous or volcanic. Hutton published the *Theory of the Earth* in 1795 in which he proposed his theory of uniformitarianism, with the processes of formation and erosion of rocks continuing over immensely long periods. Modern dating methods suggest that the rocks of the Wrekin and other similar hills in the Marches were formed about 566 million years ago. The rocks

FIG 35. The Wrekin, viewed across the Severn at Cressage. (Robin Jukes-Hughes)

are now known as Uriconian Volcanics. These are not the oldest surface rocks in the Marches: there are outcrops of gneisses and mica schists near the Wrekin that date from about 670 million years ago, but these are very limited in extent. There are of course no fossils in the Uriconian Volcanics. The chain of volcanoes that produced them were on the margin of a continental plate called Gondwana, with volcanic activity due to the subduction of an oceanic plate under the margin of Gondwana. It is tempting to think that the Wrekin and the other hills made of Uriconian Volcanics are old volcanoes, given their conical appearance from some directions, but they are actually only small remnants of old volcanoes, with the vast majority of the rock eroded away (Fig. 35).

At the time that the Uriconian Volcanics were forming, an enormous depth of sedimentary rocks was also being deposited in the adjacent downwarps. These are the famous Longmyndian rocks, with a total thickness of about 8,000 m. Darwin commented on the lack of fossils in these rocks and had no explanation that he considered satisfactory.[2] This has sometimes been referred to as Darwin's dilemma, as the fossils in rocks from subsequent periods were known to be many and varied. Abundant evidence of larger organisms has now been found in the slightly older deepwater Precambrian rocks of the Charnwood Forest, located 120 km to the east, but in the shallower water rocks of the Long Mynd no large organisms have yet been discovered. When Darwin was writing the *Origin of Species*, pit and mound structures had recently been found in rocks from the Long Mynd and attributed to the burrowing activity of a putative worm, named *Arenicolites*.[3] Recently, the specimens collected by Salter have been re-examined microscopically, together with new collections from Ashes Hollow and Cardingmill Valley on the Long Mynd.[4] Filamentous and disc-shaped microfossils were found that were most likely to have been cyanobacteria and algae. A pattern of shallow pitting found when some Longmyndian shales are split, which had been interpreted as rain prints from mud flats along an ancient coast, has as a result been reinterpreted as the product of microbial mats. The lack of evidence of macroscopic organisms in Long Mynd rocks remains a dilemma.

CAMBRIAN (544–510 MYA) – LIFE IN SHALLOW SOUTHERN SEAS

There were exceptionally widespread glaciations at the end of the Precambrian period; these lowered sea levels, exposed the Uriconian Volcanics and Longmyndian rocks and allowed extensive erosion. Gradually rising sea levels at the start of the Cambrian caused a marine transgression over the eroded Precambrian landscape. As the coastline moved eastwards, wave action created pebbly beaches. The beach pebbles were mostly rhyolite and granophyre, eroded from the Precambrian volcanoes. They became fused together to form conglomerates, which are the lowest Cambrian rocks in the Marches. Primitive planktonic algae have been found in these Cambrian conglomerates. Beach sand was deposited, so the next rocks in the sequence are sandstones called Wrekin Quartzite. This and other Lower Cambrian rocks are well exposed in quarries on the Ercall, northwest of the Wrekin. Here, the unconformity where Cambrian rocks were laid down on an eroded surface of Precambrian rocks is clearly visible. Above the Wrekin Quartzite are sandstones and then thin deposits of sandy limestone, laid down in shallow seas.

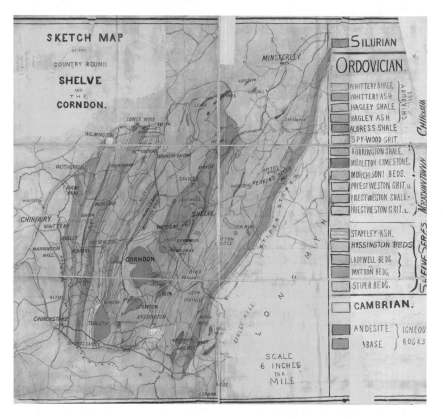

FIG 36. Lapworth's map of *Ordovicia* – he used this huge chart in lectures. (Lapworth Museum, Birmingham University)

These limestones also outcrop on the northern end of Caer Caradoc and are exposed at Comley Quarry. To the untutored eye this is an unprepossessing site, but to geologists it is very well known. It has given its name to the first epoch of the Cambrian period: the Comley Epoch. Callaway found the first examples of Lower Cambrian fossils in Britain here in the 1880s. Charles Lapworth, one of the great pioneers of Marches geology, described them and gave names to the new species. One of the Comley fossils was named *Callavia callavei* and had the distinction of being, at that time, the oldest known trilobite in Britain. Lapworth became the first Professor of Geology at Birmingham University. His archives, including hand drawn geological maps showing large parts of the Marches (Fig. 36) and collections of rocks and fossils now form part of the Lapworth Museum in the university. Dr Edgar Cobbold of All Stretton[5] made detailed studies of fossils from the Comley area in the early decades of the 20th century. Research has continued in the area, with varied finds establishing this as having one of the richest Cambrian faunas of its age in Britain. Beautifully preserved bivalved arthropods, with limbs and soft parts visible, were discovered in a trench excavated near Comley Quarry in 2003. The specimens obtained are related to ostracods and have been assigned to the genus *Phosphatogopida*. They have advanced arthropod anatomy, despite dating from the early Cambrian, and are the oldest crustaceans so far discovered in Britain.

The 20 m of strata exposed in Comley Quarry accumulated over a period of some 10 million years, between 508 and 518 million years ago. All were deposited in shallow water, in a littoral and inner shelf environment, on the margins of the vast continent of Gondwana, at about 65° south. Three divisions are recognised, which are, from base to top, Lower Comley Sandstone, Comley Limestones and Upper Comley Sandstone. The oldest trilobites appear near the top of the Lower Comley Sandstones. The Comley Limestones comprise five units, each characterised by a distinct suite of fossils, which include trilobites, ostracod-like bivalved arthropods, brachiopods and hyolithids. The overlying Upper Comley Sandstones contain fossils quite different from those in the older beds – in particular the large trilobite *Paradoxides* (Fig. 37).

Cambrian fossils from England and Wales have several species in common with those from the Cambrian in eastern Newfoundland, Nova Scotia and Massachusetts. Surprisingly, close by in western Newfoundland and western New England, a completely different suite of Cambrian fossils of 'North American' type occurs. This anomaly was explained by the famous Canadian geologist Tuzo Wilson, one of the pioneers in the development of the plate tectonic theory in the 1960s. He proposed the existence during the Cambrian of an ancient ocean separating England, Wales, eastern Newfoundland, Nova Scotia and Massachusetts

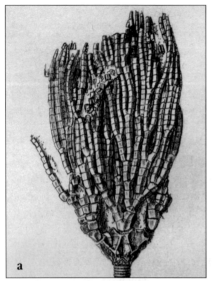

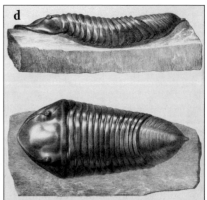

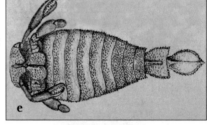

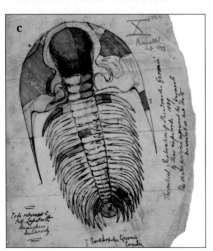

FIG 37. (a) Crinoid (*Cyathocrinus*); (b) graptolite (*Graptolithus*); (c and d) trilobites (*Paradoxides* and *Homalonotus*, respectively); (e) eurypterid (*Pterygotus*); (f) brachiopod (*Pentamerus*). (a, b, d and f: Murchison, 1839; c: original drawing by Lapworth, in the Lapworth Museum, Birmingham University; e: La Touche, 1884)

on its eastern margin from western Newfoundland and western New England on the western margin. This ocean gradually narrowed, and finally closed during later geological times. The Cambrian fossils from Comley Quarry were among those that provided important evidence in support of Wilson's hypothesis.

THE ORDOVICIAN (510–439 MYA) – LIFE NEAR THE COAST OF AVALONIA

At the start of the Ordovician period, about 510 million years ago, the rocks of the Marches still lay under the margins of a wide ocean, with the coastline lying to the southeast. Fine muds were being deposited in deep water; these have become the Shineton Shales, grey-blue in colour and up to 1,000 m thick. Until relatively recently these rocks were included in the Cambrian period, but they contain trilobites such as *Asaphellus* and dendroid graptolites such as *Dictyonema*, fossils that are more similar to those in Ordovician strata above than the Cambrian rocks below. As a result, the Tremadoc Epoch, during which the Shineton Shales were deposited, is now considered as the first epoch of the Ordovician, rather than the last of the Cambrian.

FIG 38. Ordovician trilobites from the Shineton Shales: *Shumardia salopensis*, eyeless and only 2–3 mm long (left) and *Asaphellus homfrayi*, the trilobite used to prove that the Tremadoc Epoch should be in the Ordovician rather than the Cambrian (right). (© Natural History Museum)

The Shineton Shales have proved to be a rich source of fossils (Fig. 38). Several sites where exposures have proved particularly productive have SSSI status. There are exceptionally well-preserved trilobites. The miniature and blind species, *Shumardia salopensis*, thrived for a time on the rich deposits of organic matter in the soft seabed mud, and there are large numbers of specimens in some strata. The many other trilobites belong to eight or more families and include species not previously recorded elsewhere. There are large numbers of dendroid graptolites in certain strata, again with some species first discovered in these rocks. Other species include a group of animals that is now extinct, related to chordates, named calcichordates, and a previously unknown genus of early eocrinoid echinoderms named *Anatifopsis*. One of the most remarkable findings is *Dimorphoconus granulatus*, an armoured worm with an impressive 65 spines on its 10 mm long body, presumably to protect it against predators that lived with it in the mud. The single Shineton Shale specimen is the only one that has been found anywhere.

During the early part of the Ordovician, when the Shineton Shales were being deposited, part of the continent of Gondwana, including the rocks of the Marches, split away to form a small continental plate called Avalonia. Similarities between the Ordovician trilobites found in rocks of the Marches, Wales and eastern Newfoundland show that all these areas were part of this new continent. In the new ocean to the south of Avalonia there was a constructive plate boundary, where expansion of oceanic plates was occurring. There was at the same time subduction of an oceanic plate at the northern edge of Avalonia. As a result, Avalonia moved northwards, carrying the rocks of the Marches with it, from an initial position close to the Arctic Circle, at 65° south of the equator, nearly to the tropics at 30° south by the end of the Ordovician. This was a 4,500-km movement in 50 million years, the mean rate of movement being an impressive 90 mm per year.

At the end of the first epoch of the Ordovician, movement along the Pontesford-Linley fault caused rocks to the east to be uplifted and raised above sea level. The Welsh Basin to the west remained covered by sea. This basin was a downfaulted crustal warp, orientated NNE–SSW. On its eastern edge there was a local, fault-bounded sub-basin. Sediments were deposited in this sub-basin over the period from about 488 to 456 million years ago, with a total depth of over 5,500 m. The district where the resulting rocks now outcrop, named *Ordovicia* in the previous chapter, is around the village of Shelve, west of Stiperstones. The sequence of the Ordovician rocks in the Shelve district is probably more complete than anywhere else in the British Isles, so it is very well known to geologists. Murchison described the rocks as part of his Silurian System, but the

FIG 39. *Ogygiocarella debuchi* (left), an Ordovician trilobite that was misidentified as a flatfish when first discovered in the 17th century and *Lingula lewisi* (right), a Silurian brachiopod from a genus that persists to this day, unlike trilobites. (Shropshire Museums Service)

first detailed description of the geology of the area was by Lapworth and Watts in the 1880s and 1890s. Professor W. F. Whittard[6] spent much of his life studying its fossils and wrote a monograph on the trilobites. Monographs have also been written on the graptolites and brachiopods. The rocks form a remarkable record of the life that existed in the Ordovician seas and of the evolution that occurred during that time. The animal communities that existed were still entirely invertebrate. Some of the groups that were dominant then are now extinct, such as trilobites and graptolites, or much scarcer, for example brachiopods (Fig. 39).

The oldest rocks in the Shelve district are a series of mudstones and fine siltstones. These coarsen upwards, and record a gradual shallowing of the sea, culminating in the deposition of a pale quartz arenite, known as Stiperstones Quartzite. The name suggests that it might be metamorphic, but it is a true sedimentary rock, perhaps formed as a beach deposit, or perhaps as deep slumps of beach-formed sand, with the occasional specimens of the trilobite *Neseuretus*. There are also worm trails and worm tubes with wider entrances visible on bedding plane surfaces. It is an extremely hard and resistant rock, forming the prominent crags along the Stiperstones ridge.

The overlying siltstones and mudstones were deposited from about 478 to 461 million years ago, during a long period of marine deepening with mostly low oxygen concentrations. There was a sparse fauna of benthic trilobites and some brachiopods, together with pelagic trilobites and graptolites. Higher in the sequence there are fine sandstones, siltstones and flagstones that indicate, together with their faunas, short-lived periods under oxygenated conditions. For example, the Meadowtown Formation contains 17 species of brachiopod and 20 species of trilobite, the commonest being the large ogygid species, *Ogygiacarella debuchi*.

At the beginning of the penultimate epoch of the Ordovician, about 461 million years ago, the period of sedimentation in predominantly oxygen-poor environments was terminated abruptly by an influx of storm-generated clean sands. These resulted in abundant shelly fossils, particularly brachiopods and trilobites, commonly transported and fragmentary. The change in deposition coincided with a rise in sea levels that caused the coastline to move east of the Pontesford–Linley fault. More oxygenated conditions prevailed, and the highest parts of the sequence in the Shelve district are dominated by shales, with some beds of sandstone. They contain shelly and graptolitic faunas. The spreading of shallow seas to the east of the Pontesford–Linley fault allowed sediments to be deposited here for the first time since the Shineton Shales had been laid down, about 25 million years earlier. Deposition continued for 10 million years, through the penultimate epoch of the Ordovician, named the Caradoc epoch because the type area is immediately to the east of Caer Caradoc and the Pontesford–Linley fault. Although the sequence in the type area can be correlated with that formed at the same time to the west of the fault, there are differences both in the rocks and in the fossils that they contain. For example, Acton Scott Limestone is a part of the Caradoc sequence to the east of the fault, but not in the west, where shales were being formed in deeper water at the same time. This limestone is highly fossiliferous, with many trilobites and also the distinctive brachiopod, *Nicolella actoniae*, which is the emblem of the Shropshire Geological Society.

At the end of the Caradoc epoch, Avalonia collided with Baltica, a continent lying to the northeast that is now Scandinavia. This is called the Shelveian event, after the village of Shelve. It caused uplift and extensive folding of the Marches rocks. At the same time there was a major glaciation in the southern hemisphere, which lowered the sea level. These two processes caused the coastline to move westwards, so there are almost no rocks or fossils in the Marches formed in the final epoch of the Ordovician period.

THE SILURIAN (439–409 MYA) – LIFE THRIVING IN TROPICAL SEAS

The Silurian rocks of the Marches and their fossils have been studied for over 200 years. Thomas Pennant described corals from Coalbrookdale in 1757. He sent brachiopods and other fossils to Linnaeus, who included them in his system of classification and taxonomy.[7] Arthur Aikin spent 20 years in the early part of the 19th century studying rocks in Shropshire, particularly those from the Silurian. Thomas Lewis, who had attended lectures by Sedgwick in Cambridge was the curate of Aymestrey from 1825 to 1842, during which time he studied the Silurian fossils of the surrounding area.[8] He arranged his collection according to the strata in which the fossils were found and by 1830 had distinguished five formations in the Ludlow area. He knew the sequence in which they had been deposited and the areas in which each outcropped.

Roderick Murchison first visited the Marches in July 1831. In Kington he was shown specimens of the brachiopod *Pentamerus* from local limestone and then travelled to Aymestrey to meet Thomas Lewis. The two men exchanged ideas, with Lewis able to show Murchison how the rocks and their fossils were distributed locally and Murchison sharing with Lewis some theories about the formation of these rocks over the whole of Britain. The two men visited many locations from Aymestrey across to Church Stretton and Wenlock Edge. Later in 1831, Lewis sent Murchison the first in a series of fossil-filled crates. Murchison visited the Marches again in 1832 and met other amateur naturalists who had an interest in geology, including Dr Thomas Lloyd of Ludlow, Dr Davis of Presteigne and his son Edward Davis, the Reverend John Rocke of Clungunford and Mr Proctor, a surgeon from Leintwardine. Murchison gained local knowledge and in return loaned books and arranged for expert identification of their fossils. The enthusiasm for geological research that Murchison promoted was partly responsible for the founding of the Ludlow Natural History Society in 1833, with Murchison as an honorary member. Discoveries continued to be made by local geologists and conveyed to Murchison, for example the Ludlow Bone Bed in 1834. Murchison published his great work *The Silurian System* in 1839, fully acknowledging the fossil collecting work of the Ludlow group, particularly Thomas Lewis. It is believed that one of the formations, Aymestry Limestone, was named in Lewis's honour. However, he did not acknowledge within this book the pioneering stratigraphic research that Lewis had done from 1825 onwards and Murchison has been accused of plagiarising Lewis's work. He subsequently realised the mistake and made amends in *Siluria* when it was published in 1854. Murchison could justifiably claim to be the founding father of the Silurian system, but it was only right for him to honour the work of Lewis and other gentleman amateurs.

Of the four epochs now considered to be part of the Silurian system, two have their type areas in the Marches: the Ludlow and the Wenlock, making these Shropshire place names internationally famous among geologists.

During the first epoch of the Silurian period, the Llandovery, the sea level rose and spread across the folded and eroded Precambrian, Cambrian and Ordovician rocks. Old beach lines, cliffs and sea stacks have been found around the southern end of the Longmynd, but the marine transgression eventually took the coastline eastwards beyond the Marches. The sequence of rocks indicates deepening water, with conglomerates followed by sandstones and purple shales. Brachiopod communities in these Silurian rocks from the Marches and Wales have been correlated with water depth.[9] The *Lingula* community inhabited the shallow intertidal zone, *Eocoelia*, *Pentamerus* and *Stricklandia* communities occupied successively deeper water, whilst in the deepest water at around 100 m, the *Clorinda* community was found and purple shales were being deposited.

The Purple Shales mark the end of the Llandovery and the rocks overlying were deposited in the second epoch of the Silurian. An 8 km length of Wenlock Edge, stretching southwest from Much Wenlock, is the internationally recognised type area for the rocks deposited in this epoch – the Wenlock Series. This area was chosen because the pioneering research was carried out here, and also because there is a continuous sequence of deposits, they are unmetamorphosed, with minimal faulting and the fossils are numerous and diverse. There are many easily accessible rock exposures within the type area, including those that have been selected as stratotype sections. These sections are used by the International Union of Geological Sciences to define the base of a sequence of rocks and thus an instant in geological time.

The Wenlock Series is divided into three formations. The first is the Buildwas Formation, consisting of mudstones and muddy limestones, rich in brachiopods. The second is the Coalbrookdale Formation, with soft calcareous shales, containing numerous trilobites, brachiopods and graptolites. The third subdivision is the Much Wenlock Limestone Formation. It contains one of the most diverse and well preserved of fossil assemblages. Over 600 species have been recorded, with corals (Fig. 40), brachiopods, trilobites, bryozoans and algae all well represented. The

FIG 40. Silurian corals from Wenlock Edge: *Halysites*, also known as chain coral (left) and *Kodonophyllum* (right). (Shropshire Museums Service)

tropics had now been reached, so the seas were warm and rich in dissolved calcium carbonate, which precipitated to form nodular limestones. Tabular limestones were formed from shell debris, with fragments of brachiopods, bryozoans, corals, trilobites and crinoids. A layer up to 4 m thick towards the top of the sequence consists almost entirely of crinoid fragments. The reef limestones are the most famous feature of these rocks. They were formed by patches of coral reef growing where the water was shallow enough, in the sea to the east of the Church Stretton fault – in *East Siluria*. The patches of reef are as much as 24 m thick and 50 m wide. Fossils of sponges, bryozoans, brachiopods and crinoids are found in the interstices between patches of coral reef.

Much Wenlock limestone marks the end of the Wenlock Series, the rocks overlying it being deposited in the third epoch of the Silurian. The area immediately to the west of Ludlow is the internationally recognised type area for rocks of this epoch – the Ludlow Series. As with the Wenlock Series, there is a continuous sequence of deposits, good exposures and an abundance of fossils, including bivalve and gastropod molluscs, brachiopods, corals, trilobites, bryozoa and crinoids. The international stratotype sections are at exposures near the town of Ludlow itself, in the Mortimer Forest to the west and on the Teme and its tributaries above Downton Gorge. The stratotype that has been used to define the base of the whole series is in a quarry at Pitch Coppice in the Mortimer Forest.

Shelly macrofossils of organisms that inhabited the seabed are abundant in the Ludlow Series and these, especially brachiopods, were used to define formations within the series. The first is the Elton Formation and consists of a sequence of mudstones and siltstones. Next is the Bringewood Formation, with calcareous siltstone grading into a silty limestone that is often referred to as Aymestry Limestone. The third is Leintwardine Formation, consisting of shelly limestones and calcareous siltstones often with a honeycombed appearance due to nodules of lime dissolving out as the rock weathers. The Whitcliffe Formation is the uppermost and final part of the Ludlow Series; it consists of calcareous siltstones.

The marked transitions in fossils from one formation to another are due to environmental changes in the shallow tropical waters that were covering this area and also of course to the continuing evolution of life by natural selection. Because the environmental changes are unlikely to have occurred elsewhere in the world at precisely the same times, the brachiopod and other benthic fossils are not suitable for correlating the rocks of the Ludlow Series in the type area with those elsewhere. As with the Wenlock Series, pelagic species that are affected less by local environmental change have proved more useful for this purpose. For example, the graptolite *Saetograptus leintwardinensis* ssp. *leintwardinensis* is found in the third of the four formations, the Leintwardine Formation, both in the type area and elsewhere in the world.

Although the seas that covered the type area during the Ludlow epoch were relatively shallow, they were on the edge of a basin of much deeper water to the west. This resulted in some particularly interesting features in the Leintwardine area. Former submarine canyons that cut through Aymestry Limestone were later filled with deposits from the Ludlow Series; these canyons resemble modern features that have been discovered underwater on many continental shelf edges. The distinctive fauna preserved in the rocks of these channels includes echinoids, starfish and eurypterids (Fig. 41). Church Hill Channel is the best known. Fossils of animals that sheltered in its canyon head were discovered in quarries on Church Hill, near Leintwardine. Because of the importance of these fossils, this site has SSSI status. In the 1850s, *Archaegonaspis ludensis* was found here. At the time, this was the earliest known fish and its discovery showed that marine species existed before the freshwater fish of the Ludlow Bone Bed. By the late 19th century 'a glorious list of fossils' had been recorded.[10] They included several species of starfish, graptolites and many eurypterids. The xiphosuran eurypterids are of immense interest. *Limuloides* has only been found here and only a few examples of *Pseudoniscus* have been found anywhere else in the world.

FIG 41. Silurian starfish *Lapworthura miltoni* from the canyon head of Church Hill Channel. (Shropshire Museums Service)

The basin of deeper water, into which these submarine channels led, extended westwards from the Church Stretton fault across what is now Wales. It already existed in the Wenlock epoch but was deepened by subsidence over a long period in the Ludlow. Compared with area of shallower water to the east of the Church Stretton fault, a much greater depth of sediments was laid down in this basin. The Wenlock Series is at least 500 m deep in the Long Mountain, and the Ludlow Series has a depth of over 2,000 m near Knighton. The sediments deposited in the basin were largely composed of silt, together with the remains of microscopic marine organisms and relatively small amounts of lime. Through much of the Ludlow epoch the conditions on the seabed were anoxic and in the undisturbed conditions, laminated mudstones, siltstones and fine sandstones were formed. These are dark with carbon and contain some pelagic macrofossils, such as orthocones and graptolites, including *Bohemograptus bohemicus*, the youngest British graptolite. Above these dark rocks are lighter mudstones, formed towards the end of the Ludlow epoch, as water depths decreased and oxygenation of sediments on the seabed increased. The burrowing activities of worms and other benthic organisms disturbed the sediments, so these rocks are unlaminated. Fossils are scarce, with the oxygen allowing detritivores and decomposers to dispose of organisms after death.

The rocks formed in the deep water of the basin during the Wenlock and Ludlow epochs contain fewer macrofossils overall than those of the shallower water to the east, but a remarkable exception to this general rule was recently discovered in northwest Herefordshire.[11] The site where the rocks were deposited is known as the Silurian Herefordshire Konservat-Lagerstätte. Fossils in a Konservat-Lagerstätte are of special interest because the soft parts of the animals such as limbs are preserved, in addition to their shells and other hard parts. Only 20 or so of these important sites of exceptional preservation have been discovered in the world and the Herefordshire Konservat-Lagerstätte is an extremely rare Silurian example. A sequence of unlikely events explains the exquisite preservation. Marine animals living 150–200 m deep became surrounded by volcanic ash as it settled onto the seabed some considerable distance from its point of origin. After death, clay minerals were precipitated around each animal. Calcium from the ash and chemicals from the decomposing animal remains then combined to produce calcite, which filled the voids in the clay created by decomposition. Calcite also helped to form a hardened nodule or concretion around each fossil, thereby ensuring the long-term preservation of the animals.

Three-dimensional digital reconstructions of the organisms have been made, using data obtained by grinding away 20 μm layers of the concretion to expose and record a series of sections. The most abundant animal was a small arthropod, *Offacolus kingi*. The genus name means 'dwelling with Offa'. A new species of pycnogonid was described in 2004 and named *Haliestes dasos*. It lived on the seabed, or perhaps on the surface of sponges. Pycnogonids, also known as sea spiders, are very rare as fossils and this is the oldest adult ever discovered. Another newly discovered species is an articulated brachiopod; its soft tissues are preserved along with the pedicle by which it was attached to the substrate. Smaller brachiopods are attached to its shell. A worm-like mollusc was found, with a shell, but no foot. It has been named *Acaenoplax* and has changed views about molluscan evolution. A worm named *Kenostrychus* is the best-preserved polychaete fossil ever found. Other organisms so far found in these nodules include a female ostracod crustacean with eggs (Fig. 42), a trilobite-like arthropod, a shrimp-like crustacean and a starfish.

THE LATE SILURIAN AND DEVONIAN (409–363 MYA) – LIFE ON THE OLD RED SANDSTONE CONTINENT

The rocks that were laid down after the Ludlow epoch, in the last epoch of the Silurian, are markedly different from earlier deposits. At the start of this period the continents of Avalonia and Baltica collided with Laurentia, which lay to the northwest, to form the Old Red Sandstone continent. The collision caused the joining of the rocks of Scotland to those of England and Wales and the uplifting of the Caledonian Mountains. There was a more modest uplifting

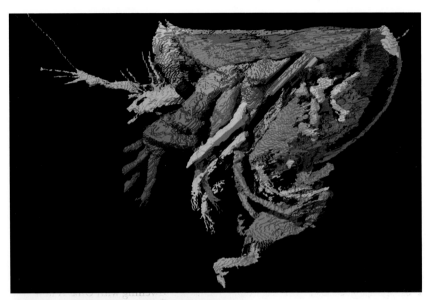

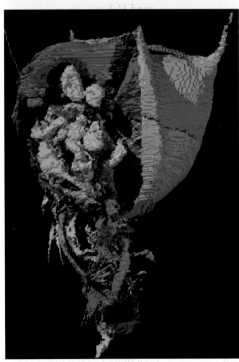

FIG 42. *Nymphatelina gravis* – an exceptionally well-preserved Silurian ostracod crustacean from the Herefordshire Konservat-Lagerstätte. This is a unique example of parental brood care in the invertebrate fossil record. Left lateral view (above) and oblique posterior view (left) with the left valve removed in each case to show appendages, brood and other soft parts. The right valve is shown in grey, the first antenna green, second antenna red, mandible blue, first maxilla pale green and second maxilla dark green. Eggs and possible juveniles are shown in yellow. (David Siveter, Derek Siveter, Mark Sutton and Derek Briggs)

of the rocks of the Marches, resulting in the disappearance of the sea that had either covered the area or been a short distance to the west since Precambrian times. Now the nearest sea was to the south, and brackish lagoons, estuaries and rivers flowing across coastal plains deposited sediments from the north. These were materials eroded from the newly formed Caledonian Mountains. These mountains continued to be uplifted to great heights and be eroded during the next geological period, the Devonian, generating huge amounts of sand and other materials that were deposited. There is therefore no clear boundary here between rocks from the Devonian and earlier ones from the late Silurian. All are collectively known as Old Red Sandstone, though various rock types are present.

Marking the point at which the change from marine to terrestrial deposition began lies the famous Ludlow Bone Bed. It contains large numbers of shiny, black, phosphate-stained fragments from the skeletons and scales of early jawless, cartilaginous fish (Fig. 43). The best-known exposure of the bone bed is at Ludford Corner on the south side of the Teme in Ludlow. A deep slit shows where geologists have excavated for specimens, but this site now has SSSI status and collecting is forbidden. The accumulation of fish fragments probably took place in shallow brackish water in estuaries. The bone bed is internationally recognised as a Lagerstätte.

An even richer source of fossils is siltstone about 200 mm above the actual bone beds. The organisms preserved in these siltstones were part of the

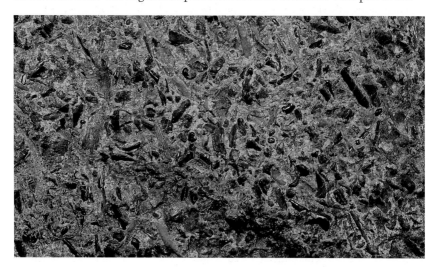

FIG 43. A typical sample of the Ludlow Bone Bed, containing teeth, scales and spines of early fish.

oldest known terrestrial ecosystem. Early land animals found here include centipedes, myriapods, tiny spider-like animals called *Palaeotarbus jerami* and large numbers of the gastropod mollusc *Turbocheilus helicites*. At the base of food chains were some of the earliest species of land plant. Fragments of one species, *Cooksonia pertoni*, have been found, but a diverse range of spore types are present, indicating that a variety of plant species grew in these late Silurian communities. A species discovered recently is different enough to be placed in a new genus: *Hollandophyton colliculum*.[12] Some of the specimens show how dehiscence of the sporangia occurred and one has a stoma – the oldest so far discovered in a spore-producing plant.

The late Silurian and early Devonian periods were particularly significant in the evolution of plants, with the first vascular species diversifying on land. Rocks found in the Marches and Wales give a more complete record of the history of these plants than any other geographical area of the world.[13] *C. pertoni*, already noted from the bone beds of Ludford Corner, has also been found in Upper Silurian mudstones at Lower Wallop Hall Quarry on the Long Mountain. *Cooksonia* and other species found at Ludford Corner belong to the earliest group of vascular land plants, called rhyniophytes. They probably had creeping stem-like structures from which hairs akin to modern rhizoids grew. They also had vertical stem-like axes, some of which were sterile and others carried sporangia.

The plant fossils that have been found in Lower Devonian rocks are more varied and include species better adapted to life on land. Nine species have been found at Targrove, north of Ludlow, four species of *Cooksonia* and five other rhyniophytes. In slightly younger rocks, exposed in the banks of a stream to the north of Brown Clee Hill, more plant species have been found than at any other single Devonian location in the world. This is despite the thickness of rock being less than a metre. The plant remains are scarcely visible to the naked eye, but are revealed by disaggregating the rock, sieving the fragments and chemically cleaning them. Fifteen species have been identified, some with characteristics not found in existing plants. The spores of some species are in pairs rather than groups of four and the leafless axes that support the terminal sporangia are branched. These are features not seen in modern mosses or liverworts, to which these tiny plants are related. The xylem tissue shows similarities with the tracheids of existing vascular plants, such as annular thickenings, but intervening walls are much thicker and, in some cases, much more complex than today. The plant remains from the site on Brown Clee Hill are regarded as phenomenal by palaeontologists, due to their exceptional preservation (Fig. 44). Perhaps surprisingly, this is because the plants were partially burned in a wildfire presumably started by a lightning strike. The fire

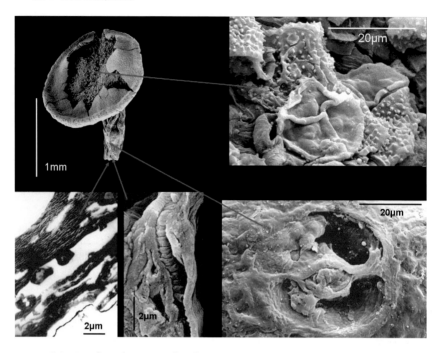

FIG 44. Scanning electron micrographs of a Lower Devonian specimen of *Cooksonia* from Brown Clee Hill: clockwise from upper left, sporangium, spores, stoma, tracheid with wall thickening and tracheid in section. (Dianne Edwards)

was slow and smouldering and so, rather than the plant material being destroyed as in a high temperature fire, it was turned to a charcoal-like material that did not decompose. The older Ludford Lane fossils also show evidence of such preservation and are therefore the earliest evidence of a wildfire worldwide. Newton Dingle, northeast of Ludlow, is yet another important site for fossils of early vascular plants. The rocks are of a slightly later date. The rhyniophyte species *Salopella allenii* has been found, together with a species of *Zosterophyllum*. The zosterphylls were a sister group of plants to lycopsids – the ancestors of modern club mosses.

These plant remains give us tantalising glimpses of the communities that existed in the late Silurian and Devonian periods. From the distribution pattern of fossils, it has been suggested that rhyniophytes may have grown close to wadi-like streambeds that were periodically or seasonally flooded and *Zosterophyllum* species in areas that were less prone to flooding. None of these plants had true roots, so they had little or no capacity to bind sediments together or promote the formation of stable soils with high organic contents. Nevertheless, there are rocks formed during the Devonian that have been regarded as fossil soils. These are limestone plaques, known locally as cornstones, formed by precipitation of soluble calcium carbonate. The process only occurred in arid areas where evaporation from the surface of sands or other materials caused calcium carbonate from lower levels to be drawn up in solution and precipitate. These areas were probably too dry for rootless plants to grow, so the materials that became cornstones were probably not organic soils.

In recent times, two changes have allowed the calcium carbonate in cornstones to move again, but in a different direction. The climate in the Marches is now damp enough for the predominant movement of water in soils to be downward. In addition, soils are now much better developed, with abundant plant roots, animals and microorganisms. Thus rainwater becomes acidified with carbon dioxide from these respiring organisms as it drains through the soil, and then percolates through the cornstones, dissolving out calcium carbonate.[14]

$$CaCO_3 \quad + \quad CO_2 \quad + \quad H_2O \quad \rightarrow \quad Ca^{2+} \quad + \quad 2HCO_3^-$$

insoluble	carbon	water	soluble	soluble
calcium	dioxide		calcium	hydrogen
carbonate			ions	carbonate ions

Where the water emerges at a spring, the calcium carbonate precipitates, forming a rock called tufa. This happens where streams emerge through the escarpment of Bishop's Frome Limestone, at Great Hudwick Dingle and other sites along the south side of Corvedale. Large deposits of hardened tufa, known as travertine, are found in northwest Worcestershire, again where streams emerge from cornstones in an outcrop of Bishop's Frome Limestone. These streams are on the southwest side of the Teme valley, between Eastham and Shelsley Walsh.[15] The largest travertine deposit is Southstone Rock, over 15 m high and containing thousands of tonnes (Fig. 45). Tufa also forms when water drains through Carboniferous rocks where porous acid and calcareous strata are interbedded. As rainwater percolates through these strata, its acidification and dissolving of calcium carbonate can occur repeatedly and large quantities of tufa have sometimes been formed. There is active deposition in Weir Coppice near Shrewsbury, Lydebrook Dingle above Coalbrookdale and in flushes at Wyre. Deposits of tufa and travertine are large enough in places for them to have been quarried and used as building stone, as in parts of Wigmore and Aymestrey churches.

The precipitation of calcium carbonate to form tufa or travertine depends on a reduction in carbon dioxide concentration in the water caused by

FIG 45. Southstone Rock: part of the huge deposit of travertine with hart's tongue fern growing below it (above) and active travertine formation with the moss *Palustriella commutatum* (below).

photosynthesising organisms. Plant roots are usually unable to penetrate the
hard deposits, so cyanobacteria and bryophytes are dominant. There are therefore
traces of these organisms in the deposits and living specimens grow on surfaces
where deposition is still occurring. Few species can tolerate the variable flow rates
and alkalinity of the water and the deposition of up to 5 mm of calcium carbonate
per year. Thus a restricted range of species occurs, strong similarities being seen
between the sites in the Marches and elsewhere in Europe.[16] As elsewhere, there
are biofilms of cyanobacteria where flow rates are greatest. The moss *Palustriella
communtatum* is dominant in moderately fast flowing water; it becomes encrusted
with tufa but grows quickly enough not to be entombed. In spray zones and
where flow rates are slower there is a wider variety of mosses and liverworts.
Five other species have been recorded at Southstone Rock, including *Eucladium
verticillatum,* another very typical moss. In the tufa flushes of Wyre *Ellipteroides
alboscutellatus,* a Red Data Book 1 species of cranefly has been found. It is confined
to this type of habitat, possibly because its larvae feed on the tufa-forming
Palustriella mosses that are associated with tufa formation. Within tufa and
travertine, the hard parts of some animals can become preserved. At Southstone
Rock, 30 species of mollusc were found, in travertine estimated by radiocarbon
dating to have been deposited 6,670 years ago.[17] There were also ostracod valves,
larval cases of caddis flies and teeth of wood mice *Apodemus sylvaticus* that may
become fossils of the future.

THE CARBONIFEROUS (363–290 MYA) – LIFE ON EQUATORIAL LAND AND IN THE SEA

At the start of the Carboniferous period there was a worldwide rise in sea levels.
It caused a marine transgression over parts of the Old Red Sandstone continent,
with limestone deposited in the warm shallow water. It is largely composed of
the skeletons of marine microorganisms, but it also contains fossils of corals,
brachiopods, molluscs, crinoids and bryozoa. The deposits of Carboniferous
limestone show that the sea spread from the north, reaching Llanymynech and just
beyond the Wrekin to Little Wenlock, and from the south as far as Titterstone Clee.
An isthmus of land was left between these areas of inundation and deposition.

Later in the Carboniferous period, river deltas spread over the shallow
seas and deposited coarse sandstones. In the Oswestry area these contain
brachiopods, and other marine fossils occur in bands formed during periodic
inundation by the nearby seas. The rocks deposited during the next part of the
Carboniferous again exhibit repeated cycles of rock formation. These are the

Coal Measures and the cycles were at least partly due to periodic glaciations in Antarctic regions. In typical cycles, rising sea levels caused the deposition of mud, followed by sand. As water levels became shallower plants were able to colonise, and ecological succession then led to the development of a tropical forest dominated by the giant lycopods and tree ferns that had evolved by this stage of the Carboniferous. The forest was eventually killed by flooding by fresh water or by rising sea levels. Remains of the forest were partially preserved as a seam of coal, and the soil below was fossilised to form rocks called seat-earth. The sequence of strata in the Coal Measures is therefore shale, sandstone, siltstone, coal and then more shale.

The seams of coal vary in their thickness and characteristics, so were easily recognised by miners. There are more than 20 named seams in the Coalbrookdale coalfield, such as Upper Lancashire Ladies Coal and Fungous Coal. There are also some narrow deposits of about 100 mm that were simply called thin coal. The thickness of individual seams varies across coalfields, as they were formed in delta areas, with braided, meandering and shifting river channels separating low-lying islands with forests and swampy lagoons. The seat-earths often contain fossil roots, and are either fireclays rich in kaolinite, or sandstones rich in silica. These deposits indicate leaching of minerals, probably by seepage of acid groundwater. Iron was leached downwards into the underlying subsoil, then reduced by bacteria to form the insoluble salts that are now part of ironstones in the shale deposits.

Plant fossils are abundant in the coal seams and large collections of them were built up while the coal was being worked. Quaker ironmaster William Reynolds encouraged local miners to collect specimens for him and paid them for their finds. Ludlow Museum, Ironbridge Gorge Museums Trust and the Lapworth Museum in Birmingham University all hold important collections. More recently, a remarkable fossil forest was found during open cast coal working in 2003 on the site of a former steelworks at Brymbo, northwest of Wrecsam (Fig. 46). The bases of many trees were discovered, including *Calamites*, a giant horsetail with bamboo-like segmented trunks and *Lepidodendron*, a giant clubmoss with diamond-shaped leaf scars on its branches. Fossilised roots of *Lepidodendron* up to 8 m long were found still attached to its trunks, that were branched and had root hairs. Other plants were discovered in large numbers such as the seed fern *Medullosales* and the tree ferns *Alethopteris* and *Neuropteris*. Efforts are being made by local geologists to preserve as much of the fossil forest as possible *in situ*, but it has proved difficult to convince those who could provide the money that the Brymbo site is of huge interest and importance.

FIG 46. Fossil forest at Brymbo – the base of a huge *Lepidodendron* trunk, with attached roots. (Jacqui Malpas)

During the Devonian and Carboniferous periods, the ocean to the south of the rocks of the Marches had been narrowing as the large southern continent that lay beyond this ocean moved north. At the end of the Carboniferous this ocean finally closed up and there was a collision between the continental plate within which the rocks of the Marches lay, and the southern continent. This ended the cycles of marine transgressions that had been such a dominant feature of the Carboniferous and caused the uplift of rocks of the Marches to create uplands called Mercian Highlands.

THE PERMIAN (290–245 MYA) AND TRIASSIC (245–208 MYA) – LIFE IN HOT DESERTS

At the start of the Permian, the rocks of the Marches were already part of a large continent and had moved north of the equator. At this latitude, there was minimal rainfall and therefore desert conditions. The Mercian Highlands were gradually eroded, the eroded fragments becoming new rocks in lower lying areas. The most extensive deposits are sandstone, composed of sand grains that are rounded as a result of being wind-blown. The cross bedding in these sandstones gives a vivid impression of how large, horseshoe-shaped dunes formed, and were gradually displaced downwind. The same process can be seen happening now in the Sahara and other sandy deserts (Fig. 47).

FIG 47. Bridgnorth Sandstone, showing cross bedding created as sand dunes migrated across an arid desert landscape at the end of the Permian period; remains are visible of a cliff house excavated in the soft rock.

At the end of the Permian there were significant environmental changes in many parts of the world, accompanied by a mass extinction of species and the appearance of ammonites and other new groups, but there were no striking changes in this region. Terrestrial conditions persisted in the Triassic period that followed. Very extensive sandstone deposits were formed; these are grey, green, cream or bright red, depending on the minerals that impregnated the deposits of sand. The rocks of the Marches had reached 20° and 30° north of the equator by this time – the latitude of the Sahara desert today.

In the middle of the Triassic period, lakes spread over the northern parts of the Marches. The siltstones formed in these lakes contain traces of lizard-like animals. In 1840, Ogier Ward, a Shropshire physician, collected fossil specimens of a small reptile from quarrymen at Grinshill, north of Shrewsbury. He sent them to Richard Owen, who described it as *Rhynchosaurus articeps*, a new genus

FIG 48. *Rhynchosaurus* forearm and ribcage from Grinshill (left) (Shropshire Museums Service) and footprints from Alveley quarry (right). (Andrew Jenkinson)

and species of reptile[18] (Fig. 48). Nearly 20 specimens have since been found as well as footprints made in soft mud at the margins of the lakes. *R. articeps* was about half a metre long with a bulky body, slender legs and a long tail. It was a member of a group of reptiles that were the dominant herbivores throughout the world in the middle and late Triassic. The dentition is unique among animals with two or three rows of teeth on both upper and lower jaws, which opened and closed without any sideways or backwards and forwards grinding action. There are also two structures that may have resembled boar's tusks, but rather than being modified teeth, they were enlarged skull bones. These were probably used for digging out roots, as were the claws on the animal's toes. Fossils of two other reptiles have recently been found in Grinshill rocks, *Isochirotherium* and *Brachychirotherium*, both about 4 m long, the former a herbivore and the latter an omnivore. Tracks of a carnivore, *Lagosuchus*, have also been found but bones are known only from other parts of the world.

After the deposits containing these reptiles were formed, conditions in the latter part of the Triassic became more arid and in northern parts of the Marches extensive salt flats developed, into which water and sediments were washed after desert storms, to form shallow playa lakes. Great depths of clay accumulated and became the mudstones known as Keuper Marl. Beds of saliferous rocks, interspersed through the strata of mudstone, form the basis for the Cheshire salt-mining industry. Dark shales containing marine fossils were formed at the end of the Triassic period when the sea that had been to the southwest spread up to cover the rocks of the Marches. Many species became extinct throughout the world at this time, among them rhyncosaurs, in another of the great global extinction events.

THE JURASSIC (208–146 MYA) – LIFE IN WARM SHALLOW SEAS

Seas covered the rocks of the Marches during the Jurassic and as they were about 30° to 40° north of the equator, conditions were similar to those of the Mediterranean today. Shales, clays and thin layers of limestone were deposited first, followed by sandy marls, calcareous mudstones, sandstones and grey shales. Thick glacial deposits cover the area of these rocks in the Marches except in the area around the village of Prees, south of Whitchurch. Investigation of these Jurassic deposits has therefore rarely been possible. A sexton collected fossils in the 19th century when graves were being dug in Prees churchyard. These came from deposits known as Middle Lias, which are rich in ammonites, bivalve molluscs such as oysters and scallops, and brachiopods. One of the few places where the Lower Lias is accessible is in the bed of the River Duckow, where it forms the county boundary between Shropshire and Cheshire near Audlem. Fossils of molluscs and echinoderm debris are present. During the building of a bypass at Prees in 1988, Lower Lias deposits were temporarily exposed in a cutting and were studied in detail by Professor Hugh Torrens. Frustratingly, all of the aragonite fossils including ammonites had been dissolved away, only calcitic fossils such as belemnites and oysters being preserved.

The rocks at Prees were laid down in the early Jurassic. Considerable depths of rock were deposited over them in later parts of the Jurassic and the Cretaceous period, covering the older rocks of the Marches. During the late Cretaceous, about 70 million years ago, the rocks of Britain were uplifted, and subsequent rates of erosion were increased. The uplift was greater in the uplands of north and west of Britain and erosion has removed more of the geological sequence, leaving older rocks at the surface. In the lowlands of the south and east there was less uplift and less erosion, so younger rocks remain at the surface. There was about 2 km of uplift in the Marches and the rate of erosion was intermediate, leaving this area on the border between upland and lowland Britain, with both older and younger rocks exposed. The uplift and tilting of the late Cretaceous followed by subsequent erosion can therefore be added to the list of reasons for the huge range of rock types in the Marches.

CHAPTER 4

Uplands

I N NORTHERN PARTS OF BRITAIN and west of Offa's Dyke there are extensive upland areas, penetrated by narrow valleys. This situation is typically reversed in the Marches. The hilltops form an archipelago of upland islands scattered across extensive lower lying plains or separated by broad valleys. These are therefore not simply small outliers of upland Britain: their natural history is distinct and worthy of description.

The contrast between the higher hills and the lower lying areas in the Marches is very striking. There is a range of altitude of more than 535 m, from 540 m above sea level at the summit of Brown Clee, to below 5 m on either side of the Dee where it reaches Aldford. A simple but striking example of the effects of altitude comes from a survey carried out by schoolchildren at Burwarton Primary School, to the east of Brown Clee. In 1984, they recorded the date when lesser celandines *Ranunculus ficaria* started flowering at different heights up the hill and showed that it was correlated with altitude. The lowest plants flowered a month earlier than those growing nearby but 180 m higher.[1] This is almost certainly due to lower temperatures at greater altitude though insolation is also less on average, a result of greater cloud cover. Some factors increase with altitude: wind speed, relative humidity, rainfall, frequency of snowfall, duration of snow cover and both frequency and persistence of ground frosts.

The hilltops have a markedly harsher climate than the low-lying land and a distinctly shorter growing season. Some upland areas, for example on Long Mountain, have deeper soils, richer in bases; these have been enclosed and there is arable farming. Nevertheless, the combination of harsh climate and thin leached soils has precluded arable or intensive livestock farming in large parts of the uplands; these are therefore unenclosed and semi-natural communities have developed. The type of community depends on slope, aspect, drainage and soil type. Most areas are grazed by sheep, occasionally by cattle or horses, so woodland cannot develop. On many of the hills the soils are thin, leached acid loams and there are species-poor moorland or grassland communities. Bracken forms extensive stands in some areas. There are also some upland areas where the soils are neutral or alkaline and the concentration of bases is reasonably high, but the soils are too thin for arable farming, so semi-natural species-rich grassland communities are found here. Soils in many parts of the uplands are freely draining, but there are also waterlogged areas, where specialised communities of plants and animals occur. Some areas are prone to drought, particularly on south-facing slopes, and distinctive grassland communities have developed here. All of these upland communities will be considered in this chapter, starting with the community that is often associated with hilltops of upland Britain.

THE MOORLANDS OF THE MARCHES

Heather-bilberry heath, often called heather moorland, is a very common community in upland Britain, forming the great grouse moors of northern

FIG 49. Heather moorland spreading into pasture at the northern end of the Stiperstones.

England, Scotland and Wales (Fig. 49). The Marches are at the edge of its distribution and there are no significant areas to the southeast. Rainfall here is at the lower end of the possible range and winter temperatures are at the upper end so this community is confined to higher ground, or as on Corndon Hill, north-facing slopes. Even on these relatively wet and cold areas, management is needed for the community to persist. The driving force in the past has been the income and enjoyment gained from grouse shooting by wealthy landowners or owners of shooting rights.

There has been some dispute about whether red grouse *Lagopus lagopus* are native to the Marches or were introduced (Fig. 50). Two pairs from Yorkshire were released on the Long Mynd in 1840, but there is a reliable report that in 1838 they were already common on the Stiperstones. It is most likely that red grouse spread naturally from Wales and have been present for centuries on hills in the Marches including the Stiperstones, Brown Clee and Titterstone Clee. During the 19th century, while labour remained easily available, it was possible to manage moorland quite intensively and maintain the conditions needed to sustain large populations. Annual bags of over 100 brace were recorded on some hills. In the second half of the 20th century a vicious cycle set in: a reduction in the number of gamekeepers led to a decrease in the management of moors and thus the size of the grouse population, hence a fall in income from shooting available to pay gamekeepers. By the 21st century, red grouse had disappeared from all hills in the Marches apart from the Long Mynd and Stiperstones; even on these former strongholds the populations were greatly reduced.

FIG 50. Red grouse camouflaged against old ling heather stems. (John Hawkins)

Periodic heather burning has been a traditional management technique, used to stimulate regrowth of young heather and prevent invasion by scrub and trees. On the Long Mynd, the burned areas were typically 15 m wide and as much as several hundred metres long. This was carried out in rotation to prevent the heather from becoming too old and woody, thus ensuring that the young shoots on which the grouse feed were available close to older areas that provide cover. The disadvantage of repeated burning is a loss of fire-intolerant plant and animal species, though low plant diversity may be an inherent feature of moorland whether or not it is burned. On the Long Mynd heather is typically dominant, with large amounts of bilberry *Vaccinium myrtillus*. Some wavy hair grass *Deschampsia flexuosa* and a small number of species of moss and lichen are also found, but no other plants. Areas of heath on the Stiperstones are a little more diverse, with bell heather *Erica cinerea*, cowberry *Vaccinium vitis-idaea* (Fig. 51) and several other species present, but still far fewer species than in most plant communities. It is perhaps therefore surprising that conservation agencies have made great efforts to conserve and even expand this species-poor plant community on both the Long Mynd and the Stiperstones. There is much to be learned from these conservation efforts and so both will be carefully considered here. There is moorland on the Clee Hills, but conservation efforts and research here are less advanced.

FIG 51. Cowberry flowers and fruits on the Stiperstones. (Ben Osborne)

Managing the moorland on the Long Mynd

The National Trust have been the owners since 1965 of a large proportion of the Long Mynd, including most of the summit plateau, when 2,000 ha of common land was bought from the manor of Stretton en le Dale. Several other areas were acquired in 1978, including Cardingmill valley and the Batch. There are currently only three National Trust properties in Britain with their own dedicated ecologist and the Long Mynd is one of these: Caroline Uff has been the ecologist since 2000. There are strong arguments for conservation of heather moorland on the Long Mynd. One is a widespread public perception that broad hilltops should be heather moors and should turn purple each August. A second is the scarcity of red grouse in the Marches. Support for this species is not a strong enough reason in itself but there are also other birds nesting in summer on the hilltops that might be expected to benefit from preservation of heather. Along with red grouse, skylarks *Alauda arvensis*, meadow pipits *Anthus pratensis* and curlew *Numenius arquata* form the most characteristic quartet of ground-nesting species. Their song flights provide some of the most evocative sounds of the high country in the Marches.

The requirements of red grouse for heather, young shoots for feeding and older plants as cover for nesting, have already been mentioned. Curlews also require cover for nesting, from dense heather or long grassland, but they prefer to feed in open areas of short grass, bilberry or heather that has recently been cut or burnt. Their numbers fell catastrophically on the Long Mynd from about 12 pairs in the mid-1990s to two pairs in 2004 and 2006.

Skylarks and meadow pipits are ground-nesting passerines that show many similarities in their characteristics, but also differences in terms of habitat requirements. They both breed on the summit plateau. Forrest commented that the skylark was very plentiful in Shropshire when he was writing at the end of the 19th century and that it made very good eating, though 'it seems a thousand pities that it should ever be destroyed for this purpose'.[2] He also wrote that the male skylark's lovely trilling song when soaring is 'the delight of all who hear it'. Male meadow pipits sing while ascending to about 30 m and then parachute rapidly downwards. The skylark and meadow pipit are birds of both the uplands and lowlands of Britain; both declined significantly in the lowland parts of their range in the 1970s and 1980s. Their conservation on upland sites is therefore particularly important. Survey transects in 1996–8 and 2004–6 did not show any significant changes in numbers of skylark and meadow pipit territories.[3] In the 1990s the skylark population was found to be between 12 and 18 pairs per km^2 on the summit plateau of the Long Mynd, which is far higher than the national average of below 5 per km^2 for upland populations.[4] The highest densities were found in areas where the heather cover was 26–75 per cent. This is because skylarks, like red grouse and curlew, have different requirements for nesting and feeding. They feed in areas of short grass and nest where there is more cover. In areas of thick old heather, with a cover of more than 75 per cent, there is too little short grass for them. A heather cover of less than 25 per cent could be due either to overgrazing, so there is not enough cover for nesting, or invasion by bracken, the height of which prevents a vital second brood from being raised during the breeding season. Heather itself does not seem to be necessary and where bilberry is not overgrazed it can also offer good habitat, provided short grass is also present. The breeding population of meadow pipits on the summit plateau is more than twice that of skylarks and they are the most numerous birds on the Long Mynd overall, though nationally the populations are of a similar size.[5] They nest in tussocky rough grass and do not have the skylark's feeding requirement for short grass. The transect survey found highest densities in areas with large amounts of heather, or bilberry with heather, and lower densities in uninterrupted areas of close-cropped grassland – meadow pipits also seem to benefit from a mosaic of plant communities.

This quartet of hilltop species therefore has differences in habitat preference, so management of plant communities aimed solely at encouraging one might harm populations of another. It would be hard to claim that the conservation of any of them is pre-eminently important. Red grouse was the original target species of moorland management, so perhaps can claim precedence. Curlews have undergone the most catastrophic recent decline on Marches hilltops. Skylarks are a UK Biodiversity Action Plan, or BAP, priority species and have undergone a steep national decline. Meadow pipits do not have any specific conservation status themselves, but a case can be made for them based on their importance to merlin. The Long Mynd is the only site in the Marches where these small falcons nest. They have done so sporadically for at least 100 years and possibly much longer. One or two pairs have been recorded in most years since the mid-1980s, but since merlin are birds of uplands and coasts, the pairs on the Long Mynd are outliers. Although they can take a range of small birds on moorland, meadow pipits are their main prey, and without a strong pipit population the merlin would almost certainly be lost. Management of the summit plateau of the Long Mynd therefore needs to be finely judged, so that each of this quartet of species survives, along with other species. Two conservation issues will be considered in relation to the Long Mynd: control of the sheep stocking rate and therefore intensity of grazing and whether heather should be burned or cut. A third issue, whether there should be control of predators, will be considered in relation to the Stiperstones.

Grazing intensity is the first management issue. In the 1980s and 1990s the Common Agricultural Policy encouraged high sheep stocking rates and it became clear that this was causing changes to plant and animal communities on the Long Mynd. Heather was failing to regenerate properly after burning, with seedlings grazed off, and any new growth on established plants also eaten, eventually killing them. This was allowing wavy hair grass and other grasses to replace the heather. Bilberry was more resilient to the intense grazing but was also diminishing, with few flowers or fruits being formed. Grassland was being grazed so intensively that it was gradually being replaced by bracken. There were about 15 red grouse territories, indicating a decrease in population of more than 90 per cent from the peak. The National Trust is the owner of a large part of the Long Mynd, yet the land is a common, with owners of property in the locality holding commoners' rights. More than 90 commoners had rights to graze a total of 27,890 sheep in the early 1990s. Only 18 of them were exercising these rights, and the total number of sheep being grazed in the summer was over 13,500. Traditionally all sheep were removed from the hill over the winter, but in the 1970s some commoners started to keep sheep on the hill and this has considerable disadvantages from the point of view of wildlife conservation. Supplementary feed is brought out to these sheep at feed stations, but there is still excessive winter grazing of heather, especially in the areas nearby. Dunging at the feed stations facilitates invasion by coarse grasses. Sheep deaths cause an excess of carrion on the hill, leading to increases in the populations of foxes *Vulpes vulpes*, carrion crows *Corvus corone* and other predators; these then harry ground-nesting birds such as curlew in the summer.

Although the numbers of sheep were reduced in the second half of the 1990s, they remained too high. The Long Mynd was part of the Shropshire Hills Environmentally Sensitive Area, or ESA. An ESA agreement began in 1999. This had been difficult to draw up as it involved the cooperation of the active commoners. As a result of the compromises that were reached, all but one commoner did agree to participate. It was a notable achievement, defying the usual preconceptions about the tragedy of the commons, though the commoners did receive payments as a part of the ESA agreement. This was a landmark agri-environment scheme as it was the first in Britain where the total payments were over £1 million. The stocking rate was reduced to a maximum of 3,341 ewes in summer and 1,670 in winter. This gives rates of 1.5 ewes per ha in summer and 0.75 in winter. It was agreed that supplementary feeding on the hill would stop at all sites. Soon after the ESA agreement was implemented, SSSI condition monitoring by English Nature showed that all of the sectors into which the Long Mynd was divided were in unfavourable condition and in more than 90 per cent of them this was due to the effects of moderate or heavy grazing. From 2002 onwards, the summit plateau of the Long Mynd turned purple again in August, with widespread flowering of heather. Whinberries, the local name for bilberries, had been abundant enough in the past to be picked on a commercial basis for use as a dyestuff and it became worthwhile to pick them again. The red grouse population was monitored from 1994 onwards by counting males calling at dawn in the heather covered areas during the winter. This indicates the number of territories and therefore gives a measure of the number of breeding pairs. The counts had risen above 30 by 2006, more than doubling the levels recorded in the 1990s. Grasses also benefited from the reduced intensity of grazing, with larger tussocks of wavy hair grass and sheep's fescue *Festuca ovina*. This did not seem to affect numbers of meadow pipit and skylark, which remained at high levels.[6] In contrast, the curlew population remained very small, almost certainly because of the large numbers of predators. Attempts were made to regenerate heather-bilberry heath in areas where it had been lost. In six trial areas where grassland had replaced heath, the turf was stripped in 2000 and heather seed was sown. By 2007, two of the plots had impressive heather growth, two had patchy growth and the other two had no signs of heather growth, perhaps as a result of winter grazing (Fig. 52). A conifer plantation at Handless on the west side of the Long Mynd was felled in 2001 and not replanted. Large parts of this site were already reverting to heathland by 2005.

Burning is the second management issue. It has been carried out for at least 150 years on the Long Mynd, but is not a natural phenomenon on Marches hills and is hard to defend on wider environmental grounds. The National Trust reduced the amount of burning and stopped it almost completely from the mid-1990s until 1999. The ESA agreement that began in 1999 involved a return to

FIG 52. Successful heather regeneration in an experimental strip on High Park, at the north end of the Long Mynd. (Caroline Uff)

burning or cutting on about half of the area of heather on the summit plateau. Small areas were burned in rotation, to establish a 15–18 year cycle and ensure that treated heather is still young enough to regrow from the base. The areas that were tackled in the early 20th century were old heather, so almost all recovery was from seed, which can be more problematical, though similar areas that were burned in 1995–6 had more than 80 per cent heather cover seven years later. Cutting began as an alternative to burning on some areas in 2001, with the cut material exported to the Netherlands for use in filtering factory waste (Fig. 53). Heather recovery is at least as good after cutting as after burning, with 75 per cent heather cover reached after only five years.

FIG 53. Heather burning at Wildmoor on the Long Mynd and bales of cut heather ready for despatch. (Nick Robinson)

To investigate the effects of cutting and burning on invertebrate populations, pitfall trapping was carried out in representative areas.[7] The results showed that species diversity was higher in areas that had been burned seven years ago than areas that had been burned one year ago. However, the lowest species diversity was found in areas of old heather that had not been burned or cut for at least 50 years, showing that cessation of heather burning is unlikely to increase species diversity. Perhaps surprisingly, diversity was slightly lower in areas that had been cut one year ago than in areas that had been burned. This survey also showed that each of the types of heather had species that were not found in the others. For example, *Xysticus sabulosus*, a crab spider, was found only in the young heather. It is an uncommon species with a scattered distribution throughout Britain, but is most abundant on heaths in southern Britain. Crab spiders rely on camouflage to catch their prey. The coloration of this species matches sand and gravel and it typically increases in numbers in the first two or three years after the burning of heathland. It is not clear from this survey whether cutting would also provide suitable habitat for *X. sabulosus*, but old heather and dense tussocky grassland certainly do not. Conversely, this survey found old heather to have large numbers of *Allomengea scopigera*, a money spider that had not previously been recorded in the Marches. It is principally a species of the north and west, and the Long Mynd is on the edge of this range. If there were no areas of old heather on the summit plateau this species might well disappear, diminishing its range in Britain. As is so often found, no single management technique will ensure the survival of all species and a mosaic of habitats should be the aim.

Of course there are many invertebrate species that are rarely caught in pitfall traps, including most flying insects. An example is *Bombus monticola*, sometimes known as the bilberry bumblebee (Fig. 54). This species has undergone a serious decline and is therefore the target of a species recovery plan in England. It is characteristic of moorland in the north and west, but there is a population on the Long Mynd and smaller populations on the Stiperstones and in the Clun Forest. Queens are produced in July and August and overwinter, emerging from hibernation to establish nests in April on high ground such as the Long Mynd's summit plateau or near its edge. Pollen is collected from bilberry plants during their flowering season from April to June and from heather in August. The workers seek other pollen sources in the gap between these two periods. This involves flying down from the summit to find western gorse *Ulex gallii*, white clover *Trifolium repens* or other suitable plants. Ideally there would be a greater diversity of flowering plants on the summit plateau, to fill the gap in flowering. Intensive grazing is a threat to this rare bumblebee, as it prevents flowering of bilberry and heather.

FIG 54. Bilberry bumblebee queen nectaring on the Long Mynd. (David Williams)

By 2009, most sectors of the Long Mynd were in unfavourable but improving condition. The ESA period ended, but was immediately replaced by a Higher Level Stewardship (HLS) agreement, reached through long and careful negotiations. All commoners joined the scheme, even though it represented a compromise between commercial and conservation interests. Grazing remains much less intensive than before and burning will continue for the moment, though there is increasing pressure to end it. The hope is that as long as grazing intensity is low enough, old heather will topple over and be able to regenerate naturally. Early signs are that the condition of moorland on the Long Mynd is continuing to improve.

Moorland on the Stiperstones and the Back to Purple project

To the west of the Long Mynd is the 10 km Stiperstones ridge (Fig. 55). SSSI designation has already been given to 588 ha here, but it has been recommended for elevation to a Special Area of Conservation, usually abbreviated to SAC, because some of its habitat types and species are threatened at a European level. An area of 448 ha is a National Nature Reserve, mostly now owned by Natural England.

The area of heather moorland on the Stiperstones is smaller than that on the Long Mynd, but its plant diversity is greater. This is partly because it is geologically more diverse, but perhaps also because of past management. Heather is dominant, with other dwarf shrubs accompanying it: bilberry, cowberry and crowberry *Empetrum nigrum*. Heath bedstraw *Galium saxatile*, tormentil *Potentilla erecta* and

FIG 55. Heather moorland on the western side ridges of the Stiperstones. The sharp demarcation between meadow and moor, and the stripes of flowering heather show the effect of management. (Natural England)

common cow-wheat *Melampyrum pratense* are characteristic herbs. Bell heather is present on south-facing slopes of valleys on the western side. As on the Long Mynd, heather burning has been practised for many years on the Stiperstones. This has continued on a rotational basis under ownership and management by the Nature Conservancy Council and its successors. Cutting was introduced as an alternative to burning in 1986, using a tractor-mounted implement called a swipe, or jungle-buster. Initially the cut material was put into rows using a hay tedder and then picked up with a forage loader wagon. More recently, to reduce the expense, the cut material has been left to decompose *in situ* and less cutting has been carried out.

An ESA agreement operated between 1994 and 2000 for the Stiperstones, but in contrast to that for the Long Mynd, its aim was to ensure that there were adequate levels of grazing, rather than to prevent overgrazing. Much of the National Nature Reserve is common land, but only three commoners have grazing rights and they grazed too few sheep and cattle to prevent tree establishment, especially rowan *Sorbus aucuparia*, during the 1980s and early 1990s. The ESA agreement established a minimum stocking rate per hectare of 1.1 ewes plus followers in summer and 0.6 in winter, with up to 40 cattle substituted for sheep at a rate of 1 cow per 6 ewes. These stocking rates are lower than those on the Long Mynd and there has actually been little or no winter grazing on the Stiperstones. As a result, tree establishment has continued. Steep and awkward slopes are most prone to this because they are less attractive to grazing animals, although the development of some small patches of woodland is welcomed. Hebridean sheep have proved better at killing tree seedlings and saplings by browsing than the commercial breeds that the commoners favour. A flock of Hebrideans is therefore kept to control tree establishment in areas where it would adversely affect the moorland. Stocking rates are still low however, and both herbicide treatment and cutting have been used to keep the main part of the moorland free of trees. Darwin pointed out how persistent young trees can be, when describing pines on a Surrey heath: 'In one square yard I counted thirty-two little trees; and one of them, judging from the rings of growth, had during twenty-six years tried to raise its head above the stems of the heath and failed.'[8]

A change in regulations prevented the ESA agreement from continuing after 2000 and so English Nature paid a subsidy directly to the commoners, encouraging them to graze the Stiperstones. Another change in regulations allowed money from the EU to be used for payments under the Higher Level Stewardship agri-environment scheme, or HLS, from 2009 onwards. As with previous schemes, the subsidies provided about 60 per cent of the commoners' income. If the payments ended, it would not be economically viable to graze the Stiperstones. Unless heroic conservation work was done annually to replace the grazing of sheep and cattle, woodland would replace moorland within about 20 years. This may well be appropriate on hills that contribute little to biodiversity, but not on the Stiperstones.

The population of red grouse has been monitored since 1989. This is done by recording the number of males calling at dawn in spring and by counting total numbers in summer. The summer censuses were originally done using dogs to point the grouse. More recently a team of volunteers linked by a rope has moved from one end of the Stiperstones to the other, dragging the rope across the ground to flush the grouse. Numbers had fallen to less than ten males in the early 1990s and extinction looked likely, but they have subsequently stabilised and increased to 15–30. However, unless the population reaches 100 or more pairs it is still viewed as being vulnerable to circumstances beyond the control of conservationists, so the aim is to help the population to increase more.

Perhaps surprisingly for a national nature reserve where red grouse was a target species for conservation, shooting of the birds continued after the reserve was bought in 1986. By contrast, it has been banned on the Long Mynd since 1990. Although English Nature and then Natural England have been the freehold owners of much of the Stiperstones, it has not been possible to buy the sporting rights and they are still privately owned. It would nevertheless have been possible to prevent grouse shooting by refusing to issue the necessary permits. The decision to allow limited shooting was taken in order to encourage the owners of the sporting rights to undertake predator control. The numbers of grouse actually shot were very small, the annual bag having fallen to two birds by 1991. Thereafter shooting was considered to be unviable, a continuation of the long downward spiral involving the lack of return from shooting and insufficient predator control. The very low grouse numbers in the early 1990s were due much more to minimal predator control by the owners of the shooting rights than to the number of birds shot. English Nature therefore stepped in and began to control crows using Larsen traps, and foxes by lamping. This continued until 2004, when the sporting rights were sold to a new owner who began an active predator control programme. He was given a permit by English Nature to shoot eight to ten red grouse in the following years. This was attempted by falconry rather than shooting, but only two birds were caught in 2006 and three in 2007. The small numbers of birds killed may ironically renew the threat to the red grouse population, as it means that intensive predator control is not worthwhile in terms of costs and benefits to the owner of the sporting rights. The overall effect of shoots or falconry on the Stiperstones is probably to increase red grouse numbers, as the annual bag is smaller than the number of birds that would be taken by predators killed by gamekeepers. This explains the apparent contradiction of allowing one of the key conservation target species in a national nature reserve to be shot or hunted. Charles Darwin offers his support for this policy in *The Origin of Species*: 'If not one head of game were shot during the next twenty years in England, and at the same time, if no vermin were destroyed, there would in all probability, be less game than at present, although hundreds of thousands of game animals are now annually killed.'[9]

Management regimes in the 1990s were successfully conserving most plant and animal species on the Stiperstones, but a much more ambitious five-year project was developed with the aim of restoring lost areas of heather moorland. Following the Rio Convention in 1992, the UK made a commitment to recreate 6,000 ha of lost heathland and the Stiperstones project, called 'Back to Purple', was part of this. Money was therefore made available from a variety of sources including the Heritage Lottery Fund and from Tarmac through landfill tax credits. Tom Wall was senior reserve manager for the Stiperstones from 1986 to 2010 and Project Officer for 'Back to Purple'. The first targets were the conifer plantations that had been at various points along the ridge. The first of these was Gatten Plantation, east of the Devil's Chair, the main summit of the ridge.

FIG 56. Moorland regeneration in the former Gatten Plantation on the eastern flanks of the Stiperstones, with conifer stumps visible.

All the conifers were felled and removed, though the stumps were left to rot. The regeneration of heather following clearance was rapid (Fig. 56). Some bracken control was necessary and regenerating trees were removed or controlled by grazing. Subsequently plantations at The Rock and Nipstone Rock were removed, to make a total of 80 ha of regenerating moorland (Fig. 57). The effect of these initiatives has been to re-establish almost continuous heather moorland along the 10 km-long Stiperstones ridge. The only interruptions are one conifer plantation and one area of farmland, where improved pasture would ideally be

FIG 57. The 'Back to Purple' project involved the removal of conifer plantations from the southwestern flanks of Stiperstones, near Nipstone Rock.

converted back to moorland. The effect on the landscape has been dramatic and benefits to wildlife, already evident, will continue to accrue.

The medium-term outlook for moorlands on the Long Mynd and Stiperstones is now good. However, their position at the limit of where this community can exist makes them sensitive to changes, especially those that are climate related. As an example, population explosions of heather beetle *Lochmaea suturalis* have been an increasing problem. The larvae of this beetle feed on leaves of heather, then pupate and metamorphose into adult beetles. Females lay up to 700 eggs, so there is always the potential for a rapid increase in population. Crop plants in monocultures are vulnerable to rapid increases in pest numbers so it would not be surprising for heather, growing with few other plants, to be affected in a similar way. Rates of predation by the ladybird *Coccinella hieroglyphica*, parasitism by the eulophid wasp *Aesecodes mento* and disease caused by the fungus *Beauveria bassiana* are all density-dependent limiting factors, helping to keep the numbers of heather beetle larvae at a level that does not cause significant damage. However, there have been several years recently when numbers have risen high enough to defoliate and kill some heather plants. There was such an outbreak on the Stiperstones in 1998–9 and another in 2006–7, similar infestations occurring on the Long Mynd over these periods. Given that there were certainly no outbreaks from 1986 to 1997 and no records of any before then either, the occurrence of two such events within a ten-year period might represent a new trend. There is some evidence that ammonia deposition might make heather more nutritious and so increase the growth rates of heather beetle larvae. Atmospheric ammonia levels are particularly high in some parts of the Marches, especially when manure is being moved or spread. Heather beetles also appear to flourish given warm wet springs and early summers. If these occurred more frequently as a result of climate change, heather moorland might not have a long-term future in the Marches despite all the conservation efforts.

BRACKEN

An obvious candidate to take over areas that are currently heather moorland is bracken. This unloved fern species already covers significant parts of hill country in the Marches. It should not surprise us that it is so widespread. Bracken is a natural part of the ground flora in the woodland that would probably develop if cutting or burning of vegetation, as well as grazing by sheep and cattle, ceased. If bracken remained within bounds, it would probably be accepted by conservationists and valued for the wildlife that it supports, but it can colonise new areas by means of creeping rhizomes. This spread is perhaps not as rapid as sometimes imagined. A careful study of bracken spreading in Belmore Ring, a small area on the Long Mynd that had been fenced off in the 1980s to prevent grazing, showed that the mean rate of advance was only 0.38 m per year.[10] The advance was also irregular, with occasional retreats. This rate of spread is too slow to account for some large areas of colonisation observed in the second half of the 20th century, for example, to the south of the road from All Stretton to High Park on the Long Mynd. Assuming that spread over hundreds of metres is not due to extremely rapid growth of rhizomes, there are two possible explanations: that there had already been many small plants scattered through an area, or that new plants have established from spores. The latter possibility might seem the more likely, but spore production has not been observed on either the Long Mynd or Stiperstones for many years. It would be interesting to find out using DNA fingerprinting methods, how large individual clones are.

Changes in agricultural practises have helped bracken to spread. It was traditionally cut by hand for use as bedding for housed livestock, but this practice ended during the 20th century when it became cheaper to transport straw from arable farms in the east of England. Overgrazing has also been cited as a possible factor as it weakens the growth of other plant species. A change in grazing from cattle to sheep may also be significant, because this reduces the mechanical damage to developing bracken croziers by trampling. Whatever the cause, bracken now covers substantial areas of hill country, so control measures are being widely used. The main areas of concern on the Long Mynd are on the summit plateau, where areas of both heather moorland and acid grassland have been colonised. About 100 ha are sprayed each year with asulam, a selective herbicide marketed as Asulox, which kills ferns but not flowering plants. Aerial spraying using a helicopter has proved to be the cheapest method (Fig. 58). Although 95 per cent of the bracken in dense stands is killed, remaining plants are able to grow in subsequent years and can soon re-establish dense cover. Follow-up treatment of the remaining plants in the years after aerial treatment is clearly needed to achieve long-term control. Contractors do this with backpacks of herbicide, although asulam is less effective at killing areas of sparse bracken. Cutting using a forage harvester has also been trialled in selected areas of both the Long Mynd and the Stiperstones and the cut material has been composted and sold to gardeners for use as mulch. Mob stocking with cattle may be used in the future. This involves putting high densities of cattle onto target areas to cause mechanical damage to the bracken by trampling.

The abundance of bracken in the communities where it occurs is very varied. It forms a closed canopy in some areas, with few plants able to grow beneath.

FIG 58. Bracken control on the Long Mynd by helicopter spraying of broken ground at Bilbatch and by cutting of relatively level areas at Plush Hill. (David Cowell)

Bracken leaves can synthesise allelopathic compounds and release them during the summer to inhibit the growth of other plant species, but evidence that this actually occurs in the Marches is as yet lacking. A deep blanket of leaf litter tends to develop in dense stands, giving the bracken rhizomes protection against frost damage. A leaf litter depth of 860 mm has been measured at Beeston Castle to the north of the Peckforton Hills in Cheshire.[11] The allelopathic compounds synthesised by the leaves may persist in bracken litter and therefore inhibit the germination and growth of other plants. The author's pupils at Shrewsbury School carried out experiments with composted bracken that showed heather germination to be impeded by freshly made bracken compost but not if the compost is stored for a few years. In other areas bracken is less dominant and a few flowering plants such as sheep's fescue, heath bedstraw, tormentil and

common dog-violet are able to gain a foothold or sometimes just a toehold.
There are also areas where the bracken fronds are small and scattered.
Trampling, shallow soils, waterlogging and exposure to frost or drought can each
impede bracken growth enough for it to lose its dominance. Not enough litter
accumulates in these sparse stands to protect against frost or have a significant
allelopathic effect on other species. The growth of other plants attracts grazing
animals and therefore increases damage due to trampling. Positive feedback
mechanisms can therefore both operate to either increase or decrease bracken
density. The critical question is what determines the type of feedback that
operates in an area.

The most conspicuous patch of bracken in the Marches is probably the ring-
shaped area on the northwest side of the Lawley, visible from both the road and
railway between Church Stretton and Shrewsbury (Fig. 59). It was described a
quarter of a century ago and is still very prominent.[12] The ring is presumably a
single clone that has spread out from one original plant in the centre. Computer
analysis of aerial photos on various dates in the past shows that the ring spread
outwards by 10–15 m between 1981 and 1999, but by 2009 there had been no
further spread. In the centre of the ring, where there must at one time have
been vigorous growth, the bracken is now depauperate, raising the possibility
that dense stands of bracken currently suppressing all other plants elsewhere
in the Marches may in time become sparser. A comparison of aerial photos of
the Stiperstones taken in the 1950s and in the same areas in the 1980s showed

FIG 59. The bracken ring on the Lawley is a natural feature that is not the result of bracken
control by spraying, and is presumably a single bracken clone.

that the total area of bracken was about the same, but there were differences in the location of dense stands. Bracken had therefore spread into some areas and disappeared from others. The reasons for the degeneration of some stands are worthy of investigation as they could lead to improved techniques for bracken control, with benefits for other species.

Bracken can wage chemical warfare against both plant and animal species. The leaves synthesise a cocktail of secondary compounds that are toxic and act as feeding deterrents to many plant-eating insects, mammals and other animals. There is a select group of herbivores that can feed on bracken. A very small number feed exclusively on it, for example larvae of the brown silver-line moth *Petrophora chlorosata*, a species that is common wherever bracken occurs in the Marches. Other species feed mostly on bracken, such as larvae of the small angle shades *Euplexia lucipara* and the broom moth *Melanchra pisi*. Both of these species are fairly common. There are nonetheless far fewer herbivores able to feed on bracken than those associated with other plant species.

Many species of butterfly use bracken as a habitat, but not a food source. Dark green fritillaries *Argynnis aglaja* have in the past been found widely in the hill country of the Marches and are still present, but as elsewhere in Britain they have suffered a decline in distribution. They can use common dog-violets *Viola riviniana* as their larval food source; these grow in stands of bracken that are not too dense. Dark green fritillary larvae can also benefit from denser stands of bracken where leaf litter has built up. They bask on dead bracken fronds in the spring and the decaying litter provides a source of warmth. It must be stressed that dark green fritillaries are not confined to areas of bracken and can use other sites as long as there are violets present, such as areas of upland grassland and heath. Small pearl-bordered fritillaries *Boloria selene* are occasionally recorded in sparse stands of bracken where there is some damp ground. A strong correlation has been found between their population density and the percentage cover of marsh violets *Viola palustris*, the main larval food source, but not with dog violets, suggesting that they are not used.[13] On the Long Mynd there have been few small pearl-bordered fritillaries recorded, possibly because areas of suitable habitat are too scattered for a population to be supported. High brown fritillaries *Argynnis adippe* have only been recorded in the Marches in habitats dominated by bracken. The larvae are beautifully camouflaged against the dead bracken fronds on which they bask in spring. Bracken litter is vital in helping to raise body temperature and thus increase growth rates. Bircher Common in northwest Herefordshire was the last site in the Marches with a population, but from the early 21st century onwards there have only been very occasional sightings of adults and no records of breeding.

This mirrors the overall picture in Britain – a huge decline in distribution during the 20th century and high browns becoming a national BAP priority species. The larval food plant is common dog-violet found growing in sparser stands of bracken. Therefore, like the dark green fritillary, good habitat is a mosaic of sparse bracken with violets and dense bracken with accumulations of litter. Bircher Common was recently surveyed and found to have just such a habitat. Poor weather conditions in spring and during the adult's flight period in summer may partly explain the disappearance of high browns from this and all other former sites in the Marches. Longer growing seasons may have resulted in bracken areas becoming grassier, with bluebells rather than violets. Commons grazed with cattle were mostly abandoned after the Second World War and the bracken became too dense for fritillaries. For these butterflies, spraying with asulam is too drastic. Cutting, as occurred widely in the past, should be enough to weaken stands of bracken and trigger the positive feedback mechanisms that reduce dominance and promote species diversity. In the light of its role in sustaining these species of butterfly we should perhaps discard the idea of bracken as an all-conquering army that must be resisted by all possible methods.

UPLAND GRASSLAND

Much of the hill country has been traditionally used as sheep walks, with grassland therefore prevailing. Cattle have also been grazed. Grassland was mostly pasture rather than meadow, as steep gradients, rocky outcrops and summer rainfall made haymaking difficult. Manure and fertiliser were rarely applied and pastures were not usually ploughed up or resown. The upland grasslands were therefore semi-natural communities as much as agricultural areas. In the 20th century some of these grasslands were planted with conifers, particularly in northwest Herefordshire. Others have been resown in recent decades, for example on the northeast side of Caer Caradoc, but much semi-natural upland grassland still remains. Almost all of this is acid, with the limited areas of limestone occupied by woodland, ploughed up for arable farming, quarried, or too low lying for upland grassland.

Several types of acid upland grassland can be recognised in the Marches. The type dominated by mat-grass *Nardus stricta* that covers so much of upland Britain is present in patches on the summits of the Long Mynd and the Clee Hills (Fig. 60). The rainfall at below 1,200 mm per year is not high enough, drainage is too good and peat only occurs patchily, so the conditions that favour mat grass are lacking.

FIG 60. Mat grass with its distinctive ivory colour in winter, near the Gliding Station on the Long Mynd. This is one of a series of photos taken to monitor whether the grass is spreading. (Caroline Uff)

During the years of the ESA agreement on the Long Mynd, mat grass appeared to become more widespread. It had probably been present before, but its leaves had been grazed down to a low level. This is an indication that the Long Mynd had been seriously overgrazed as the mat-grass leaves are very unpalatable to sheep! Fixed-point photography is being used to monitor this grass. Large expansions in its range in place of heather and bilberry would be undesirable, indicating that grazing intensity is possibly too low.

Far more widespread here is a type of upland acid grassland in which the dominant species are sheep's fescue and common bent *Agrostis capillaris*, with heath bedstraw the most common dicot herb. According to the National Vegetation Classification, or NVC, this is U4 grassland. Rainfall of at least 800 mm per year is required for it to develop, so it is confined to the north and west of Britain, including the hills of the Marches but not low-lying parts. Further north and west conditions on hilltops are too wet and cold so this community is mainly found on hillsides. In the Marches U4 grassland can extend onto the summits and is found very widely, including parts of the Long Mynd, the Lawley and Caer Caradoc (Fig. 61). It is also found on Hopesay Hill, Stapeley Common and the Breidden Hills.

This is a rather species-poor community, but other grasses and dicot herbs can be present with the three species already mentioned. Sweet vernal-grass *Anthoxanthum odoratum*, wavy hair grass, harebell *Campanula rotundifolia* and tormentil are often found. Mountain pansy *Viola lutea* is confined to this type of grassland in the Marches and is not found further to the southeast in Britain. Waxcap fungi are a distinctive feature of this type of upland acid grassland.

FIG 61. Upland grassland dominated by sheep's fescue and common bent, on Hope Bowdler Hill, one of the Stretton Hills, with Caer Caradoc in shade and the Lawley in the distance. (David Williams)

They appear during the autumn in such a wide spectrum of bright colours that it looks almost as though a capricious creator has been at work, but as good biologists we must look instead for explanations in terms of natural selection. One waxcap, sometimes called the pink ballerina *Hygrocybe calyptriformis*, is a Shropshire BAP species. It was at one time also a national BAP species, but suffered the indignity of delisting for being too common.

As mentioned earlier, some upland bird species require areas of short-cropped grassland in which to feed. However, this type of turf does not usually provide enough cover for skylarks or other ground-nesting birds to breed. Upland field boundaries, where they occur, are usually fences and any hedges tend to consist only of scattered relict hawthorns giving little protection for nesting birds. Upland pasture therefore tends to be used by birds for feeding rather than breeding. Carrion-feeding birds are particularly numerous on these areas of upland grassland. Buzzards *Buteo buteo*, carrion crows and ravens *Corvus corax* are all now frequent. Sheep carcases are an abundant food source in all seasons but especially during winter. They were at one time collected and sold to knackers' yards, but this was banned during the outbreak of BSE in the early 1990s. Defra and English Nature still require removal of carcases but there is no incentive for farmers to do this and so it often does not happen. Pheasants *Phasianus colchicus* are another food source that has increased greatly, more than 50 per cent of the birds released for shooting being taking by predators or carrion feeders. Ravens became extinct here in the 19th century; the last pair occupied a nest in Ashes Hollow on the Long Mynd and, after boys stole their eggs in 1884, they did not breed again.[14] The same site was used once again when ravens returned to breed on the Long Mynd in 1918, after which a long and gradual increase in numbers took place. In the 1990s flocks of ten or so were very occasionally seen, but flocks of 30 are now common and a flock of 58 was counted in the area to the east of Norbury Hill in July 2006. Red kites *Milvus milvus* also became extinct in the Marches in the 19th century but it took much longer for them to return, although by 2010 the breeding population in the Shropshire Hills AONB was greater than ten pairs (Fig. 62). Their apparently effortless agility in the wind over upland grassland and other habitats is an increasingly frequent delight for naturalists.

FIG 62. Red kite with rufous plumage and forked tail. (Tom Osborne)

THE LONGSTONES PROJECT

The hills of the Marches were described at the start of this chapter as upland islands separated by lowland valleys. In some cases the valleys are sufficiently high that they do not totally separate the hills, so larger upland areas exist. The area between the Long Mynd and the Stiperstones is an example. This is undulating country with valleys formed by tributaries of the River Onny and isolated farmsteads. It still has an upland feel, though the land is enclosed, unlike open hilltops. The success of the 'Back to Purple' project has encouraged the proposal of an ambitious scheme for this area. The overall aim is to recreate natural links between the Long Mynd to the Stiperstones, so it is known as the 'LongStones Project'. The total area that would be linked up is 16,000 ha. It is an example of what has become known as landscape scale conservation. The Upper Onny Wildlife Group, established in 2004, identified some target species and measures needed to conserve them. Mountain pansy was the first plant species selected. This tract of country was renowned in the past for its upland hay meadows and pastures. The *Ecological Flora of the Shropshire Region*[15] speaks of 'a succession of well-grazed fields whose ancient turf was rich in flowers; heath bedstraw, bitter-vetch, bird's foot trefoil, moonwort and the hauntingly beautiful mountain pansy were all common'. Charles Sinker wrote nostalgically of this area: 'In the 1940s it was still possible to walk from Ratlinghope via Squilver and Shelve to Bromlow Callow through field after field washed pale with mountain pansies.'[16] Almost all of these fields were ploughed up and resown during the post-war drive to increase food production. Mountain pansy can be found in a few pastures that escaped ploughing and resowing (Fig. 63). There were estimated to be 50,000 plants flowering in a 1.5-ha field on the western flanks of the Stiperstones in 2006 and smaller numbers

FIG 63. Mountain pansy on the Stiperstones, at the eastern edge of its upland range in Britain. (Ben Osborne)

in some other fields. As with so many upland plants, this species is at the edge of its distribution in the Marches. Elsewhere it is usually found on calcareous rocks, yet it is a mild calcifuge. The soils in the Upper Onny area seem to suit it, perhaps because of applications of lime in the past. Very acidic soils are unsuitable. It cannot compete with tall-growing plants, so does not survive in fields used for hay or silage making, or where large amounts of fertiliser are applied. On the other hand, it does not thrive in nutrient-deficient soils and can benefit from moderate applications of manure. It fails to flower if grazing is very intensive.

Another target species is the curlew. According to one author in the 1940s, there were few moments in spring and early summer when curlews could not be heard in the Upper Onny area.[17] Surveys carried out in 2005 and following years located as many territories and nest sites as possible; they also monitored breeding success. A total of 25 territories were identified in the area between the Long Mynd and the Stiperstones. The behaviour of breeding pairs was observed at the end of June, to deduce whether young had been successfully raised, the success rate being about 50 per cent. The average number of young fledged per pair per year could not accurately be determined because of their diversionary and retiring behaviour patterns. It was certainly less than the figure of 1.77 fledged young per year, which has been calculated to be the minimum needed for a population not to decrease. The population was therefore in decline, persisting only because of curlews' longevity and not through recruitment by breeding success. Of the 13 nests located in 2007, eight were in hay or silage, four were in rushy pasture and one was in rough grazing. Damp areas in fields left to grow into a hay or silage crop were the most attractive to breeding birds. Unfortunately, in these fields nests with eggs or hatched chicks are very vulnerable to agricultural operations. The meadows are often rolled or harrowed in spring and then mown for hay or silage later in the season. Unless breeding can be completed between these two operations, it will almost certainly be unsuccessful. Farmers in the Upper Onny area, especially those on whose land curlews have attempted to nest, were therefore given advice on how they could help. The following measures were included in the advice:

- Removal of stock and completion of rolling and harrowing before mid–late April.
- Leaving stock for as long as possible on fields that will be cut early, to encourage nesting in other fields.
- Delaying cutting for hay or silage until mid-July or later if possible.
- Cutting hay or silage from the middle of the field outwards, so that chicks are encouraged to escape into hedges or adjacent fields.

It remains to be seen whether enough farmers are willing to carry out these measures for populations of curlew to persist on upland fields.

FLUSHES AND VALLEY MIRES

In the uplands of the Marches there are areas of impeded drainage where soils are very wet and peat has accumulated. Valley mires are found at the heads of small valleys and often form the beginnings of hill streams. Flushes occur on many hillsides where impervious rock causes water to emerge from springs and seep down the slope through the soil. These sites are typically small, sometimes just a few square metres in extent, but there are large numbers of them, over a hundred on the Long Mynd for example. The presence of soft-rush *Juncus effusus* indicates where soil is saturated with moving water. It is unpalatable and spread during the years of overgrazing on the Long Mynd but, having established, was able to grow more vigorously when grazing intensity was reduced. Some areas have been strimmed recently as they had become too thick for ground-nesting

FIG 64. Flush community on Hopesay Hill, containing the very rare liverwort *Jamesoniella undulifolia*. (Fred Rumsey)

birds. Plant diversity is usually greater where the grazing regime prevents soft rush from becoming the dominant species. These areas are often lawn-like, with marsh St John's-wort *Hypericum elodes*, blinks *Montia fontana*, bog pimpernel *Anagallis tenella*, bog asphodel *Narthecium ossifragum*, creeping forget-me-not *Myosotis secunda*, round-leaved sundew *Drosera rotundifolia*, common butterwort *Pinguicula vulgaris* and heath spotted-orchid *Dactylorhiza maculata* growing among closely cropped or trampled grasses (Fig. 64). The seeping water is sometimes richer in bases than the surrounding hill soils, allowing species such as tawny sedge *Carex hostiana* and lesser skullcap *Scutellaria galericulata* to grow. A survey sample of ten flushes on the Long Mynd recorded 160 plant species, including two RDB listed and five nationally scarce.[18] There are also characteristic birds,

FIG 65. Plants of flushes and valley mires: clockwise from upper left, bog pimpernel; round-leaved sundew (Caroline Uff); *Jamesoniella undulifolia* (Fred Rumsey); marsh gentian at Cramer Gutter (Gareth Thomas).

including reed bunting *Emberiza schoeniculus* and snipe *Gallinago gallinago*, though the latter is now very scarce.

The largest area of upland peat deposition is on Catherton Common, to the northwest of Titterstone Clee. This can be attributed to the relatively cool and wet climate and to impeded drainage in soils derived from the underlying Carboniferous rocks. The peat is only about half a metre deep, but is unusually widespread for Marches hill country and could be described as incipient blanket bog. Shropshire Wildlife Trust recently acquired the 200 ha of Catherton Common, with the aim of conserving and restoring the special communities there, including the blanket bog. Burning has been used to control gorse and old heather, but this will now be discouraged as it harms the peat-forming *Sphagnum*, which is present but not abundant. A number of plants are present at Catherton that are much commoner in the colder, wetter uplands of Britain, including deergrass *Trichophorum caespitosum* and hare's-tail cottongrass *Eriophorum vaginatum*. However, there are also similarities with plant communities of the milder south and west. Humid gorse heath occurs on parts of the common, with western gorse, heather and purple moor grass *Molinia caerulea*. Until recently this community had only been recognised in Devon, Cornwall and South Wales. Many-stalked spike-rush *Elocharis multicaulis* is present despite being more associated with western and southern coastal counties. Marsh gentian *Gentiana pneumonanthe* is chiefly found in eastern and southern coastal counties, but also grows at Cramer Gutter on the margin of the common in a base-rich flush (Fig. 65). This colony is far from any others in England or Wales. Catherton Common is fascinating area, epitomising the natural history of border country, and if management by Shropshire Wildlife Trust is successful it will be an increasingly important area in years to come.

SPECIES-RICH DROUGHT-TOLERANT GRASSLAND

The next upland community to be described is in some ways anomalous. It is a type of grassland that covers a much smaller area of the Marches than the communities so far described, but is nonetheless of considerable interest. It usually occurs on south-facing slopes where the rock is close to the surface and the soil is thin and drought-prone. The grassland that develops is species rich, with growth and flowering peaking in spring rather than summer. It is a type of plant community that has become increasingly scarce in Britain, but is still relatively well represented in the hill country of the Marches. There are about 30 ha of it in total on the Long Mynd, made up of many individual small areas.

There are also areas on Earl's, Clee, Lyth, Haughmond, Corndon, Roundton and the Breidden hills.

Although often missed because of the lack of large and showy plants, the diminutive plants that grow in this type of grassland are well worth our attention, even if this involves getting down on hands and knees. Sheep's fescue, common bent and sheep's sorrel *Rumex acetosella* are almost always present, often with early hair grass *Aira praecox*, common whitlowgrass *Erophila verna* and mouse-ear hawkweed *Pilosella officinarum*. A variety of other perennials occasionally occur, including some uncommon or decreasing species, for example maiden pink and rock stonecrop *Sedum fosterianum*, the latter being an uncommon native, though widely naturalised in Britain. Species of *Cladonia* and other lichens are often present. As in deserts, there is a group of ephemeral species that complete their life cycle while water is still available, in this case before the summer. They are known as winter annuals and are very characteristic of this type of grassland (Fig. 66). Shepherd's cress *Teesdalia nudicaulis*, upright chickweed *Moenchia erecta* and bird's-foot *Ornithopus perpusillus* are typical examples. Shepherd's cress has declined in many parts of Britain but is still abundant here. Upright chickweed has gone from most of the Midlands but persists here. Many other annual species are present, including some that are declining nationally, such as small cudweed *Filago minima* and knotted clover *Trifolium striatum*. Their decline is linked to the widespread loss of species-rich drought-tolerant grassland from much of the lowlands, caused by agricultural intensification and the use of artificial fertilisers. In the NVC classification this community is U1, a category of upland grassland, yet it is more characteristic of warm dry lowland sites. This is why it is areas on the fringes of the uplands that have become strongholds rather than the true uplands.

FIG 66. U1 grassland on the Long Mynd, with red inflorescences of sheep's sorrel.

The U1 grassland sites on the Long Mynd have been more carefully surveyed than most, so it is possible to draw conclusions about the ecological factors that determine their distribution.[19] They occur most commonly on the lower parts of sun-baked slopes with an aspect between southwest and southeast. They are absent from areas with thick soil, where taller growing plants including bracken become established. Even on thin soils, grazing has to be tight to prevent taller plants from competing. Sheep graze the Long Mynd, but rabbits graze sites on some other hills tightly enough, providing bare soil in which the winter annuals can germinate. Species composition is variable and various types of this grassland have been identified. A type in which winter annuals are particularly frequent, occurs in areas that are trampled by humans or animals but not very tightly grazed. Another type, in which lichens are more frequent, is found where there is little trampling and particularly tight grazing. These two variants, rich in winter annuals and lichens respectively, were originally described on dry sandy soils in the Breckland, but are now increasingly recognised in the Marches, albeit with differences in species composition. Upright chickweed is frequent here but not found in the Breckland and the typical lichen species here is *Cladonia subcervicornis* rather than *Cladonia arbuscula*.

Most U1 grassland occurs where the rock gives rise to acidic and base-poor soils. There are other variants of U1 grassland on hills where the rock and soil types are base-rich, for example Corndon and Roundton hills. Wild thyme is an indicator of these communities. There is a nationally important area of U1 grassland on Craig Breidden, near Welshpool, that contains some real rarities. The underlying rock is dolerite with calcite crystals, on which unusual base-poor but calcium-rich soils develop, allowing both calcicole and calcifuge species to thrive. Thin soils found near the summit as well as on rocky outcrops on the south and west sides of the hill provide the drought-prone conditions that favour species-rich grassland. In the Breidden version of U1 grassland, which is probably unique, cat's ear *Hypochaeris radicata* is one of the characteristic species, with common stork's bill *Erodium cicutarium* agg., common rock-rose *Helianthemum nummularium*, rock stonecrop and bloody crane's-bill *Geranium macrorrhizum*. Some extremely rare plants join this unusual assemblage on some parts of the hill: sticky catchfly *Lychnis viscaria*, spiked speedwell *Veronica spicata*, rock cinquefoil *Potentilla rupestris* and shaggy mouse-ear hawkweed, *Pilosella peleteriana* ssp. *subpeleteriana* (Fig. 67). The latter taxon is a subspecies that occurs nowhere else. The mosses *Schistidium pruinosum*, which is extremely rare in the southern half of Britain, and *Schistidium helveticum*, only recently recorded in Britain, have also been discovered on exposed rock. There are also some interesting whitebeams on the crags, including *Sorbus*

FIG 67. Craig Breidden's special version of U1 grassland: bloody crane's-bill (left) and shaggy mouse-ear hawkweed (right). (Simon Cope)

anglica and *S. rupicola*. Another species recently discovered at Breidden has been named Stirton's whitebeam, *Sorbus stirtoniana*.[20] There are 35 or more individuals present on the west crags and just two on the north crags. This whitebeam has not been found elsewhere, so is another Breidden endemic.

NATURAL HISTORY OF THE BATCHES

Batches, beaches and hollows are the small, steep-sided valleys that are a distinctive feature of some hills here. They will all be called batches in this account. The best-known examples occur on the east side of the Long Mynd, but there are similar valleys on the west side of Stiperstones and also some to the west of Corndon Hill and Stapeley Common (Fig. 68).

The batches were probably clothed in the past with scrubby oak woodland, but almost all of this has been cleared. A little remains at Resting Hill on the north side of Crow's Nest Dingle on the Stiperstones, but elsewhere there are other communities, maintained by sheep grazing. Wood-sorrel *Oxalis acetosella*, bluebells *Hyacinthoides non-scripta* and creeping soft grass *Holcus mollis* persist in some places as woodland relicts. Because the batches mostly run eastwards or westwards, their steep sides face north or south. North-facing slopes tend to have grassland at low altitudes, dominated by sheep's fescue and common bent, with heath bedstraw also present. A heath community is usually found higher up the slopes, with bilberry, heather and an understorey of mosses and lichens. This merges into the moorland community of the summits. On the warmer south-

FIG 68. Ashes Hollow, one of the finest of the batches, with meandering stream, steep sides and scattered gnarled hawthorns. (Andrew Jenkinson)

facing slopes, both U1 grassland and thickets of gorse *Ulex europaeus* occur at lower levels. Grassland starts at a higher altitude than on the north-facing slopes, but it is similar in species composition. On both the south- and the north-facing slopes there are patches of bracken, especially where the soil is deeper.

Mosses and liverworts have been surveyed in the batches and several nationally or locally rare species found. *Grimmia montana* is a moss of acid rocks, with a very scattered distribution in Britain. It occurs on south-facing rocky outcrops, but it is not clear what it is about these sites that suits it.[21] *Schistostega pennata* grows in rocky crevices and rabbit burrows, which provide the low light intensities to which it is adapted (Fig. 69).

Very characteristic of the batches are the large gnarled hawthorns *Crataegus monogyna*, scattered through grassland, heath and bracken. There are thousands of them in total, so they are a significant landscape feature and habitat. A survey in Callow Hollow on the Long Mynd, where there is a particularly high density, found over 1,600 hawthorns in an area of about 200 ha, with a height of up to 5 m.[22] Tree rings in cores taken from a sample of trunks showed that the smaller hawthorns were 30–50 years old but larger specimens were probably over 100

FIG 69. *Schistostega pennata* in an abandoned burrow on the Long Mynd, with reflective lens-like cells of the protonema that make it shine like cat's eyes. (Dean Wrench)

years old. There have therefore been several recruitment periods, presumably at times when the intensity of grazing was low. Recently grazing has been much too intense so there are no youngsters on the Long Mynd. Some rowans are now establishing where dense stands of heather or bracken prevent sheep from gaining access.

A detailed study of the upland birds of the Long Mynd has shown the importance of the batches with their hawthorn trees to a group of bird species, most of whom are summer visitors.[23] About 60 pairs of tree pipits *Anthus trivialis* nest here each year. Each territory includes areas of bracken with a few hawthorns or other trees for use as singing posts. The density of territories is greater where there is also some heath or grassland, which provides the sparse vegetation for feeding that dense bracken cannot. Redstarts *Phoenicurus phoenicurus* also establish territories in the batches where there are hawthorns or other old trees that have suitable holes for nesting. They also have the highest density of territories where there is a mosaic of bracken and heath or grassland. The number of pairs has fluctuated between about 30 and 70. There are typically about 100 pairs of whinchats *Saxicola rubetra*. They establish territories and nest on steep bracken-covered slopes in the upper regions of the batches. Whinchats use the hawthorns as singing posts but can also use taller bracken fronds and heather, and thus occupy treeless areas. Water seems to be important to them as their nests are never far from a stream or other source. They are one of the few bird species that seem to benefit from the presence of bracken in the hills. Stonechats *Saxicola torquatus* have a westerly and coastal distribution; the Long Mynd population is an outlier. Here they site their nests either in the upper regions of the batches or on the summit plateau, with a typical count of about 20 pairs. Similar numbers of wheatears *Oenanthe oenanthe* nest in the batches, but with different territory preferences as they nest in rabbit holes. Their territories are either in, or are adjacent to, areas of short grassland, so unlike some species they benefit from high sheep stocking rates.

Until recently, a population of ring ouzels *Turdus torquatus* returned to the batches of Long Mynd to breed each year[24]. This population was an outlier and its song was distinguishable from that of other ring ouzel populations to the west in Wales and elsewhere in upland Britain. The batches provided suitable areas of heath for nesting and grassland for feeding. In 1998 there were 13 pairs, after which the population went into a catastrophic decline. By 2003 there were no more than two pairs and in 2004 only a single male bird was recorded. This was a bird that had fledged from a nest near Light Spout waterfall in 2003. There have been no sightings since then apart from migrating birds passing through and ring ouzels are presumed extinct as a breeding bird in the Marches, for the moment at least. Climate change may be implicated but the principal cause appears to be increased nest predation by crows, foxes and stoats *Mustela erminea*. Compared with other ring ouzel populations, smaller proportions of pairs raised second broods or even reached the stage where a first brood fledged. The only pair found in 2002 built five nests and laid eggs in at least three of them, all of which were taken by predators. Other factors may have contributed to the ring ouzel's decline, but whatever their influence, no species could survive this level of predation. The problem of increased numbers of predators, stemming from the lack of control by farmers and gamekeepers, has already been discussed in relation to other bird species. Although not its purpose, control of predators may have helped species such as the ring ouzel and many conservationists therefore argue that it is desirable. A programme to control crows on the Long Mynd has now been instigated.[25] A less contentious conclusion from studies of breeding birds in the batches is that a patchwork or mosaic of different plant communities is needed to provide a habitat for the range of bird species that still visit in summer, as has also been found on the summit plateau of the Long Mynd.

About 70 species of bees, ants and wasps have been recorded on the Long Mynd, mostly in the batches. South-facing slopes are favoured by many of the solitary bees including the nationally notable species *Andrena apicata* and *Andrena similes*. Another nationally notable bee species, *Nomada lathburniana*, is a parasite of *Andrena cineraria*. Grayling butterflies *Hyparchia semele*, which had formerly been recorded in the batches, were not found when careful surveys were done in 1996, presumably because the intense grazing was leaving too little of their larval food plants, especially sheep's fescue and early hair grass. During the ESA agreement period from 1999 to 2009, annual counts were done on a ridge with plenty of suitable habitat. These showed a return of graylings and then a huge increase in numbers – a particularly welcome finding, as this species has been declining in much of Britain. Another butterfly that has been declining in parts of its range is the green hairstreak *Callophrys rubi*. It is present in large numbers in some of the batches, using western gorse as its main larval food plant. Largest numbers of larvae are found on the topiarised gorse bushes that result from repeated browsing, as these have plenty of soft young growth. There have been concerns that gorse is spreading in the areas of species-rich drought-tolerant grassland, which would reduce habitat for grayling. The National Trust has therefore used burning to control gorse, but only where the unbrowsable thicket that has developed is unlikely to support green hairstreaks. Areas of scattered gorse bushes with grassland between are left. This management approach may need to be reviewed, as gorse is very well adapted for re-establishment in burned areas. Burning has been found to be counter-productive in New Zealand, unburned gorse thickets eventually growing very tall and degenerate, allowing other communities to re-establish. As dense gorse thickets senesce here, they are likely to be replaced by grassland with scattered gorse, if grazing or trampling is persistent enough. The biodiversity of the batches, and indeed of all upland habitats in the Marches, depends on careful management, based on detailed understanding of ecological processes.

CHAPTER 5

Legacies of Ice Ages

THE LANDSCAPES AND NATURAL HISTORY of the Marches have been hugely influenced by ice ages. Many of the species that currently find a habitat in the Marches do so because of the varied ways in which frosts, snow, ice and meltwater have changed the environment.

Ice ages are periods when the Earth's climate becomes cold, and extensive ice sheets spread over land and sea. There have been four of these periods since the Precambrian. The first three occurred hundreds of millions of years ago. The fourth began about 15 million years ago in the Tertiary period and continued into the current Quaternary period, which began about 2.5 million years ago. Rather than continuous coldness in this fourth ice age, there has been an alternation between colder and warmer phases, with cold phases starting at approximately 100,000-year intervals. Whereas in previous ice ages the rocks of the Marches were too close to the equator for ice to spread over them, by this one they had moved northwards far enough for it to happen in some but not all cold phases. The spread of ice during a cold phase is a glaciation, the most recent of which was the Devensian. In all parts of the Marches reached by Devensian ice sheets the effects of previous glaciations were obliterated, such was their destructive power. Of the areas covered by this book, only southeast Shropshire, northeast Herefordshire and northwest Worcestershire were spared. In these regions deposits remain not from the previous glaciation, the Wolstonian, which did not spread further than the Devensian, but from the one previous to this, the Anglian. These deposits are over 250,000 years old, are much eroded and do not influence the natural history or landscape of the Marches significantly. This chapter will instead be concerned with the effects of the Devensian glaciation. In the hills of northwest Herefordshire and south Shropshire, bedrock is still the dominant influence, but there are also some fascinating periglacial features that have created distinctive habitats. A thick mantle of glacial deposits overlies the North Shropshire–Cheshire Plain, hence being the dominant influence. This is a classic area for the study of glacial geomorphology and it has therefore been selected to be the type area in the British Isles for the Devensian.

THE DEVENSIAN GLACIATION

The cycle that has occurred repeatedly during the current ice age is for a long period of fluctuating but cooling conditions to be followed by a rapid temperature rise, a brief warm period, and then a return to cooling conditions. The positive feedback mechanisms that cause warming or cooling are partially understood, as are the tipping points that cause the switch from warming to cooling and vice versa. A warm interglacial period occurred 125,000 to 120,000 years ago, with cooling starting after that. Although the whole of the cold period that followed is called the Devensian glaciation (see Table 1), it was only towards the end of it that conditions were cold enough, and there was enough precipitation, for ice to spread over Britain as far as the Marches. The glacial maximum occurred 23,000 to 18,000 years ago with temperatures about 10 °C lower than now. The ice started to retreat after this, initially more as a result of decreased precipitation than temperature increases. The climate warmed rapidly between 14,000 and 13,000 years ago and the last remains of the ice in the Marches disappeared. There was another phase of rapid warming about 10,200 years ago, with a rise in summer temperatures of about 8 °C in only 50 years. Maximum temperatures were reached between 8,000 and 6,000 years ago. A switch to cooling conditions may have occurred then.

MEGAFAUNA OF THE DEVENSIAN

The ice sheets of the last glaciation were not devoid of animal life. The species that dominated were large mammals, as in today's polar regions. Remains of these animals have been found in peat deposits, river terraces and former kettle holes. Skulls of wild oxen have been found at many sites, including the Berrington estate north of Leominster where, in the 1870s, alluvium was being excavated during drainage work. A woolly rhinoceros tooth was found at Dinmore, south of Leominster, so this species also lived here. Mammoth bones were found during the excavation of the Ellesmere Canal at Wrenbury in 1803.

However, a more exciting discovery took place in 1986, when a dog-walker noticed some large bones in a pile of clay and peat that had been dug out of

FIG 70. Mandible of woolly mammoth found at Condover, showing the single tooth on each side, with grinding ridges. (Shropshire Museums Service)

a gravel pit in a former kettle hole near Condover, south of Shrewsbury. After careful excavations, the almost complete skeleton of an adult male woolly mammoth and parts of three young mammoths were discovered. The mammoths are now in Ludlow Museum (Fig. 70). The adult was 30–32 years old and would have had a shoulder height of 3.4 m, which is tall even for a mammoth! There has been much speculation about how these mammoths met their fate; Peter Toghill gives a full account of the most likely hypothesis.[1] They are remarkable

TABLE 1. The timescale of the Pleistocene

DATES (BP)	GLACIATION	EXTENT OF ICE
300,000–250,000	Anglian Glaciation	Thames Valley
250,000–195,000	Hoxnian Interglacial	None in Britain
195,000–130,000	Wolstonian Glaciation	?
130,000–120,000	Ipswichian Interglacial	None in Britain
120,000–10,000	Devensian Glaciation	Marches
10,000–0	Flandrian Interglacial	None in Britain

because of the grouping of adult and juvenile bones, which has not been found anywhere else in Europe, and also because of their date. It had been assumed that mammoths became extinct in Britain about 18,000 BP (before present), but radiocarbon dating gave an age of 12,700 years, showing that mammoths survived for 5,000 years longer. This corresponds to the period when the ice sheets were rapidly disappearing; the remains of beetles adapted to warm climates, found in the same deposits as the mammoths, confirm that the climate had warmed by this time. Interestingly, the plant remains in these deposits were arctic species – a demonstration that animals can migrate faster in response to climate change than plants. Some plants that are regarded as glacial relics remained for a remarkably long period in the Marches. Rannoch-rush *Scheuchzeria palustris* survived on Clarepool Moss until the 19th century. Least water-lily *Nuphar pumila* clings on still at Crose Mere, its only site in England or Wales.

THE ICE SHEETS OF THE DEVENSIAN GLACIATION

A period of ice coverage is referred to as a glaciation, but most of the ice in the Marches formed sheets covering wide areas, rather than discrete glaciers. There were cirque glaciers in cols on the mountains of Berwyn and on the Clwydian range to the west and north, but the hills of the Marches were not high enough for glacier formation. Most of the valleys have the V shape of fluvial geomorphology, rather than the U shape with steep rocky sides formed by glaciers. Ice sheets can be very extensive, and exhibit movement from colder higher areas, where precipitation increases the mass of ice, to lower warmer areas, where the ice tends to melt.

There has been considerable interest and research into the ice sheets that spread across the Marches during the Devensian. The origin of ice and its direction of movement can be deduced from scratch marks called striae, and from deposits of rock, or material derived from rock, that have been brought from another area. Striae have been reported from Charlton Hill near the Wrekin and Sharpstones Hill near Shrewsbury, but far more has been learned from glacial deposits. The grinding action of ice sheets produces a rock flour with particles that range from fine sand to clay, depending on the parent rock. It is typically mixed with worn and fresh rock lumps that also vary in size from small fragments up to boulders. The whole mixture is called till. Two main types occur in the Marches. One is generally a brown or grey clay, or silty clay, with rocks of Welsh origin, including greywacke and quartz-rich sandstones. These displaced rocks are known as glacial erratics and they can easily be found during field walking. The Bellstone in Shrewsbury is an example of a large glacial erratic, composed of andesite probably from Snowdonia.

FIG 71. Fluvioglacial sand and gravel deposits at Bromfield Gravel Pit, near Ludlow, with sand martin nest holes (left) (Andrew Jenkinson), and the Bellstone on display in Shrewsbury (right).

Charles Darwin was shown it as a young man (Fig. 71). When told that that there was 'no rock of the same kind nearer than Cumberland or Scotland', and that 'the world would come to an end before any one would be able to explain how it came where it now lay', Darwin[2] commented: 'This produced a deep impression on me, and I meditated over this wonderful stone.' The other type of till is clayey or sandy and reddish in colour, indicating the products of erosion of the Triassic or Permian sandstones that occur extensively from Shropshire northwards to Lancashire and under the Irish Sea to the west. Lumps of granite and other glacial erratics from the Lake District and Southern Uplands of Scotland are present. These deposits show that ice moved into the Marches from two sources: eastwards from Wales and southwards from the northern England and Scotland. The latter is called Irish Sea ice, as the ice sheet from which it originated extended over what is currently the Irish Sea, though it was at the time entirely ice-covered.

Irish Sea ice
The North Shropshire–Cheshire Plain was covered by Irish Sea ice moving south. Its maximum thickness has not been determined, but granite erratics have been found at 250 m above sea level on Wenlock Edge and at over 300 m near Pulverbatch, north of the Long Mynd, so a depth of at least 400 m on the North Shropshire–Cheshire Plain seems likely. The ice therefore covered both the low-lying areas and Triassic sandstone escarpments. Because of the dip of strata in the Cheshire basin, scarps face south in north Shropshire and west in the mid-Cheshire ridge. They did not therefore obstruct the southward movement of the ice sheet and were not destroyed by it, as any north-facing scarps of soft sandstone will have been. Wenlock Edge, facing northwest, formed a partial

barrier to the ice, although there is glacial till to the south in Hopedale, indicating some penetration by the ice sheet. The ice passed to the east and west of the Wrekin, but not over the summit ridge. It penetrated what is now the Severn Valley, reaching slightly further than Bridgnorth but not as far as the Clee Hills. This is shown by the presence of many granite cobbles and pieces of unweathered coal in deposits west of Bridgnorth. It reached to the northern slopes of the Long Mynd but not the summit plateau, also moving southwards down the Church Stretton valley, as far as where Marshbrook now lies. The Irish Sea ice extended westwards about as far as the position of Offa's Dyke from Treuddyn to Wrecsam and then a line extending from Wrecsam to Ellesmere and on to Shrewsbury. Welsh ice occupied the area further west than this.

Welsh ice

The movement of Welsh ice is more complicated because of the hilly topography. Glacial deposits are found on high ground to the west of Offa's Dyke, but there are no such deposits on the tops of hills to the east: the Breidden Hills, the Long Mountain and *Ordovicia*. We conclude that this ice sheet, having its centre in Mid-Wales, covered all the hills and valleys west of the dyke. Lobes of ice emerged to the east and were diverted around the hard rocks of the Marches hills. One of the main flows from Wales was along the Severn Valley and this is sometimes called the Severn glacier. However, unlike a typical glacier this ice divided and moved east along several valleys, before coalescing to form the extensive sheet that reached as far as Shrewsbury. The main lobe passed north of the Breidden Hills, joining with ice from the valley of the Vyrnwy. One lobe passed along the valley between the Breiddens and the Long Mountain, another along the Marton valley between the Long Mountain and *Ordovicia* to Worthen and beyond. South of these, one lobe originated in the Kerry area, moved along the valley beyond Church Stoke between *Ordovicia* and *West Siluria*, before being baulked by the west-facing scarp at the southern end of the Long Mynd. Further south still, Welsh ice emerged from the valleys of the Clun, the Teme and the Lugg, while ice from the Wye Valley spread northwestwards to block the gap in the hills at Aymestrey. Devensian ice did not penetrate into northeast Herefordshire, so any deposits here must be from an earlier glaciation (Fig. 72).

ICE SHEET LANDSCAPES

The landscapes that were created by the Welsh and Irish Sea ice sheets will be described in the remainder of this chapter, together with the natural history that

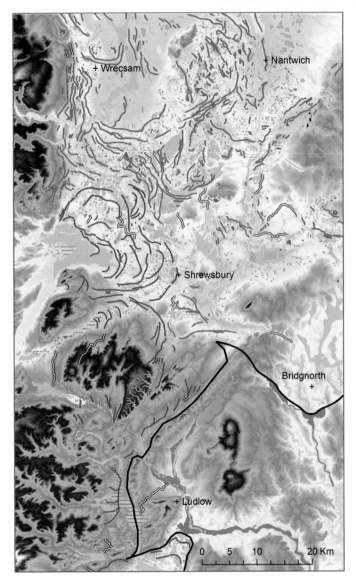

FIG 72. Glacial features of the Marches, draped over Fig. 17: black lines are the maximum extent of Devensian ice, with purple areas showing fluvial deposition beyond the maximum. Brown areas are moraines and light purple are sandur; blue and brown lines show stages in the retreat of Irish Sea ice and Welsh ice respectively; white lines show gorges and red lines eskers; blue hatching shows proglacial lakes. (Map constructed by Geoff Thomas)

is associated with them. The hill country will be considered first, followed by the lowlands to the north and south.

Nunataks and blockfields

Isolated peaks of rock that project above ice sheets in Greenland are called nunataks. The highest hilltops of the Marches show some features of nunataks, suggesting that they remained above the ice sheets during the Devensian. They would have been exposed to conditions very different from ice-covered areas. Extreme cold at night would have caused water to freeze deep into rock and soil. Temperatures could then rise in daylight, melting the water. Freeze-thaw action causes rapid erosion of rocks on exposed hilltop crags, with blockfields or screes accumulating below. Where there is a covering of soil on hilltops, rock can be shattered below the soil, leading to the formation of coarse material called head. This material covers much of the summits of the Long Mynd and the Clee Hills. It can move slowly down slopes by a process called solifluction. Head is found at the base of the scarp of Wenlock Edge, for example. Areas that are not ice covered, but which are close to ice sheets are periglacial. The Marches were at the edge of the Devensian ice sheets and the ice was relatively thin, so there were periglacial areas at a much lower level here than in areas to the west and north. This explains why hilltops with relatively modest altitudes can seem like mountain summits, with some of the natural history associated with high country.

A classic example of a periglacial landscape is seen on the Stiperstones, with its frost-shattered tors (Fig. 73). There are deposits of head along the ridge, in the form of orange clay containing angular lumps of quartzite and shale. On the soil surface are widespread areas of scree, within which polygonal areas of stone can be discerned and also stone stripes, formed as a result of lateral and downslope sorting of rock by ice. These periglacial features are particularly prominent on either side of the main ridge between Cranberry Rock and the Devil's Chair. Screes and areas of larger rocks known as blockfields are found on the Breidden Hills, Titterstone Clee, Corndon, Todleth and Roundton hills. There is an area of scree below crags on Earl's Hill near Pontesford and although this hill seems too low to have escaped ice coverage, little material is now being added from the crags above, suggesting a periglacial origin, as with the other sites.

Exposed rock is colonised by lichens, as soon as weathering has roughened the surface and created the small fissures needed for germinating spores to gain an anchorage. The species that colonise depend on aspect, altitude and the nature of the rock. On Stiperstones quartzite screes two foliose species are prominent and encrust large areas of rock: *Parmelia saxatilis* is greenish grey and is common in much of Britain, whereas *Parmelia omphalodes* is darker in colour and has a more westerly distribution. Other lichens present on the boulders are *Xanthoparmelia conspersa, Porpidia macrocarpa* and *Porpidia crustulata*. A lichen characteristic of rock crevices is *Pseudovernia furfuracea*, which consists of branched strap-shaped structures, grey with black undersides. The Stiperstones quartzite is so hard and resistant to weathering that there is little accumulation of mineral fragments or organic matter where lichens grow on the rock surfaces. Mosses such as species of *Racomitrium* might be expected to join the lichens after they have been growing for some time, but this does not seem to occur. A few

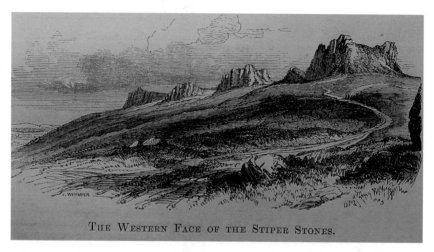

THE WESTERN FACE OF THE STIPER STONES.

FIG 73. Above: A periglacial landscape – an engraving in Murchison's great work *Siluria* of tors on the Stiperstones ridge. Below: The same view photographed over 150 years later from Shepherd's Rock.

mosses and leafy liverworts grow in shaded and humid conditions in crevices between the boulders, including species more typical of western parts of Britain. A recent discovery was *Lepidozia cupressina*, a leafy liverwort whose symmetrical leaves are beautiful when viewed with a hand lens. Leafy liverworts may look superficially similar to mosses, but their leaves are in two or three ranks rather than being in bunches or spirally arranged.

The most extensive blockfields in the Marches and one of its most remarkable habitats are on the north and west sides of Titterstone Clee Hill (Fig. 74). There are about 5 ha covered with angular dolerite boulders ranging in size from about 100 mm to a metre or more. Although the boulders are on a steep slope, there is little sign of movement and only a few additions formed by frost shattering from the craggy outcrops above. The rock is hard and very resistant to weathering, but it is not as hostile as quartzite and its surface becomes completely covered with a rich assemblage of lichens, mosses and liverworts. There is no sign that ecological succession is progressing any further, although small amounts of one alien moss, *Campylopus introflexus*, have appeared relatively recently. Given that 10,000 years have elapsed since the blockfields were established, it seems unlikely that the current community will ever be replaced, though some lichenologists are concerned about the possible effects of atmospheric deposition of nitrogen. Both

FIG 74. Blockfields on Titterstone Clee, looking steeply downhill with cloud in the valley below. Individual blocks are over a metre across.

the lichens and mosses that are present are calcifuge species, subtly coloured in whites, greys and browns, unlike the bright yellow, green and terra-cotta coloured species that are found on base-rich rocks elsewhere. Notable lichens are species of *Lecanora polytropa*, *Stereocaulon vesuvianum* and *Lasalia pustulata*.

The most prominent mosses are *Racomitrium* species, including *R. lanuginosum*, which is rare in lowland Britain but abundant here (Figs 75 and 76). It forms grey woolly patches on most boulders; these look scarcely living until viewed with a hand lens. Another moss more typical of mountains, but present in large amounts is *Grimmia incurva*. The next nearest population is far away on the Glyders in North Wales. It forms tight dark green cushions on rock surfaces in full sun, both on the blockfield and on the rocks that form the embankment of the hill fort on the summit of Titterstone Clee. *Rhabdoweisia crispata* is another small cushion-forming species, but it grows in shady crevices where a little soil has accumulated. Also in these crevices is *Tetraplodon mnioides*, with small bright green leaves and prominent capsules. It will never be abundant, as it grows on the faeces or decaying remains of mammals. In other habitats these materials are consumed or decomposed too quickly for a moss to colonise them, but here they form a very specialised but exploitable niche. Both of the latter moss species are at the southeastern extremes of their ranges; so too is the leafy liverwort *Gymnomitrium obtusum*.

There are other leafy liverworts growing in the humid conditions of the crevices and on shady sides of the boulders, including species of *Marsupella* and *Gymnomitrion*. Some lichens also favour crevices where there is a little soil, for example *Cladonia* species and *Cetraria aculeata*. The crevices between the dolerite boulders offer the only opportunities on the blockfields for vascular plants,

FIG 75. Titterstone Clee blocks covered with the woolly lichen *Racomitrium lanuginosum*.

FIG 76. Oak fern growing in a crevice. (John Bingham)

having with small pockets of soil, as well as protection from dehydration and grazing. Parsley fern *Cryptogramma crispa*, oak fern *Gymnocarpium dryopteris*, beech fern *Phegopteris connectilis* and mountain male-fern *Drypoteris oreades* have all been found in the blockfields on Titterstone Clee, where they are all the southeastern extreme of each of their ranges, as is fir club-moss *Huperzia selago*, a lycopod that is currently found nowhere else in the Marches.

There are other smaller but nonetheless interesting blockfields in the Marches. The areas on the east side of Corndon Hill have similarities with Titterstone, as the rock is dolerite, and lichens, mosses and ferns again dominate. Scaly male-fern *Dryopteris affinis* is characteristic of the edges of the Corndon blockfields. All four of the Titterstone ferns mentioned above occur here. Mountain male-fern also occurs in similar conditions at Earl's Hill, another outcrop of dolerite.

The origin of the batches

The formation of the batches of the Long Mynd and other Marches hills is at least partly periglacial. There was permafrost on the hilltops that protruded above the ice sheets during the Devensian glaciation. Water close to the surface will have melted during the summer, but lower layers remained frozen. Summer rainfall and meltwater could not therefore drain downwards as it now does and instead will have flowed laterally off the hilltops. The peak flow rates and erosive power of the streams draining the summits would therefore have been high, causing rapid downcutting into the rocks of the Long Mynd. Given the hardness of the rocks of the Long Mynd, it seems unlikely that this recent origin could entirely account for the depth and steepness of the valleys. Another contributing factor may be the tropical weathering to which the rocks of the Long Mynd were repeatedly subjected in the past. This involved softening of the rocks by penetration of rainwater and organic acids to a depth of 100 m or more along the lines of interfluves. There may therefore have been a preformed pattern of softened rocks, into which the periglacial torrents could have cut with relative ease.

Glaciated valleys

The batches are narrow and rather intimate. Separating the main groups of hills are some much larger U-shaped valleys, the most famous of which is at Church Stretton (Fig. 77). These valleys are broad, often with hummocky terrain in their base. Watersheds cross a number of them, with streams flowing in opposite directions to both ends of the valley. Some have streams flowing along both sides, rather than a dominant watercourse in the centre. These are clearly not typical river valleys and the streams that currently flow in them are mis-fit streams,

FIG 77. Hummocky terrain in Church Stretton valley bottom. The Church Stretton Fault runs along the far side of the valley, with the Stretton Hills beyond. (Robin Jukes-Hughes)

having too little erosive power to have formed the valleys. The origin must instead be presumed to be glacial, during the time when ice moved westwards from Wales and southwards from the Irish Sea. It is no coincidence that these broad glacial valleys are all located where there are soft underlying rocks, mostly Ordovician and Silurian mudstones. Streams and rivers in the past will have cut down through these rocks, creating valleys along which ice could move during the last and other previous glaciations. The lowest ice in the lobes that moved along the valleys carried rock fragments, which abraded the underlying rocks, deepening the valleys.

The ice brought large amounts of clayey till and deposited it over extensive areas in these valleys. This impedes drainage and makes arable farming difficult, so pastures grazed by cattle and sheep predominate. When warming conditions caused the ice to retreat, terminal moraines were left in some areas, creating a hummocky landscape. This is particularly noticeable in the many hidden dips on the road at Middletown, in the valley between the Breidden hills and the Long Mountain.

The Church Stretton valley is more complicated in its origins.[3] According to current interpretations, it was deepened by meltwater in the Wolstonian glaciation, which occurred before the Devensian. Borehole evidence shows a V-shaped valley that was formed, considerably deeper than the current level. Irish Sea ice entered the Church Stretton valley during the Devensian, but was at its southern limit and only penetrated as far as Marshbrook. Rather than deepening the valley, the ice sheet raised its floor by deposition of 30–60 m of clay, sand and gravel. The current U-shaped profile is therefore due to deposition rather than glacial erosion. Much of the valley floor has the hummocky terrain that is characteristic of glacial deposition, but there is also a level marshy area that is a former lake and also some small wooded rocky outcrops that protruded above ice. Despite its overall U-shape, the Church Stretton valley is therefore not a typical glacial valley.

Proglacial lakes

In some glaciated valleys there are extensive level areas, rather than a hummocky terrain. Examples include the Marton valley south of the Long Mountain and the Church Stoke valley south of *Ordovicia*. It has long been suggested that the level areas are former lakes. Evidence for this is provided by the presence of varves; these are laminated clays that are laid down by sedimentation in the base of lakes. Seasonal variation causes a cycle of deposition, hence the layers or lamination. There is a fine exposure of such deposits beside the Severn at the Field Studies Council headquarters at Preston Montford. About 2 m of laminated clay are visible, with dropstones distributed through it. These dropstones are present thanks to small icebergs that became separated from the Welsh ice sheet to the west, floated across a glacial lake and then melted, dropping stones trapped in the ice (Fig. 78).

FIG 78. Laminated clays with dropstones at Preston Montford, with local glaciologist David Pannett describing them, and the author on the left. (Geoff Thomas)

It is not certain how long particular lakes existed, but their origins are understood. The ice sheets dammed up valleys at certain points during the late Devensian, preventing or delaying the drainage of meltwater and causing lake formation between the ice and higher ground. Some of the meres that exist today may be proglacial lakes that have survived, but all the larger lakes were drained when the blocking ice sheets melted. There were two proglacial lakes in valleys to the east of the Vale of Montgomery where ice in the vale prevented meltwater from flowing to the Severn. A lake formed in the Presteigne basin when Welsh ice emerging from the Wye Valley spread northwestwards to block the Lugg valley at Byton. The Welsh ice also blocked the gap in the hills at Aymestrey, preventing the southwards flow of water and causing the formation of Lake Wigmore to the north (Fig. 79). Ice from the same source blocked the flow of water southwards in the area around Orleton and Brimfield, forming Lake Orleton to the north and possibly extending to Ludlow and beyond. Though large, these lakes would have been modestly proportioned in comparison with the first periglacial lake to be postulated: Lake Lapworth. Professor Wills of Birmingham University was its proponent, in the early years of the 20th century. He argued that the Irish Sea

FIG 79. The Vale of Wigmore, viewed from Croft Ambury hill fort. Lake Wigmore filled the level area in the middle distance. Beyond are the valleys and conifer-covered hilltops of West Siluria. (Xiaoqing Li)

ice sheet blocked the escape of meltwater northwards to form a huge lake. At its maximum, Lake Lapworth would have occupied much of central Shropshire. Although the sites of smaller periglacial lakes have been discovered within this area, including Lake Melverley at the confluence of the Severn and the Vyrnwy, there is now strong evidence that Lake Lapworth itself did not exist.

Being level and low lying, the sites of proglacial lakes are still prone to flooding in winter, but the soils underlying them are potentially fertile, especially where silt is deposited by the floodwater. Most of these areas are used for cattle grazing. In places a semi-natural grassland community persists that is dominated by creeping bent *Agrostis stolonifera* and marsh foxtail *Alopecurus geniculatus*, with tubular water-dropwort *Oenanthe fistulosa*, brown sedge *Carex disticha*, small water-pepper *Persicaria minor* and other plants that are tolerant of inundation. Floating water plantain *Luronium natans* was recently found in a damp hollow in cattle pasture on a part of the site of Lake Melverley.

Gorges and dingles

Not only can ice form dams and prevent the flow of water, it can also force water to change direction and follow new routes to the sea. The route taken by the Teme downstream of Leintwardine is a famous example. We have already seen that its original route southwards to join the Lugg and the Wye became blocked at Aymestrey and Lake Wigmore was formed. This lake grew to about 20 km², eventually overflowing to the northeast. Recent research suggests that rather than cutting a new channel through the ridge of Aymestry Limestone on the north side of the Ludlow anticline, the valleys of two pre-existing streams were commandeered. One was the valley of the Burrington Stream, which used to flow southwards in the opposite direction to the current flow of the Teme and had already cut a channel through the Aymestry Limestone. The other was the valley of the Pre-Teme that flowed northeastwards in the same direction as the Teme does in the present day.[4] The col between these two valleys was composed of hard Whitcliffe Formation sandstones and limestones. It formed a sill that was eventually overtopped as the level of Lake Wigmore rose. Flow of water from the lake gradually cut down through these hard rocks, reducing the level of the lake until it was emptied, and creating Downton Gorge with its sheer cliffs. The gorge is spectacular but little known and rarely visited (Fig. 80).

Though a National Nature Reserve, Downton Gorge is privately owned and a permit is required to enter. It has SAC status, because of the importance of its geology, woodlands and river. The woodlands contain both small-leaved *Tilia cordata* and large-leaved lime *Tilia platyphyllos* together with ash *Fraxinus excelsior* and elm *Ulmus glabra*. The ground flora includes wood fescue *Festuca altissima*,

FIG 80. Downton Gorge, through which the Teme has flowed since the last glaciation. Large- and small-leaved limes grow on the sides of the gorge. (Andrew Jenkinson)

violet helleborine *Epipactis purpurea* and lily-of-the-valley *Convallaria majalis*. A variety of ferns grow on the cliffs, though fewer than before the depredations of 19th-century collectors. An account of a visit in 1869 by the Woolhope Naturalists' Field Club[5] states: 'The majority of the ladies chose fern-hunting. The delicate Oak Fern abounds here and many were the roots carried off.' The gorge was part of the Downton Castle estate, inherited by Richard Payne Knight in 1772. He was a leader of the picturesque movement and created a landscape park with paths up the gorge, grottos, tunnels and caves. From Downton Gorge the Teme now flows on to Ludlow. It might then be expected to flow south to join the Lugg at

Leominster, but was diverted again at Wooferton, its path being blocked by the Wye Valley glacier, and it has since flowed eastwards to join the Severn below Worcester. A small stream is now all that flows through the wide former river valley between Wooferton and Leominster.

The Lugg was also diverted from its original course through the gap in the hills at Byton. A new route was formed by the formation of gorges at Kinsham and Lye. The Onny, which rises in the hills around the Stiperstones, was diverted in a similar way and instead of flowing westwards to join the Camlad it now flows eastwards, except in extreme floods. Its escape route was cut just to the south of the Long Mynd though Silurian mudstones, which are softer than the Longmyndian rocks, forming the Plowden Gorge. The Camlad, which flows from Lydham to Church Stoke, was itself diverted when its westward flow to the Severn was blocked by ice. A new route northwards was cut through relatively soft Ordovician shales to form the steep-sided Marrington Dingle. This takes the Camlad northwards, joining the stream that drains western parts of the Marton valley. It then heads westwards to join the Severn near Fflôs and Berriew.

Another extraordinary diversion is seen in the northwest of our region. The Afon Alun flows northwards to the east of the Clwydian Range, heading for the coast of North Wales. It then turns via a gorge cut through Carboniferous limestone, flowing southeast to Mold, south towards Wrecsam and then east over the Cheshire plain to a confluence with the Dee. The explanation once again is the blockage by ice of the original and much more direct route to the sea.

We now turn to the diversion of a river's course, more dramatic than any of the above. The original route of the Severn from Welshpool was northwards to the Dee estuary and the Irish Sea. This route became blocked by ice, but rising water levels and the overflowing of a proglacial lake is not now thought to have led to the subsequent diversion of the Severn. Meltwater flowing in channels below ice sheets is under great pressure and can carry large amounts of abrasive rock fragments. It therefore has a powerful capacity to cut into rock or sediments beneath the ice, creating deep sub-glacial channels. An example, now filled with clay and other sediments, starts at Melverley, passes east to Shrewsbury and then southwestwards towards Ironbridge. Called the Severn Trench, its base is up to 120 m below current ground levels and more than 50 m below sea level. The base of the trench runs against the gradient in places, but because the water flowing in it was confined below the ice sheet, it was able to flow uphill, unlike surface watercourses. This upward flow is reminiscent of the rise of water in an artesian well. Herein lies the probable mechanism for the diversion of the Severn and the origin of Ironbridge Gorge. Water could have flowed up what would have been the northeastern section of Wenlock Edge to gouge out an extension to the Severn Trench. As soon as flow was established, there would have been a rapid downcutting through the limestone of the escarpment and the softer rocks beyond, creating 10 km of gorge, a new route to the sea in the Bristol Channel, and Britain's longest river. The old route to the Dee estuary is much shorter and therefore has a steeper gradient, but it has never been readopted.

The gorges created by river diversion typically have steep wooded sides. There are also many smaller wooded valleys in the Marches, known as dingles. These have the V-shaped profile expected of valleys eroded by streams. Some are cut into solid rock and others into glacial deposits. The depth of a dingle is typically only 30–60 m – much less than the batches previously described. It seems likely that many dingles are recent features, probably formed when new patterns of surface water drainage were established at the end of the last glaciation. They have since been deepened by the erosive actions of the streams in them and are often difficult to access thus rarely visited. Though individually narrow, there is a considerable total length of dingles, making them collectively significant.

Moraines

We now move away from the hills and valleys, to the parts of the Marches that were totally covered by the ice sheets of the Devensian. This includes the whole of the North Shropshire–Cheshire Plain. Here there is an almost continuous mantle of glacial deposits. Geological maps show most of the ice-covered area shaded in pale blue, indicating clayey till. Agriculture is a challenge here, as the soils are cold, heavy and poorly drained. Dairy farming is particularly prevalent. The abundance of milk has led to the development and production of Cheshire cheese not only in the county of Cheshire but also in the part of north Shropshire around Whitchurch. More recently, Müller Dairies has made vast numbers of yoghurts at a factory in Market Drayton.

Thicker deposits were left at the furthest points reached by the ice sheets. These deposits are called end moraines. There is a large complex of them in a band from Wrecsam in the west, to Ellesmere and then on eastwards to Whitchurch and Bar Hill. These end moraines mark the limit of the Irish Sea ice sheet at one stage during its retreat. The streams and small rivers flowing northwards through this area of moraines have cut deeply down through the deposits to create steep-sided valleys. Checkley Brook located north of Woore is an example, as are the Wych Brook and the River Duckow. There are also end moraines near Shrewsbury, at the limit of Welsh ice. These moraines are typically oriented north–south and in some areas there is a series of them, each formed in a single summer, revealing the rate of retreat of the ice sheet (Fig. 81).

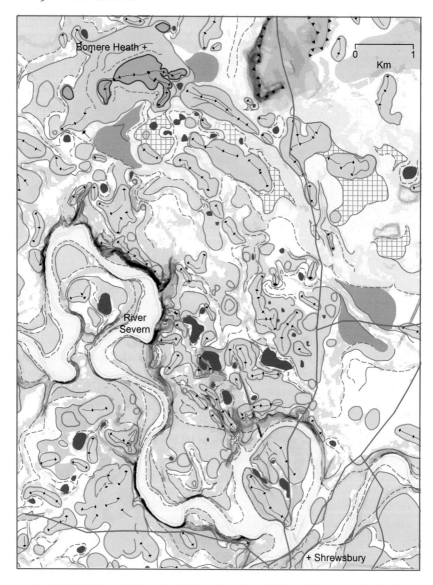

FIG 81. Glacial features to the north of Shrewsbury, formed during the retreat of Irish Sea ice: browns show moraines with black lines at the crests; blue is sandur formed from sediment carried by meltwater flowing parallel to the moraine fronts in a southeasterly direction. Dark grey areas are kettle holes; light grey indicates rock at the surface; river terraces are green and recent river alluvium yellow; red lines indicate A roads. (Geoff Thomas)

Eskers, sandar and sandy heaths

Extensive areas of the Marches are covered by deposits of sand or gravel. The soils are free draining and usually very base-poor in these areas. There may have been woodland or heath communities here in the past, but as elsewhere in Britain, few have survived with anything approaching natural communities. The ice sheets transported sand and gravel and deposited it in various ways, leading to the formation of two distinctive landscape features, eskers and sandar.

Eskers are raised steep-sided ribbons of sand and gravel that can extend for long distances. They are formed when tunnels created by meltwater under ice sheets became infilled with gravel and other coarse material. The word is of Irish origin but after being described in Ireland, they were found elsewhere in the world. The Dorrington esker, a curving ridge to the west of Condover, is a well-known example. It has been extensively quarried for sand and gravel. A series of eskers have been found near Newport in east Shropshire, including the wooded ridge north of Aqualate Mere. There is another excellent example at The Wauns, near Gwersyllt, to the north of Wrecsam.

Sandar are broad, flat deposits of gravel and other coarse material, washed out of the front of ice sheets. The name is Icelandic and the singular of it is sandur. In the area known as the Wrecsam delta plateau, which originally covered about 50 km², there were extensive sandar. Most of these have been lost due to quarrying. The workings at Borras are the second largest sand and gravel quarry in Britain. There are many sandar in north Shropshire, often with a place name recording the existence of a former heath. An example is Knockin Heath, to the west of Ruyton XI Towns. Its vegetation was recorded in the late 18th century, when it still had the characteristics of a heathland community, but over-intensive agriculture had already damaged the site and inland dunes had formed from eroded sand.[6] There were even damp hollows between the dunes with royal fern and other plants of mires growing in them. Almost all other lowland heaths in the Marches have suffered a similar fate, with agriculture or quarrying destroying the heathland communities.

Sands and gravels give rise to light, warm and hungry soils, but root and cereal crops can be grown. The level surfaces and sharp drainage of sandar made them attractive for the construction of airfields before and during the Second World War. An excellent example of sandur underlies RAF Shawbury (Fig. 82). Material was fed to it from the ice sheet to the north via the Lee Brockhurst channel that cuts through the Hawkstone scarp. RAF Tern Hill and RAF Cosford are also underlain by sandar, as are the former airfields at Borras, Rednal, Peplow and Atcham. Prees Heath near Whitchurch is another sandur site and former airfield; so far saved from quarrying, it is of considerable conservation importance as it supports the only population of silver-studded blue butterflies *Plebeius argus* in the West Midlands. The nearest colony is at Great Orme on the North Wales coast. At Prees Heath, adult butterflies emerge in June and fly until the end of July (Fig. 83). They use bell heather as a nectar source. Eggs are laid on both bell and ling heather, but

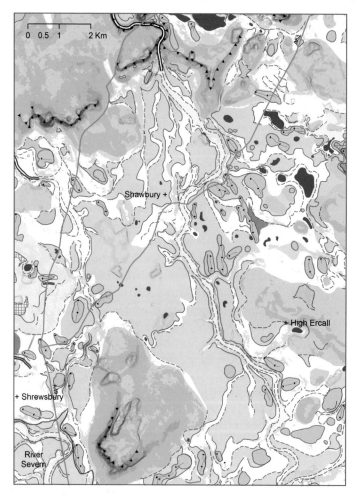

FIG 82. Glacial features of the Shawbury area, using the same colour code as Fig. 81. During the retreat of Irish Sea ice, the ice margin lay to the north of the sandstone escarpment between Grinshill and Hodnet. Pro-glacial drainage escaped via a rock-incised channel or gorge at Lea Brockhurst. This fed a large, terraced sandur fan running towards what is now the Severn and its recent terraces. The Roden now flows in this rock-incised channel. (Geoff Thomas)

FIG 83. Adult male silver-studded blue butterfly at Prees Heath (Danny Beath) and newly emerged adult with attentive black ants (Stephen Lewis).

ling is preferred. Bird's-foot trefoil, gorse, broom and some grasses are also used for egg laying. The eggs over-winter and hatch in April. Like other blues, this butterfly has developed a mutualistic association with ants. Black ants *Lasius nigra* collect the caterpillars, then feed and protect them inside their nests. In return, the caterpillars produce a sweet secretion from special glands, on which the ants feed.

The survival of the silver-studded blue at Prees Heath is fortunate, being partly due to the construction of concrete runways when the site was used as an airfield during the Second World War. The airfield was decommissioned in 1945 and two large areas of the heath were ploughed up in the 1970s, and copious quantities of chicken manure spread to increase crop yields. This caused eutrophication and the loss of all the heathland plants from these areas. Although the main runways were broken up in the 1970s, large lumps of concrete were left; these prevented conversion to arable farming, so an area of heathland survived. This area has the ants and all the plants needed to allow silver-studded blue butterflies to complete their life cycle: ling heather, bell heather, bird's-foot-trefoil *Lotus corniculatus* and heathland grasses such as squirreltail fescue *Vulpia bromoides*, with some broom *Cytisus scoparius*, gorse and western gorse *Ulex gallii*. Pyramidal orchid *Anacamptis pyramidalis*, slender St John's-wort *Hypericum pulchrum* and heath dog-violet *Viola canina* are also present. There are populations of small copper *Lycaena phlaeas* and small heath butterflies *Coenonymphia pamphilus*, as well as several day-flying moths.

The Prees Heath population of silver-studded blues has been appreciated for many years, yet it is still vulnerable. The annual count of adults is 500 on average, but there is considerable fluctuation: from over 1,000 in 2006, to as few as 140 in the cold wet summer of 2007. After many attempts, Butterfly

FIG 84. Heath regeneration at Prees Heath after deep ploughing and scattering of heather brash. (Stephen Lewis)

Conservation bought part of Prees Heath common in 2006, including the main runway area and adjacent arable areas. An ambitious project is now underway to recreate heathland on the arable areas. Deep ploughing was used to bury the topsoil under the 900 mm of sand and gravel that had been below it. Sulphur was spread, to lower the pH. Approximately 100 t of heather brash from Cannock Chase was spread over the surface of one arable area, to re-establish populations of heather and other heathland plants from seed. A seed mixture collected from a local area of acid grassland, at Melverley Farm, was sown on another. Initial results from both areas are promising. Large amounts of yellow-rattle *Rhinanthus minor* are established in the grassland area, which should prevent any vigorous grasses from becoming too dominant (Fig. 84). The natural plant community that eventually develops on Prees Heath, if appropriate management continues, will probably be similar to that of the Brecklands in East Anglia. If the re-creation of heath at this site is successful, perhaps some other lost heaths of the Marches could be re-established, hence allowing more populations of silver-studded blues and other heathland species to return. Nightjars *Caprimulgus europaeus*, for example, reported to be numerous in northwest Shropshire in the late 19th century,[7] were probably on some of the lost heaths. Steel Heath, owned by Shropshire Wildlife Trust, but invaded by scrubby pine woodland, is an obvious target.

Drumlins and kettle holes

Drumlins and kettle holes both contribute to the hummocky landscape in parts of the Marches. Drumlins are mounds composed mostly of till, typically shaped like a half egg. They are formed when ice sheets move over flat, wet terrain and the pressure under the ice sheet is variable. The end facing the direction from which the ice sheet moved is steeper. There is an extensive area of drumlins to the west of Shobdon in northwest Herefordshire, filling what was probably the valley of the River Lugg before the last glaciation. To the east of Shobdon, as far as Orleton, there are features that have been described as drumlinoid, as have some of the hummocks in the Church Stretton valley. The area north of Welshpool, between the rivers Severn and Vyrnwy, is a classic area for drumlins.

Kettle holes are hollows or basins, formed towards the end of the last glaciation. When the ice sheets retreated, large immobile ice blocks were left behind in some places when the surrounding ice had melted. Sand and gravel washed out from the retreating ice sheet covered the stranded ice blocks, which may have remained for long periods. A kettle hole was formed when each block did eventually melt, into which any overlying glacial deposits dropped. There are hundreds of them in the Marches, in the areas once covered by both Welsh and Irish Sea ice. They are very variable in width from a few metres to many hundreds. They also vary in depth. Some of the best known are in the area around Ellesmere. Here drumlins, eskers, end moraines and kettle holes combine to create a giddy, disorientating landscape. Charles Sinker described this area as being bewilderingly complex.[8] The drumlin field to the west of Shobdon is another very three-dimensional landscape, featuring many small water-filled kettle holes.

An important group of 40 kettle holes was formed on part of the delta plateau to the northeast of Wrecsam. They perfectly illustrate the great variation in drainage, diameter, depth and shape that is possible. The westernmost of these kettle holes, in the Pant-yr-Ochain area, have become water filled (Fig. 85). The group that is furthest to the east, including Vicarage Moss, are also mostly water filled. Some of the water-filled kettle holes are steep sided with little marginal vegetation. Others shelve much more gently, allowing colonisation with different plants at different depths and therefore zonation. Another possibility found in some of these

FIG 85. The Pant-yr-Ochain group of kettle holes on the outskirts of Wrecsam.

FIG 86. Dry kettle holes of the Holt Estate are in the centre of this aerial photo taken in 1989, with Pant-yr-Ochain kettle holes to the right, Vicarage Moss lower left and Borras sand and gravel quarry upper left. (© Crown: Ordnance Survey)

kettle holes is for the water to become completely covered by bog plants, especially *Sphagnum* and cottongrass. Kettle holes with open water are usually known as meres and those with bogs are known as mosses. Not all kettle holes hold water. The central part of the Pant-yr-Ochain area is known as the Holt Estate. From the air, its delicate moon-like landscape of dry kettle holes is revealed (Fig. 86). Despite their great geological and ecological interest, only one of the 40 kettle holes in the Wrecsam group has any statutory protection – Vicarage Moss has SSSI status and is a GeoConservation Review site as it is deemed to show some of the best developed kettle hole features. Sadly, Wrecsam County Borough Council, owner of the mineral rights, has given planning permission for the Holt Estate to be quarried and its subtle but beautiful landscape will be lost. As the meres and mosses are two of the most important features of the natural history of the Marches, they will be described separately in the next two chapters.

CHAPTER 6

Meres

THE MERES OF THE NORTHERN MARCHES are a distinctive and important group of natural lakes. It is impossible to say how many there are in total, unless an arbitrary lower size limit is defined. There are over 100 meres with an area of 1 ha or more and many smaller pools. All are post-glacial in origin. There are comparable groups of lakes in other parts of the northern hemisphere including Poland, Germany, Denmark, Minnesota, Wisconsin and Indiana, but nowhere in Britain is there any area that approaches the concentration in the Marches. The meres have been described as England's third Lake District, but given that the Norfolk Broads are not natural in origin, perhaps they should be promoted to the position of England's second natural Lake District. English Nature recognised the significance of the meres when defining natural areas in England by creating the Meres and Mosses natural area. This covers most of Cheshire, the northern half of Shropshire and part of northwest Staffordshire. Forty meres have SSSI status and 20 are part of the Midlands Meres and Mosses Ramsar Site (Fig. 87). They vary in their size, depth, hydrology, pH and nutrient concentrations. Aqualate Mere is the largest at 80 ha and Rostherne Mere the deepest at 30 m. The management of both open water and the use of surrounding land also differ. Because of these differences and the large number of meres, there are great opportunities for comparative studies. There has been increasing research interest, with some intriguing recent findings, but there is plenty of scope for further work to disentangle the ecology of the meres. Current knowledge will be reviewed in this chapter and some of the unanswered questions will be identified. There are two questions to answer first: what is the origin of the basins in which the meres are located and why has water has collected there?

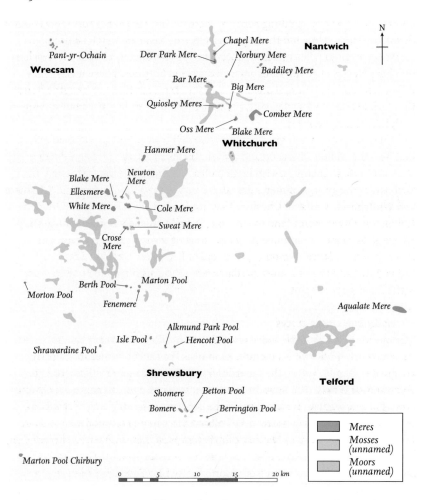

FIG 87. Map of the main meres of the Marches. There are distinct groups of meres, for example in the Ellesmere area, and also some isolated meres such as Aqualate.

The origin of the mere basins

Six types of origin have been suggested for basins in which the meres are located.[1] Three of these are found elsewhere in the world but not here: vestigial meltwater lakes, englacial plunge pools and periglacial pingoes. In central and north Cheshire, post-glacial subsidence hollows have been formed where salt dissolved out of saliferous mudstones lying close to the surface, with meres known locally as flashes filling some of these basins. However, most meres do not lie on saliferous rocks and the two other types of basin are much commoner.

Many of the smaller meres are located in approximately circular depressions that have steeply shelving sides and relatively flat bottoms. These meres show little correlation between diameter and depth. Most are likely to be kettle holes, the stranded ice blocks all having had approximately vertical sides but varying in both height and diameter.

These meres occur in groups where there were deep sub-glacial channels that became infilled with sand and gravel. Sizeable masses of ice could lodge at depth in these channels, with kettle holes forming when the ice melted. In Shropshire the groups of meres are centred on Shrewsbury, Baschurch, Ellesmere and Whitchurch, whilst in Cheshire they are around Delamere, Knutsford and Congleton. Other meres tend to have more shallowly shelving sides, suggesting an origin as moraine-dammed hollows. Some of the largest meres have one or more distinctly deeper regions, for example Blake Mere and Cole Mere, each probably originating as a moraine-dammed hollow within which one or more kettle holes were present.

Hydrology of the meres

The question of why kettle holes or other basins filled with water can be answered using Micawber's dictum. As long as the flows of water into a basin are greater than flows out, the water level will rise and a mere will be formed. Hydrologists refer to the flows in and out as recharge and discharge. An obvious means of recharge is a stream. Few of the meres in the study area of this book have substantial inflowing streams; shallow meres more commonly have them than deeper ones, perhaps because of differences in their origin and surrounding topography. Aqualate Mere, which is large but very shallow, has three inflowing streams. A small stream flows from Marton Pool into Fenemere, both shallow meres. Flow rates in most of the streams carrying water into and out of meres are typically low and often there is little or none in summer. Few of the deeper meres receive significant amounts of water by inflowing streams. Inflowing streams tend to bring silt or clay particles into a mere; these sink to the bottom and gradually fill the mere, which partly explains the persistence of meres that do not have streams. The rates of infilling will only have been great while the landscape was still bare after the last glaciation. Most meres that survived until a cover of vegetation was established will have remained as meres, unless subsequently in-filled by other processes. More recently agricultural activities have increased rates of infilling in some meres, with deltas developing where ditches and streams bring in silt, as at Bar Mere.

A second possible means of recharge is surface drainage. However, because gradients are very shallow and surrounding soils and underlying glacial deposits are usually permeable, typically little or no water enters meres in this way, except briefly after heavy rain. The other two methods of recharge are direct rainfall and groundwater drainage. Seepage of groundwater into meres is very difficult to measure but it certainly occurs widely. The annual rainfall in the Marches is typically 650–700 mm whilst evaporation has been estimated at 500 mm, giving a net gain of at least 200 mm of water per year, suggesting that supplies of groundwater might not be essential to maintain water levels. If meres were fed only by rainwater, they could be likened to dew ponds on the downs of southern England. However, the chemistry of rainwater and water in the meres is very different, apart from Oakmere, and even here it is only vaguely similar. It seems that all meres are recharged by groundwater in addition to direct rainfall. Even at Oakmere, the similarities in water chemistry are likely to be due to the very sandy, nutrient-poor surrounding deposits through which the groundwater percolates, rather than to the mere being recharged only by rain. Another factor, only partially understood, is transpirational water loss. Bankside trees, emergent plants and even floating leaves may increase the rate of water loss from a mere, but the amount is difficult to estimate. In small meres, where the ratio of plant cover to open water is usually highest, the effect may be significant. However, there is still likely to be an excess of rainfall over evapotranspiration in larger meres. This makes it perhaps surprising to find dry and water-filled kettle holes in close proximity, as for example in the Pant-yr-Ochain area, north of Wrecsam.

Dry kettle holes presumably receive more water in rainfall than they would lose by evaporation, but the excess drains down to the water table through pervious substrata. This is prevented where the water table in the surrounding glacial deposits is above the base of the kettle hole, or where there is an impervious layer such as clay underlying or lining the kettle hole. Clay, found in White Mere amongst many others, was deposited in the post-glacial period, when there was much redistribution of glacial deposits. The result can be a perched water table – the surface of the mere is higher than the water table of the surrounding area. Boreholes have shown the existence of this phenomenon at Brown Moss near Whitchurch, explaining the presence of large pools where they might not otherwise be expected (Fig. 88). The Isle Pool, a 6-ha mere located in a huge loop of the Severn near Shrewsbury, is another example. The bottom of the mere is above the level of the river, but it holds water throughout the year and groundwater appears to drain into it. When a dry summer lowers the level of the mere, wet weather does not immediately cause a rise, presumably as groundwater levels must first be restored. Once this has been accomplished, the level of the

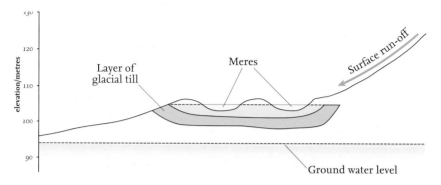

FIG 88. Perched water table at Brown Moss. A layer of impervious glacial till that holds water in meres, which would otherwise drain down to the lower ground water level.

pool suddenly starts to rise. There are also examples of this phenomenon in Breckland meres.

Dams have been constructed to raise the levels of some meres, for example Titley Pool, a Herefordshire Nature Trust reserve and Comber Mere in Cheshire. There are also some entirely artificial open water bodies, created by the construction of dams to hold back the water of streams, interesting and historic examples being in Fishpool Valley at Croft Castle. However, these man-made pools and lakes are not a special feature of the Marches and their hydrology is different from that of true meres so they will not be considered further.

Not only do most meres lack an obvious method of recharge, they also lack streams as a means of discharge. Meres that receive water through a stream are more likely to have discharge through a stream. Aqualate Mere has a small outflowing river. Marton Pool near Chirbury is a good illustration of the individuality of the meres: it lies on a watershed and has two outflowing streams carrying water in opposite directions, to Wales and to England. Rostherne Mere has a small and sluggish outlet, Blackburn's Brook, which has been known to flow backwards, bringing water into the mere after heavy rain.

Drains have been constructed to provide an outlet for a few meres and some of these have artificially lowered the mere surface. Ellesmere discharges via a culvert that runs through the town. The Isle Pool was completely drained in 1793, miners being employed to build a 300 yard brick-lined tunnel through the perched water table of the mere and down to the nearby Severn. The tunnel became blocked at some stage during the 19th century and the mere refilled, though only to about half its former area. Elaborate schemes have been constructed to overcome the sluggish drainage in some parts of north Shropshire and Cheshire. For example, a series of culverts was constructed in 1864 to carry water from Crose Mere to the River Roden over 3 km away, lowering the surface of the mere by 2–3 m. Nonetheless, most meres lack a stream or drain to provide a means of discharge. Presumably excess water, from a period of heavy rainfall for example, can still seep away through surrounding sands and gravels.

WATER LEVEL FLUCTUATIONS AND DRAWDOWN ZONES

Variations in water level might be considered to be typical of reservoirs rather than lakes. However, recharge and discharge rates are not equal through the seasons of the year, so the water level of a mere does tend to fluctuate. A variation in level of 440 mm was found during a 27-month study of White Mere in the 1990s.[2] Changes in level may not be obvious in steep-sided meres, but when the sides shelve shallowly, there can be a large drawdown zone. This zone dries out during summer, supporting a distinctive associated flora and providing a habitat for certain invertebrate species. Good examples of drawdown zones are found around some of the pools at Brown Moss near Whitchurch. Characteristic plants are orange foxtail *Alopecurus aequalis*, small water-pepper, fine-leaved water-dropwort *Oenanthe aquatica*, lesser marshwort *Apium inundatum*, marsh St John's-wort and bog pimpernel (Fig. 89). There are also two rare liverworts at this site: cavernous crystalwort, *Riccia cavernosa*, a nationally scarce species, and channelled

FIG 89. The main pool at Brown Moss is shallow with extensive drawdown zones, seen here in late Summer 2005. (Alex Lockton)

crystalwort *Riccia canaliculata*, with Red Data Book or RDB status and recorded nowhere else in England. (Red Data Books are lists of threatened species, held by the International Union for Conservation of Nature.) Both inhabit peaty mud close to the shore of the mere, where conditions are neither heavily shaded nor permanently desiccated. In 1990 one of the most despised alien plants was recorded for the first time at Brown Moss: New Zealand pigmyweed, *Crassula helmsii*. It has since become established on the main pool there, but has not spread to the others. In the winter of 2003/4 English Nature and Shropshire County Council carried out management work to attempt to eradicate it. The plants and topsoil were scraped from the margins of the pool, dumped on an arable field and sprayed with herbicide. The regrowth was also sprayed in the following summer. These measures reduced but did not eliminate *Crassula* from Brown Moss and by 2010 there were again large amounts.

Changes in water level are tolerated by some plants but are essential for others, including shoreweed *Littorella uniflora*. It grows in shallow water, but is wind pollinated so has emergent flowers. Seeds only ripen if the fruit dries out for at least two weeks. The seeds germinate on damp mud, which then needs to be inundated for growth to continue. Shoreweed has disappeared from many lowland sites in England and Wales but is still found at Brown Moss. It has recently colonised oligotrophic pools on higher ground in the Marches, most notably on the Long Mynd. Six-stamened waterwort *Elatine hexandra* also requires fluctuating water levels. Unless it is exposed in summer it cannot flower and set seed to complete its annual life cycle. It becomes a short-lived perennial if it remains submerged, holding out for the exposure that its pollinators need to reach it. Leighton described six-stamened waterwort seeds in his 1841 *Flora of Shropshire* as 'most beautifully ribbed and transversely striated' (Fig. 90). It is a rare plant in Britain, mostly found around the western

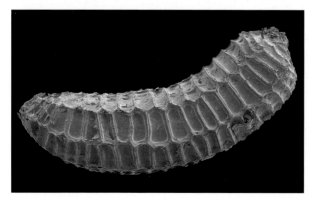

FIG 90. Scanning electron micrograph of six-stamened waterwort seed, 0.6 mm long, showing the ribs and transverse striations admired by Leighton over 100 years before the invention of the electron microscope. (Wolfgang Struppy, © Board of Trustees RBG Kew)

fringes.[3] It was first recorded in Britain at Bomere in 1798 and still occurs around the north and east margins, although shading trees threatens this historic population. The water level at Bomere does still fluctuate, but not in an entirely natural way. Two abstraction licences exist that allow large volumes of water for irrigation to be pumped out during relatively short periods in some summers. The recharge rates are scarcely enough to replace this water in following seasons unless they are particularly wet, but little if any water is abstracted in wet summers. There is therefore between-year variation in level as well as within-year. The Environment Agency is currently investigating the impact of these licences.

Fluctuations in water level have been greatly reduced or even prevented in some meres. Reynolds found that the annual variations at Crose Mere were less than 200 mm over a period of nearly ten years. As has been explained, this mere has an artificial outfall that limits rises. At the Isle Pool, near Shrewsbury, an ingenious siphon system was installed in 1877 to prevent the level from rising more than was wanted. It consists of an iron pipe, 6 inches in diameter, running from the pool to the nearby Severn, which is at a lower level. The system is still in operation. If the level of the pool is perceived to have risen excessively, a pump is used to fill the siphon, which then may flow for weeks without any need for further pumping.

There are various reasons for wanting water levels to vary little. Farmers do not usually wish fields adjacent to meres to become periodically waterlogged. Muddy drawdown zones look unattractive to some owners and visitors. Anglers like to build permanent jetties that remain at a constant height above the water surface. There is, on the other hand, strong evidence for the ecological benefits of fluctuations of as much as 1 m through the year. Plant and animal diversity is increased and a swampy marginal area may develop, which will tend to harbour denitrifying bacteria and reduce nitrate levels, helping to prevent excessive growth of algae. Invasion of this marginal area by trees may be prevented by the periodic inundations. Trees currently line the banks of many meres, shading out other plants in the shallows and depositing large quantities of leaves and dead wood in the water. These trees have been cleared as a conservation measure in some cases, but they are killed very effectively by a rise in water levels, with far less effort required. There has been a trend in recent years for the water level in some meres to rise and this has killed trees growing on the banks, including many alders *Alnus glutinosa* and oaks, resulting in easily recognisable spike tops. Shrawardine Pool demonstrates this process. It had been suffering from a fall in water levels due to the effects of an artificial drain and looked to be developing into alder carr, but blockage of the drain has reversed the process. Fluctuations in water level should therefore be considered natural and desirable in the meres, being allowed to occur wherever possible.

NITROGEN AND PHOSPHORUS IN THE MERES

The concentrations of nitrogen and phosphorus are critically important in the ecology of the meres and these two nutrients have been the focus of much research. Typically, concentrations of nitrogen are relatively low, often so low in summer that they are undetectable by normal test methods.[4] However, some inflowing streams and groundwater sources have high concentrations, especially where fertilisers are applied to surrounding farmland. The nitrogen concentrations of rainwater falling on to meres can also be significant, partly as a result of two anthropogenic sources: nitrate from nitrogen oxides in vehicle exhausts and volatilised ammonia from livestock. The low nitrogen concentrations found in the meres must therefore be due to losses from the water. Photosynthetic organisms absorb nitrates or ammonia for use in biosyntheses. Perhaps more significantly, certain groups of bacteria convert nitrates to nitrogen gas by the process known as denitrification. Denitrifying bacteria occur both in anaerobic deposits in the base of meres and in surrounding wetlands that have not been artificially drained.

The trends with phosphorus are different. Direct rainfall contains little or no phosphorus. Groundwater is sometimes assumed to have high phosphorus concentrations, but samples from tube-wells installed to intercept groundwater flowing into White Mere had levels of only 16 μg per litre.[5] Inflowing streams at base flow can have relatively high phosphorus concentrations as much of the water has seeped through soils, dissolving out phosphorus. Concentrations are much lower when streams are at flood flow, after heavy rainfall, when much of the inflow to stream-fed meres occurs. This is because a large proportion of the stream water is derived from surface run-off, so there is a dilution of nutrients dissolved out from soils. Given the low phosphorus concentrations of water entering the meres, the concentrations within them are surprisingly high. In a survey of 18 meres, the mean annual concentration was more than 300 μg per litre.[6] It was as high as 2,000 μg per litre in White Mere during parts of the year – more than two orders of magnitude higher than the groundwater or any of the other inflows.[7] Stream-fed and groundwater-fed meres do not differ significantly in phosphorus concentrations, both typically having high concentrations. This appears easier to explain in stream-fed meres, although anthropogenic sources of phosphorus such as pollution from sewage, effluent from livestock and leaching from overloaded arable farmland, are actually uncommon in streams that recharge meres.

The high phosphorus concentrations in groundwater-fed meres are not the result of excessive inputs, but of long periods of accumulation. This is indicated by long residence times. Residence time is how long water spends in a lake on average. It depends on the size of a lake as well as the rates of recharge and discharge. Little Mere in north Cheshire has a residence time that can be as low as 0.03 years, but this is an artificial stream-fed mere created by damming the outflow of Mere Mere. It behaves more like a wide stream of small volume than a true mere, so its figures should be regarded as highly atypical. True stream-fed meres have longer residence times, for example Cole Mere at 0.29 years and Crosemere at 1.06 years. More of the meres of the Marches are groundwater fed and these have longer residence times, for example White Mere at 2.6 years, Ellesmere 3.57 years and Bomere as much as 4.5 years.[8] Long residence times are due to low rates of both recharge and discharge, the low discharge rates resulting in little phosphorus being washed out each year.

The concentrations of phosphorus and the changes during the year are far greater than can be accounted for by nutrient recycling by the community of living organisms in meres. Data were obtained from White Mere over a depth range of 11 m, during an 18-month period from 1993 to 1994.[9] The results show marked fluctuations and differences between deep and shallow water (Fig. 91). Concentrations of phosphorus were highest in summer months, due to its release in anaerobic conditions from sediment surfaces at the base of the mere. The deeper water in meres such as White Mere is known as the hypolimnion, the water above being the epilimnion. There is little mixing between these layers during the summer months so oxygen in the hypolimnion is used faster than it is replaced, creating the anaerobic conditions that promote phosphate release into the water. In the autumn, cooling at the surface causes mixing of deeper and shallower water, so the hypolimnion becomes oxygenated. This results in the formation of insoluble iron phosphates, which precipitate into basal sediments. Losses in discharge from the mere during winter are therefore reduced. The precipitated phosphate can be released into the water again in the following summer. It is easy to see that if slightly more phosphorus is released into the water and then precipitated each year, the concentration in White Mere could have built up gradually over the centuries, or even millennia, to the current high levels. Similar processes of accumulation will have occurred in other meres.

Phosphorus

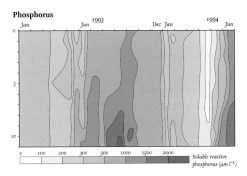

Nitrate

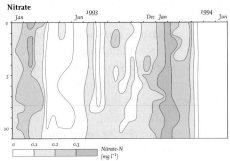

Ammonia

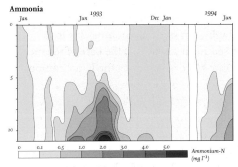

Chlorophyll

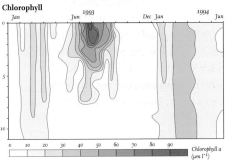

FIG 91. Concentration of mineral nutrients and chlorophyll in Whitemere from 1993–4. The vertical axis shows water depth in metres. Modified from Hameed *et al.*, 1999.

NUTRIENT CYCLES AND PHYTOPLANKTON

There are vast numbers of microscopic photosynthesising organisms in the water of the meres, collectively known as phytoplankton. Chlorophyll a occurs in all photosynthesising cells, including both eukaryotic algae and blue-green bacteria. Measurement of this pigment's concentration in the water thus indicates the overall density of phytoplankton. Rapid rises in chlorophyll a concentration indicate how quickly the populations of phytoplankton can increase. The cells of some species can double in size and divide every few days when conditions are favourable. The standing crop in the meres is often greater than 20 g per m^2, which is higher than in many lakes elsewhere. The amounts of organic matter produced are also larger than might be expected. The production of phytoplankton in the 15 ha of Crose Mere has been estimated to be between 11 and 30 t per year[10] and other meres are likely to be comparable in their productivity. The community of phytoplankton can alter much more quickly than the plants of a terrestrial habitat. Whereas the trees of a forest could maintain their dominance over other plants for hundreds of years, in an aquatic environment there can be changes both from year to year and through the seasons of a single year. Reynolds described an annual succession that he considered typical of larger meres that are surrounded by sandy drift, such as Crose Mere, Cole Mere, Hatch Mere and White Mere. Five main groups of phytoplankton are involved. Four of these are eukaryotic algae: diatoms, cryptomonads, green algae and dinoflagellates.

Diatoms and cryptomonads can grow even in low light intensities and temperatures, starting to do so early in the year, utilising the high nutrient levels that build up in winter. They can increase in number rapidly and reach quite large population densities, in what is known as the spring outburst. There are several reasons for other groups superseding them after a few weeks. Nutrient concentrations in the water become lower, favouring groups that are more efficient at nutrient uptake. Diatoms and many cryptomonads are vulnerable to grazing by zooplankton, whose numbers increase in spring. The cell walls and cytoplasm of phytoplankton are denser than fresh water, potentially leading to the problem of their settling to the base of the meres. Although cryptomonads can use their two flagella to stay in suspension, diatoms are non-motile. They also have dense siliceous cell walls so have a fast sinking rate. Eddy currents set up by winds blowing over the water surface help to keep diatoms suspended in spring, but as thermal stratification becomes established during the summer, it becomes much more likely that diatoms will sink beyond the reach of these currents. Diatoms will then need to reproduce quickly just to maintain numbers near the surface and rapid growth can be self-limited by exhaustion of the dissolved silicates needed for cell wall production.

The green algae are efficient at nutrient gathering and some are motile, thus able to remain near the water surface. They are also more buoyant than diatoms and so even the non-motile types can be kept in the upper layers of water by eddy currents during spring and summer. They have larger cells and many have thick cell walls so are less vulnerable to ingestion by grazers. Despite a relatively low growth rate, they can therefore build up to high population densities in late spring or early summer. Numbers of dinoflagellates tend to build up later in the summer when the water is warmer and the vitamins that some species require are being produced by summer bacteria. Like the green algae they are efficient at nutrient gathering, are large enough to resist grazing, build up in numbers relatively slowly, and can reach high densities. They use their flagella to swim up and down so that they can reach nutrients at different levels. Many species can feed by ingesting organic matter, in addition to photosynthesising when light levels are high enough.

The other group of phytoplankton is the cyanobacteria. These organisms are sometimes called blue-green algae but as they have a simple cell structure with no nucleus, they are not algae and are classified instead with bacteria. They thrive when the water has warmed up in the summer. Some have air-filled gas vesicles, the production and collapse of which can influence buoyancy. An excess of sugar accumulates when cyanobacteria are near the surface, because photosynthesis rates are rapid but a lack of nutrients prevents the sugars from being converted to substances needed for growth. The sugars cause a rise in turgor pressure and the collapse of the gas vesicles. The cells therefore sink to depths where nutrients are more abundant, sugars can be used up, turgor pressure falls and gas vesicles can reform, allowing a rise back to the surface. At the surface cyanobacteria resist grazing in two ways: by forming chains or other groups of cells that are too large for zooplankton to ingest, and by producing toxins. They can therefore build up to high population densities, but as long as they remain spread over a range of depths, this may not be apparent. However, a phenomenon known for over 100 years can make the cyanobacteria become all too visible.

The breaking of the meres

In 1884 William Phillips[11] reported to the Shropshire Archaeological and Natural History Society on a phenomenon known locally as the breaking of the meres: 'The water first assumes a brownish tint, which becomes more yellow, then more green. The matter then rises and forms a scum on the surface. Some of this is blown by the wind and stranded on the shore or caught among the reeds along the margin of the lake. The rest sinks to the bottom and disappears. The water then becomes perfectly clear again. During the earlier stages the water gives off a very offensive smell and is quite unfit for household use.'

The phenomena that Phillips was describing are often called algal blooms, but given that cyanobacteria often cause them, rather than eukaryotic algae, they are better referred to as surface blooms (Fig. 92). They are still very common in the meres but our attitude to them has changed since the 19th century and there are various commonly held beliefs:

- they are due to a population explosion of cyanobacteria
- they have very harmful ecological consequences
- they pose severe dangers to livestock and pets
- they are due entirely to human activity
- they are getting much worse.

All of these perceptions can be challenged in relation to the meres. If the water in a mere becomes particularly turbid, light penetration is reduced. A longer period of gas vesicle production results, as cyanobacteria have to rise further in the water column to reach light intensities high enough for the vesicles to start collapsing. The number of vesicles produced can then be so great that they fail to collapse properly, so the cyanobacteria remain very buoyant, resulting in the green floating scum that characterises surface blooms or the breaking of the meres. The cause of the turbidity that sets off this process is usually an abundance of phytoplankton. This could be due to a population explosion of cyanobacteria, but it could also be due to large numbers of other types of phytoplankton. In any case it is the flotation of the cyanobacteria rather than an increase in their numbers that is the direct cause of rapidly developing surface blooms. Reynolds

FIG 92. Surface bloom at Cole Mere. The water of the mere has turned as green as paint and the blue-green bacteria have risen to the surface and been blown to the lee shore. (Ewan Shilland)

collected evidence to support this during the 1960s. On 21 July 1966 he predicted that a break would occur at Crosemere and spent the whole of the following night taking samples at different depths. By morning more than half of the population of cyanobacteria, mainly *Microcystis aeruginosa*, had risen to the top 100 mm of water and the surface of the mere was covered with patches of scum, yet there had been no overall increase in numbers of cyanobacteria[12] (Fig. 93). Once cyanobacteria are floating at the surface, exposure to ultraviolet light often leads to their mass mortality. Large clumps of decomposing cyanobacteria accumulate on the lee shore of meres; these are unsightly and malodorous, but the ecological effects do not seem to be great. Fish are not observed to die from lack of oxygen in the water, and unlike some other parts of the world, there are very few reports of harmful effects on livestock from toxins in the cyanobacteria. A small number of cattle were reported to have died at Rostherne Mere, but there has not been widespread or frequent mortality.

Phillips's report shows that there were already surface blooms in 1884. This is long before the advent of modern intensive agriculture, though it is also before mains drainage and effective sewage treatment, so there may have been more pollution with organic wastes then than now. Even extensive agriculture can

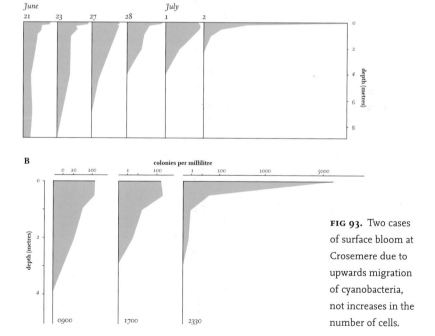

FIG 93. Two cases of surface bloom at Crosemere due to upwards migration of cyanobacteria, not increases in the number of cells.

cause some nutrient enrichment when forests are cleared and their capacity to hold nutrients is lost. Studies of photosynthetic pigments in the sediments from Cole Mere[13] and White Mere[14] suggest that surface blooms were a feature of the meres even before any forest clearance or extensive agriculture had occurred in the Marches. The study of White Mere involved using a corer to obtain a 4-m depth of sediment samples, shown by radiocarbon dating to have been formed over approximately the past 6,500 years. Pigments were extracted, separated and identified. Echinenone, a pigment produced almost solely by cyanobacteria, was found throughout the 4-m depth of sediments. β-carotene, a pigment that is produced by all phytoplankton, was also found throughout. The ratio of echinenone to β-carotene showed that cyanobacteria have formed a significant proportion of the phytoplankton of White Mere over at least the last 6,500 years. Surface blooms will almost certainly have occurred throughout this period and they are therefore not solely due to recent human activity. The reasons for them being such a longstanding feature of the meres deserve consideration. The question of whether they have become more frequent or more severe will be left until the final section of this chapter.

Limiting factors on phytoplankton

In considering the phytoplankton of the meres, it would be wrong to focus exclusively on cyanobacteria. In a survey of 23 meres, cyanobacteria made up 22.8 per cent of biovolume on average, with a range of from 0 to 71 per cent.[15] Other groups of phytoplankton were therefore usually more abundant. These other groups can reach high population densities, but as they do not form surface blooms they are less noticeable. Diatom populations usually peak in spring, green algae in early summer and dinoflagellates later in the summer. If the population of any of them was excessive and there was significant mortality, the decomposition of the phytoplankton would deplete the water of oxygen and fish-kill would be expected. There must be factors that usually limit these types of phytoplankton before their populations become excessive, and because of the conservation implications it is important to consider what they might be.

Ecologists have often found that the concentrations of nitrogen, and phosphorus in the form of phosphates, are the limiting factors on the growth of phytoplankton and therefore classify lakes according to them. Dystrophic lakes have the lowest concentrations of nitrogen and phosphorus and the lowest rates of algal and plant growth. They occur in areas of peat formation and so have peat-stained water. There are examples at Clarepool Moss and at Abbots Moss, but these are not typical meres. Oligotrophic lakes have slightly higher but still very low nutrient concentrations, followed by mesotrophic and then eutrophic lakes, which have successively higher concentrations and growth rates. Eutrophication is an increase in the availability of either nitrogen or phosphorus or both of these elements to levels where they promote vigorous growth. Photosynthetic organisms need nutrients other than nitrogen and phosphorus, but they are rarely the limiting factor on growth. The density of phytoplankton populations at any instant in time is not of course determined by growth rates alone – the rate of consumption by zooplankton is also significant.

The factors controlling the growth of phytoplankton in the meres have been investigated since the 1880s. Two contrasting possible mechanisms are referred to memorably as bottom-up and top-down control. The concentration of a nutrient in the water is usually the limiting factor in the bottom-up mechanism. The characteristically high phosphorus concentrations of the meres prevent this from being the usual limiting factor on growth of phytoplankton in the meres. This is in marked contrast to lakes studied elsewhere, including the Broads, where phosphorus has usually been found to be the most significant limiting factor. Limnologists have described the meres as lakes that defy conventions about nutrients.

If phosphorus concentration does not limit growth, perhaps nitrogen does. A study of 24 meres in the early 1990s did indeed provide evidence for nitrogen rather than phosphorus as a limiting factor, but only in deeper meres.[16] In meres deeper than 3 m, phytoplankton biomass was positively correlated with the winter concentrations of nitrogen in the form of dissolved nitrate or ammonium. There was no correlation between phytoplankton biomass and phosphorus concentrations. It is well known that deeper meres become thermally stratified in late spring and remain so until autumn. The warmer epilimnion is mixed by wind, but is separated by a thermocline from the colder hypolimnion below, which remains largely unmixed. Wind-generated currents cause mixing of the shallow and deep water from autumn until spring, bringing nutrients up from the base of the mere. Phosphorus concentrations are typically high, but nitrogen levels are low in winter and virtually undetectable in summer. This is the case even in deep meres where there are surface streams bringing in appreciable amounts of nitrogen. The hypolimnion becomes anoxic soon after its formation in spring and nitrates will therefore be converted to nitrogen gas by denitrifying bacteria. Phytoplankton in the epilimnion presumably absorb nitrates and ammonium so efficiently that these nutrients become exhausted, limiting further growth. The cyanobacteria that cause surface blooms would be able to escape this limitation if they fixed their own nitrogen supplies. However, there is no obvious relationship between the cyanobacteria present as a percentage of total planktonic biovolume and nitrogen levels, either summer or winter; neither is it clear to what extent freshwater cyanobacteria actually do fix nitrogen. Recent research[17] found that cyanobacteria populations were relatively greater in meres with higher nitrogen concentrations, in contrast to general expectations. Dinoflagellates are favoured by relatively low nitrogen and higher phosphorus concentrations; this is because they can migrate to different levels in the epilimnion and sometimes feed heterotrophically to boost their nitrogen supplies. When nitrogen concentrations are too low to be detected, but there are appreciable concentrations of phosphorus, dinoflagellates and cyanobacteria are co-dominant. If the concentration of both nutrients is too low to be detectable, cyanobacteria are favoured, maybe because they can adjust their density using gas vacuoles and sink to the hypolimnion to obtain phosphorus. Dinoflagellates are prevented from doing this by the low oxygen concentrations and low light intensity of the deeper water.

The evidence from deeper meres suggests that phytoplankton are limited by nitrogen concentrations, an example of bottom-up control. By contrast, top-down control has been found to operate in shallow meres. No correlation was found between the concentration of either nitrogen or phosphorus and phytoplankton biomass in meres with a mean depth of less than 3 m.[18] Clearly there must be some fundamental differences between deep and shallow meres. Shallow meres do not become thermally stratified, because wind causes mixing of water throughout the year. Concentrations of nitrate and phosphate were found to be higher on average in shallow meres, allowing a greater biomass of phytoplankton to develop in the growing season. In 12 shallow meres, the mean concentration of chlorophyll *a* was 30.3 μg per litre, with a maximum of 80.1. The mean was 18.0 μg per litre and the maximum was 30.5, in 12 deep meres. The lack of correlation between nitrogen concentrations and phytoplankton biomass in shallow meres suggests that another factor is limiting. The most significant correlation was found between the biomass of phytoplankton and that of zooplankton. The correlation was negative, with lower phytoplankton biomass in meres that had higher zooplankton biomass. This suggests that grazing by zooplankton was the limiting factor. The maximum zooplankton biomass in shallow meres was nearly 8 mg per litre compared with 2 mg in deeper meres. This difference cannot be entirely accounted for by the greater availability of phytoplankton. There were also more submerged plants growing in shallow meres; these provide shelter for zooplankton and reduce predation by fish. The lower numbers of phytoplankton per litre in meres deeper than 3 m means less light is absorbed by them, yet submerged plants still cannot easily grow, because more light is being absorbed by the water itself and organic substances dissolved in it. Zooplankton populations are therefore smaller, ensuring that bottom-up rather than top-down control is dominant.

Despite their ecological importance, zooplankton are under-recorded, under-researched and do not enjoy the protection that is accorded to more charismatic groups. The records that do exist show considerable variation both between meres and between different sample dates in the same mere. This could simply be due to the recorders having different interests, expertise, sampling methods or collection techniques. Reynolds listed the species of rotifer, cladoceran and copepod that he found to be the most ubiquitous and abundant.[19] Population densities of zooplankton follow annual cycles. Some species have two annual peaks, in spring and in late summer, following peaks in phytoplankton populations. The rapid growth of phytoplankton allows the zooplankton feeding on them also to multiply rapidly, reaching relatively large standing crops. The dry biomass was found to range from 3 to 10 g per m^2 for most of the year in Crosemere, with a peak of up to 25 g in spring.[20] The zooplankton may briefly outweigh the phytoplankton at this point, giving an inverted pyramid of biomass, but annual production of zooplankton is of course lower than that of phytoplankton.

SUBMERGED PLANTS

There is a clear relationship between the nutrient status of the meres and the submerged plants that grow in them. The only submerged plant found in highly eutrophic meres such as Crosemere is horned pondweed *Zannichellia palustris*. Moderately eutrophic meres, for example Cole Mere, can support other submerged plants: autumnal water starwort *Callitriche hermaphroditica*, rigid hornwort *Ceratophyllum demersum*, small pondweed *Potamogeton berchtoldii*, fennel pondweed *Potamogeton pectinatus*, spiked water-milfoil *Myriophyllum spicatum* and fan-leaved water-crowfoot *Ranunculus circinatus*. Several species of giant algae in the genus *Chara* also occur.

More species can join the underwater sward in meres that are mesotrophic, for example Marton Pool, Chirbury, Newton Mere and Bomere (Fig. 94). Blunt-leaved pondweed *Potamogeton obtusifolius*, needle spike rush *Elocharis acicularis* and six-stamened waterwort have been found in some. Six-stamened waterwort has already been mentioned as a plant of shallow water and exposed sandy margins. Its discoverer at Bomere Pool was Edward Williams, who also found quillwort at the same site.

Quillwort *Isoetes lacustris* has been described as a glacial relic at Bomere Pool and it is no longer found anywhere in the Marches though there are stable populations to the west in Wales. The oligotrophic conditions that it requires are not now found in any mere. Another submerged plant requiring oligotrophic

FIG 94. Bomere is a mere that has been a very significant site for hydrophytes in the past and could be again in the future. (Iain Diack)

conditions that was formerly found at Bomere in the early 19th century is water lobelia *Lobelia dortmanna*. It was recorded at several other meres in the 19th and early 20th centuries but as with quillwort we need to look westwards to Wales to find it now. Quillwort, water lobelia and also shoreweed are out-competed in alkaline water where hydrogen carbonate ions are abundant. This is because whilst other aquatic plants can use hydrogen carbonate in photosynthesis, they can only use carbon dioxide.[21] They obtain it mostly from sediments, having high root to shoot ratios, and root adaptations for carbon dioxide uptake. Increases in hydrogen carbonate concentrations cause their demise as a result of competition, whilst rapid deposition of fine silts also kills them because with small size and slow growth rates they are easily buried. These species are a challenge for all those involved with conservation in the meres.

We can expect eutrophication of a mere to lead to the loss of some species of submerged plants. In a recent study that included some of the shallower meres in the Marches there was a negative correlation between the concentration of nitrogen in the winter and the overall species diversity of submerged plants.[22] Experiments have been carried out to test whether nitrate enrichment causes a loss of diversity.[23] Artificial ponds were set up, each containing water and sediment from a lake and the same range of submerged plant species. The ponds were all enriched with sufficient phosphorus to ensure that it was not limiting, and a range of different concentrations of nitrate. The results over two years showed that the more nitrate added to a pond, the more species of submerged plants were lost. Even the lowest nitrate concentration tested, which was 50 times lower than the EU limit for safe drinking water, caused the loss of some species. The maximum nitrate concentration that would have allowed the survival of all submerged plants was estimated to be between 0.6 and 0.65 mg of nitrate per litre. Nitrate enrichment caused an increase in phytoplankton suspended in the water and also in the slimy green layer of periphyton growing on surfaces, including those of submerged plants. Light that would otherwise have reached the leaves of the submerged plants was therefore intercepted. These experiments were carried out using water and sediments from Hickling Broad in Norfolk, but it seems very likely materials from the meres would give similar results.

There are other possible reasons for poor light penetration. Silt washes into meres from surrounding farmland. Bottom-feeding fish can stir up sediments, the worst culprits being the carp that anglers have introduced. Bottom-feeding fish can also destroy submerged plants by uprooting them. Coots *Fulica atra*, tufted duck *Aythya fuligula* and great crested grebes *Podiceps cristatus* all dive and feed partly on submerged plants. All of these species are very commonly seen on the meres, the latter two increasing considerably in the latter part of the 20th century, but their populations seem too small for them to have much overall effect.

FLOATING PLANTS

The explanations offered for the poor species diversity of submerged plants in eutrophic meres do not apply to floating plants, yet their diversity is also negatively correlated with winter nitrogen concentration.[24] As with submerged plants, some floating species thrive in eutrophic meres. An example is yellow water-lily *Nuphar lutea*, which can produce submerged leaves but grows longer petioles, allowing its leaves to float on the surface where there is shelter from wind and the water is calmer. White water-lily *Nymphaea alba* is less tolerant of eutrophication, producing only floating leaves. It requires still water and on larger meres there is too much turbulence caused by wind and waves, especially on the windward shores. It is also unable to tolerate disturbance by boats on meres used for sailing or water-skiing. A third species of water-lily is one of the great rarities of the Marches: least water-lily (Fig. 95). It has been recorded on Blake Mere, Kettle Mere and Cole Mere, but nowhere else in England or Wales. It is now found only on Cole Mere where there is still a small population. Further

FIG 95. Least water-lily at Cole Mere. (Alex Lockton)

north, in Scotland, it is associated with oligotrophic or mesotrophic conditions and as Cole Mere is eutrophic, and it is used by a sailing club, the population has looked vulnerable for many years (Fig. 96). Its loss would be highly regrettable, especially as it was the first emblem of the Shropshire Conservation Trust. Overhanging alders, sycamores *Acer pseudoplatanus* and rhododendrons have recently been cleared from the shore closest to the plants, in an attempt to reduce shading and encourage its growth. This has been successful and the number of plants is increasing in both of the areas where there are colonies. It is likely that there would originally have been reedswamp between the water lilies

FIG 96. Cole Mere, with fringing woodland, some of which has been cleared as part of an effort to conserve the least water-lily.

and surrounding carr, which would have reduced shading by the carr. It would therefore be worth investigating reasons for the loss of reedswamp, so that measures can be taken that allow it to regenerate.

Another possible threat to the least water-lily is hybridisation with yellow water-lilies. All the plants at Cole Mere are purebred, but hybrids between the least and the yellow water-lilies were recently discovered at both Betton Pool and Hatch Mere. These were probably introduced rather than local hybrids. Indeed, the population of least water-lilies at Cole Mere is such an outlier that it may be a 19th-century introduction rather than a rare survival.[25]

Floating water-plantain has been recorded from meres in the past. Like the previous species it requires oligotrophic or at least mesotrophic conditions. It can grow either entirely submerged or with its leaves floating in shallow water. Floating water-plantain is rare and threatened globally, the Marches populations being a significant part of the British range. It has been described as the most significant plant species in the meres and is one of the main reasons for their SAC status.[26] Currently, floating water-plantain only just clings on, with recent records from Bomere Pool and the pools at Brown Moss, but there are also populations in disused canals.

FISH

Although many meres have no connection to streams or rivers, nevertheless they contain a variety of fish species. Fish may arrive as eggs or fry on the feet of ducks, though there is no proof of this. Some species were probably deliberately introduced in the past as a source of food. Perch *Perca fluviatalis* are described as 'best for the table in the winter' in the *Fauna of Shropshire*.[27] Pike *Esox lucius* were also consumed in the past and occasionally still are. Carp are a non-native species, introduced as a source of food. Like perch and pike, they are usually now regarded as a coarse fish, though there are reports that anglers from Eastern Europe have recently been eating carp of up to about 4 kg. Meres have sometimes been stocked with brown trout *Salmo trutta* and rainbow trout *Oncorhynchus mykiss*, but with little success. Information on fish introductions from the past is at best patchy and often non-existent. There are records of the stocking of specific meres with bream *Abramis brama*, roach *Rutilus rutilus*, tench *Tinca tinca*, rudd *Scardinius erythrophthalmus*, pike, trout, common carp *Cyprinus carpio* and crucian carp *Carassius carassius* from the 1970s onwards, but anglers are notoriously secretive about their activities and there will have been other introductions. Attempting to discern the natural distribution of fish in the meres is therefore a futile exercise. We should instead focus on actual distributions and the natural history of the species that now thrive. There is currently a shortage of good data on populations, despite their ecological importance. Single counts have not proved reliable and the status of a species can only be evaluated after repeated surveys in a mere over several years. Permission from landowners and from the Environment Agency is often very hard to obtain, especially for the most unbiased survey methods using gill net fleets.

One of the conundrums of ecology is how the many species of fish in some lakes can all find ecological niches, for example the cichlids of Lake Malawi, of which there are hundreds of species. There are far fewer species in the meres so it should not be so difficult to decide how each species earns its living. The principal species that are ubiquitous or nearly so are pike, tench, bream, roach and perch.[28] Research over the last 20 or 30 years has revealed various trends.[29] The number of species present increases with the size of the mere and with the amount of submerged aquatic macrophytes. Numbers of bream and tench have both declined in some meres due to the progressive loss of macrophytes and spawning substrates. Roach and tench have generally increased in abundance in recent years, probably because of increased spring temperatures.

Pike spawn in the spring, while the water is still quite cool. The young fish feed on zooplankton and then on insect larvae. As they grow older they feed increasingly on other fish, especially roach in spring and perch when the water is more turbid in the summer. They also feed on amphibians and the young of waterfowl. They tend to lie in wait for their prey, either among plants in shallow water, or near the surface further from the shore if the water is turbid enough to offer the necessary concealment. There are reports of a black-headed gull *Chroicocephalus ridibundus* being taken by a pike at Cole Mere, but pike do not grow as large here as in some other habitats in Britain, rarely reaching more than 10 kg.[30] Populations declined during the 20th century and pike are now absent from some meres.

Tench require water temperatures of about 20 °C to spawn, so this does not occur until summer and in some years not at all. As with most other species of fish in the meres, they prefer areas of shallow water where there are plants that offer protection and zooplankton on which to feed. Numbers have fallen in meres where these macrophytes have declined. Tench are cyprinids – members of the carp family. They share with other members of this family the characteristic of becoming bottom feeders as they grow larger, and they tolerate low oxygen levels. They can penetrate up to 70 mm in sediments to obtain worms, non-biting midge larvae, crustaceans and molluscs. They sometimes disturb the sediments deliberately in order to expose their prey, of which there can be huge numbers. A survey of Cole Mere showed that there were 16,860 oligochaetes, 5,720 chironomid larvae,

2,710 ostracods and 300 ephemoptera per m² of sediments.[31] Tench also feed on submerged water plants and are associated with habitats where these are abundant.

Bream spawn in warm shallow areas where water plants provide cover. A survey at Ellesmere, Cole Mere and Tatton Mere in 1983 showed that recruitment to the population had only occurred in 1959, 1966, 1969 and 1973. Water temperature in these years during July and August was above 16 °C, which apparently is the minimum for successful spawning. Further surveys showed repeated failures of recruitment to the population until the warm summer of 1989. Given that successful spawning occurs so irregularly, the survival of bream in the meres depends on their being particularly long-lived, specimens aged 20 or more years being found in Ellesmere. As with other species of cyprinid in the meres, growth rates of bream are typically high, owing to the abundance of the invertebrates on which they feed. Young bream feed on zooplankton and then when older on invertebrates in bottom sediments, particularly worms and non-biting midge larvae.

Roach are very common in many meres, though their numbers have fluctuated, and size class studies suggest that there can be a series of years when few fish are added to the population. Since the mid-1980s there have been significant population increases, with a particularly good spawning season in 1989. Roach often swim in shoals, spawning in spring or early summer in the shelter of water plants. They show similarities in feeding behaviour with their fellow cyprinids, tench and bream. Young fish rely on phytoplankton including cyanobacteria and zooplankton in open water. Older fish continue to feed on zooplankton but are also bottom feeders, preying on non-biting midge larvae and other invertebrates in the sediments. Larger roach can also feed on water plants, as well as crustaceans, insect larvae and molluscs in open water, and are therefore rather more varied in their diet than bream. They also appear to cause less turbidity in the water by disturbing sediments while feeding. Hybrids between roach and bream occur in some meres, specimens with lengths of over 500 mm being caught at Aqualate Mere. They are popular with coarse anglers as they fight more than either of the parent species.

Perch spawn by laying ribbons of eggs on submerged water plants. The young form shoals, feeding on zooplankton and then successively larger prey, including insect larvae, crustaceans and fish larvae. As they grow, perch spend more time in beds of water plants close to the shore where they feed on small fish and invertebrates, either picked off the bottom or from the surface of plants. As they grow larger, perch feed increasingly on fish, so indirectly reduce zooplankton consumption, but in turbid waters growth to a large size rarely occurs. They do not themselves cause water to become turbid, as their feeding methods do not disturb bottom sediments. Perch were abundant in the meres until the mid-1970s when a disease reduced their numbers greatly. They remained scarce in the 1980s, after which they recovered somewhat. Studies elsewhere have suggested that perch numbers tend to fall when lakes become more eutrophic, roach gaining the competitive advantage.

Although the five species so far described are the most abundant, others are found in many meres. Eels are the only species that lives in the meres but does not spawn there, yet it does not need to be restocked artificially as the young fish arrive through migration, either in streams or across land if it is damp. At one time eel traps were set in White Mere, showing that meres without outflowing streams could be reached. It has been reported that more females than males reach the meres. While still young, their main food items are non-biting midge larvae, crustaceans and other invertebrates, but larger eels eat smaller fish and molluscs. They feed mostly on the bottom, yet cause little disturbance of sediments.

Rudd feed on invertebrates and plants, mostly near the surface. They are another cyprinid species and, like bream and roach, older rudd take some invertebrates from open water. However, they feed less in bottom sediments than these other species, more often finding food close to the water surface and in beds of water plants close to the shore. Research at Little Mere found that they could co-exist with roach as long as perch were also present, but that the loss of perch led to a severe decline in numbers of rudd.

Common carp are also cyprinids, showing similarities in their feeding behaviour to tench, bream and roach. The young feed on zooplankton, but older fish grub around on the bottom of the meres feeding on biting midge larvae, crustaceans and molluscs. Carp have an extensible tubular mouth, which can penetrate into bottom sediments, stirring them up and making the water very turbid. They sometimes rise to feed on insects at the surface, unlike tench and bream, which are more exclusively bottom feeders. Carp require a water temperature of 18 °C or more for spawning, choosing warm sheltered shallows to do so. There has been some discussion about carp's ability to reproduce successfully in the meres, but local anglers are well aware that they can. Aqualate Mere with its shallow water and extensive reedswamp is one of the likelier sites, the 2 kg carp caught there probably being the product of spawning. What is certain is that carp can grow very rapidly in the meres, with anglers judging their prowess by the size of specimens that they have caught. An obsession can develop for catching large carp, with anglers sometimes camping on the lakeshore and fishing continuously for many days, using large quantities of groundbait. The larger fish in some cases have been given names and are always returned after being caught. Most meres have had carp introduced, large numbers of fish or very large specimens being released in some cases.

The fish of the meres are a powerful draw for anglers. Most meres are leased to angling clubs and the Prince Albert Angling Club in particular has become a very dominant force. The club recently bought Oss Mere at auction, outbidding Shropshire Wildlife Trust and raising concerns about the future ecological status of this SSSI. The positions around meres that are used for fishing are known as pegs and paths are maintained to allow access to them. Anglers need unobstructed access to open water at their pegs and this sometimes necessitates the cutting of bankside vegetation. Sometimes the bank of the mere is built out with soil or rubble inside a revetment, or alternatively wooden staging may be constructed to reach beyond the outer edge of the swamp. The closer that pegs are to each other, the greater the effects that they have on the communities of shallow water and banks, principally swamp and carr and the species that live there. Predators of fish are of course unwelcome, including otters *Lutra lutra*, mink *Mustela vison* and some birds. Mink rafts are used to test for their presence and to trap them on some meres. Poor water quality is another threat, especially in warm summers. Bales of barley straw are sometimes put into the water with the aim of reducing the growth of phytoplankton, but there is no properly controlled experimental evidence for the efficacy of this method (Fig. 97). In the 1990s the Fire and Rescue Service was called in to oxygenate the water in Isle Pool by pumping water out of the mere and allowing it to cascade back in. Canisters of potassium permanganate have also been used for artificial oxygenation. It is not

FIG 97. Marbury Mere, with bales of barley straw placed in the water by the angling club that manages the mere, in an attempt to prevent surface blooms.

clear whether these measures are necessary to prevent death of fish from anoxia and it is difficult to find reliable evidence of significant numbers of fish deaths being attributable to poor water quality.

BIRDS

These are perhaps the most extensively studied inhabitants of the meres, a wealth of data being obtained on their feeding, breeding and roosting. Coots, tufted duck and great crested grebes are all frequently seen diving to feed on animals and submerged plants. Coots are mainly vegetarian but also eat smaller quantities of fish fry and eggs, insects, molluscs and worms. In contrast, tufted ducks eat mostly animals such as small fish, frogs *Rana temporaria*, molluscs, larger insects and insect larvae, but also small quantities of submerged plants and duckweed. Great crested grebes also feed mainly on animals, including small specimens of all of the species of fish, insects and insect larvae, crustaceans, molluscs and some submerged plants. Ruddy duck *Oxyura jamaicensis*, regarded as feral as they are not native, also dive to feed on aquatic insects and seeds of water plants. Herons wade in shallow water throughout the year, hunting for fish, especially perch and eels, as well as roach, small pike or carp and frogs, young coot and ducklings. Mute swans *Cygnus olor* feed in shallow water on algae, submerged plants and the rhizomes and roots of emergent plants. Some animals are eaten, for example small amphibians, molluscs and more rarely small fish. Canada geese *Branta canadensis* do feed to any extent on plants growing in the meres, but grass in adjacent fields is a more important food source for them. Over a thousand birds have been recorded at Cole Mere in winter, depositing large quantities of faeces on surrounding fields and causing significant damage to crops. Similarly high winter numbers have been recorded around the pools at Brown Moss. Waders are rare on the meres, due to a lack of shallow water.

Hirundines often visit in large numbers over the meres giving spectacular aeronautical displays as they hawk for insects. Sand martins *Riparia riparia* are the species most frequently seen from their arrival in March until early September. Large numbers may be seen together, for example 300 on Ellesmere in April 2003. Sand martins and house martins *Delichon urbicum* sometimes feed in mixed flocks. House martins arrive slightly later in April and stay a little longer until September or October. Swallows *Hirundo rustica* also hunt for insects on the wing over the meres, but sometimes pick them from the surface or sip water as they skim over it. Swifts *Apus apus* come down to feed on insects or to sip water, but they usually feed higher than the hirundines.

Most of the birds that breed on the meres choose areas of emergent plants or dense shrubs for their nests, where they find some concealment. Water rails *Rallus aquatica* breed in such seclusion at Aqualate and Rostherne Meres. Moorhens *Gallinula chloropus* are more conspicuous, and are ubiquitous on the smaller meres and ponds. Nests are constructed among plants in shallow water or on the bank, but food is obtained both from water plants and areas around the meres. Coot both feed and breed in water, preferring larger areas of open water than do moorhen and their nests are built among emergent vegetation on the margins of meres. Great crested grebes also build their nests among such plants, usually on meres that are larger than 2 ha, with several pairs typically on the largest waters. Tufted duck is another species that favours the banks of meres where there are shrubs or emergent plants. Small numbers breed on Aqualate and some other large meres. Mute swans breed around some meres, sometimes in sheltered areas of emergent plants, but occasionally also in open, relatively unprotected sites. Mallards *Anas platyrhynchos* do not confine their nests to waterside sites either, being seen with their young soon after hatching on the water of most meres. Shelduck *Tadorna tadorna* are scarce summer visitors, with breeding records for a few meres including Cole Mere and Newton Mere, and northern shoveler *Anas clypeata* breed at Aqualate Mere in small numbers.

Ruddy duck bred in captivity for the first time in Britain at Walcot near Bishop's Castle in 1936. They bred in the wild in the Marches from the 1960s onwards, constructing their nests in shallow water reed-beds. The meres became their most prolific area in Britain. Notable records include five nests on Crose Mere in 1981 and 19 individuals on Ellesmere in January 2002. However, ruddy duck have caused problems elsewhere in Europe by crossbreeding with white-headed duck *Oxyura leucocephala*. The UK Government acceded to pressure from the EU and Spain, agreeing to a programme of eradication. A five-year programme was carried out, costing £4.6 million. The ruddy duck population was estimated to be 4,400 when the programme started in 2005, and by 2010 it had been reduced to a few hundred. It seems hard to believe that if this sum of money had been available for the conservation of meres, it could not have been more effectively spent!

Some birds nest in trees adjacent to meres. The heronry at Aqualate Mere is known to have existed on its current site for hundreds of years and currently has 40–45 pairs nesting each year. The heronry at Ellesmere has only been on its Cow Island site since the 1970s, adjacent to the visitor centre at Ellesmere. It is perhaps the best place in Britain to view breeding grey herons *Ardea cinerea*, telescopes and video cameras being in operation from March to the middle of

May, after which tree leaves obscure the view (Fig. 98). The island is artificial, created by dumping material on the ice when the mere was frozen in the year of Napoleon's retreat from Moscow. There are very few natural islands on the meres but species such as Canada geese that often nest on island sites seem to be able to breed nonetheless. Canada geese are sometimes culled at Aqualate and other nature reserves, partly because their aggressive territorial behaviour during the breeding season deters native birds from nesting. The cormorant *Phalacrocorax carbo* is another species now breeding in larger numbers than some would wish (Fig. 99). Trees near the heronry at Aqualate Mere are used, for example, over 30 nests being recorded in 2006.

FIG 98. Courtship display by herons at the heronry at Cow Island, Ellesmere. (John Hawkins)

FIG 99. Cormorant roost at Rostherne Mere, with alder trees killed and coloured white by cormorant guano.

All of the breeding birds so far mentioned spend time on or in the water, but there are other species that keep out of the water but are still dependent on it for nesting sites. Reed warblers *Acrocephalus scirpaceus* are at the western extreme of their range in the Marches. They nest in reed-beds around the margins of meres, even in quite small stands. The population at Rostherne Mere, north of the area covered by this book, is perhaps the best-studied in Britain.[32] There are also strong populations at Fenemere and at Aqualate Mere where there are between 30 and 50 pairs. Many other meres have smaller numbers, typically of between five and ten pairs, because extensive areas of reedswamp are currently lacking. Sedge warbler *Acrocephalus schoenobaenus* also nest in reedswamp, but favour drier, scrubbier areas. Numbers tend to be smaller than reed warbler even though its range extends much further westwards. Reed bunting often also breed in reedswamp or in rough areas of wetland adjacent to the meres.

Many birds use the open water of the meres as a safe place to roost. Some are residents that disperse over the meres to breed in spring and summer but become more sociable during the rest of the year when they are no longer tied to the nest. Others are winter migrants that arrive in the autumn, remaining until spring and then returning north or to the sea to breed in summer. Many of the birds that roost on the meres feed elsewhere during the day. The numbers of birds roosting on the larger meres is very variable but can be huge. Gulls form perhaps the most impressive congregations in the winter months. Numbers are notoriously difficult to estimate in fading evening light, the different species intermixed and black-headed gulls in almost constant motion, but the totals on Ellesmere can be well in excess of 10,000. Herring gulls *Larus argentatus* and black-headed gulls are usually present in the largest numbers; lesser black-backed gulls *Larus fuscus* and common gulls *Larus canus* are also often present in substantial numbers. It is unclear whether the roosting gulls contribute significant amounts of guano to the water. The favoured meres are close to landfill sites, because they are used for daytime feeding. Betton Pool, south of Shrewsbury, was a favoured roost until the nearby municipal tip was closed. Another prominent group of roosting winter migrants are the ducks. Counts of dabbling ducks on the larger meres are up in the hundreds for widgeon *Anas penelope*, and in the tens for northern shoveler and gadwall *Anas streptera*. For the diving ducks, counts of 30 are typical for pochard *Aythya farina*, but numbers of scaup *Arythya marila* and goldeneye *Bucecephala clangula* are much less. Twenty is a typical maximum count for goosander *Mergus merganser* and smaller numbers for smew *Mergellus albellus*, both of these being sawbill ducks.

The numbers of some species of bird that breed on the meres are augmented in winter by migrants. On Ellesmere, 300 tufted duck were recorded in February

2004 for example and 45 great crested grebe in January 2004. Teal *Anas crecca* breed in small numbers in pools, both on the mosses and the hills, but appear in much larger numbers on the meres in winter; 100 were recorded on Ellesmere in January 2001 for example. Some juvenile and breeding cormorants spend the summer in the Marches, but others join them from the coast in winter, using trees adjacent to some meres for their roosts. Large numbers are sometimes seen, for example over 130 on Ellesmere in January 2004. Starlings *Sternus vulgaris* are well known for spectacular aerobatic performances seen when they come in to roost in winter. Reed-beds are occupied around some meres, with up to 150,000 recorded from Aqualate Mere in November 2006.

Although the meres already have a rich avifauna, let us consider how it could be enhanced in the future, either naturally or by reintroduction. Waders such as common sandpiper *Actitis hypoleucos* would be able to feed in draw-down zones if these were re-established. Bittern *Botaurus stellaris* might breed in reed-beds around the meres if they were extensive and secluded enough. One or two birds already over-winter at Aqualate Mere and some other sites in the Marches but currently they breed elsewhere, probably in the Netherlands. An area of 10 ha is regarded as the minimum for bittern to breed; none of the meres currently has this. Clear water would allow osprey *Pandion haliaetus* to feed and perhaps nest by undisturbed meres. Already ospreys visit Aqualate Mere, where they are seen to catch bream and other species of fish. New species might colonise the meres, especially if climate change continues. Bearded tit *Panurus biarmicus*, currently found only to the east, might be tempted to extend its range to the meres, provided there was suitable reedswamp for nesting and scrubby carr close by for feeding. Little egrets *Egretta garzetta* might nest around some meres. Black-winged stilts *Himantopus himantopus* nested at a pool near Northwich in Cheshire in 2008 and if we ensure that the conditions are right, they and other species may become part of the biodiversity of the meres in the future.

SWAMP AND CARR

In water shallower than about 1–2 m around the margins of a mere can be found a group of plant species that grow with roots in the sediments and leaves projecting above the water surface. These are known as emergent plants and the community is usually called swamp. Wave action, grazing by cattle, shading by trees and the activities of anglers prevent its development or cause its loss along shores of some meres. Many other meres have only a narrow band of swamp composed of common reed *Phragmites australis* or lesser bulrush *Typha angustifolia*, because the bed is steeply shelving. A small number of meres have extensive areas of shallow water, where wider swamps can develop. Fenemere has quite large areas, whilst Aqualate Mere has 8 ha of swamp, the largest of any mere. Where the bed of a mere shelves shallowly there can be clear zonation, according to the depth tolerances of the emergent plants (Fig. 100).

The classic description of a swamp adjacent to a mere was written about the western end of Crose Mere.[33] This recorded zonation of emergent plants over a 10-m distance started with common club-rush *Schoenoplectus lacustris* in the deepest water, followed by common reed, lesser bulrush, great fen-sedge *Cladium mariscus* and then greater tussock-sedge *Carex paniculata*. Saplings of alder were growing among greater tussock-sedge and in places there were areas of alder carr developing. Charles Sinker also described Sweat Mere, which lies to the east of Crose Mere. Here swamp has developed into mature alder carr. Sweat Mere is a famous site in the history of ecology, Tansley describing it as the classic example of a hydrosere – ecological succession through swamp to carr and finally drier woodland.[34] The implication of Tansley's account was that all shallow areas of the meres would gradually develop in this way. It is now clear that artificial lowering of water levels in both Crose Mere and Sweat Mere, mentioned earlier in this chapter, precipitated the changes that took place at Sweat Mere. Given that the meres were formed 10,000 or more years ago, open water can clearly persist for very long periods without ecological succession converting it into something else. Where carr has developed recently, we must always consider whether human activities were the cause. Drainage is one obvious factor; eutrophication is another. Hencott Pool, north of Shrewsbury, is currently occupied entirely by a dense and impenetrable carr of alder and willow carr, yet botanical records show that it was a mere in 1796, and remained so through much if not all of the

FIG 100. Circular zonation of plant communities in a kettle hole at Pant-yr-Ochain, near Wrecsam.

FIG 101. Hencott Pool, north of Shrewsbury, where conditions have changed from acidic oligotrophic open water with rare plants to eutrophic alder carr.

19th century (Fig. 101). Awlwort *Subularia aquatica* was found there, indicating that the water was acidic and oligotrophic. Hencott Pool is the only site where this plant has ever been found in the English lowlands. Floating water-plantain, requiring oligotrophic or mesotrophic conditions, was also present, as were some plants of peaty mires: hare's-tail cotton grass, white sedge *Carex curta* and lesser bladderwort *Utricularia minor*. These plants are all long gone and those currently present, including common duckweed *Lemna minor* covering the water surface, indicate that conditions are now eutrophic. A recent survey showed that many invertebrate species are present at Hencott, including some notable water beetles adapted to mesotrophic conditions, but no species associated with oligotrophic lakes.[35] Intensive agriculture in the area around Hencott Pool is the likely cause of eutrophication, the entry of nutrient-enriched groundwater leading to the transition from open water to carr. Agricultural drainage will have changed the hydrology of Hencott Pool, reducing the volumes of water entering the pool each year, particularly in winter, so there will no longer have been the periodically high water levels that kill trees and prevent succession to carr. Many of the meres now have areas of alder carr around them; wherever this has appeared or enlarged recently we may suspect eutrophication and changes to hydrology.

EUTROPHICATION OF THE MERES

The losses of species that have occurred at Hencott Pool and other former oligotrophic or mesotrophic meres can certainly be explained in terms of eutrophication. There is much recent data on nitrate and phosphorus concentrations, with measurements from the 1990s onwards for many meres. For a few meres there are measurements from the 1970s and for Rostherne

Mere and Hatchmere from the 1950s.[36] These records show an overall trend of rising concentrations of both nitrogen and phosphorus, but the evidence for eutrophication is not as unequivocal as one might expect. This may be because some meres are naturally eutrophic and others had already become so by the 1950s. There are suggestions that by the late 19th century surface blooms of algae were occurring in the meres during a greater part of the year, and with greater intensity than before.[37] It would be interesting to know whether this was due to eutrophication in the 19th century; unfortunately, we do not have measurements of nitrogen and phosphorus from that period. We must rely on indicator species to provide estimates of past nutrient concentrations.

Evidence for overall increase in fertility of the meres has been obtained using botanical records of aquatic plants.[38] Every plant species has indices assigned to it known as Ellenberg values, which indicate environmental tolerances to pH, light and other variables. The only Ellenberg value to have increased for aquatic plants on average in the meres over the past 200 years is that for mineral nutrient concentrations. All meres that had important groups of species adapted to oligotrophic conditions have lost them, apart from Bomere and the pools at Brown Moss. Many meres have gained groups of species that thrive when the water is eutrophic. However, these changes did not begin recently – they were already happening in the 19th century, so modern agriculture is not entirely to blame. In addition, they have not occurred to an equal extent in all meres.

Earlier in this chapter, distinctions were made between nitrogen and phosphorus concentrations in the meres. Attempts have been made to deduce past changes in these nutrients in the meres. The siliceous cell walls of diatoms can remain preserved in sediments for long periods of time and species can be recognised under the microscope using cell wall characteristics. As the phosphorus requirements of particular species are known, the phosphorus concentration in the water at the time of their growth can thus be estimated. Studies have been carried out at various meres, including Oxon Pool, Ellesmere and Kettle Pool.[39] These suggest that phosphorus concentrations have fluctuated in response to changes in the management of the catchment areas, but have generally been high over the last 100–150 years. Results from White Mere suggest an increase in phosphorus from about 25 µg per litre 1,200 years ago, to 100 µg today, the rate of increase accelerating over the last 100 years.[40] These estimates need to be treated with some caution, as current measured concentrations in White Mere are closer to 1,000 µg, but the trend that they indicate is almost certainly real.

Another study involved chironomid larvae, collectively known as non-biting midge larvae.[41] The levels of environmental variables were measured in water samples from 33 meres in the Marches and 11 lakes in Wales; chironomid larvae were also collected and identified. There was a strong correlation between the distribution of chironomid species and phosphorus concentration of the water. One particular mere was then chosen for further study. This was Betton Pool, to the south of Shrewsbury (Fig. 102). Surface blooms certainly happen here, but not every year. The owner, who farms the surrounding land, reports that the water can turn as green as paint over just a few days and then clear just as quickly. A 900 mm core of sediment was taken from the deepest part of the mere. The different levels in the core were deposited over the period extending back to 1830. Remains of the chironomid larval head capsules were collected from different levels in the sediment and then identified. The changes in the phosphorus concentration of Betton Pool were inferred from these remains. An increase is evident, particularly since 1950, and current levels are high. Possible contributory factors are: the ploughing of surrounding fields up to the water's edge, grazing by cattle with poaching of the banks of the mere, and the use of the mere as a roost since the late 1980s by a population of gulls. This ingenious study gives convincing evidence of a large increase in phosphate concentrations. However, it is nitrogen rather than phosphorus that appears to be the limiting factor at both Betton Pool and White Mere. Ironically, small rises in nitrogen concentration or nitrogen input might be harder to demonstrate but are much more significant to the ecology of the meres.

FIG 102. Betton Pool, south of Shrewsbury. In the foreground is a cereal crop, separated by a furrow from the 10 m-wide buffer strip of permanent grassland adjacent to the mere.

CONSERVATION OF THE MERES

Even without proof of increases in nitrogen concentration, it seems obvious that management aims for the meres should include the reduction in concentrations of nitrogen and phosphorus. According to the concept of limiting factors, reducing the level of the nutrient that is already in shorter supply is more likely to have an effect than reducing the level of the nutrient that is more abundant. This may seem counter-intuitive. Natural England has defined targets for phosphorus and nitrogen concentrations in 14 meres and has identified some strategies for achieving these. There is considerable variation in the needs of the various meres. One measure appropriate for meres that are surrounded by arable land is the establishment of a 10 m wide buffer strip of grassland that is either grazed or cut for hay. This has already been established at Betton Pool. The aims are to reduce diffuse pollution caused by ploughing and to intercept nutrients in groundwater before they reach the mere. It is not certain how effective these buffer strips will be, as groundwater may not enter uniformly around the edge of meres, but through deeper routes that circumvent the buffer zone. Whole-catchment management schemes may be necessary to make a real difference. Another measure is the establishment of wetlands adjacent to meres; this encourages bacteria that thrive in waterlogged soil to reduce nitrate concentrations by denitrification. Reduction in nitrate levels should be the key to the conservation of the deeper meres where there is bottom-up control of phytoplankton.

In shallow meres with top-down control, the key strategy is likely to be boosting zooplankton populations by re-establishing healthy populations of submerged plants. The abundant and diverse communities of submerged plants that existed in many shallow oligotrophic meres in the past have largely been lost. The disappearance of awlwort, quillwort and water lobelia, as well as the precarious state of floating water-plantain and least water-lily, can be attributed to eutrophication. The loss of animal species such as the otter and the peregrine falcon has led to government legislation and vigorous action by conservation agencies, with successful outcomes – the loss of plant species often seems to be accepted with a shrug. Given the importance of submerged plants in the control of phytoplankton in shallow meres, bold action is surely justified to re-establish the oligotrophic conditions that they require.

Aqualate Mere

An example of bold action to promote conservation is planned for Aqualate Mere. It is the largest of the meres, but now also one of the shallowest, with a depth throughout its 80 ha of about 1 m. The water depth was 2–3 m as recently

as the 1930s and before the middle of the 19th century, when large amounts of
silt started entering the mere, the depth was probably about 3–4 m. The problems
began with the opening of the Shropshire Union Canal, east of the mere. Silt-
laden water from the canal began to be discharged into the Wood Brook, one of
three streams that flow into the mere. This has happened for over 150 years and if
it were allowed to continue the mere would become totally in-filled.

Aqualate Mere has SSSI status, but its condition is currently classed as
unfavourable. The shallowness of the water in the mere reduces the diversity
of animal species. Dabbling ducks thrive, but diving ducks do not usually stay
for long. More seriously, the shallowness allows water movements caused by
wind to stir up the sediments and make the water turbid. Submerged plants
are unable to grow in these conditions and therefore the top-down control of
phytoplankton is unable to operate. Despite the obvious vulnerability to surface
blooms, in most years they have not occurred, possibly because of the turbidity of
the water. Fish mortality has been confined to small numbers of larger fish in hot
weather. However, there have been problems in the Meese, the outfall river from
Aqualate. It is not unusual for blooms to develop in this sluggish and silty river,
but that of July 2008 was the worst for at least 20 years. Cyanobacteria caused a
turquoise discoloration of the water that stretched for 8 km downstream of the
mere. Oxygen saturation, routinely monitored at Skew Bridge in the village of
Forton, is often 100 per cent, but during this algal bloom dropped below 10 per
cent. Dead fish seen in the water included large pike; it was the smell of their
decomposition that caused the first reports to the Environment Agency of this
pollution incident. Unusual weather conditions may have set off the bloom by
causing phosphate-rich sediments in the mere to be stirred up. The prime source
of phosphate in these lake sediments is the water flowing into Aqualate Mere, in
particular the treated effluent from Barnhurst Sewage Works in Wolverhampton.
Equipment has recently been installed to strip phosphates and nitrates from
the effluent, and the phosphate concentration of the treated effluent has
dropped from 8 mg per litre to less than 1 mg. This is a useful step, but it will
not be enough to restore the mere to favourable status, with clear water, healthy
populations of submerged plants and a diverse fauna.

Improvements to the quality of water entering the mere from the 50 km^2
of farmland in the catchment area are being made using the Higher Level
Stewardship Scheme. This involves 40-m buffer strips and other measures to
reduce leaching of nitrates into the mere. British Waterways Board is planning
work that will reduce or prevent silt passing from the Shropshire Union Canal
into the mere, but the problem of the 1–2 m depth of silt already there remains.
Surveys have shown that, without its removal, the mere will continue to have

unfavourable conservation status. Tim Coleshaw, Senior Reserve Manager since Aqualate became a National Nature Reserve in 1991, has developed a scheme for pumping out the silt and restoring the mere to a depth of 3–4 m. The estimated volume of material, which will be used to improve soils on four large areas of nearby farms, is 3–4 million m³. There will inevitably be a period during which the ecology of the mere is disrupted, but it should emerge from this in a far better state and start to achieve its full potential as an internationally important site. Let us hope that this ambitious and important conservation work is done as soon as possible.

Conflicts of interest

Two meres, Aqualate and Rostherne, are located in National Nature Reserves so their wildlife is of paramount importance. Other meres have multiple uses and conservation is rarely the main priority, even where there is SSSI status. Greater impetus for conservation should come from the Water Framework Directive, European Union legislation that dictates that all natural freshwater bodies must be in good ecological health by 2015. When English Nature surveyed 33 meres with SSSI status in 2006, only eight were judged to be in favourable condition. Widespread measures are therefore needed to improve the ecological health of the meres, even if they have multiple uses. Cole Mere, part of a country park, is an example of successful mixed use. An extremely rare plant survives there, the least water-lily, even though the mere is used by a sailing club and by anglers. There was over-fishing by a large angling club in the past, so a fishing ban was introduced. However, there were problems of enforcement as fishing only becomes illegal when a fish is actually taken from the water. A better policy has now been found: the fishing rights are leased to a small syndicate of anglers, who act as bailiffs and prevent illegal fishing.

Although anglers often release fish into the meres, stocking for conservation reasons has rarely been done, but there is abundant evidence from elsewhere that it can be effective. A ranking of fish species in terms of their desirability in SSSI sites has been devised.[42] The ranking for species commonly found in the meres, from least to most desirable, is common carp, bream, tench, roach, rudd, perch, pike and finally eel. The least desirable species are bottom feeders that make the water turbid by stirring up sediments, promote high densities of phytoplankton and contribute to the elimination of submerged water plants. The most desirable species do not cause water to become turbid. They allow submerged water plants to thrive and control the populations of zooplanktivores, thereby indirectly controlling the densities of phytoplankton. This is most significant in the shallower meres with top-down control. In the past eels would have been able to recolonise, but numbers of elvers are so reduced that artificial introductions might now be justified. Pike should ideally be reintroduced if they are no longer present. Bream, tench and roach should not be reintroduced, though it would be hard to justify deliberate control measures, as they may be native to the meres. The most useful conservation measure in meres would be the removal of carp and the prevention of their reintroduction. The Environment Agency has acknowledged that carp are an introduced and destructive species and it seems inconceivable that meres with SSSI status can be restored to the good ecological status required by the Directive without carp removal. Experiments are needed to establish whether meres can be managed both as carp fisheries and for nature conservation. However, the hold that carp fishing has on the angling community is very strong, and there will be determined and effective resistance to measures that threaten this sport.

Perhaps we should abandon some meres to carp fishing and accept that they will have little interest, as long as enough other meres are managed for their wildlife. Only Aqualate and Rostherne are currently National Nature Reserves and, in various respects, they are not typical. There is a clear need for one or more National Nature Reserve to conserve and restore meres that are not fed or drained by streams. There should be enough surrounding land in each reserve to ensure that the entire catchment of their meres can be taken out of intensive agriculture. Both deep and shallow meres should ideally be represented. Bomere, with its fascinating and varied group of surrounding kettle holes, would be ideal for this initiative. Another obvious target for integrated conservation action is the Crose Mere–Sweat Mere–Whattall Moss complex (Fig. 103).

FIG 103. Crose Mere with fringing reedswamps. (Chris Walker)

CHAPTER 7

Mosses

IN NORTHERN PARTS OF THE MARCHES there are more than 200 sites with the word *Moss* in the name, for example Lin Can Moss, Shemmy Moss and Lindow Moss. The original meaning of this word in Old English is bog, but it also came to be used for the plants that were characteristic of bogs. Ecologists now refer to these sites as mires and botanists use the word moss for one group of bryophytes. In this chapter the word will be reclaimed and used for sites that are mosses in the original sense (Fig. 104).

The mosses are scattered across the North Shropshire–Cheshire Plain. They are not evenly spread but instead are clustered in certain areas, as the distribution map shows. They vary in size from as small as 10 m in diameter at Brown Moss, to 950 ha for the whole Fenn's complex of mosses. Many are secluded and scarcely visited. Impeded drainage and accumulation of acid peat make the mosses unpromising for agriculture, which explains their survival in a region that has been farmed for thousands of years. Large numbers have succumbed to drainage schemes and conversion to agriculture, forestry, or peat cutting, but enough mosses remain to form a significant feature of the natural history of this part of the Marches. Seventeen have SSSI status. Wybunbury Moss and the complex consisting of Fenn's, Whixall and Bettisfield mosses are National Nature Reserves, as is Chartley Moss to the east in Staffordshire. Ten mosses form part of the Midlands Meres and Mosses Ramsar site. Two groups of mosses are SACs, the Fenn's Complex for its lowland raised mire and Clarepool, Wybunbury, Chartley and Abbot's mosses for quaking bog and transition mire. In the same region as the mosses there are other types of peatland, for example those areas named moors. These were moors in the sense that they were unenclosed and uncultivated, because the soil is peaty and the drainage poor. The fact that they were distinguished in name from mosses is significant and their origins and natural history are different. The scope of this chapter will be extended slightly, to cover all the lowland sites where peat formation has occurred, including both mosses and moors and a small number of other types of mire. Leaching of nutrients from surrounding farmland and sewerage from housing has affected some mosses whilst airborne deposition of nitrogen is a more general problem. These and other conservation challenges for the mosses will be considered later in the chapter.

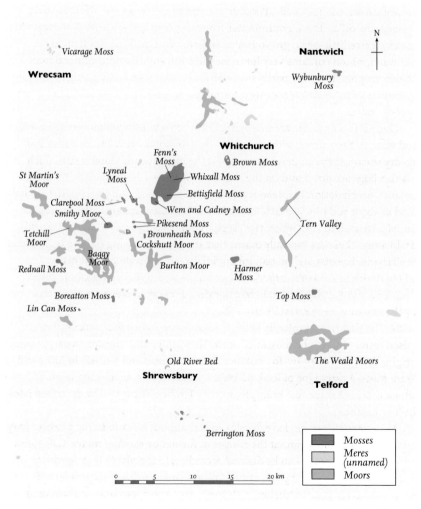

FIG 104. Map of the main peatlands of the Marches, with mosses and moors distinguished.

PEATLANDS

A defining feature of mires is the accumulation of semi-decomposed plant material or peat. All the sites described in this chapter have this accumulation of peat and it has many consequences for their natural history. Relative rates of production and decomposition of peat determine how much accumulates. A depth of at least 500 mm is the minimum for a site to be regarded as a mire. Decomposition is restricted in all mires by the low oxygen concentrations present in waterlogged soils. Possible sources of the water are direct rainfall, surface run-off and true groundwater from seepages and springs. Ombrotrophic mires receive little or no groundwater and are principally dependent on rainwater, which contains very low concentrations of dissolved mineral ions. Minerotrophic mires are partly supplied by groundwater, containing significant quantities of minerals. Markedly different communities are found in these two types of mire.

Ombrotrophic mires are most commonly found in the uplands of the north and west. In these areas, with annual precipitation greater than 1,200 mm and no dry season, they can develop on all but the most steeply sloping sites. Such blanket bogs are not found on the North Shropshire–Cheshire Plain. As in the uplands precipitation is spread relatively evenly through the year, but the annual total at about 700 mm is much lower. Ombrotrophic mire formation can occur, but is restricted to sites where the precipitation, mainly rainfall, cannot quickly drain away. These are typically basins that are either low lying or have impervious underlying deposits and no natural outfall for surface water, or flat plains where drainage has been impeded by glacial deposits. In ombrotrophic mires decomposition is also inhibited by low mineral nutrient concentrations and by the low soil pH that results from the presence of carbonic acid and organic acids. The peat may eventually form a raised dome, hence the name lowland raised mire. Most of the mosses of north Shropshire and Cheshire were probably originally in this category, for instance Fenn's, Whixall and Bettisfield Moss and Wem Moss. A rarer type of lowland mire is quaking bog or schwingmoor, of which there are some fine examples in the Marches. These will be described later in the chapter.

Minerotrophic mires have developed throughout Britain. In the Marches they are mostly found in basins at the fringes of former or existing meres. Categories of minerotrophic mire can be defined according to the plants that dominate. Swamps are dominated by one or two tall-growing species of narrow-leaved herb such as reeds or bulrushes, with their roots and sometimes parts of their shoots in water. They remain inundated all year round. Areas with a wider range of herbs, where peat has accumulated sufficiently to reach the water surface and where the water level drops below the peat surface in dry periods, are called fens or fen meadows. They are described briefly in the next section of this chapter. Areas where trees dominate and the soil is waterlogged and peaty are known as carr. In the remainder of this chapter the natural history of the fens, lowland raised mires and schwingmoors will be described, including some of the finest examples of each.

FENS

The development of swamp communities at the margins of meres was described in the previous chapter. When the level of organic matter accumulates sufficiently for it to reach the water surface, plants other than swamp species are able to colonise, allowing a more diverse fen community to develop. This can be seen at Hatchmere, Norbury Meres and Quoisley Meres in Cheshire, at Ellesmere, Colemere, Crosemere and Oss Mere in Shropshire. Species of monocotyledon are usually dominant: greater tussock-sedge, great fen-sedge, lesser pond-sedge *Carex acutiformis*, sharp-flowered rush *Juncus acutiflorus* or blunt-flowered rush *Juncus subnodulosus*. Many other species are seen, including ragged-robin *Lychnis flos-cuculi*, meadowsweet *Filipendula ulmaria*, wild angelica *Angelica sylvestris*, fen and common marsh-bedstraws *Galium uliginosum* and *G. palustre*, marsh pennywort *Hydrocotyle vulgaris*, common and marsh valerians *Valeriana officinalis* and *V. dioica*, marsh willowherb *Epilobium palustre*, bittersweet *Solanum dulcamara*, skullcap *Scutellaria galericulata*, hemp-agrimony *Eupatorim cannabinum* and marsh helleborine *Epipactis palustris*. Both common spotted-orchid *Dactylorhiza fuchsii* and southern marsh-orchids *Dactylorhiza praetermissa* occur at some sites, together with interspecific hybrids showing a combination of characteristics and in some cases impressive size due to hybrid vigour. Meadow thistle *Cirsium dissectum*, on the northwest edge of its range, and marsh fern *Thelypteris palustris* are sometimes also found. Mereside fen communities like this are less common than they used to be. More commonly, there is now carr directly abutting the open water of a mere. This is because fen communities only develop and persist where summer grazing or haymaking is practised. In some cases the fields surrounding meres have been converted to arable farming, with consequent loss of all former fen. At other sites, for example Norbury and Quoisley Meres, carr is found on the margins of meres, with fencing separating it from adjacent grazed areas of fen in the adjoining fields.

Some of the largest peatlands in the northern Marches are on river flood plains, where there has been periodic bursting of the river's banks and deposition of sediments to form level areas with impeded drainage. It has been suggested that larger river flood plains, as at Baggy Moor and Weald Moors, may have been fen before their drainage and conversion to agriculture. Pollen analysis of the peats from Baggy Moor has shown that alders and willows were present with some reeds and sedges. The natural state of these extensive flood plains was therefore presumably at least partly swampy woodland or carr rather than fen. Clearance of the carr took place in the post-Roman period but the waterlogged conditions and deposits of peat discouraged much agriculture and these sites remained unenclosed until relatively recently. Since then drainage and cultivation have led to rapid loss of peat and the retreat of the natural communities to ditches and other small areas (Fig. 105). It is impossible to know precisely what species had previously been present, but there will have been minerotrophic mire communities, sufficiently distinct for local people to call most of these sites moors rather than mosses.

The largest existing example of fen on flood plain is the Old River Bed, a former meander of the Severn that runs for 3 km through north Shrewsbury. It was cut off about 5,000 years ago.[1] The Old River Bed was almost certainly carr when Leighton published his *Flora of Shropshire* in 1841, but this was cleared during the First World War, in a failed attempt to convert the land to intensive agriculture.

FIG 105. Exposed tree roots due to loss of peat at Pen-yr-estyn on Baggy Moor. (Iain Diack)

Only a small stream now flows though the middle of the site, but it frequently floods and peat formation has been extensive. Sedges dominate most of the area. Moving from wettest to driest parts, the sequence of species is: bottle sedge *Carex rostrata*, lesser pond-sedge, brown sedge, tufted-sedge *Carex elata*, then common sedge *Carex nigra* and in surrounding grassland, hairy sedge *Carex hirta*. A rich diversity of other plants grows among the sedges, including many of those found in the mere-side fens described above. The community now present there would almost certainly revert to carr if it were not grazed or cut for hay at least biennially.

Much scarcer as locations for fen development in the Marches are areas where the substrata are alkaline. There are a few areas where plant communities suggest the presence of calcareous glacial deposits through which groundwater percolates to emerge at springs or seepages. One example is the species-rich fringing fen at Fenemere. Nearby is the Yesters, where there are remnants of a type of fen dominated by great fen-sedge and purple moor-grass that does not occur elsewhere in the Marches. There is also fen-meadow where blunt-flowered rush prevails at this site. The fen communities at the Yesters are lowland in character, but there are also a small number that are more characteristic of the uplands. Trefonen Marshes to the west of Oswestry has a particularly fine spring-fed alkaline fen with a full complement of brown mosses, butterwort *Pinguicula vulgaris*, dioecious sedge *Carex dioica*, tawny sedge *Carex hostiana*, few-flowered spike-rush *Eleocharis quinquefolia* and broad-leaved cottongrass *Eriophorum latifolium*. There is also some formation of tufa.

Sweeney Fen to the southwest of Oswestry is an important site. The underlying rock is carboniferous limestone, but a deposit of boulder clay retains the base-rich run-off from the hills, creating conditions wet enough for fen species to thrive and peat to develop. The peat has a depth over 800 mm in places and a slightly alkaline pH. From a distance the vegetation looks rank and neglected but closer inspection shows how diverse and special it is. Blunt-flowered rush, meadowsweet, bogbean *Menyanthes trifoliata* and marsh valerian are prevalent in some areas, but many other species are also present, notably globeflower *Trollius europaeus* at the edge of its northwestern upland range, marsh helleborines in abundance, many fragrant orchids *Gymnadenia densiflora* with their sweet smell of cloves and huge numbers of common spotted-orchids (Fig. 106). As elsewhere, this community is dependent on carefully controlled levels of grazing, which prevents invasion by trees while minimising poaching of waterlogged ground caused by excessive trampling. There are some sites in Cheshire on Mercian Mudstones with a similar fen community and peat development, for instance at Hatherton in the upper Weaver valley. However, fens are scarce in the Marches, have only occupied small areas and tend to be transient communities.

FIG 106. Conservation work over many years has resulted in fine displays of orchids at Sweeney Fen, including fragrant orchid (left) and marsh helleborine (above). (Ben Osborne)

In contrast to fens, ombrotrophic mires are far more prevalent and so deserve a much more detailed account. Many classifications of mire types have been published but here the term lowland raised mire will be used for the typical mosses of north Shropshire and Cheshire.

THE DEVELOPMENT OF LOWLAND RAISED MIRES

Only about 5 per cent of Britain's peatlands are raised mires. To find the reasons why this uncommon type of mire has developed on many sites in the Marches we must look at the climate, topography and drainage, together with the solid and drift geology. The monthly mean air temperature on the North Shropshire–Cheshire Plain varies from about 3 °C in January to 16 °C in July. These means are lower in winter than areas to the west and lower in summer than areas to the south and east. Annual rainfall in the Marches is typically 650–700 mm, which is marginal for lowland raised mire formation. Evapotranspiration is unlikely ever to exceed rainfall during the colder half of the year from November to April. From May to October, there will often be a shortfall in rainfall, but over the year as a whole, it usually exceeds evapotranspiration and, where the water does not rapidly drain away, enough is available for lowland raised mire to develop. Mean soil temperatures are close to the mean air temperatures and low enough to tilt the balance away from peat decomposition and towards accumulation.

The North Shropshire–Cheshire Plain, where the mosses are located, is gently undulating and low lying with large areas less than 100 m above sea level (Fig. 107). Restricted surface drainage has led to the development of mosses in three types of site. The first is in moraine-dammed hollows, for instance in the Shrewsbury area, where linear basins lie between NW–SE oriented morainic ridges. Fenn's, Whixall, Bettisfield, Wem and Cadney Mosses lie in a shallow valley between a moraine of clay to the southwest and to the northwest a ridge of sand

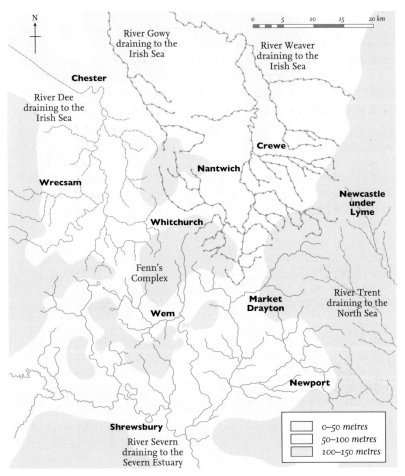

FIG 107. Since the last glaciation, rainwater falling less than 50 km from the Mersey estuary on parts of the North Shropshire–Cheshire Plain has flowed instead to the North Sea or the Severn Estuary.

deposited at a later date as the ice sheet retreated. Kettle holes are the second type. Vicarage Moss (Fig. 108), northwest of Wrecsam and with SSSI status is an example, but many others exist. Post-glacial subsidence hollows are the third and scarcest type of site. They form where the underlying rock contains layers of salt. If the salt in these rocks dissolves and is washed away, voids can be created underground into which overlying material above can collapse, creating crater-shaped basins. Elongated or linear basins can also be formed, by subsidence along the line of an outcrop of saliferous rock. Bagmere and Brookhouse Moss are good examples of mosses in crater and linear subsidence basins respectively and Wybunbury Moss has also probably been a site of subsidence.

It might be expected that most mosses would only develop in areas of poorly drained glacial till, but instead more are located on sands and gravels. The factors affecting are the same as for meres and there is evidence that all the sites now occupied by mosses were once meres. The processes by which they developed into mosses can be studied by taking vertical cores and by recording the sequence of deposits. Laminated clays, usually found at the base of the sequence, will have washed into the basin during the period after the last glaciation when there was sparse vegetation and major reworking of glacial deposits. The clay will have sealed the basin, allowing water to accumulate and a mere to be formed. Above the clay, there are dark sediments known as

FIG 108. Vicarage Moss, near Wrecsam, with cottongrass fruiting and woodland on a moraine to the north and west.

gyttja. These contain large amounts of organic matter, especially the remains of diatoms, and are typical of nutrient-rich lakes. Overlying the gyttja in a typical core there are peaty deposits formed from sedges or other monocots, often with fragments of wood from trees that are tolerant of waterlogging such as alders. These organic deposits are derived from minerotrophic swamps or carr. They will have continued to accumulate as long as the surface of the swamp or carr was at or below the water table of the basin and water could still penetrate either as groundwater or from streams. Sweat Mere, Hencott Pool and Shrawardine Pool all have areas of carr with peaty deposits and partially decomposed fallen wood starting to accumulate. In each of these cases, environmental changes caused by human activity instigated the succession from open water to carr. In sites that are now mosses, this succession took place thousands of years ago and was almost certainly natural. The upper parts of typical cores from mosses are deposits that are formed in raised mires, especially *Sphagnum* peat. The change from minerotrophic swamp or carr to ombrotrophic mire occurs when accumulation of peaty deposits raises the surface high enough to prevent the entry of groundwater or stream water, and allows the downward drainage of rainwater to leach out nutrients. This is not a sudden switch – it will tend to occur gradually, probably over decades, starting at the centre of a basin and working outwards. Where there is still some penetration of groundwater containing nutrients, and grazing or cutting for hay, transition mire can develop, with a community that is intermediate between species-rich and poor fen.

If transition mire is a temporary stage between minerotrophic and ombrotrophic mires, all natural examples should be long gone in the Marches. There are in fact important examples of this fen type here, including Berrington Moss and areas around Berrington Pool, to the south of Shrewsbury, characterised by bottle sedge, bladder-sedge *Carex vesicaria*, bogbean, marsh cinquefoil *Potentilla palustris*, slender sedge *Carex lasiocarpa*, some of the more base-tolerant species of *Sphagnum* and mosses such as *Calliergon cordifolium*. Where transition mires have developed recently we must assume that anthropogenic environmental change has reset the clock in terms of succession. Many basins with no natural inflows or outflows had culverted outflows built in the 19th century as part of drainage schemes. Some of these culverts have ceased to drain basins effectively and a process of re-flooding has occurred.

In the Bomere complex, whose importance was mentioned in the last chapter, there is a kettle hole to the south of Shomere Pool where there appears to have been a significant rise in water level, several mature oaks now dead in standing water. An artificial means of draining the kettlehole presumably became blocked. There are stands of bulrush *Typha latifolia* and soft-rush along some of the margins of the open water and also areas dominated by *Sphagnum fallax*, waterlogged but not underwater, featuring heather, cross-leaved heath *Erica tetralix*, hare's-tail cottongrass and white sedge. Between the open water and *Sphagnum*-dominated areas there is a transition mire community of bottle sedge, marsh cinquefoil, bog pondweed *Potamogeton polygonifolius* and the bryophytes *S. fallax*, *S. squarrosum*, *Straminergon stramineum* and *Calliergon cordifolium*. This site is particularly interesting because there is an apparent expansion into the open water of floating rafts comprising *S. fallax* and associated species of ombrotrophic mires. This raises the prospect that a raised mire or quaking bog might eventually replace all of the open water, without an intervening stage of minerotrophic swamp or carr.

Flooding of small basins and establishment of transition mires, with increasing prevalence of *S. fallax* leading to ombrotrophic conditions, may also have occurred at Lin Can Moss and some of the Delamere Forest mires and pools. Rafts of *S. fallax* floating on minerotrophic water are found at some other sites, including Berrington Moss and Boreatton Moss.

The evidence that ombrotrophic mosses can develop from minerotrophic communities raises a tantalising possibility: we might induce swamp, carr, fen and even open water to change into ombrotrophic mosses if we blocked artificial drains built in the 19th and 20th centuries and then left them for long enough – probably hundreds of years. The Crose Mere–Sweat Mere–Whattall Moss complex is an obvious target for this ecological experiment, but there are others where it would be fascinating to see the response to a return to natural water levels. In particular, more could be learned about the factors that determine why some basins still retain the open water of a mere whilst others develop into minerotrophic and then ombrotrophic mires.

PEAT FORMATION AND PEAT CUTTING ON THE MOSSES

Once the change to ombrotrophic conditions is complete and groundwater no longer seeps into mires, the rate of peat formation tends to increase. As the peat continues to build up, the surface gradually rises, hence the term lowland raised mire for the mosses. Accumulations of peat on lowland raised mires can be considerable and some of the north Shropshire–Cheshire mosses have depths as great as any in the world. Uncut parts of Bettisfield Moss have over 8 m of peat and one of the domes of Wem Moss is 10 m deep. Even greater depths have been recorded: in 1878 the depth in the centre of Danes' Moss was found to be 40 feet, or 12.2 m. These are greater depths than are found in the blanket mires of the uplands where 8 m is the usual maximum and that only occurs where there are depressions in the substrate.

The upper layer of raised mires, about half a metre in depth, tends to be porous, with water able to drain through rapidly. It is called the acrotelm and consists of the layer of growing *Sphagnum* and other mire plants, together with dead plants immediately below and the upper uncompacted layers of peat. Decomposition of plant matter can occur in the acrotelm but is severely inhibited as prolonged waterlogging ensures that the concentration of oxygen remains low. Phenolic compounds contained in plant tissues inhibit the enzymes that carry out decomposition. Another enzyme, phenol oxidase, can eliminate these phenolic compounds, but requires oxygen to be able to do so. Undecomposed material at the base of the acrotelm becomes compacted and less porous, making water movement through it much slower, and it then becomes part of the underlying catotelm. Decomposition slows to a negligible rate in the catotelm, preserving the peat indefinitely. Analysis of the pollen preserved in the catotelm can be used to trace the post-glacial vegetational history of the Welsh Marches. The central area of lowland raised mires is usually wettest, because of slow lateral movement of water. The greatest accumulation is therefore expected here, making the mire surface convex or dome shaped, with slopes at the edges known as rands. This is not clearly seen on most of the north Shropshire–Cheshire mosses, which are relatively flat surfaced. This could be because human activity has caused the loss or collapse of the domes or there may have been differences in mire development from the typical pattern. The rate of accumulation in mires varies, but if we assume that the 8 m depth of peat at Bettisfield Moss was formed in less than 10,000 years, the mean rate would be 0.67 mm per year.

When the successive layers of peat in the mosses are examined, variation can be seen, not only in the rate of peat formation, but also in its colour and composition (*see* Table 2). W. P. M. Hamilton gave an early account of this in a paper to the Caradoc and Severn Valley Field Club after a visit to Whixall Moss in May 1900:[2]

'*At one foot nine inches below the surface the substance, light in colour, consisted entirely of the aforementioned species (Sphagnum imbricatum) in a sufficiently good state of preservation to admit of a microscopical examination of the leaves in section. At two foot three inches down the stratum was of a much deeper colour but consisted of the same species more closely compacted. In another cutting where the black peat was being cut into bricks to be dried for fuel, I took a specimen at a depth of five feet. The man at work there informed me that stumps of trees were often found in this lower black mass. There are two points to be noticed with regard to the peat of Whixall Moss, although probably not peculiar to it. The first is that the stratum of light-coloured or red peat does not merge gradually into that of the black below it, but is divided by a distinct line of demarcation. The other point to call for remark is that the species of which the red peat consists, viz, Sphagnum imbricatum, is now extinct in the locality and is a rare occurrence in the British Isles.'*

Differences in the composition of peat have been interpreted in terms of climatic shifts and changes in groundwater penetration. These can alter the types of plant that contribute the organic matter and the extent of its decomposition. Decomposition in the acrotelm can occur when the water table falls below the surface for part of the year, as happens when the climate is drier. Penetration of groundwater carrying nutrients can also increase decomposition rates. Peat made up of more decomposed or humified plant matter is a blackish colour. In contrast, the peat from wetter periods with wholly ombrotrophic conditions is much less humified and is a lighter colour – peat cutters called it white peat, though Hamilton describes it as red. In the mosses of the Marches it is typically rich in the remains of *Sphagnum imbricatum*, a tussock-forming species, but some layers can be found that are dominated by bog pool species – *Sphagnum cuspidatum* and *Scheuchzeria palustris* (Rannoch rush). The latter is another plant now extinct in the Marches, though it was recorded in the 19th

TABLE 2. Peat cutters' and ecologists' names for layers of peat.

PEAT CUTTERS'	ECOLOGISTS'	CAUSE OF DEPOSITION	START OF PERIOD OF DEPOSITION
White peat	Poorly humified ombrotrophic peat	Deposition of organic matter from Sphagnum, with limited decomposition in a relatively cold and wet climate	2,500 BP (years before present)
Grey peat	Well humified ombrotrophic peat	Deposition of organic matter from sedges and other monocots, with partial decomposition in a relatively warm and dry climate	7,000–5,000 BP
Black peat	Fen peat	Deposition of organic matter in swamp or carr	8,000–10,000 BP
Black coal	Gyttja	Lake clay with diatomaceous sediments	10,500 BP

century from both Clarepool and Wybunbury Mosses. Since Hamilton's time, the sequence of layers of peat has been investigated repeatedly (Fig. 109).

Hamilton's sharp line of demarcation was between the poorly and well humified peat – the grey and the white. It seems unlikely that there was a sudden climatic shift and yet there appears to have been a rapid transition in plant communities and the type of peat being formed. This rapidity may have been partly caused by the properties of *Sphagnum*: it grows rapidly to fill surface hollows and channels thus reducing surface runoff by blocking rapid flow pathways; its surfaces whiten during dry periods causing reflection of sunlight and reducing temperatures and evaporation; its hyaline cells make it highly effective at retaining moisture, even after death. Just 1 g of *Sphagnum* can retain up to 20 g of water. *Sphagnum* also secretes hydrogen ions as it absorbs mineral nutrients. So, when the shift to a wetter climate occurred 2,500 years ago and it became established on the mosses, the waterlogging and the acidity of the acrotelm will have been increased by *Sphagnum* itself, favouring its further spread – an ecological version of positive feedback.

FIG 109. Exposed peat at a hand cutting on Whixall Moss. Black peat is at the base, with grey and white peat above. Cut blocks of peat are stacked on the surface. (Joan Daniels)

Each individual moss will have its own particular variant of this basic sequence of layers. For example, on parts of Fenn's and Whixall Mosses there is a layer of pine stumps in the grey peat, indicating that trees were able to establish and grow on the moss for a time, presumably because of a lowering of the water table (Fig. 110). Overlying the stump layer is peat known locally as nog. It contains large pieces of partially decomposed cottongrass, indicative of very wet conditions, which probably accounts for the death of the pines.

The volumes of peat that developed in the mosses of the Marches were prodigious. If we estimate conservatively a mean depth of 3 m over the whole of the Fenn's, Whixall, Bettisfield, Wem and Cadney Mosses, the total volume would be 30 million m³. These peat deposits have proved very attractive to the local population and the history of peat winning is a long and fascinating one. It can only be mentioned briefly here. No moss seems to have been completely unexploited but the extent of peat cutting varies considerably from minimal amounts, leaving scattered pits on Wem Moss for example, to complete removal of peat, as in some of the smaller Cheshire mosses. Many uses have been found for the peat. The upper layers of white peat proved useful as horse and poultry litter and also for production of a molasses-based cattle feed. Black peat has most commonly been used as a fuel as it dries to a dense coal-like material, but it has also been distilled to produce paraffinoids and other chemicals. It has been used

FIG 110. Peat cutting on Whixall Moss with exposed pine stumps. This indicates a period of drier conditions and a time when *Pinus sylvestris* was native to the area. (Joan Daniels)

for building internal and, even more remarkably, external walls of houses. In the 1950s, these varied uses were almost entirely superseded by horticultural ones, with the upper white peat being the most desirable. Each of the mosses had its characteristic tradition of peat cutting. On Whixall Moss for example, the 9 × 7 × 4 inch peat blocks were known as Whixall bibles, as they had the size and shape of a family bible. The usual practice was to remove surface vegetation and then cut the blocks with a short handled spade from a pit that was about 10 foot wide by 20 foot long, going as deep as the summer water table allowed. The 'bibles' were then wheelbarrowed to a drying area where they were stacked on edge. If dry enough before winter, the stacks were dismantled and carted off the Moss (Fig. 111).

A limited amount of peat cutting by this method may actually have enhanced the biodiversity of the mosses. Abandoned pits became water-filled and were soon colonised by plants and animals adapted to permanent inundation. However, methods started to change in the 1920s on some of the larger mosses, with the arrival of peat cutters from Holland. These mosses were divided up into a regular pattern of trackways, drains and peat cutting areas. The drainage allowed much deeper cutting and when demand for horticultural peat increased from the 1960s onwards, machines were introduced to speed up the peat cutting process. Only on the larger mosses was commercial exploitation using machinery viable: Risley Moss, Lindow Moss and Danes Moss in Cheshire and Fenn's Moss in Flintshire. Each of the three Cheshire mosses has mostly been lost and Fenn's Moss nearly suffered the same fate. Its reprieve and restoration is described later in this chapter.

FIG 111. Abbie Austin hand cutting on Fenn's Moss. The Austin family continue to cut small amounts of peat. (Joan Daniels)

PLANT COMMUNITIES OF THE MOSSES

The differing conditions and management history of the mosses mean that there is considerable variation in their plant communities. Nonetheless, several core groups of plants can be identified that form recurring themes. Species of *Sphagnum* are of course critically important both for their capacity to retain water and for their contribution of organic matter to peat formation, but a select group of flowering plants able to thrive in wet, nutrient-poor, acidic conditions is also present. The precise composition of the plant community at any particular location can be related most closely to the degree of waterlogging (Fig. 112).

At the wettest extreme are the pools that remain filled throughout the year with dystrophic acidic, peat-stained water. Pools are less common than on mires further north and west in Britain and many that exist are of artificial origin, usually peat cuttings. Small shallow pools often contain submerged plants of *Sphagnum cuspidatum*, a green or slightly brownish bog-moss, whose appearance in the water is often likened to that of a dead kitten. Where this species grows vigorously, it can eventually fill pools with a dense mass of shoots. Lesser bladderwort is also occasionally found submerged in the water. This is a fascinating plant that is usually regarded as being carnivorous. There are obvious advantages in catching prey rich in proteins and thus nitrogen in the nutrient-poor environment of the mosses. Lesser bladderwort has slender stems bearing small bags or vesicles that are probably modified leaves. The vesicles or bladders are about 2 mm in diameter and have a hinged door, usually closed, with sensitive hairs to trigger opening. Water is removed from the bladders, creating suction. When an aquatic invertebrate touches the hairs, the door opens and sucks the

FIG 112. Bog pool on Whixall Moss, with the brown leaves of common cottongrass adjacent to the pool and *Sphagnum cusidatum* in the water. (Joan Daniels)

invertebrate into the bladder. The expectation is that the invertebrate dies and is digested, but living algae and zooplankton have been observed inside bladders, raising the possibility of a mutualistic rather than carnivorous relationship. Leighton describes a second function of the bladders in his 1841 *Flora of Shropshire:*[3]

> *'When it becomes necessary for the plant to rise to the surface of the water for the expansion of its blossoms, the vesicles on the leaves, which before contained water, are by some unknown means now filled with air, which after fecundation, again gives place to water and the plant descends to ripen its seeds at the bottom.'*

Extensive areas of *Sphagnum fallax* (*S. recurvum*) are sometimes present at the edges of pools and in other permanently wet localities. These areas tend to have a flat surface, with few other species present and so are sometimes called *Sphagnum fallax* lawns. The first emergent species in pools on the mosses is usually common cottongrass, spreading by means of creeping rhizomes through the peat underlying the pool. Its leaves stand 200 mm or more above the water surface. Air spaces in its roots allow oxygen to diffuse down to cells absorbing nutrients from the water, but even so, the cottongrass growing in the pools typically show signs of nutrient deficiency: the triangular leaf-tips often make up much of the leaf with only short lengths of wider channelled blade below. A more hummocky type of *Sphagnum* lawn is found on other areas that are still wet but which may periodically dry out. Both *S. papillosum* and *S. tenellum* are found is such areas. Another bog-moss, *S. magellanicum*, is sometimes also present, usually with a dull crimson colour (Fig. 113). This type of *Sphagnum* lawn typically has more flowering plants than a *Sphagnum fallax* lawn. The most characteristic are cranberry *Vaccinium oxycoccos*, round-leaved sundew and hare's-tail cottongrass. The stems of cranberry scramble over the surface of the bog-moss and have to be renewed annually as they are buried by the growth of *Sphagnum* shoots. The small, widely spaced leaves have a thick layer of cuticular wax. Paradoxically these are adaptations typical of drought-tolerant desert plants. The root system of cranberry plants avoids the anaerobic conditions below the surface by remaining shallow, with many narrow hair roots. The plants would succumb to desiccation without a low rate of transpiration during dry periods. The pink flowers in June or July are followed by disproportionately large berries, which are eaten by a variety of birds and have also in the past been harvested by the human population. This plant is close to the southeastern edge of its main range in Britain. Round-leaved sundew is another plant that supplements its nitrogen intake by insectivory. Hare's-tail cottongrass can be distinguished from common cottongrass *Eriophorum angustifolium* by its needle-

FIG 113. Bog mosses from Fenn's and Whixall Mosses:
a. *Sphagnum cuspidatum* (Joan Daniels); b. *Sphagnum fallax* (Jonathan Sleath);
c. *Sphagnum magellanicum* and *Sphagnum papillosum* (Colin Heyes); d. *Sphagnum capillifolium*
ssp. *rubellum* (Colin Heyes); e. *Sphagnum pulchrum* (Ian Atherton); f. *Dicranum bergeri*
(Jonathan Sleath).

like narrow leaves, by its having only one cottony head per flower stalk instead of a cluster of several and also its tendency to form tussocks rather than spread by means of rhizomes. It also tends to remain green in winter whereas common cottongrass turns wine-red in October. Indeed, without any showy displays of flowers the plants of these wet areas can be surprisingly colourful: bog-mosses range from bright green, to yellow, red, orange and brown, sundews are a vivid red colour and cottongrasses provide splashes of white from summer through to winter. White beak sedge *Rhynchospora alba*, occasionally present in open parts of the wetter areas, has narrow yellowish-green leaves and bright white V-shaped inflorescences.

The plant community changes again as we move to higher and drier areas, with pinkish coloured *Sphagnum capillifolium* ssp. *rubellum* forming hummocks. There is again a select group of flowering plants, from a very select number of families, which also thrive in these conditions, with bog rosemary *Andromeda polifolia* and cross-leaved heath very typical. Both of these species, like cranberry, are members of the Ericaceae – the heather family. For reasons explained above, members of this family have adaptations that might be expected in dry rather than waterlogged conditions. They also have ericoid mycorrhizal infections of the roots, helping them to absorb nitrogen and phosphate from the mineral-deficient peat. Bog rosemary has stems that straggle through the bog-mosses with small alternate greyish leaves and pink bell-shaped flowers. It is here close to the southern extremity of its range (Fig. 114). Cross-leaved heath also has greyish leaves and rose-pink bell-shaped flowers, but the leaves are narrower and are arranged in whorls of four. Bog asphodel shares a preference for damp rather than waterlogged conditions and is abundant in some parts of the mosses. It has

FIG 114. Cranberry (above) and bog rosemary in bud (right). (Ben Osborne)

bright yellow star-shaped flowers in July followed by persistent tawny coloured fruits. The highest areas are too dry for bog-mosses though other bryophytes and lichens are often present. The most characteristic flowering plants are purple moor-grass and ling, another member of the Ericaceae, as well as crowberry, a close relative. Seedlings of birch and Scots pine are also frequently seen on some mosses where there are seed sources.

The relatively small numbers of plant species on the mosses and their distinctive appearances make it easy to identify the various communities. Where human intervention has been least there can be large areas of a single community, but more commonly there is a complex mosaic of communities, revealing how each part of a moss has been managed. Plants are ideal for use as indicator species, but the animal communities of the mosses are also distinctive and deserve careful consideration.

FOOD CHAINS AND THE FAUNA OF THE MOSSES

In contrast to surrounding agricultural land, the mosses support a wide diversity of animal species, including some that have become very scarce elsewhere. Many species visit them for use as temporary feeding grounds, but for others the mosses are more of an obligatory habitat, as breeding sites or because of the presence of vital food plants. Although less productive than some other types of ecosystem in the Marches, significant flows of energy do occur along food chains and three or four trophic levels are sustained. Decomposition rates are low, but nevertheless the proportion of annual plant biomass production converted to peat is small and animals consume much more of it.

The bog pools and *Sphagnum* lawns of the mosses are an obvious starting point. Dark peat-stained water and closely packed bog-mosses mean that these are worlds usually hidden from view. The acid conditions and low nutrient levels are inhospitable to most organisms, yet certain species are able to thrive and fit into the food chains of the mosses. Bog pools typically have shallow water, which warms quickly, and there are usually no shading trees, so light intensities at the surface can be high. Few organisms consume the *Sphagnum* floating in the water or in surrounding lawns, apart from a few worms and insect larvae, but many other organisms feed on the macrophytes in or around the pools and on algae in the water. There are also vast numbers of unicellular photosynthetic organisms growing on the surface of the *Sphagnum* – blue-green bacteria, diatoms, desmids and other algae. Filamentous algae often coat submerged plants of *Sphagnum cuspidatum*, like epiphytic mosses on a tree trunk.

A variety of unicells graze on the microscopic producers: flagellates, ciliates and amoebae. Multicellular consumers continue the food chains, particularly rotifers, cladocerans, copepods and water mites. Omnivorous caddis fly larvae are often present, including *Limnephilus luridus* with its case made of small fragments of plant matter. The larvae of some cranefly species are also present, for example *Phalocrocera replicata*, a nationally scarce species. These feed on plant roots and decaying organic matter. There are herbivorous and carnivorous species of water beetle both in the bog pools and the surrounding *Sphagnum* lawns. Silver beetles of the family Hydrophilidae are so called because of the mirror-like effect of the layer of air, held by the hairs on their underside, from which they absorb oxygen. They are often found in large numbers, adults feeding mainly on decomposing plant matter. Water beetles belonging to the family Dytiscidae are present, all fierce carnivores, including the RDB species *Acilius canaliculatus*, associated with holes left by fallen trees on bog surfaces but also found in a wider variety of pools on the mosses. The larvae of *Atylotus plebeius*, also predators of smaller aquatic animals, are sometimes found in pools with floating *Sphagnum*. This species has RDB1 status and is known as the Cheshire horsefly because of its association with the post-glacial kettle-hole mosses of that county and of north Shropshire.

There are also water bugs such as the common backswimmer, *Notonecta glauca*, a voracious carnivore. This is another species that copes with the low oxygen conditions of bog pools by collecting air at the surface of the pond and holding it on its ventral surface, this being upper-most as it swims upside-down. A similar strategy for coping with low oxygen levels is used by the water spider *Argyroneta aquatica*, but in a rather more sophisticated way. This species is widespread on the handcuttings of Whixall Moss and elsewhere on the mosses. It spins a curved silk platform, attached to underwater plants, then brings bubbles of air down to it from the surface. A large supply of oxygen is thus built up and may well be replenished by photosynthesis in the nearby plants. The water spider feeds on small crustaceans and insect larvae in the water. Another famous spider frequently seen around the margins of bog pools or on *Sphagnum* lawns is the raft spider *Dolomedes fimbriatus*. This grows to a large size – up to 20 mm long excluding appendages – with handsome yellow stripes down each side. Although *Dolomedes* can retreat underwater for a few minutes, it hunts on the surface, catching small prey animals by surprise and rapid pursuit.

Continuing the list of voracious carnivores are at least 17 species of dragonfly or damselfly that breed in bog pools, often in large numbers. Some of these also breed in habitats away from the mosses, for example the large red damselfly, azure damselfly and common hawker, but others require the acid conditions offered by bog pools on the mosses. The black darter, *Sympetrum danae*, Britain's smallest dragonfly, chooses larger un-vegetated pools, laying its eggs at the water-line, especially where there is bare peat. Its larvae live and feed on the bottom of pools, but can survive temporary drying of a pool by burrowing into damp *Sphagnum*. Closely related, but much rarer, the white-faced darter, *Leucorrhinia dubia*, breeds in shallow bog-pools where there is both open water and cover from *Sphagnum* (Fig. 115). The mosses are one of the main strongholds for this species in Britain. A serious threat to this and all of the other bog pool species in the past was the drainage of the mosses for peat cutting. Another potential threat was the collection of *Sphagnum* for use in the horticultural trade, as white-faced darter larvae were unintentionally removed with the moss. However, the necessity of allowing harvested moss to dry next to the pools gave the larvae time to return to the water and indeed the removal of some *Sphagnum* may have helped to maintain the open water required by this species. The emerald damselfly *Lestes sponsa* selects pools with open water and also some emergent plants for egg laying, preferably common cottongrass. The larvae hunt small invertebrates, mostly high in the water, but as they are very active during daylight hours they are vulnerable to predation themselves and often seek shelter against the green coloration of the purple moor-grass leaves. A significant advantage of pools on the mosses to all dragonfly and damselfly larvae is the absence of fish. The water is too acidic for any fish species, so the larvae are safe from their main potential predators. This helps to explain the large population sizes and high biodiversity of dragonflies and damselflies on the restored and undrained mosses. On emergence, adults are immediately

FIG 115. White-faced darter male at Whixall Moss. (John Balcombe)

vulnerable to predation, for example by hobbies *Falco subbuteo* (Fig. 116). This summer visitor preys on swallows, swifts and martins, but the main components of its diet are large insects, especially dragonflies. Hobbies are most often seen in the afternoon, from April to September, when dragonflies are on the wing.

Moving from the pools to consider insects of the drier areas, there are again some species seen widely elsewhere whilst others are confined to the mosses. Compared with the wettest areas there is an increased proportion of generalists. One of the best examples of a moss specialist is the large heath butterfly *Coenonympha tullia*; this is the only British butterfly that is confined to acid boggy sites. The large heath and its larval food plant, hare's-tail cottongrass, are both at the southeasterly edge of their range, as with so many species on the mosses. Eggs are laid on the leaves of cottongrass tussocks and the larvae feed on them from late July until September. By this stage they have reached the second or third instar and hibernate low in the tussocks. Winter inundation kills the larvae, so excessively wet areas on the mosses, particularly with unstable water-tables, are unsuitable. The handsome green striped larvae continue to feed from March onwards, passing through the remaining instars and then pupating in late April or early May. Adults are seen flying from late June to early August, using cross-leaved heath as a nectar plant. Their wings are grey with brown and white flashes, and with prominent eyespots on the underside that mimic the dead flowers of the cross-leaved heath very precisely. The presence of these eyespots shows that the large heaths on the

FIG 116. Hobby perching on a compartment marker post at Whixall Moss. (John Hawkins)

mosses belong to the lowland subspecies, *Coenonymphia tullia* ssp. *davus*. Some individuals also have unusually extensive white marbling of the grey on their hind wings, a form known as *cockanei*. A survey of populations on three mosses gave an estimate of 28 per cent for individuals of this form. The large heath has suffered a serious population decline in England and Wales and is not present on all of the mosses. Those who have attempted to photograph it will know that it is a restless butterfly, rarely settling anywhere for more than a few seconds. Despite this, large heaths have been found to remain within a relatively small area during their adult lives. They rarely move more than 100 m from where they emerged from a pupa. They therefore require both of their food plants to be in close proximity and this precludes them from many areas where one or other species is absent. Hare's-tail cottongrass inhabits wetter areas and cross-leaved heath drier, so the complex microtopography of some of the mosses with wetter hollows and drier raised areas provides ideal habitat for this vulnerable species (Fig. 117).

There are rather more moss specialists among the moths than the butterflies. Listed below are examples, with larval food plants:

- Haworth's moth (*Glyphipterix hawarthana*) – seeds of common cottongrass.
- Manchester treble-bar (*Carsia sororiata anglica*) – cranberry and bilberry.
- Grey scalloped-bar (*Dyscia fagaria*) – cross-leaved heath and ling.
- Heath rustic (*Xestia agathina*) – cranberry and ling.
- Haworth's minor (*Celaena haworthii*) – common cottongrass.
- Marsh oblique-barred (*Hypenodes turfosalis*) – probably cross-leaved heath, perhaps *Sphagnum*.
- Argent and Sable (*Rheumaptera hastata hastata*) – birch seedlings and bog-myrtle.

FIG 117. The lowland subspecies of large heath butterfly: adult with prominent eyespots (Barry Probin); green and white-striped larva (Joan Daniels).

Although the total number of moths recorded from the mosses is huge, an even greater number of beetles have been found, including some that are specialist species. Many of these are nationally scarce or RDB species, for example *Agonum ericeti* and *Enochrus affinis*, both associated with *Sphagnum*. *Mycetoporous calvicornis*, *Pterostichus nigrita*, *Dyschinius globosus* and also *Donacia* spp. live in the air-filled spaces at the bases of the roots of common cottongrass. There are also nationally scarce species of true fly, for example the craneflies *Idioptera linnei* and *Idioptera pulchella*, found in *Sphagnum* or wet peat, dance flies such as *Rhamphomyia curvula* and muscid flies, notably *Phaonia jaroschewski*. The bog bush cricket, *Merioptera brachyptera* is found in wetter areas, feeding on small insects and singing from late afternoon into the night by rubbing its wings together. The many insect species known on the mosses cannot all be listed here, and there are doubtless many species still to be discovered and much work to be done before we have a complete picture of their ecology.

There are many other invertebrates. Two millipedes are often encountered, *Pteroiulus fuscus* and *Polydesmus angustus*, but spiders are the most diverse group, with over 150 species found on some individual mosses. Many of these species also occur in other habitats, but some are specialists. Two aquatic moss specialists have already been mentioned, *Argyroneta aquatica* and *Dolomedes fimbriatus*. A wide variety of money spiders is found in *Sphagnum* lawns and tussocks. *Glyphesis cottonae* is a nationally scarce species, found in some Shropshire and Cheshire mosses in *Sphagnum* tussocks. *Carorita limnaea*, an even rarer money spider, has only ever been found in Britain in damp *Sphagnum* on one moss in Shropshire and one in Cheshire. *Bathyphantes setiger*, an uncommon species of wet *Sphagnum*, has not been recently recorded but may well still be present on some of the mosses. Spiders have been an under-recorded group in large parts of the Marches; money spiders such as these are easily missed, given their minute size and concealment in bog-moss. Wolf spiders are much more prominent, especially when they are hunting on the surface of *Sphagnum* lawns or carrying egg-sacs. Species of *Pirata* are the commonest lycosids on the mosses, making tubular webs in the *Sphagnum* from which they emerge to chase and catch their prey. *Pirata tenuitarsis*, *P. hygrophilus*, *P. uliginosus* and *P. piscatorius* are all found. *P. tenuitarsis* is absent from much of Britain but has one of its strongholds on the mosses, especially near pools and in the wettest areas. *P. piscatorius*, even more patchy in its distribution, is another species found in the wettest parts of the mosses where, despite its name, it catches insects and not fish. *P. hygrophilus* and *P. uliginosus* also have inappropriate species names, the former being found away from open water on the mosses and the latter preferring areas that are drying out. *P. uliginosus* is another species with a very patchy distribution in Britain. Several species of jumping spider are also found, frequently including *Neon reticulatus*, a species with widespread but localised distribution, and *Sitticus floricolus*, recorded in Britain only on the north Shropshire–Cheshire mosses and on two sites in southwest Scotland. It is found over-wintering deep in *Sphagnum*, or on tall vegetation such as cottongrass seed heads. *Xysticus ulmi*, a crab spider with a local distribution, is on the northeastern edge of its range on the mosses.

Turning now to the vertebrates that form the latter parts of food chains on the mosses, there is a clear trend for more generalist species, familiar from other habitats, and fewer species confined to the mosses. Most mammal species seen are foraging visitors: foxes, badgers *Meles meles*, brown hares *Lepus europaeus*, rabbits *Oryctolagus cuniculatus*, common and soprano pipistrelle *Pipistrellus pipistrellus* and *Pipistrellus pygmaeus* and Daubenton's bats *Myotis daubentonii*. Water voles *Arvicola terrestris* are present on some mosses where there are old peat cuttings or drain sides in which they can excavate the burrow systems that they inhabit. Small mammals such as common shrews *Sorex araneus*, pygmy shrews *Sorex minutus* and water shrews *Neomys fodiens*, field voles *Microtus agrestis*, bank voles *Myodes glareolus* and wood mice are often present and attract predatory birds and reptiles. Adders *Vipera berus* have been eliminated from some mosses by fire, sometimes started deliberately by peat-cutters fearing bites. Good populations still remain on other mosses though. The other herptiles most likely to be found are palmate newts *Lissotriton helveticus*, common frogs, grass snakes *Natrix natrix* and common lizards *Zootoca vivpera*. Viviparous species such as adder and common lizard can breed in acid conditions that affect the eggs of non-viviparous species.

The mosses can sometimes seem almost devoid of birds, especially in winter, but nonetheless for some species they are an important habitat. A variety of dabbling ducks, such as mallard, appear where there is open water, with teal particularly characteristic, but diving ducks only make brief appearances because of the shallowness of the pools. The three species of wader most frequently seen are curlew, lapwing *Vanellus vanellus* and snipe, although less common species such as greenshank *Tringa nebularia* and spotted redshank *Tringa erythropus* frequent restored mosses. Curlews are most often present between February and August, with a few winter records. They nest on the ground, especially on dry islands in wetter areas where they are protected from predators. They are sometimes present at high densities. Lapwings are semi-resident on some mosses, with numbers highest from January to October. They may breed, especially in areas of open water and bare peat (Fig. 118). Snipe may be present as winter visitors in significant numbers. The males' drumming displays, beginning in March, show that breeding is sometimes at least attempted. As feeding grounds for waders the mosses are poorer than many other wet areas, with relatively low densities

FIG 118. Lapwing feeding on bare peat at Whixall Moss. (John Hawkins)

of suitable invertebrate prey living in the peat. Swifts are often seen overhead in large numbers whilst swallows and house martins both hawk for flying insects. Skylarks and meadow pipits are the main ground-nesting passerines, feeding on invertebrates and seeds. Both are resident, favouring the open areas with few trees that characterise the mosses. Cuckoos *Cuculus canorus* are attracted by the meadow pipits and also by reed buntings, both of these species being targeted for nest parasitism. Whinchats are mostly birds of the uplands but they do occur on the mosses as summer visitors, breeding regularly, particularly in areas with some trees or shrubs. Buzzards and kestrels are the raptors that most commonly hunt on the mosses, at any time of year. Sparrowhawks *Accipiter nisus*, peregrines, long-eared *Asio otus* and short-eared owls *Asio flammeus* also hunt over the mosses, the latter species mostly as a winter visitor. Marsh harrier *Circus aeruginosus*, hen harrier *Circus cyaneus*, merlin and great grey shrike *Lanius excubitor* are more occasional, either as birds of passage or as winter visitors hunting in open areas.

With these birds of prey we have reached the end of the food chains of the mosses. Before moving on to conservation, a special and intriguing type of moss will be considered – quaking bogs or schwingmoors.

QUAKING BOGS

The surface of some mosses undulates alarmingly if one walks across it, revealing that instead of being acrotelm overlying peat, the surface consists of a thin mat of vegetation and some peat, floating on a body of water. The water can be very deep, more than 8 m at Clarepool Moss and 15 m in the centre of Wybunbury Moss for example.[4] The typical community of plants suggests that conditions in the floating layer, away from the margins at least, are ombrotrophic. Because the surface of this type of moss is essentially flat, it cannot be regarded as lowland raised mire and is usually known as quaking bog, though ecologists often use the German equivalent, schwingmoor. Clarepool, Wybunbury and Abbot's Mosses are well known examples, but other less known but nonetheless fine quaking bogs exist, making this an important speciality of the North Shropshire–Cheshire Plain (Fig. 119).

These sites are particularly treacherous places, and they can not effectively be visited in wet seasons. They are located in basins, often with woodland clothing the steep basin sides and frequently alder carr towards the bottom. Next to the carr and around the margins of the schwingmoor there is usually a moat-like region, with standing water or bare waterlogged peat. Transition fen, discussed earlier in the chapter, may be present where groundwater enriched with nutrients seeps in. At Wybunbury Moss there is an excellent example of the complete zonation from alkaline fen through transition mire into an ombrotrophic quaking bog community. Greater tussock-sedge and other species characteristic of base enrichment may be present, together with fallen and rotting trunks from the adjacent carr if it is present. If the visitor is intrepid enough to cross this moat, the floating mat is reached. Extensive lawns of *Sphagnum fallax* are usually present, with hummocks of *Sphagnum papillosum*,

FIG 119. A floating bog at Massey Lodge, near Delamere, with green *Sphagnum* moss and drowned birches. (Iain Diack)

Sphagnum capillifolium ssp. *rubellum* and other bog-mosses of drier conditions. As on the other mosses, cranberry, bog rosemary, crowberry, common and hare's-tail cottongrass, cross-leaved heath and round-leaved sundew are also usually present. Oak, birch and Scots pine seedlings frequently germinate on these quaking bogs, pines sometimes grow to a height of 5 m or more, but a very characteristic feature is the presence of standing dead pine trees. The reason for their death may be that, upon reaching a certain size, they grow too heavy to be supported by the quaking bog and sink into it, the acid and anaerobic conditions below the surface proving fatal to their roots. In these conditions, the roots and wood of pines fail to decompose, leaving the upper portions of the tree protruding as spike-tops. These have a ghostly appearance, as their bark is quickly lost, leaving the pale wood exposed.

Another intriguing question is why quaking bogs have developed at some sites rather than raised mires with a solid body of peat. Lake deposits underlying quaking bogs and raised mires indicate that they both develop from meres. It could be hypothesised that in all cases *Sphagnum* has spread over the mere surface and gradually deposited peat into the water below. Quaking bogs might then be the result of greater depth of water in a mere, slower deposition of peat or faster decomposition. The evidence does not support this. A small central pool at Wybunbury Moss became covered with *Sphagnum fallax* lawn during the second half of the 20th century yet, during the same period, *Sphagnum* has not grown out over the surface of the pool at Clarepool Moss. There are sites in the northern Marches where *Sphagnum* is growing out over open water, for example parts of Fenn's and Whixall Mosses, but the water at these sites is always relatively shallow, or the pool diameter very small. To explain the presence of *Sphagnum* growing over deep water in the quaking bog at Clarepool Moss we must postulate that at some stage in the past water levels at Clarepool were much lower than they are now and that *Sphagnum* spread over the water to form a moss community, beginning the process of peat formation. After some peat had accumulated the water level rose, with the peat and the moss community floating on top of it, creating the quaking bog. At Wybunbury it also seems likely that the water depth was much shallower in the past and a moss community became established. In this case however, rather than the pool surface rising, the floor of the basin subsided as a result of salt dissolving out of the rock below. The hypothesis that *Sphagnum* can only spread over relatively shallow water, perhaps less than 2 m, is reinforced by observations from further north in Cheshire, where lawns of *S. fallax* only spread over small water-filled basins in the Delamere Forest after drainage schemes had reduced water depths. It must be unusual for the necessary substantial increase in water depths subsequently to occur, which partly explains the relative rarity of quaking bogs in much of Britain (Fig. 120).

The layer of peat and moss must have a density lower than that of water if it is to float on the surface of a quaking bog. At Flaxmere, which despite its name is a moss, black sedge peat was found to lie below the water body, with lighter coloured *Sphagnum* peat in the floating surface raft,[5] a pattern also found elsewhere. Presumably, when the increase in water depth occurred the peat body split along the sharp line of demarcation between the two peat types. The floating of the upper layer of peat indicates that its density is less than that of water. This could be due to the lack of humification of this peat but it could also be caused by the accumulation of gas in the peat. Inflammable gas has long been known to emanate from waterlogged sites, hence the name marsh gas. A mural in Manchester Town Hall shows John Dalton supervising the collection of marsh gas in glass jars by a boy balanced on a plank over a bog pool near Manchester. This gas is now called methane. Its production is a biological process, involving methanogenic bacteria, which are only active under certain conditions. In particular, the low pH conditions of ombrotrophic mosses wetted only by rainwater usually prevent methanogenesis.

Western transect

Eastern transect

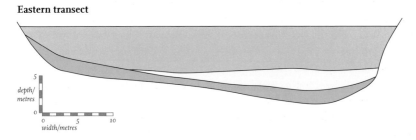

FIG 120. Sectional diagrams of Wybunbury Moss. The Western Transect shows how peat and surface vegetation float on water in a quaking bog (brown, peat with wood fragments; yellow, sedge peat; blue, water; pink, *Sphagnum* peat).

FIG 121. Quaking bog at Wybunbury Moss with a lawn of *Sphagnum* over a thin layer of peat, with metres of water below. (Iain Diack)

Groundwater, which can maintain a slightly higher pH, and mesotrophic conditions are needed. Little methane is produced if nitrogen or phosphorus concentrations are low in the peat. This is also the case if lignin or other phenolic compounds are at relatively high concentrations, as in the strongly humified peat found at greater depths. It seems that peat will only remain buoyant enough for a quaking bog to exist if conditions are acidic enough to allow *Sphagnum* to grow but discourage other plants, yet not so acidic or nutrient poor that methanogenic bacteria stop working. Microbial activity must be inhibited enough for there to be slow decomposition rates and accumulation of peat, but not so inhibited that methanogens are prevented from flourishing. With such a delicate balance needed, it is not surprising that natural quaking bogs are uncommon and the sites in the Marches are therefore all the more precious (Fig. 121).

RESTORATION OF LOWLAND RAISED MIRE – A CASE STUDY

Most of the mosses of the Marches have remained confined to the basins where they originated, but the Fenn's, Whixall, Bettisfield, Wem and Cadney Moss complex developed from a group of individual mosses that spread out and merged to cover a much larger area (Fig. 122). The discovery of the trunks of fallen oak trees preserved beneath the peat suggests that the domes of raised mire waterlogged the surrounding land, allowing the mire to expand into areas of prehistoric wildwood – a process now known as palludification. Without using this modern term, J. D. Sainter gave a graphic description of the process in 1878, when writing about mosses in the Macclesfield area:[6]

*'Peat accumulates wherever stagnant water prevails. It has a tendency to
accumulate in all swamps and hollows; and wherever stagnant water prevails
there it increases, filling up lakes, choking river courses, entombing fallen forests
and spreading over every surface having moisture sufficient to cherish its growth.'*

The total area now covered by peat at Fenn's, Whixall, Bettisfield, Wem and
Cadney Mosses is 948 ha. It is of international importance for its wildlife,
with the SSSI citation[7] picking out the 'extensive and exceptional invertebrate
fauna' for special note. More than 1,700 invertebrate species have been recorded
including about 30 that are RDB listed.

Fenn's Complex has been altered by drainage for canal and railway
construction, agriculture and forestry, has been repeatedly burnt and has even
been used by the RAF as a bombing range. There is a long history of hand cutting
of peat. Larger scale mechanical extraction began in 1968 but, after a change of
ownership in 1989 and the introduction of new machinery, it was scaled up from

FIG 122. Aerial view showing Wem Moss in the foreground, with Bettisfield Moss in the
middle ground before removal of its cover of pines. In the distance beyond the Ellesmere
branch of the Shropshire Union Canal is Fenn's Moss on the left of the view and Whixall Moss
on the right. (Clwyd-Powys Archaeological Trust)

20,000 m³ per year towards a planned 50,000 m³. The severe damage that this rate of exploitation was causing soon became apparent. Widespread protests and a highly effective campaign by ecologists and environmentalists led to intervention by the Nature Conservancy Council, which bought the freeholds of the exploited areas in December 1990 and established a new National Nature Reserve. The period of intensive peat extraction was brief and much future damage was prevented. Intensive efforts have been made to 'mend the mire' by English Nature and Natural England, partly on behalf of the Countryside Council for Wales. Management techniques have included: damming drains, clearing scrub and conifer plantations, and removing sources of nutrient-rich water. Marked changes to communities of plants and animals are already obvious, with species characteristic of raised mires returning or increasing in number. The process is a huge and ambitious experiment with Senior Reserve Manager Joan Daniels as its tireless and devoted leader. The final results will not be known for many years, but it is already possible to assess progress across the various parts of Fenn's, Whixall, Bettisfield, Wem and Cadney Mosses, with the question in mind: can the mire be mended?

The largest area of mechanically cut peat and thus the most severely damaged area was on Fenn's Moss (Fig. 123). This extended to 140 ha, with a repeating pattern of strips created by the peat extraction techniques. Deep drains had been dug at 10 m intervals. The vegetation and surface layers of peat were removed from a strip beside each drain, leaving bare peat. The materials removed were

FIG 123. Fenn's Moss, showing the regular pattern of strips created by mechanical peat extraction, now rewetted, with cottongrasses and other bog plants re-established. (Joan Daniels)

dumped to form another higher and drier strip alongside. On strips that had been left to give access for the machinery, relatively undamaged peat and vegetation survived, unlike mosses elsewhere in Britain where the surface-milling technique was used, and the entire surface of the moss was destroyed. There were other encouraging signs. Although the acrotelm had been lost, peat remained to a depth of 3 m on average, giving a substantial capacity for water storage. The peat surface was of moderately humified 'grey' *Sphagnum* peat, making restoration of raised mire communities more likely than if the surface had been black fen peat.

One of the first objectives was to block the drains, in order to re-establish as far as possible the natural hydrology and hydrochemistry. Ironically, much of the machinery used was bought from the company that had been extracting the peat and several of the workers from this company were employed, bringing with them a detailed knowledge of conditions on Fenn's and Whixall Mosses and, especially useful, the locations of the drains. Birch scrub was removed before damming work was started, in case it became impossible to get machinery on to the site subsequently because of raised water levels. To form the dams, black peat was excavated from the base of the drains and used to form 3–4 m wide plugs at about 40 m intervals along the drains, compacting it with the mechanical excavator to reduce leakage (Fig. 124). The success of damming on Fenn's Moss and adjacent areas has been assessed using a network of tubes called dipwells. These show that even in dry years, the water table is in the upper 200 mm of peat for 60 per cent of the time and in wet years it is always within the top 300 mm. There are year-to-year variations depending on rainfall and evapotranspiration, but winter levels are always high and crashes in summer are shorter and less dramatic. A twice-yearly survey of water levels in drains has shown little change in winter, which was already high because of back-flooding due to the limited capacity of the drainage network, but higher levels in summer after damming.[8]

FIG 124. Damming drains with excavated peat to re-wet and mend the mire on Fenn's Moss. (Joan Daniels)

The raising of the water table on the commercially cut areas of Fenn's Moss has led to dramatic changes in plant communities. A survey in 2000 showed 10 per cent cover of *Sphagnum cuspidatum*, compared with less than 1 per cent in 1991. The total cover of cottongrasses in 1991 was less than 1 per cent but by 2000 there was 11 per cent cover of hare's-tail cottongrass, mostly in the strips that had been bare peat and 20 per cent cover of common cottongrass mostly in the former drains.

Round-leaved sundew, scarcely present in 1991, had become frequent by 2000, especially on bare peat. Purple moor-grass had increased on the access strips and the drier strips where scraped-off vegetation was dumped. Increases in purple moor grass have been used to indicate where further management is needed to raise water tables. The importance of a high water table for re-instatement of communities dominated by *Sphagnum* has been shown by survey work on Fenn's and Whixall Mosses. Dipwells have been installed at many sites to allow water levels to be monitored. Vegetation was surveyed at 93 of these sites and the results were grouped according to water depths recorded in the dipwells. The results showed that for *Sphagnum* to colonise, the water table must be within 100 mm of the surface for most of the year. Colonisation is much greater if the water level is slightly above the surface than below it.

Fenn's Moss and Whixall Moss meet at the English–Welsh border, which is marked only by a 1 m-wide drain. Although these two mosses are part of a single larger peat mass, differences in the way that Fenn's and Whixall Mosses have been exploited make the areas on either side readily distinguishable now. There has been extensive peat winning on Whixall but, in contrast to Fenn's Moss, individual peat cutters worked it by hand and so the consequences were not the same. About 20 local men each rented a 'turf bank' of about an acre, but there were variations in the way that they worked. The pits left behind by cutting remained wet and were important reservoirs of the scarcer mire species. In the years since 1990 these species have been encouraged by careful management to spread back out over the rest of the mosses. There has been more success with some species than others. Lesser bladderwort has increased following work to flood more of the old peat cuttings on Whixall Moss by damming of the drains, but it is still not widespread.

The white-faced darter has spread out more widely from the hand cuts and by 2000 there were 12 known areas where larvae could be found, including some in the restored commercially cut areas of Fenn's Moss. The northern footman moth, *Eilema sericea*, an RDB species, has disappeared from almost all of its known sites on the mosses, but light trapping on Whixall Moss has produced good numbers of adults and shows that the population is being maintained in areas of old hand cuttings here. Adults are small and grey, with orange margins to their in-rolled wings. Only one caterpillar has ever been found at Whixall and the larval food requirements are not yet known. Other footman moth larvae feed on lichens and this is the likeliest food of the northern footman. In the areas where it is found there is extensive cover of lichen on dry ridges of bare peat and a tide-line of lichen on vertical sides of peat cuttings. In contrast to other species that are conservation targets, the northern footman could be threatened by any restoration measures that cause water levels to rise. Lichens on the vertical sides of cuttings would be drowned and mosses or other plants would replace those on the bare peat ridges. If a raised mire community with lichen-rich hummocks were to be re-established on parts of Fenn's and Whixall Mosses, the northern footman would probably be able to form populations there and be much less vulnerable. Until then, refugia are being maintained where water levels are not raised. Given the importance of conserving the northern footman and the very limited understanding of its requirements, there is a clear and urgent need for further research.

Different conservation challenges have been met on two small parts of Fenn's and Whixall Mosses, named Oaf's Orchard and the Cranberry Beds. These areas are unusual in that they have never been cut for peat and therefore have a higher peat surface than surrounding cut areas. This has made them prone to drying out and allowed heathland communities to develop, with many birch trees. Nevertheless, they formed important refugia for the large heath butterfly because enough hare's-tail cottongrass remained to sustain populations. Large heaths have been able to spread out from here and recolonise large areas of Fenn's and Whixall mosses following their restoration. As the name suggests there is an abundant population of cranberry plants in the area called the Cranberry Beds and within living memory, the fruits were harvested. Two mosses found here are of conservation importance. There are large patches of *Sphagnum pulchrum*, a rare species that grows in shallow pools or over damp peat. Waved fork-moss, *Dicranum bergeri*, has RDB status and is in marked decline nationally, but is quite abundant on the Cranberry Beds in some of the drier areas, forming tussocks, particularly over old heather stems. Oaf's Orchard is notable for having a depth of more than 8 m of peat, with white, grey and black peats all still intact. This makes the area particularly valuable for any research that requires a complete sequence of layers of peat. The drying of the upper layers and the loss of the acrotelm, particularly by burning, threatened this, so Oaf's Orchard was an early target for rewetting. Birches and other woody plants have been cut annually. Drains on surrounding cut areas were dammed and embankments of peat, lined with waterproof polythene sheeting, used to block drainage from old peat cuttings. Water levels have been successfully raised and a major increase in bog species followed, including hummock-forming *Sphagnum* species such as

S. magellanicum and *S. papillosum* that are the core vegetation of lowland raised mires. The liverwort *Odontoschisma sphagni*, also characteristic of raised mires, became established in significant quantities. Restoration of Oaf's Orchard has been particularly successful and a proper mire community is re-establishing with the precious peat record safe beneath.

There are more extensive areas of uncut peat to the west of Fenn's and Whixall Mosses, resulting in another large area of raised mire: Bettisfield Moss, which covers 57 ha. It is connected to Fenn's and Whixall Mosses by the peat that underlies the Llangollen Branch of the Shropshire Union Canal. The part of Bettisfield Moss in Wales is almost all uncut, with peat depths greater than 8 m. The English part has been hand-cut for peat in the past, the remaining layers being up to 3.5 m deep. Bettisfield Moss was regularly burned to keep it clear of trees for peat cutting, but when this ceased self-sown pine trees colonised the Moss. For a few years they were kept clear by the young pines being cut for sale as Christmas trees, but by 1991 they had grown to form a dense cover, up to 15 m high. Two areas remained more open, one of which on the English side had been dynamited in the past in an attempt to create a duck pond. This area was very wet with only small trees, bog-mosses and white beak-sedge *Rhychospora alba*. Another area in the centre of the Bettisfield Moss on the Welsh side near the canal was the last to be colonised. In this area bog-mosses were and still are dominant including *Sphagnum pulchrum*, *Dicranum bergeri* and *Sphagnum magellanicum*. Other species characteristic of raised mire also persisted. However, a survey showed that shading from the pines had destroyed much of the former mire community in other parts of Bettisfield Moss, only bare ground remaining where the pine forest was most developed.[9] Two water-level recorders were installed in 1995, one in a small clearing and one under adjacent mature pine canopy, to assess the effect of trees on the hydrology of the area. These showed that the water level in the peat under the closed pine canopy was lower for much of each year, especially the summer and autumn.

Removal of the forest was clearly needed if water levels and the mire community were to be re-established. Small-scale attempts had begun in 1992, but the size of the trees, the difficulty of access and the wetness of the site made the task very challenging. Contractors were employed from 1999 onwards and a variety of machinery used. Brash was used to make tracks for vehicles moving across the site and an aerial cable was used to remove some of the timber (Fig. 125). All of the forest had been cleared by May 2002, except for a marginal band. Since then pine seedlings have been removed by hand pulling and tree regrowth has been prevented by herbicide treatment of stumps. Birch, bramble and willowherb have also been sprayed with herbicide. Within two months of the forest clearance,

FIG 125. Tree clearance on Bettisfield Moss with aerial cables to allow timber extraction without heavy machinery crossing the delicate mire surface. (Joan Daniels)

curlews were breeding again on Bettisfield Moss. Water levels have risen, especially in autumn, and plants of raised lowland mires have spread. Permanent quadrats were set up in 2002 to monitor changes to plant communities. By 2005 these were already showing significant increases in positive indicators of moss vegetation: *Sphagnum*, cross-leaved heath and both species of cottongrass. They were showing significant decreases in negative indicators including purple moor-grass, bracken and the moss *Aulocomnium palustre*.[10]

The Ellesmere branch of the Shropshire Union Canal, constructed between 1797 and 1804, separates Bettisfield Moss from Fenn's and Whixall Mosses. The canal and adjacent British Waterways land became part of the National Nature Reserve in 2005, in recognition of its wildlife interest. It is deeper than most canals, was cut directly into the peat of the mosses and was never sealed with clay. The water of the canal is close to neutral and richer in nutrients than water on the mosses. The diverse range of species that thrive in the water of the canal include numerous dragonflies and damselflies that could not survive in the acid bog pools, such as the banded demoiselle. Alder woodland known as The Quob has developed along both sides of the canal, because of nutrients leaching out from the canal water. Many plants characteristic of fens and swamps thrive here and, although unnatural in origin, this community may resemble natural woodland called lagg or lagg fen that typically is present beyond the rands of raised mires. If there were lagg communities around the edges of Fenn's, Whixall and Bettisfield Mosses they have long since been lost to agriculture, so the cutting of the canal across the mosses ironically may have saved species that have elsewhere been lost as agriculture encroached on the margins of the mosses.

An example of a species mostly confined to the margins of the mire and also to The Quob is alder buckthorn. Found on drained peat and along ditches that are nutrient rich, it is the foodplant of brimstone butterfly larvae *Gonepteryx rhamni*. Adult brimstones that have over-wintered are seen flying from March onwards, with the new generation of adults visible in August. Other species of butterfly and many species of bird inhabit the margins rather than the main body of the mosses. Hobbies breed on the margins and nightjars are still heard churring at dusk in most years.

Another notable example of species of the margins is *Hagenella clathrata*, a caddis fly, with RDB status, that is found at only three locations in Britain (Fig. 126). This species has very particular requirements. The larvae live in the bases of tall grass tussocks, especially purple moor-grass, in areas ranging from open to wooded. As the larvae are aquatic and live through the winter and spring, the tussock bases must be flooded during this period. Pupation takes place under water, but for the adults to be able to emerge in late June or July they need the tussocks to dry out. *Hagenella clathrata* is adapted to the conditions found in the rands and laggs around the margins of raised mires. These have been lost to agriculture, but the caddis flies have survived in three parts of Whixall Moss where conditions further into the mire have been altered and are now similar enough to a rand or lagg. One of these is an area of old peat cuttings and the other two are former bullock fields that have been drained in the past and are now reverting to birch woodland. The larvae have been found to inhabit wet vole runs in these areas. Populations are monitored each year by counting both larval cases and adults. Although the numbers are holding up well, there is long-term concern about the future of this very rare species. *Hagenella clathrata* will remain vulnerable at Whixall unless it spreads out over larger areas, especially those that

FIG 126. The rare caddis fly *Hagenella clathrata*: encased larva (left) and adult (right). (Barry Probin)

have long-term stability in their vegetation and annual water-level cycles. There are other apparently suitable areas that are not occupied and more research is needed to trace the factors currently preventing colonisation of them. In the areas where it is currently found the cover of trees and shrubs is increasing and water levels are vulnerable to change. The work that has been done over much of Fenn's and Whixall Mosses to re-wet the mire is not being done here; instead, attempts are being made to prevent any further increase in tree and shrub cover and to maintain the existing annual cycle of water levels.

Hagenella clathrata provides another example showing how critical water levels are to the wildlife of the mosses. The area of Fenn's, Whixall, Bettisfield, Wem and Cadney Mosses is so large that management can be organised to ensure that the variety of water levels is wide enough to suit the diverse needs of the species present. While some areas should be kept drier, most areas must be re-wetted to allow the natural species of the mosses, especially *Sphagnum*, to thrive again. Not only will this help to conserve these species, but the mosses will also act as a gigantic sponge, storing up and purifying water and helping to restrict flooding in surrounding areas. Finally and very significantly, it will become a carbon sink again and be a part of the vital drive to reduce atmospheric carbon dioxide levels, thereby limiting global warming. There are concerns that if carbon dioxide levels rise to a certain level then a 'tipping point' will be reached. The next part of this chapter is devoted to another case study, that of Wem Moss, where a tipping point, hydrological this time, may already have been passed and conservation may therefore be extremely difficult.

WEM MOSS, CADNEY MOSS AND THE HYDROLOGY OF THE MOSSES

Wem Moss forms the southwestern extreme of the linked complex of mosses and is the last part to be described here. Cadney Moss has been completely reclaimed for forestry and agriculture, and once continued directly into the north dome of Wem Moss. The cutting of the English–Welsh border and marginal drains round the mosses has caused the collapse of the domes of peat and led to extensive drying out. Wem Moss became a Shropshire Wildlife Trust reserve in 1973. It has scarcely been used for commercial peat extraction, nor has much peatland on the margins of the Moss been reclaimed for agriculture. Small amounts of peat were taken in the past using the Whixall bible-cutting technique and this has left shallow pits scattered over parts of the Moss, but most of the surface is unaffected. The Moss consists of two raised areas, separated by a narrow central strip. The range of elevation between the middle and the edges of the raised areas is currently around 0.8 m – less than is typical for raised mires and almost certainly less than it once was.

Charles Sinker described the communities present on Wem Moss and his account still forms a useful benchmark.[11] The raised areas were mostly drier than expected for raised mire and were dominated by ling, cross-leaved heath, hare's-tail cottongrass and purple moor-grass. These are fire-tolerant species, suggesting that in the past Wem Moss was burned to prevent scrub encroachment and ensure that some grazing was available for commoners with rights of pasture. Sinker referred to the surface of much of the raised areas as 'desiccated and fire-swept', but there were also some wetter patches where the dominant plants were the bog mosses *Sphagnum cuspidatum* and *S. papillosum* and common cottongrass. The most varied plant communities were in the damp hollows left by peat cutting. All three British species of sundew were present: *Drosera rotundifolia* most abundantly, and *D. intermedia* and *D. anglica* more infrequently, with each hollow tending to be occupied exclusively by one species. The central strip of Wem Moss showed a transition from a tongue of willow carr at the eastern end to an area with plants characteristic of mesotrophic fens, including royal fern *Osmunda regalis*, meadow thistle and slender sedge. Bog-myrtle *Myrica gale*, an uncommon plant in the Marches, was also present. Further west this community gradually merged into that of the acid mire. Sinker deduced that there was penetration of nutrient-enriched water from agricultural land to the east through this central strip, and therefore called it the soakway. Birch scrub was prevalent around the margins of Wem Moss, but the eastern side was fringed by a lagg community of dense carr dominated by grey willow *Salix cinerea*, with alder and alder buckthorn *Frangula alnus* (Fig. 127).

In the decades after 1962 carr spread across the soakway to form a central lagg, as a result of the continued or increased penetration of nutrient-enriched water from slurry entering the farm drains on the eastern margin of the Moss. The open fen community that Sinker described in 1962 has disappeared. Bog-myrtle has spread over large parts of the central lagg and other parts of the Moss. This success may be down to its ability to form root nodules in which *Frankia*, a filamentous bacterium, resides. *Frankia* has vesicles at the end of its filaments in which it maintains low oxygen levels and fixes nitrogen. Some of this fixed nitrogen is used by the bog-myrtle, giving it a competitive advantage over other plants in conditions where levels of phosphate and potassium are adequate, but nitrogen is deficient. Alder also has root nodules containing *Frankia*, enjoys a mutualistic relationship with this bacterium, and thus grows vigorously in low nitrogen conditions. Shropshire Wildlife Trust removed much of the tree cover from the central lagg in the late 1990s, but this has not led to the re-establishment

FIG 127. Aerial view of Wem Moss, showing the two peat domes, left and right, separated by a central lagg along which birch woodland has invaded.

of the fen community. Birch has rapidly grown up instead, together with invasive plants such as rosebay willowherb *Chamerion angustifolium*. With continued nutrient penetration from surrounding farmland this is not surprising.

Desiccation was Charles Sinker's other concern about Wem Moss and the signs of this have been increasingly obvious. A survey in 1999 found only 5 ha of *Erica tetralix–Sphagnum papillosum* raised mire and a very small area of *Sphagnum cuspidatum–recurvum* bog pools. *Drosera anglica* has not been seen since 1998 and *Drosera intermedia* is also now probably extinct at Wem. Accompanying changes have taken place in the animal community, for example the raft spider *Dolomedes fimbriatus* has become much scarcer. The drying of Wem Moss seems to be relentless and unless reversed will eventually lead to the loss of all the species of lowland raised mires. A study in 2003 showed that the water table was as much as 0.6 m below peat surface level near the peripheral drains, 0.2 m below in the northern dome and 0.4 m below in the southern dome. As no surface drains extend across the Moss to connect with the peripheral drains and Wem Moss is 500–600 m across, it is surprising that the peripheral drains could have lowered the water table to such an extent. The boundary zone on the mire side of a drain is the region in which the water level in the mire is lowered. This zone is usually only about 5 m wide in raised mires.

A partial explanation of the desiccation of Wem Moss may be that before peripheral drains were dug, groundwater drained from surrounding basin into the mire and that this helped to maintain a high water table. This water no longer reaches the mire as the peripheral drains intercept it. Also, when the south drain was deepened in 1985 it was cut below the base of the peat, into coarse sands and gravels. This sand and gravel underlies the peat of much of the south dome and water may therefore drain down through the peat into the sand and gravel and then laterally through it to the deepened south drain. This could occur at a much more rapid rate than the natural slow rate of drainage through the peat itself. Another highly significant factor is the loss of the *Sphagnum* from much of the surface of the Moss. The role of *Sphagnum* in increasing the wetness of mires was described earlier in this chapter as an ecological version of positive feedback. The cycle of desiccation is also positive feedback but in the opposite direction – if some *Sphagnum* is lost, the consequent drying of the Moss will cause further loss. If Wem Moss was only just wet enough to survive as an ombrotrophic mire dominated by *Sphagnum* then an apparently innocuous change could have set off the downward spiral of drying. This critical point is sometimes referred to as a tipping point. The initial loss of *Sphagnum* could have been initiated by some factor other than desiccation, for example, burning. The cessation of grazing is another possibility. Grazing can help to maintain both *Sphagnum* cover and moisture levels, by reducing the leaf areas of competing plants with high transpiration rates such as purple moor-grass. Cattle grazing occurred on the moss until at least the 1970s but after then little if any has taken place, indeed a management agreement has prevented grazing rights being used by a neighbouring farmer.

The lack of wood in the upper 2 m of peat at Wem Moss shows that for some considerable time no trees grew on the raised areas of the Moss. High water tables, grazing and fire can prevent establishment of tree and shrub seedlings. The water table has certainly fallen and fires are not now raised on Wem Moss. It is therefore not surprising that there has been increasing invasion by trees in recent years, especially birch. This has been identified as another possible cause of drying, but it is by no means certain that this is the case. Results from Bettisfield Moss show that clearance of dense stands of conifers can the raise water table of mires, yet the tree cover at Wem has been much less complete during the years in which desiccation became a problem. Scattered trees or small stands of birch trees might intuitively be expected to increase evapotranspiration during May to October when they are in leaf, but there is no experimental evidence to show that this is the case on Wem Moss and evidence from other similar sites is scant. A possible increase in transpiration from the birches has to be set against any reduction in transpiration by plants growing beneath them, as a result of shading and wind shelter. Another consideration is the interception of rainfall. Some intercepted rainfall runs down the trees to the plants or peat below, but some of it also evaporates and is lost. Despite this complexity of factors, it seems very likely that the replacement of communities dominated by *Sphagnum* with alternative ones dominated by trees will lead to an increase in overall transpiration and a consequent drying of the Moss.

Another exacerbating factor is the development of cracks and natural pipes in the peat. The collapse of the domes themselves has led to a wrinkling of the surface, effectively forming 1 m deep cracks leading to the Border Drain, further drying the surface. Continued shrinkage of the peat during drying has created fissures and natural pipes, which greatly speed up drainage rates through the peat. The fissures give the peat surface the appearance of crazy paving and can widen to form gullies. Natural pipes are underground channels, roughly circular in cross section through which water can run; these can become collapse pits if the natural pipe becomes very wide. Rapid drainage reduces the chance for rainwater to be absorbed into the peat, especially when there has been heavy rain after a period in which the peat dried out.

Paradoxically, because there has been so little damage to Wem Moss by peat extraction, the high peat surface makes re-wetting it more difficult. Shropshire Wildlife Trust has carried out conservation work on Wem Moss since the 1970s. Attempts at clearance of trees and shrubs have so far been largely unsuccessful, with rapid recolonisation. On the south side of the moss a French drain has been installed in the adjacent fields, to intercept and remove groundwater from the agricultural land. This allows the deep open drain on the margin of the moss to be dammed, preventing it from draining the moss. Vertical sheet-piling has been carried out extensively to block lateral flows through surface gullies and natural pipes into the open drain on the north side of the moss. Cutting and herbicide treatments have been used to control scrub; controlled grazing may then be used to prevent its re-establishment.

As with all examples of positive feedback, the desiccation of Wem Moss is an inherently unstable situation and may be very difficult to reverse. Considerably more work may be needed to wet the mire sufficiently for the acrotelm, dominated by *Sphagnum*, to be re-established. Once this starts to happen, changes could be rapid and the domes of peat may swell and rise up once again. If attempts at rewetting are not successful then the Moss community described by Charles Sinker will be permanently lost.

WETLAND VISION: THE MERES AND MOSSES STRATEGY

In 2007, Natural England published an ambitious 50-year vision for freshwater wetlands, with plans that go far beyond a limited number of nature reserves. The aim is to conserve a whole landscape of peatlands. A map of all extant and relict peat-filled basins is being produced. Significant amounts of money are being made available for conservation projects, some but not all of which are on SSSI sites. Farmers are of course currently able to obtain payments for conservation of mosses through Higher Level Stewardship. Major restoration work has been carried out at ten sites in the Meres and Mosses area. Trees have been removed and ingress of raw sewage overflowing from a septic tank has been prevented at Lin Can Moss, a site that was in the past categorised as a schwingmoor.[12] At Clarepool Moss, a most important site,[13] £35,000 has been spent on the removal of a failed conifer plantation on peat-covered areas that necessitated use of overhead cables to extract the timber and brash. Several areas of schwingmoor were re-found. A boundary ditch and several internal ditches have been blocked with interlocking plastic sheets. Trees have also been removed from Hodnet Heath, a wet heath that had been colonised by birch. In the Bomere complex, trees and rhododendrons are being removed from around Shomere. The depth of organic sediments at this site is greater than 8 m, with several metres of gyttjas followed by fen deposits and then peat from ombrotrophic mire vegetation.[14] The aim is to re-establish *Sphagnum*-dominated mire. There are plans for future projects, for example the establishment of grazing marshes on Baggy Moor, which could help reduce flooding problems in Bewdley and other places on the Severn.

Unfortunately, these on-site works cannot successfully tackle off-site pressures such as nutrient enrichment in catchments and changes in agricultural systems that make mosses practically worthless to landowners. There is a Catchment Sensitive Farming project seeking to address soil and nutrient management, but it is struggling to make much headway. Drainage schemes installed in the past still affect most mosses and whilst the water level changes that they caused could be reversed, there would be significant impacts on surrounding land. As so often, bold conservation measures are needed. To restore the mosses that were once part of the important Crose Mere–Sweat Mere–Whattall Moss complex for instance, water levels would need to be raised by over a metre, with some loss of agricultural land, but the benefits to the natural communities of the meres and mosses in this complex would be immense. If Wetland Vision succeeds, not only will an inland archipelago of many mosses be established across which wildlife can thrive, but peat formation will restart on a large combined area, sequestering carbon from the atmosphere and helping to combat global warming.

CHAPTER 8

Woodland

THE CLIMATE, TOPOGRAPHY AND SOILS OF THE Marches are suited to the growth of trees, so without human intervention woodland would be almost ubiquitous. At the start of the 21st century, slightly more than 8 per cent of the total area was wooded, of which 5 per cent was broadleaved and 3 per cent conifers. Although most of the woodland of the Marches is made up of relatively small fragments, there are some more extensive areas. The largest area is in Wyre, much of which is broadleaved. Wyre has its own dedicated study group and is easily the most intensively recorded area in the Marches. The other large areas of woodland are mostly post-war conifer plantations, especially in northwest Herefordshire (Fig. 128).

Most of Wyre is ancient woodland. Sites are regarded as ancient woodlands if they were wooded in 1600 and still are today. Their distribution in the Marches is very uneven.[1] There are many ancient woodland sites in Herefordshire and south Shropshire, but parts of north Shropshire and south Cheshire have none. These are areas with flatter land and drift deposits, so are amenable to agriculture. It is no surprise that almost all this land has been cleared at some stage and the limited amount of woodland that now exists is almost all secondary and of relatively little natural history interest. There has been an increase in small woodlands on farmland as a result of grant structures, but far more woodland, and almost all ancient woodland is still located where agriculture proves unrewarding. Some sites are in steep-sided gorges and many are in the narrow deeply incised dingles that are so characteristic of the Marches. These gorges and dingles often have the topography of the uplands, but the diversity of tree and shrub species of lowland woodlands. Other areas of ancient woodland have survived because the soil is thin and the underlying rock is usually close to the surface. There is great variation in rock type, so the woodland is accordingly

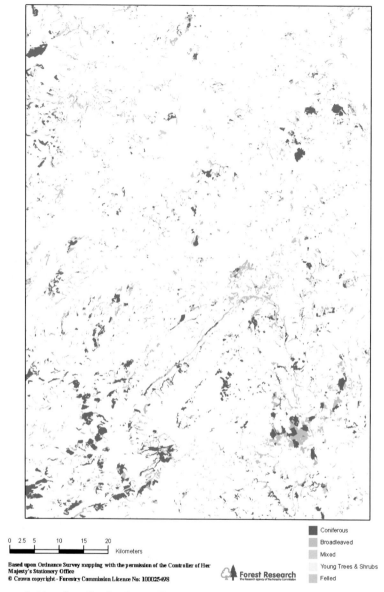

Coniferous
Broadleaved
Mixed
Young Trees & Shrubs
Felled

0 2.5 5   10   15   20
Kilometers

Based upon Ordnance Survey mapping with the permission of the Controller of Her Majesty's Stationery Office
© Crown copyright - Forestry Commission Licence No: 100025498

Forest Research
the Research agency of the Forestry Commission

FIG 128. Map of woodland in the Marches, showing the large area of Wyre forest (lower right), partly coniferised, the extensive coniferisation of hilltops in *West Siluria* (lower left), the 30 km wooded length of Wenlock Edge and the relative paucity of woodland on the North Shropshire–Cheshire Plain. The area is as in Fig. 18, with an additional 10 km to the east. (Forest Research)

very varied. Some of this variation may be due to historical accident – how owners have chosen to manage a site – but there are many sites where recent management has been limited enough for natural influences to come to the fore.

WOODLAND TYPES

Attempts to classify woodlands into specific types have been made many times and in many ways. The most detailed and widely used system in Britain currently is the National Vegetation Classification (NVC)[2]. The EU Habitats and Species Directive has a different classification, which has been used for the UK Biodiversity Action Plan (BAP)[3].

Woodlands in the Marches often do not conform either to NVC categories or to BAP habitat definitions. This is partly because conditions here are different from elsewhere, so we can expect the woodlands to be different. Another reason is that discrete types of habitat or community do not exist and instead the variation is a multidimensional continuum, admittedly with particular parts of the continuum more commonly found than others. This pattern of variation is reflected in the ordination of woodland stands that was carried out during the research for the *Ecological Flora of the Shropshire Region*.[4] The results are fascinating but do not reveal distinct woodland types, even in the restricted area covered. So, without attempting to reclassify the unclassifiable, this chapter will attempt to tease out relationships between underlying rock, soil type, topography, altitude, climate and the type of woodland that prevails. Only natural or semi-natural areas will be considered and initially only common plants that are useful indicators of particular conditions will be mentioned. Woodlands on the well-drained sites are considered first, in order of increasing soil fertility, followed by woodlands on waterlogged soils.

SESSILE OAK WOODLAND

The ability of trees to grow almost anywhere in the Marches is illustrated by the oaks that cling to the steep upper slopes of hills, where the soils are thin, sharply drained and acidic. The acidity is mainly due to the underlying rock on these sites. There is a variety of these rocks in the Marches: Precambrian rhyolite and granophyre, as well as Ordovician and Triassic sandstones. The surface layers of soil are more acidic than the deeper horizons, because calcium and other bases are leached downwards, causing the formation of podzols or acid brown podzolic soils. Sessile oak dominates and pedunculate oak is rarely found. Silver birch

Betula pendula is usually present in these woodlands in the Marches, whereas further west into Wales there would usually be downy birch instead. This type of sessile oak woodland is about as dissimilar from tropical rainforest with its many layers as it is possible to get. There is little or no understorey of smaller trees or shrubs. Rowan and holly *Ilex aquifolium* may be components of a shrub layer, but more usually they are part of the main canopy. Usually there are signs of long periods of past coppicing, with the larger stools of oak 1 m or more wide and with multiple trunks, sometimes numbering as many as eight to ten. Coppicing is now rarely practised, so the oaks grow to their maximum height. This height varies, but where the soils are thinnest and the exposure to wind is greatest on the crests of the slopes, it can be little more than 2 or 3 m. The woodland in such sites has a true upland feel, as one would experience when not far below the tree line. Growth of moss is typically patchier, both on the ground and on trunks, than in woodland further west where conditions are more humid and epiphytic mosses are luxuriant. The large pale hummocks of *Leucobryum* seen in the west make a rare appearance here in the form of *Leucobryum juniperoideum*.

The sparse canopy of tree foliage allows a heathy ground flora to develop that is similar to the moorland hilltops. Wavy hair-grass is frequently present, often accompanied by creeping soft-grass and annual common cow-wheat. The latter plant parasitises these grasses using its haustoria, but also photosynthesises so is regarded as a hemiparasite. Bilberry, ling heather, wood sage *Teucrium scorodonia*, heath bedstraw and scattered fronds of bracken are also often present (Fig. 129).

This is a rather exclusive company of trees, herbs and mosses. There are several possible reasons. The poor acid soils and sharp drainage exclude many species. Most sites have been grazed, eliminating herbs that are intolerant of grazing or trampling. Also, the coppicing cycle excludes woodland species that establish slowly and do not tolerate the open conditions immediately after coppicing, or grazing where it is allowed. The dominance of oak may be due to its relative tolerance of soils deficient in nitrogen and phosphorus. Another possible explanation is the elimination over long time periods of undesirable tree species, as part of the management of the coppiced woodland.

Good examples of heathy sessile oak woodland are to be found at Dale Coppice and Oilhouse Coppice, both in Ironbridge Gorge. Other examples are at Resting Hill, which is part of Stiperstones National Nature Reserve, or NNR, on the northwest side of the Ercall and upper parts of Lurkenhope near Knighton, both of which are parts of Shropshire Wildlife Trust reserves. In the NVC, these areas of woodland are closest to the W16 type (*Quercus* spp.-*Betula* spp.-*Deschampsia flexuosa* woodland). Some Marches woodlands show features of more westerly sessile oak woodland – the W17 type (*Quercus petraea-Betula pubescens-Dicranum*

FIG 129. W16 sessile oak woodland with a heath-type ground flora at Lurkenhope near Knighton, now a Shropshire Wildlife Trust reserve. (Sarah Bierley)

majus woodland), an example of which is Woodhampton Wood, in northwest Herefordshire. The upper parts of Oaks Wood near Habberley have been described as intermediate between W16 and W17. The latter two sites can only visited by permission of the owners but there are similar areas nearby in Montgomeryshire that are Wildlife Trust reserves and can be visited.

MIXED DECIDUOUS WOODLANDS DOMINATED BY OAK

Oak is still the commonest tree in these woodlands, but conditions are less harsh and wavy hair-grass is replaced as the dominant part of the ground flora, usually by brambles *Rubus fruticosus*. This indicates that soils are deeper, with a little more nitrogen and phosphate and less tendency to drought. These conditions are often found lower down on slopes, on level ground or where slopes are less steep. Soils are still well drained but are not podzolised. They are acidic, but rather less so than those of heathy oak woodland and are classified as brown earths. Typical underlying rocks are the Ordovician quartzite and Silurian siltstones of south Shropshire and Herefordshire, the Carboniferous shales and sandstones of southeast Shropshire's Coal Measures and the Devonian red sandstones of Herefordshire. Suitable soils are found widely in the Marches but as they are reasonably fertile, there is far more farmland on them than woodland. Oak is frequent, sometimes with ash and sycamore. Holly, rowan, hazel *Corylus avellana* and hawthorn *Crataegus monogyna* are typical of the understorey. Honeysuckle *Lonicera periclymenum* climbs where it can, but ivy is usually absent. Bracken is still present, typically in denser stands than in the oakwoods described above, but there are also brambles, often in large quantity. A variety of other herbs can be present, including bluebells, wood anemone *Anemone nemorosa*, wood millet *Milium effusum*, tufted hair-grass *Deschampsia cespitosa*, wood-sorrel *Oxalis acetosella*, climbing corydalis *Ceratocapnos claviculata* and broad buckler fern *Dryopteris dilatata* (Fig. 130).

These woodlands are generally placed in NVC category W10 (*Quercus robur-Pteridium aquilinum-Rubus fruticosa* woodland). In the Marches both pedunculate and sessile oak can be present, as well as hybrids showing characteristics of both species. Oak has effectively been a crop in these woodlands and so selection of species and characteristics has been artificial to a large extent for centuries. There have been suggestions that pedunculate oak, grown from imported seed, was widely planted in the late 19th and early 20th centuries. It would be interesting to know more about the origin and distribution of both the species and hybrids. DNA profiling would probably throw new light on what is currently

FIG 130. W10 sessile oak woodland on the eastern side of the Ercall, near Telford.

a rather murky area. Among the many examples of mixed deciduous woodland dominated by oak are: parts of Poles Coppice, a reserve owned by the County Council at the north end of the Stiperstones; the east side of the Ercall, which is a Shropshire Wildlife Trust reserve; Lady Wood in Ironbridge Gorge; and Clay Vallet Wood near Lingen, a Herefordshire Nature Trust reserve.

Further south and east through England and across Europe, we would expect hornbeam *Carpinus betula* to be present as a part of this type of woodland, but it is considered not to be native in the Marches so must have been planted where it is present. It is nonetheless present in some areas of ancient woodland, for example the upper reaches of Lydebrook dingle. This is not the only tree species that has been planted on sites where mixed deciduous woodland dominated by oak would naturally be present. There are some very attractive areas of mature beech woodland *Fagus sylvatica*, including those examples on Wenlock Edge and on the Croft Castle estate. Despite its not being native, beech regenerates here. If summers become warmer and drier in the future, beech woodland may actually thrive better in the Marches than in the areas further south and west where it is regarded as truly native. Sweet chestnut *Castanea sativa* was planted in the past on some sites and coppiced. These sites have almost all now become what is known as stored coppice, with one or two large chestnut trunks allowed to develop from each of the coppiced stools, for example at Farley Coppice near Buildwas and Stanway Coppice on Wenlock Edge.

Some sessile oak woodlands that failed to fit into the W16 type also differ from W10 and can be regarded as intermediate between the two. Examples include semi-natural woodland on the tops of Permian sandstone hills of north Shropshire and Cheshire, for example Bickerton and Peckforton Hills, and also large parts of the plateau of Wyre.

MIXED DECIDUOUS WOODLANDS DOMINATED BY ASH

Continuing the trend of increasing fertility, we now move to areas of freely drained base-rich soils. These occur typically on sloping ground, especially on the lower parts of the slopes. In the Marches, the underlying rock types are Silurian limestones and calcareous shales, Devonian marls and Carboniferous limestones. The soils on these sites are classified as brown calcareous earths or clayey brown earths. The surface layers tend to dry out during the summer and be rewetted in autumn, causing clay minerals to be leached downwards. These soils are deeper and have more moisture available at depth than those of the previous woodland types, so a greater variety of trees can thrive. This, together with differences in management, explains the variable nature of these woodlands. Ash usually forms a significant part of the canopy. Sessile oak is often present too but, although typically a more significant component than in similar woodland to the north and west, it is not usually dominant. Pure pedunculate oak is rarely found, unlike similar woodland communities to south and east, but there are sometimes oaks showing some pedunculate ancestry. Both large-leaved and small-leaved limes may be present as native species, sometimes in stands of many individuals. Small-leaved lime occasionally dominates whole woodlands. Wych elm is very frequent but large trees are now rare and this species tends to be a member of the understorey, repeatedly growing, dying back and regenerating. Field maple *Acer campestre* is sometimes present and sycamore is frequent – indeed so well naturalised that it seems hard to believe that it could have been introduced as recently as the 16th century. The prominence of sycamore in these woodlands in the Marches is an indication that the climate here is wetter than to the south and east, where this species is less frequent. Silver birch is often scattered through, where there have been gaps in the canopy from wind-thrown trees. Pure stands of silver birch are sometimes found where this type of woodland has been felled and not replanted. Birch recolonises quickly, but in time would almost certainly be replaced by ash. Yew *Taxus baccata* and field maple are also often found as a part of the understorey rather than the canopy. Wild service-tree *Sorbus torminalis* and crab apple *Malus sylvestris* may be dotted through. Wild cherry *Prunus avium*, celebrated by Housman in *A Shropshire Lad*, is quick to establish but being short lived and shade intolerant, it is rare in mature stands (Fig. 131).

The shrub layer is denser than in the previous woodland types, with hazel as the commonest element, but also dogwood *Cornus sanguinea*, guelder-rose *Viburnum opulus*, goat willow *Salix caprea*, spindle *Euonymus europaeus* and spurge-laurel *Daphne laureola*. Hawthorn is often present and sometimes arborescent, with single dominant trunks growing to 10 m or more. Where elder *Sambucus nigra* is found the soil is likely to have been enriched by starling roosts or a badger sett. The herb layer is richer than in oak woodland and very variable, but it usually contains dog's mercury *Mercurialis perennis*, often in abundance, with herb robert also reliably present. Enchanter's-nightshade *Circaea lutetiana*, early dog-violet *Viola reichenbachiana*, lords-and-ladies *Arum maculatum* and sanicle *Sanicula europaea* are good indicators of this type of woodland; woodland orchids and herb-paris *Paris quadrifolia* are also associated with it. Hart's-tongue *Phyllitis scolopendrium* is more often present than in similar woodlands to the south and east. Ivy *Hedera helix* often carpets the woodland floor and climbs successfully up many trunks. There is some evidence of its increase in the Marches, perhaps in response to warmer winters. Bluebells are often present if there is good drainage

FIG 131. W8 Mixed deciduous woodland with bluebells and ramsons at Beechfield Dingle, near Worthen. (Mark Duffell)

and the shade is not too deep. In contrast, ramsons *Allium ursinum* is found where the soil is deeper and moister, especially towards the bottom of slopes.

In pockets that become waterlogged in winter, anaerobic conditions allow bacteria to reduce metal ions in the soil, especially iron. The reduced ions being more soluble and mobile then migrate through the soil. Rusty-red spots or streaks appear when the soil dries in summer, because the iron and other metals are reoxidised. This process is called gleying. It usually happens at depths of 150–300 mm in the brown earths under woodlands in the Marches. Tufted hair-grass is an indicator of these gleyed woodland soils.

There are many examples of mixed deciduous woodland in the Marches, especially on Wenlock Edge and in the hills to the west of Oswestry, including the east side of Llanymynech Hill. There is another area on the east side of Earl's Hill near Pontesbury. Mere Hill Wood near Aymestrey and Fishpool Valley at Croft Castle are examples in northwest Herefordshire. The woodlands of Benthall Edge Wood and Tick Wood in the Ironbridge Gorge are important sites, having substantial populations of large-leaved lime that are regenerating from seed.

These and other similar woodlands are usually assigned to the NVC category W8 (*Fraxinus excelsior-Acer campestre-Mercurialis perennis* woodland), though sessile oak and wych elm are sometimes both present, and this is not expected in W8. Some stands contain rowan, for example on Wenlock Edge, which is also not being expected in ash-dominated W8 woodland on limy soils. Further west in Wales, rowan would usually form a significant part of ash-dominated woodlands, but these are classified as W9 (*Fraxinus excelsior-Sorbus aucuparia-Mercurialis perennis* woodland) rather than W8. There are a few sites in the Marches that could be regarded as W9 woodland, including Worns Wood in the Unk Valley near Clun, part of Big Wood on the Halston estate near Oswestry and part of Lower Woodhouse near Knighton, all in private ownership. However, where rowan is present in the Marches there is usually also field maple, which is not expected in W9 woodland. An example is Stanway Coppice, on Aymestry Limestone near Wilderhope Manor, with areas of mixed rowan and field maple. We should of course not be surprised for woodland types here to be intermediate between those elsewhere, given that the Marches is a region of transitions.

WET WOODLANDS

Waterlogged soils present special challenges to trees and distinctive woodland types develop on them. There are some fine examples in the Marches, showing variations in species composition related to environment and management. Birch is the dominant tree species in some bog woodlands in the Marches, where there are acidic peaty soils with very low concentrations of phosphate and potassium, but alders are almost always present and are usually dominant, even on stagnant waterlogged sites. Alder roots growing below the water table are spongy. The gas that can be squeezed out of them contains more than 15 per cent oxygen by volume, which has diffused from the air above. This oxygen allows aerobic respiration to continue despite the anaerobic conditions. Denitrifying bacteria break down nitrate ions in waterlogged soils. Alders develop root nodules containing nitrogen-fixing bacteria of the genus *Frankia* and so have their own private supply of fixed nitrogen. They therefore gain the competitive advantage over other trees.

Lacustrine alder woodland develops around the margins of the meres in north Shropshire and Cheshire. It has a wonderfully primeval air and can be almost impossible to explore. The underlying soil is peaty, base rich and waterlogged. Alder is dominant but grey willow is often also present, either in the canopy or the shrub layer. Downy birch is sometimes also represented. Ash may be found on drier areas. If any oak is present, it is pedunculate. There are often large areas of bare peaty soil, which may be flooded for part or all of the year. The alders often rise out of the water or waterlogged peat on small eminences, formed by a fringe of strut roots arising from near the base of the trunk, which have a mangrove-like appearance (see Fig. 101). These roots have been taken to indicate a falling water table caused by artificial drainage and consequent soil shrinkage or loss of peat. However, they are in fact adventitious roots, which stabilise the tree in soft unstable peat and absorb oxygen by growing at or close to the water table. Otters have built holts in these large alder bases around Aqualate Mere and elsewhere in the Marches, although on riverbanks the less dense root systems of ash and sycamore are favoured over alder.

When a ground flora is present in lacustrine alder woodland, it is usually dominated by some spectacular species of swamp vegetation, including greater tussock-sedge. Lesser pond-sedge and yellow iris *Iris pseudacorus* are often present. Broad buckler fern and marsh fern are abundant on some sites, for example Wybunbury Moss NNR. Characteristic dicotyledons are marsh-marigold *Caltha palustris*, bittersweet and common nettle *Urtica dioica*. Both red and black currants *Ribes rubrum* and *Ribes nigrum* are often present, and though they are usually regarded as escapees from cultivation, it has been argued that they could both be native in the Marches. In 1841 Leighton recorded black currant growing in an apparently wild state at Alkmond Park north of Shrewsbury.[5] It still grows in the alder woodland there, to the east of Park Pool.

There are examples of lacustrine alder woodlands, also known as alder carr, on the east side of Cole Mere, on the north side of Fenemere, and at two sites of significance in the history of ecology – Hencott Pool and Sweat Mere. These woodlands are probably in the NVC category W5 (*Alnus glutinosa-Carex paniculata woodland*).

Riverine alder woodland is found in valley bottoms beside streams and small rivers. Alders are well adapted to survive waterlogged conditions during the periodic floods that occur on these sites. Alluvium is deposited, but alder can tolerate rises in soil level because of its ability to form adventitious roots. Typically, these riverine woodlands are a metre or more above the summer water level in the adjacent watercourse and as the silty soil drains freely, it can dry out when there has been little rainfall. Organic matter therefore decays and peat does not form.

The swamp plants that characterise the peaty alder woodlands are consequently absent or much less frequent (Fig. 132). The herb layer is instead dominated by common nettles, with other plants such as tufted hair-grass. Monk's-hood has recently been shown to be truly native in riverine alder woods in Herefordshire and just across the border into south Shropshire on both the Ledwych Brook and the Gosford Brook, which are tributaries of the Teme[6] (Fig. 133). Other records of this species occurring in different habitats in Shropshire appear to be the hybrid *Aconitum × cammarum*, rather than *A. napellus*. Himalayan balsam is spreading in some riverine alder woods over areas of bare,

FIG 132. W6 riverine alder woodland in Downton Gorge, with deposited silt and stinging nettles.

FIG 133. Monks-hood (left) growing beside the Ledwyche Brook to the west of the Clee hills (Mark Duffell) and bird cherry (above) in flower in damp woodland at Fenn's Bank near Whitchurch.

newly deposited alluvium. Where cattle or sheep are allowed to graze, the natural ground flora is replaced by damp pasture.

There are examples of riverine alder woodland beside many streams and rivers in the Marches, including the Lugg between Mortimer's Cross and Leominster, Dowles Brook in Wyre, and Loamhole Brook in Loamhole Dingle near Ironbridge. They are probably in the NVC category W6 (*Alnus glutinosa-Urtica dioica* woodland). These and other remaining areas are small in comparison with the extensive areas that probably existed in the past, especially on the flood plains of the Severn and its tributaries. Large groves of alders in the Rea valley were felled to provide fuel for the iron industry in the 16th century. Pengwern, the ancient British name for what is now Shrewsbury, means 'place at the end of the alder swamp', but there are now only scattered trees beside the river where it flows through the town. Pollen records from Baggy Moor, near Ruyton XI Towns, show that about 7,000 years ago alder woodland developed across an extensive flood plain on the site of a former lake. This woodland persisted until clearance in Roman times. The Weald Moors, north of Wellington, probably also had many square kilometres of alder woodland.

Further evidence for alder woodland on flood plains comes from a study of cores taken from the flood plain of the Severn between Worcester and Tewkesbury.[7] There was a metre depth of peat, formed over several thousand years by alder carr, starting about 6,000 years ago. The pollen record suggests that woodland dominated by lime occupied the river terraces above the flood plain, until it was cleared by early farmers around 5,500 years ago. At a later date the alder woodland on the flood plain was first coppiced and then cleared 2,500 to 1,000 years ago. Above the peat there is over a metre of silty clay, deposited during floods. Its position above the peat is strong evidence that deforestation and other human activities have caused the soil erosion that results in alluvial deposits such as these. An obvious conclusion is that reforestation is needed, and in particular that large areas of riverine alder woodland should be re-established. There would be environmental benefits for humans in reducing downstream flooding, for wildlife whose habitat is alder carr and also more widely if peat formation with its associated carbon capture restarted.

Another type of alder woodland is found where there are waterlogged mineral soils but little deposition of alluvium. These conditions are found alongside small streams and on sloping ground where moisture levels remain high because of springs, seepages or flushes. There are two types of site in the Marches where suitable conditions are found. The first is on Carboniferous rocks of the Coal Measures, with a complex succession of strata, water draining out through pervious layers overlying impervious ones. The second type of site is found in areas of deep glacial drift deposits, in north Shropshire and Cheshire. Water flows easily through gravelly and sandy strata but not through clays. Where sands and gravels overlie clays there are often springs on valley sides above the clay strata, the spring water then draining down in a flush over the clay. The water is not very base-rich or eutrophic. The woodland on these sites is probably W7 (*Alnus glutinosa-Fraxinus excelsior-Lysimachia nemorum* woodland) according to the NVC. It develops on steeper slopes and higher up on slopes than is usual in other regions of Britain. Alders dominate, but ash is frequent and there can also be birch, usually downy rather than silver. Pedunculate oak may be present in drier areas. The shrub layer is variable, depending on wetness. Hawthorn, hazel, elder, blackthorn *Prunus spinosa* and rowan are found in drier regions; elsewhere there is guelder rose, grey willow and sometimes an abundance of bird cherry *Prunus padus* (Fig. 134). The herb layer is often diverse too with yellow flag, pendulous sedge *Carex pendula*, remote sedge *Carex remota*, common nettles, brambles, marsh-marigolds, large bitter-cress *Cardamine amara*, yellow pimpernel *Lysimachia nemorum* and great horsetail *Equisetum telmateia*.

Because of the dense growth of plants and the wet soil, these woodlands tend to be difficult to traverse, rights of way have not developed and many are rarely visited, despite being beautiful. They can form wonderful refuges for wildlife in areas that are primarily agricultural. Some might argue that beauty is wasted if unseen by humans, but these alder woodlands are very delicate sites, so perhaps it is best in this case not to encourage visitors. There are examples at Weir Coppice,

FIG 134. W7 alder
woodland near
Whitchurch with bird
cherry in the shrub
layer.

near Hook-a-gate and in the woodland between the Ercall and New Works. There are also superb examples to the west and north of Whitchurch, as well as in the base of some batches in the hill country of the Marches.

A fourth type of alder woodland in the Marches is neither lacustrine nor riverine. It is found instead in depressions or other low-lying areas on plateaux, where there is a thin layer of peaty soil. This is W4 downy birch–purple moor-grass woodland according to the NVC. Birches are indeed usually present with the alders, but silver birch is much commoner than downy in the Marches. Purple moor-grass is not always present, in which case NVC classification seems like opting for bacon and eggs for breakfast without the bacon, or the eggs. The two *Sphagnum* species, *S. palustre* and *S. fallax*, are characteristic, as is tufted hair-grass and lesser skull-cap. There are examples on the summit plateau of Haughmond Hill and the floor of an abandoned quarry at Poles Coppice, at the north end of the Stiperstones. As alder seeds have air bladders, which aid water dispersal, it is perhaps surprising that these alder woodlands exist away from either flowing or standing water.

Where there is a greater depth of peat, with lower pH and mineral nutrient concentrations, birches replace alders. This is bog woodland, as defined in EU documents. Bog woodlands can be found in kettle holes and other basins, which abound in the landscape of north Shropshire, Cheshire and parts of northwest Herefordshire. The existence of woodland in bogs is rather paradoxical, as the acidity, lack of nutrients and anaerobic waterlogged conditions normally prevent the growth of trees. Indeed, actively growing bogs or mires can kill trees by palludification. Trees are nevertheless invading some mosses in the Marches. The invading species is often silver birch rather than downy birch, with Scots pine too if there is a nearby seed source. Trees can start to invade if artificial drainage reduces the water table of the mosses and the peat dries out. Conservationists regard this process as undesirable but find that removal of trees is only a very temporary solution and that there is rapid reinvasion unless the peat is rewetted at the same time. Continued tree growth causes further drying of the peat and other species including pedunculate oak can then invade. Purple moor-grass is often present in the herb layer but broad buckler fern or bracken can also be dominant. If *Sphagnum* is present, it is usually the woodland species *S. fimbriatum, S. squarrosum* and *S. palustre*.

The birch-dominated bog woodland that currently exists in the Marches all seems to be on sites where the water table has been lowered by artificial drainage. An example is the birch woodland at Sweat Mere, which Tansley wrongly described as part of a natural hydrosere.[8] There are similar areas at Wybunbury Moss in the southern and eastern drained sections and around the margins of Fenn's, Whixall and Bettisfield Mosses, where deep ditches show that there has been artificial drainage. There was an example at Shomere, in the Bomere complex of kettle holes. Evidence from the 8.5 m depth of peat at this site indicates a classic development from mere to moss. Succession to bog woodland occurred relatively recently though there is no natural outfall for artificial drains, so the causes of drying are not obvious. Much of this woodland has now been removed, as it has at Bettisfield Moss, showing that bold conservation measures can reverse decades of habitat degradation. Clearance of bog woodland should be carried out at Wybunbury and probably at all areas where it currently occurs in the Marches.

SCARCE PLANTS OF MARCHES WOODLANDS

The plants mentioned so far in this chapter have been the stalwarts – typical plant species that form abundant food sources for herbivores and allow recognition of particular woodland communities. There are other species that are notable because of their scarcity. Some species are scarce in the Marches because they are at the edge of their range, but are commoner in adjacent areas, so need not be as much of a conservation priority as species that are scarce or declining elsewhere. An example is herb-paris, which has been lost from many sites in Britain but still occurs in many ancient woodlands of Herefordshire and south Shropshire (Fig. 135). Lily-of-the-valley is naturalised in woodland in

FIG 135. Herb Paris in fruit on Wenlock Edge (left) and narrow-leaved helleborine in Wyre forest (right). (Rosemary Winnall)

parts of Britain, but local botanists regard it as native in at least some parts of the Marches, including sites in Wyre and northwest Herefordshire. Spreading bellflower *Campanula patula* grows in open woodland and is a speciality of the southern Marches, spreading up into north Herefordshire. Common wintergreen *Pyrola minor*, a charming but unassuming plant, occurs in woodland in north Herefordshire. It was recently rediscovered in Wyre, growing in woodland along a disused railway track, one of the characteristic habitats for this species. Lesser hairy-brome grass *Bromopsis benekenii* is very scarce in Britain but has one site in Horton Hollow on Wenlock Edge. Narrow-leaved helleborine orchid *Cephalanthera longifolia* declined markedly in the 19th and 20th centuries in Britain. It has disappeared from some sites, but still occurs in woodland on limestone near Ironbridge. It also persists in a number of parts of Wyre where there were deer lawns in the past that were limed, making the soils less acidic than is typical in this area. Coppicing may have suited it very well in the past at Wyre. It was recently refound in oak woodland with bracken at a site just to the west of Offa's Dyke in Montgomeryshire. Two other rare helleborines occur on parts of Wenlock Edge, but not elsewhere in the Marches: narrow-lipped *Epipactis leptochila* and green-flowered helleborines *Epipactis phyllanthes*. Both favour areas of moderately dense woodland, where there is an abundant ground cover of mosses, but other potential competitor plants are shaded out. Although the sites occupied are ancient woodland, they have often been disturbed, for example by quarrying. Both orchids appear only sporadically and there is a strong possibility that they can be fed underground by their mycorrhizal fungi for one or more years, when there is insufficient light available in shady woodland for productive photosynthesis.

Three other scarce species of Marches woodland have evolved to be permanently freed from the need to obtain light: yellow bird's nest *Monotropa hypopitys*, bird's-nest orchid *Neottia nidus-avis* and ghost orchid *Epipogium aphyllum*. They are so rarely found that they have achieved almost mythical status (Fig. 136). Each of them occasionally produces brownish or yellowish flowering stems. They contain little or no chlorophyll, and use rhizomes or roots to obtain nutrients saprotrophically from leaf litter. Toothwort and broomrapes are superficially similar, but they are root parasites rather than saprotrophs. Yellow bird's nest pops up sporadically in woodland on shallow limestone soils and tends to be recorded for a few years and then disappear. The most recent find was on mine spoil, under mature goat willow, which resembles its alternative dune slack habitat. Yellow bird's nest has not been seen for some years but is very easily missed and is probably still present in the Marches. Bird's nest orchid is recorded a little more frequently in north Herefordshire and south Shropshire. It is found in woodland on limestone, particularly where there is deep leaf litter and dense shade. The ghost orchid is the most elusive of the three and has only ever been

FIG 136. Woodland plants without chlorophyll: (a) yellow bird's nest (Kate Thorne); (b) ghost orchid (Stephanie Thompson); and (c) bird's-nest orchid (John Robinson).

recorded in Britain in the Chilterns and in the Marches. The original site in the Marches was Upper Evens, a part of what is now known as the Mortimer Forest. It was recorded there three times between 1876 and 1892. The ghost orchid was found again at Haugh Wood in Herefordshire in September 1982.[9] A single stem produced two flowers. There then followed a 23-year period during which there was increasing concern that there would never be another sighting, but in 2009 a single stem with one flower was discovered at an undisclosed location – a most welcome apparition!

WOODLAND BIRDS

Deciduous woodland typically has large numbers of breeding birds. Some species are almost ubiquitous, such as robin *Erithacus rubecula*, chaffinch *Fringilla coelebs*, great tit *Parus major* and wren *Troglodytes troglodytes*.[10] Others are only found in certain woodland types, for example willow tits *Poecile montana* in wet woodland of birch, alder or willow, where there is standing rotten timber and nest holes can be excavated. Marsh tits *Poecile palustris* also favour carr. They are more common than willow tits in the Marches and are dominant, often taking their nest holes. Buzzards are now a very common sight and their calls an almost ever-present sound in rural parts of the Marches. They often nest in woodland trees. Red kites are now breeding again in woodland of north Herefordshire and south Shropshire.

Three species are regarded as indicators of typical sessile oak woodland with upland character: pied flycatcher *Ficedula hypoleuca*, redstart and wood warbler *Phylloscopus sibilatrix*. Pied flycatchers were at the eastern edge of their range in the Marches during the 19th century, but they have spread further across Shropshire and Herefordshire and there is now a strong population, in contrast to some other areas of Britain. They are a very characteristic presence in upland oak woodlands from May to August, breeding naturally in tree holes, but often preferring nest boxes, if available. Many boxes have been put up in Wyre, in the Clun valley, the Upper Onny valley and in Shobden Hill and Mary Knoll woods in northwest Herefordshire. Redstarts are also summer visitors and tree hole nesters, but they prefer more open deciduous woodland than pied flycatchers, or even isolated trees (Fig. 137). Their population in the Marches is stronger than in many parts of Britain. Wood warblers are summer visitors that particularly favour the oak woods of the Marches, especially where there is a dense canopy and an open forest floor, with few shrubs, brambles or bracken. Mixed woodlands with conifers and broadleaves are also attractive as long as there is 10 per cent or

FIG 137. Birds of upland woodland, photographed in Wyre: (a) wood warbler; (b) pied flycatcher; and (c) redstart. (John Robinson)

more of broadleaves. Sloping sites are preferred with as few humans as possible, especially dog walkers, as wood warblers are ground nesters and sensitive to disturbance.

INSECTS IN WOODLAND

The diversity of insects in Marches woodland is immense, including bugs, flies, bees, wasps, ants and above all beetles. Peter Thompson, founder of Kew's seed bank, recorded 253 species when as a retirement project he trapped and identified macromoths every night for a year in the wooded valley where he lived at Horderley in South Shropshire.[11] Over 1,200 species of lepidoptera have now been recorded in Wyre, the fourth longest list in Britain, with only the New Forest, Portland Bill and Dungeness having more. Some of these species are nationally rare, including the alder kitten, angle-striped sallow, common fanfoot and great oak beauty. Among the rare beetles in the Marches is *Pyrrhidium sanguineum*, the Welsh oak longhorn beetle, with its strikingly bright red coloration. It was originally known only from Moccas Park in the Wye Valley but was then found in the Forest of Dean. In the 1980s it was found in northwest Herefordshire in Brampton Bryan Park and near Llanvairwaterdine.[12] The larvae feed on dead oak at the bark–wood interface, making tunnels parallel to the grain of the wood. Branches with a diameter of between 150 and 300 mm are preferred. It turns up occasionally in fuel wood; over 300 emerged recently from a batch of logs from an unknown source delivered to a family near Clun.

We might not anticipate finding caddis flies in woodland, but one species in Britain has terrestrial larvae, *Enoicycla pusilla*, which was discovered in Wyre in the 19th century. Norman Hickin refound it in the 20th century.[13] The population in Wyre is still strong and it is now known from other woodland sites in Warwickshire and adjacent counties, but not elsewhere in Britain[14] (Fig. 138). Ninety species of cranefly have been found in Shropshire woodlands, many with very specific requirements.[15]

The predominant species of wood ant in the Marches is *Formica rufa*. It is common throughout Wyre and other forests, especially on the edge of woodland paths where these face south. A species of wood ant with a more northerly distribution is *Formica lugubris*. Its most southerly site in Britain is in woodland on the west side of Stiperstones in an area of old oak coppice. It appears to be

FIG 138. The land caddis of Wyre, *Enoicycla pusilla*, as a larva (Rosemary Winnall) and adult (Harry Green).

benefiting from the extra light and warmth that penetrates recoppiced areas. *Formica rufa* nests as large as 1.8 m in diameter and 0.7 m high have been found in Wyre. *Formica lugubris* colonies are rather smaller, but are still substantial structures. The warmth and food supplies offered by these nests are attractive to other species. The shining guest ant *Formicoxenus nitidulus* has been found in wood ant nests in Wyre and may occur elsewhere.[16] It lives in small colonies within the nest, obtaining food from the wood ants either by soliciting or stealing, but is nevertheless rarely attacked (Fig. 139). Wingless males and winged females emerge to mate on the surface of the nest in late summer and early autumn, which is therefore the best time to search for them. The females fly off after mating to establish colonies in new wood ant nests. The relationship between the guest ant and its host has been described as commensalism by some authors and parasitism by others. The deciding factor is whether the guest does harm to its host. As the guests take food that the host workers collected and would have fed to host larvae or adults there does seem to be some harm done. A clearer case is seen with the blood-red slave-making ant *Formica sanguinea*. This nationally scarce ant is found in Wyre and carries out raids on the colonies of black ants, either *Formica fusca* or *F. lemani*, carrying worker larvae and pupae back to their own nest where they rear them along with their own young. When the black ant workers emerge from their pupae they help with foraging and other tasks.

Among species of butterfly, there are two that inhabit the canopy of mature broadleaved woodland. Purple hairstreaks *Neozephyrus quercus* are handsome butterflies that are quite common in the Marches, but rarely observed. The larvae feed on oak flowers and adults tend to remain high in the canopy of oak trees, where they can obtain energy from honeydew. White-letter hairstreaks *Satyrium w-album* have a similar habitat but in elm rather than oak. This species, close to the western edge of its distribution in the Marches, declined as Dutch elm

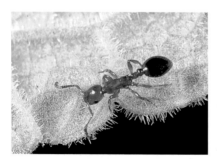 

FIG 139. Ants of Wyre: the shining guest ant (left) and the blood-red slave-making ant (right). (John Bingham)

disease spread. Other butterflies live at lower levels in woodland. White admirals *Limenitis camilla*, silver washed fritillaries *Argynnis paphia* and speckled wood butterflies *Pararge aegeria* all occur in the Marches and adults can be seen taking nectar from bramble flowers along rides and in glades. White admiral larvae feed on honeysuckle in shady woodland. This species only just reaches the Marches but it is increasing in Wyre and has also been recorded a little further north in Chorley Covert. Silver washed fritillaries are large and beautiful butterflies that are being found more and more widely in the Marches. They require broadleaved woodland with not only shady areas containing dog-violets to feed the larvae, but also clearings or rides where adults can find nectar. This species has a southern range in Britain, explaining why warmer oak woodland sites on south-facing slopes and sites with gaps in the canopy are favoured. Speckled woods were once scarce in the Marches but have become widespread and common. The larvae feed on grasses in woodland, such as false brome *Brachypodium sylvaticum* and cock's-foot *Dactylis glomerata*. Adults feed on honeydew in the canopy of trees.

Small pearl-bordered fritillaries, pearl-bordered fritillaries *Boloria euphrosyne* and wood whites *Leptidea sinapis*are are all characteristic of woodland margins, rides and areas of temporary open space within managed woodland. All of these species have disappeared from former parts of their ranges in much of central and eastern England, but they have fared relatively well in the Marches (Fig. 140). Wood whites are at the northwest edge of a range that extends far to the south and east through Europe. They were only known in the Marches from a handful of sites during much of the 20th century, but latterly have been increasing both in

FIG 140. Woodland butterflies: wood whites courting (left) and a pearl-bordered fritillary (above). (Danny Beath)

numbers and in the number of occupied sites, particularly in the Clun valley. Bury Ditches in south Shropshire and Wigmore Rolls in northwest Herefordshire are two strongholds. These are both Forestry Commission conifer plantations. Efforts are being made to increase the amount of suitable habitat, with rides expanded from a typical width of about 4 m, to as much as 15 m, particularly on south-facing slopes. This allows in more light and encourages growth of the larval food plants – meadow vetchling *Lathyrus pratensis* and bird's-foot-trefoil. The vegetation is cut along approximately 10 km of rides to prevent scrub invasion. This was initially done on a four-year rotation, but birch and willow growth was found to be excessive by the fourth year, so a three-year rotation has been adopted. Wood whites can travel along the widened rides and extend their population range. Small pearl-bordered fritillaries can be seen in glades and clearings in Wyre. This is at the western limit for woodland populations of this species, though further west it occurs in rush pastures. The closely related pearl-bordered fritillary has suffered a catastrophic decline nationally, but it still has one of its most important national strongholds in Wyre. Conservation involves ensuring that both larval and adult food plants are available.[17] Violets are the larval food plant and these are most abundant in recently coppiced or cleared areas of woodland. The pearl-bordered fritillary clearly benefits from the active management of woodland, the demise of which during the 20th century helps to explain this butterfly's plight.

COPPICING

The traditional management for most oak woodland in the Marches was coppicing. This was a major activity on many estates during the winter months. For example, over 100 men were employed in coppice woods on the Bateman estate at Shobden in northwest Herefordshire in the 18th century. Cordwood from coppices was used as a fuel, either directly or after making into charcoal, and bark was used by the tanning industry. Although demand for coppice products continued through the 19th century, it was by then declining and coppicing had all but died out by the Great War. The resultant changes in woodland had major consequences for many species, including the butterflies described earlier and also birds.[18] There have been experimental attempts to re-establish a programme of coppicing in some areas. The Greenwood Centre was set up in the late 1980s in Coalbrookdale, one of its main aims being to promote coppicing. Some of the few coppice workers who had kept traditional methods alive have passed on their skills in short courses organised by the trust and an apprenticeship scheme has also been developed. After some very lean decades, there are more coppices being cut commercially each winter.

Coppicing has also been reintroduced for conservation reasons, with variable but generally beneficial results. The most substantial recent programme has been in Wyre. There have been smaller scale trials in several nature reserves. An area of old oak coppice at Resting Hill, part of Stiperstones NNR, was recoppiced in 1992, partly in the hope that tree species diversity would increase. Oak regrew strongly from the cut stools and in 15 years formed a closed canopy, with a height of over 5 m (Fig. 141). There was some initial growth of brambles and bracken but the ground flora has since returned to its previous state, dominated by wavy hairgrass. Grazing had been excluded from 1984, but there was still no recruitment of tree species other than oak, either before or after coppicing. Other areas were coppiced in 2005, again with grazing prevented. Seedlings of silver birch have appeared in these areas and it seems likely that some of these may grow quickly enough to join the oaks in the canopy that develops. Experimental plots have been cut at Clunton Coppice, a Shropshire Wildlife Trust reserve in the Clun Valley. Deer grazing damaged oak regrowth, and bracken grew strongly, outcompeting the weakened oak. Small sapling oaks were planted and protected by

FIG 141. Sessile oak coppice re-growth with sparse W16 ground flora, at Resting Hill in Stiperstones National Nature Reserve.

plastic tubes but were also killed by deer. Subsequent coppicing has had to be protected by fenced exclosures, which has allowed successful oak regrowth. The finding that grazing animals must initially be excluded is of course not a new one and it was a standard part of coppice management in the past for hedges or barriers made of dead brushwood to be used to 'protect the spring' for between four and seven years.

WOODLAND MAMMALS

In comparison to many other parts of the world, there are rather few mammal species in Marches woodland. Hedgehog *Erinaceus europaeus*, common shrews, pygmy shrews and moles *Talpa europaea* are present, but none of these species can be regarded as woodland specialists because they inhabit other habitats and there is little local data about them in the Marches. The rodents of woodland are grey squirrels *Sciurus carolinensis*, bank voles, wood mice, yellow-necked mice *Apodemus flavicollis* and dormice. Common rats *Rattus norvegicus* may be more abundant than generally recognised, as they are not caught in small mammal traps and are very rarely the focus of research. As elsewhere in England and Wales, wood mice are the most abundant and widespread rodent species in woodland, but bank voles are also present in large numbers in many woods. Yellow-necked mice have a more restricted and rather unusual distribution (Fig. 142). They were found in all the sites where trapping was carried out in Herefordshire and

FIG 142. Yellow-necked mouse. (Gareth Thomas)

Shropshire during a survey in the 1990s, but not at any sites in Cheshire.[19] They were also absent from Wales and central England. Relative abundance was higher in the Marches population than anywhere else in Britain, for reasons that are not clear. Mixed deciduous woodland dominated by oak or ash seems to be the most suitable type. Woodland of ancient origin is more likely to be inhabited by yellow-necked mice than newer plantations; managed woodland is favoured over unmanaged and old coppice over new. Yellow-necked mice are more frequent in woodland with relatively small amounts of ivy on trees, but this and the other findings are mere correlations. Further research is needed to find the actual determinants of the distribution and aspects of the Marches that suit yellow-necked mice so well.

The other native species of rodent found in woodland in the Marches is the dormouse. Dormouse sites extend further north in the Marches than in Wales or most of England to the east. It has been found in sites scattered throughout Herefordshire, whilst of more than 50 sites surveyed in Shropshire from the late 1990s onwards, dormice have been found on nearly half. A north–south transect of sites in the Marches showed an abrupt decrease in dormouse abundance between south and north Shropshire.[20] There are of course populations much further north in Cumbria and Northumberland and a population has also been successfully established in the Wych Valley in southwest Cheshire. Fifty-four captive-bred adults were released in 1996–7. They have increased to over 100 with the help of 250 nest boxes, and have now spread westwards into adjacent parts of Wales. Habitat rather than climate is therefore likely to be excluding dormice from some areas.

Broadleaved woodland with oak, hazel, brambles and honeysuckle has usually been regarded as ideal, but populations have also been found in conifer plantations on ancient woodland sites, for example Aston Common in Mortimer Forest and Radnor Woods. A programme of research into dormice and conifers in Ribbesford Wood, to the south of Wyre, began with the finding of a single dead individual in the 1980s. A variety of conifer species had been planted in the 1970s after clear-felling a previous conifer crop, though broadleaved trees remained along ride edges. Thirty nest boxes were put up in 1993 to find out if the single dead individual had been part of a viable population. In the following year, 12 dormice were found in them, including juveniles. Further nest boxes were put up and in 1997, a peak number of 96 dormice was found in the 300 nest boxes then installed. Intensive nest boxing, with the boxes at 20 m × 20 m intervals in 17 ha of plantation, confirmed that dormice are indeed able to thrive in areas of conifers with little or no oak, hazel or fruiting brambles. The home range of individual dormice was studied using radio transmitters. This was found to be about 1 ha, an area similar to that in broadleaved woodlands, suggesting that the quantity of suitable food was also similar. The scarcity of hazel nuts and bramble fruits seemed to be compensated for by the availability of insects on conifer trees. Bright yellow dormouse faeces was observed in May and June, presumably when male cones containing yellow pollen are being consumed. Radio tracking also showed that a wide variety of hibernation sites were being used, situated just below the leaf litter on the forest floor. Although usually considered to be totally arboreal for most of the year, dormice were found sometimes to venture on to the ground to collect dry grass for nest building. Tracking has shown that an individual typically builds four or five nests and all are used intermittently during the active season. One individual built as many as ten nests during the summer–autumn period. Research began in 2003 to establish how best to return conifer plantations on ancient woodland sites to native broadleaves, while maintaining dormice populations. Nests on the ground are particularly vulnerable during forestry operations. It was found that harvesting machines, which can extract timber at a distance without moving over the whole site, destroy fewer dormouse nests than more labour-intensive methods.

Ironically the rodent species most likely to be seen in Marches woodland is the alien grey squirrel. It was not mentioned in accounts of the fauna of Shropshire and Cheshire at the end of the 19th century and instead red squirrels were common throughout. Red squirrels started to decline after this, before the arrival of greys, despite the common belief that the grey squirrel drove out the red. Infection with parapoxvirus may have been the cause. There was a population of grey squirrels to the west of Welshpool in Montgomeryshire for some years in the first half of the 19th century, but it died out. The first recorded successful introduction in Britain was in 1876 to the park at Henbury Hall in northeast Cheshire and grey squirrels were also released at Rossett near Wrecsam in 1903. Although both of these introductions gave rise to populations that expanded into surrounding areas, most of the Marches was colonised by a much more rapid spread from the southeast.[21] Grey squirrels were in Gloucestershire in the 1920s and had spread north and west to reach Hereford by 1948. They had not been seen in Bringewood near Ludlow in 1951, but arrived by the following year and in subsequent years spread up through Shropshire to merge with the Wrecsam and Cheshire populations. Red squirrels *Sciurus vulgaris* disappeared from the Marches as the greys spread, with the remnants of the population gone by the end of the 1960s. Grey squirrels are now abundant in all areas of woodland, unless actively controlled.

Bats are important members of the woodland community, foraging in the tree canopy and roosting in cracks, holes and crevices in the bark of trees. There is considerable interest in this group, though there is some evidence from a recent distribution atlas of under-recording or under-reporting of records in the Marches, compared with other regions.[22] Bat detectors have made it much easier to study foraging behaviour, but much survey work is done on a fee-paid contract basis and the results are unpublished. Brown long-eared bats *Plecotus auritus* and both pipistrelles, both common and soprano, are often recorded feeding along the woodland edge and in open woodland, but other species are more particularly associated with woodland. Brandt's bats *Myotis brandtii*, whiskered bats *Myotis mystacinus* and Natterer's bats *Myotis nattereri* all feed in woodland habitats and other habitats with trees, but there are also recent records for whiskered and Brandt's bats from open and urban areas in the Marches. This group of bats all roost in tree holes and in buildings and there are almost certainly more roosts than have so far been recorded. This is also the case with noctule bats *Nyctalus noctula*, our largest species. A large pre-maternity roost was recently found in a block of flats at Dothill in Telford that were scheduled for demolition, but are now preserved. The roost is only used for about a month in spring each year. It was one of the first discoveries of a site other than a tree hole or nest box being used by this species. Barbastelles *Barbastella barbastellus* seem to be spreading northwards in the Marches. They are not easy to detect but there have already been a few records, for example from Earl's Hill in Shropshire in 1994 and more recently from Ludlow Castle and other sites in south Shropshire. Their maternity roosts are in trees and they forage over water or in wooded sites within about 250 m of water.

Of the carnivores, stoats and weasels *Mustela nivalis* are common in woodland but are also found widely in other habitats and foxes are opportunists that do use woodlands, but prefer the margins and small wooded areas rather than large tracts. About 20 per cent of badgers' setts are in woodland, usually within 50 m of the edge. A far higher percentage of setts are in hedgerows and most foraging is in grassland. Pine martens *Martes martes* are the only specialist carnivores in Marches woodland. They became locally extinct in the 19th century, but there have been occasional sightings in recent years in both north Herefordshire and the Clun area, so there may now be a small resident population. Pine marten boxes have been set up in some Forestry Commission plantations but have not so far been occupied. There have been reports of large cats in Marches woodland, presumably panthers or lynx. Some country dwellers are adamant that they exist, but there is no firm evidence.

The final group of mammals to be considered is the even-toed ungulates. Wild boar *Sus scrofa* have not yet returned to Marches woodlands so the representatives of this order are all deer. Roe deer *Capreolus capreolus* are the

only extant native species. Their distribution is very patchy and there are large areas where they are absent. As in much of Britain, hunting and deforestation in the Middle Ages caused their disappearance and at the end of the 19th century there were still none present in Shropshire[23] or elsewhere in the Marches.
In the late 1960s, a small group were reintroduced to a conifer plantation in north Herefordshire. They found abundant sources of food and thrived, often producing twins rather than single fawns. They have since spread northwards to Bishop's Castle, south to Shobden and east to Wyre, though they have not yet re-established a large breeding population there. It is impossible accurately to count roe deer, but there are probably about 1,000 in total in north Herefordshire and south Shropshire. Despite the activities of many keen stalkers, numbers will probably continue to rise and their range to expand. Roe deer are more of a woodland species than fallow deer, emerging less frequently to feed on agricultural land. Although essentially shy of humans, they sometimes choose less secluded sites: a pair lived on a traffic island in Telford for a time.

Fallow deer *Dama dama* were introduced by the Normans for hunting in royal forests, so they are not truly native. The Mortimer family established and maintained herds in their deer parks in Herefordshire and Shropshire. Uncontrolled hunting, deforestation and the demise of deer parks in the Middle Ages caused them almost to die out in the Marches, but a group of fallow deer seems to have clung on in the area that we now call the Mortimer Forest. This formed the nucleus for the thriving population that in the 20th century spread out through north Herefordshire and south Shropshire. There are currently an estimated 1,000 fallow deer in this area. There are also populations in deer parks re-established in the 19th century, such as Attingham, Loton Park and Cholmondley. The herd of fallow deer in Wyre probably descends from a mass escape from a park at Mawley Hall in about 1880.

A variety of fallow deer with a winter coat of hair that is twice as long as normal has been known to exist in the Mortimer Forest for centuries.[24] The whole coat is longer than normal in the winter and when it is shed for the summer, long hairs persist on the forehead and on the tails, doubling their apparent length (Fig. 143). This variety was brought to the attention of the scientific community by a Forestry Commission ranger, Gerald Springthorpe, in 1956. It was named in his honour as *Dama dama springthorpii* and has not been discovered anywhere else. Researchers from Reading University set up enclosures in which the mode of inheritance and adaptive value of the long coat could be studied. A dominant allele was found to be responsible, presumably formed by a mutation in one individual and passed on to its descendents. The long hairs were found to be finer and more easily wetted, causing the coat to cling to the skin and

FIG 143. Long-haired fallow deer in Mortimer Forest, with the long hairs showing particularly on the forehead, neck and tail. (Gareth Thomas)

provide less heat insulation. Long-haired fawns had a lower body mass on average than normal short-haired ones, presumably because more of their available energy is used to maintain body temperature. Natural selection therefore favours the commoner short-haired individuals. When fallow deer are culled in Mortimer Forest, long-haired individuals are spared, to maintain them in the population. As some long-haired individuals have lived to an age of 30 or more, it may only be deleterious in fawns, with their high surface area to volume ratio.

Fallow deer will emerge from woodland to feed on grass and herbs and on arable crops. They also browse in woodland on brambles, shrubs and parts of trees within reach, creating a browse line. This is even sometimes seen on yew trees, which are the food source of last resort in winter. Severe damage to deciduous trees is seen in some parts of the Marches, with leaders and lateral branches browsed off and bark stripped by peeling upwards from below. Rubbing antlers against bark, known as thrashing or fraying, can cause further damage. Tree seedlings and coppice regrowth are particularly palatable to fallow deer, so much so that natural regeneration of woodland can be completely prevented.

The ground flora can also be altered considerably with a reduction in brambles and a spread of tufted hair-grass, which is unpalatable. Roe deer also cause damage, but it tends to be less intense, because they are territorial rather than living in herds as fallow deer do.

Reeves' muntjac deer *Muntiacus reevesi* have spread through parts of the Marches and according to some estimates numbers are increasing by about 10 per cent per year, but damage to ground flora does not seem to be severe so far. There are two centres of population, one near Tenbury and another at the north end of Wenlock Edge. Elsewhere reports have been of single young adult males that are probably moving through the Marches in search of a mate. Muntjac deer are territorial but there have been suggestions that they cannot easily establish territories where there are roe deer, because the roebucks are so much more aggressive. The presence of roe deer may therefore explain the absence of muntjac from parts of the Marches and the scarcity of roe deer in Wyre may explain the presence there of about 100 muntjac.

Chinese water deer *Hydropotes inermis* survived for a time in the wild, after escaping in the 1960s from Walcot Hall, formerly Lord Clive of India's home in south Shropshire. Hard winters and fox predation caused the disappearance of this species after a few years, but the trend is for populations of all other deer to rise. There are various reasons for these increases. Their natural predators, wolf, lynx and brown bear, have all been extirpated and there are restrictions on hunting. Less woodland is used to shelter and graze livestock in winter so the understorey and herb layer provides more food, as do autumn-sown crops. Winters and springs tend now to be warmer. Another factor is the quietness of the countryside. Mechanisation of agriculture means that many arable fields are deserted for most of the year, with occasional operations by a single tractor, whereas in the past farm workers would often have been present, disturbing and driving away deer.

The population of fallow deer in Wyre rose to about 700 by the mid-1980s and there was significant damage to regenerating oak woodland, regrowth of coppiced areas and the ground flora. The population of fallow and roe deer in the Mortimer Forest also rose to levels where there was damage. Two of the earliest deer management societies were set up to monitor and control populations in these forests. Both societies carry out annual culls, with does rather than bucks the main target. The aim in Wyre is to keep fallow deer numbers in the winter herd down to 250–300. There have been smaller culls in recent years, as mortality from a variety of other causes has increased. Bucks are vulnerable to poaching and illegal night shooting, because of the trophy value of their antlers and the high carcass weight when sold for venison. A typical price for a fallow deer carcase from a game dealer is currently about £50, whereas smaller roe deer fetches only £25. Whereas a fallow buck would naturally live for 12–15 years, few are surviving beyond three years.[25] Debate continues on the optimal size of deer populations and the number that should thus be culled each year. It might be expected that foresters would prefer there to be no deer, but Forestry Commission managers in the Marches welcome moderate levels of grazing by deer and regard a population of about four or five per 100 ha as ideal. Research has shown that limited numbers increase biodiversity, as the dominance of some plant species that grow on the forest floor such as bracken and brambles is reduced, allowing weaker competitors to survive. Glades are kept open, allowing animal and plant species to thrive that are excluded from areas of mature closed canopy woodland. A study of moths and butterflies recorded in Wyre showed that 18 per cent of species were associated with heathland of the type that develops in clearings where forest regeneration has not occurred.[26] There has been much recent debate about how extensive glades would have been within woodland before humans started to alter the ecological processes. Even if it is natural for glades to exist, there must be some tree regeneration for woodland to persist. Experiments using fenced enclosures in Wyre have shown that deer grazing only had moderate effects on the herb layer, but could prevent the growth of birch and oak saplings.[27] This is not the only current factor currently hampering natural regeneration of woodland

REGENERATION OF WOODLAND

Areas of semi-natural broadleaved woodland that have been left unmanaged might be expected to develop into a climax community, with trees growing to maturity, dying and being replaced. We might also expect mixed ages of tree, because it seems intuitively obvious that trees will die and be replaced at different times. Large numbers of young trees should therefore be present, springing up in gaps that have appeared in the canopy. The overall species composition should remain more or less unchanged with all tree species successfully regenerating.

This prospect of endlessly sustained native woodland, uninterrupted in time or space is not currently seen in the Marches. Oak woodland in particular is not persisting in this way. Many areas of woodland have remained unmanaged in recent years, so mature oaks do topple over and saplings sometimes grow up to replace them, but these are rarely oaks. Both sessile and pedunculate species produce crops of acorns containing viable seed, but seedlings almost always succumb to a host of possible fates, often in combination: deer, voles, rabbits or other herbivores including geometrid moth caterpillars, lack of light, frost damage and mildew. Instead, gaps where light reaches the ground are filled by ash, sycamore and birch seedlings, some of which grow up to become saplings. Ash and birch typically grow well, occasionally forming mixed aged stands, but sycamore is often badly damaged by grey squirrels. It therefore seems as though oak will gradually disappear from these areas of closed canopy mixed woodland. It is possible that conditions have changed in the Marches to favour ash and sycamore instead of oak. Enrichment of the soil by atmospheric nitrogen deposition could be involved. Deposition of dissolved nitrate from nitrogen oxides in vehicle exhausts is relatively small, but a recent survey found that more ammonia from agricultural sources is deposited in woodland in Welsh border counties than anywhere else in Britain. Even in areas of woodland in the Marches containing only oaks, there is usually little or no oak regeneration and in none of these areas are there trees at a range of ages that would indicate a cycle of continuous natural regeneration. As in mixed woodland, gaps tend to be filled by sycamore, ash or birch. Perhaps we should abandon the concept of a climax community here and accept that the prevalence of oaks in the past has been due to management at least as much as its ability to outcompete other species. Peterken[28] and others have argued that all woodland is dynamic and cyclical, affected by catastrophes such as disease, windthrow and other climatic events; a rotation of species is therefore not unexpected. Birch and oak may alternate naturally as oaks germinate and grow successfully under the sparse canopy of birch and eventually outlive it. Gaps created by fallen oaks are quickly colonised by birches. Young oaks also grow very successfully in open areas, including grassland and clear-felled areas. A patchwork of communities may be needed for oaks to regenerate strongly, with clearings and scrubby areas among areas of closed canopy woodland. Maybe we should even regard oaks as a pioneer rather than the main component of a climax community and oak woodland as a temporary or seral stage, albeit one that may persist for hundreds of years.

The need of oak seedlings for open conditions and high light intensities explains the success of an approach to woodland regeneration that is being used in the parts of Wyre, owned by Natural England and managed as a National Nature Reserve. The approach is a modified version of the traditional coppice management that was used in Wyre. Each winter relatively small areas of about half a hectare of woodland are felled, leaving a few mature trees to act as seed sources, sometimes called mother trees. An adjacent area is felled in the following winter. The results have been very variable but there is usually vigorous regrowth from the oak stumps and often prolific growth of sessile oak from seedlings. The ground flora is completely shaded out in the densest areas of oak saplings, which can have as many as 25 oaks per m². Self-thinning occurs, the survivors developing straight upright trunks and no low side branches – ideal for timber production.

Deer browsing can cause significant damage in Wyre. Tall fencing has been used around some areas to prevent this by excluding deer completely. Lower fencing has been used around other areas – this reduces damage by simply deterring deer. It is noticeable that oak regeneration has sometimes been just as successful outside fenced areas as within them. To reduce costs some areas have been left entirely unfenced and vigorous oak regeneration has still occurred. This may be partly due to deer avoiding areas where there is disturbance from dog walkers, but deer management policies generally are dispersing the population more and preventing hot spots of excessive damage. The result of these methods has been some vigorous regeneration, of both coppiced oaks and maiden trees. This is a sight that in recent years has been all too rare in the Marches. For reasons that are not entirely understood, oak regeneration sometimes fails initially and silver birch becomes established instead, along with a dense growth of bracken. It is anticipated that oak will eventually become dominant in these areas and, as conservation rather than commercial forestry is the aim, we should not regard a delay before oak is established as necessarily undesirable.

The difficulties that oaks have in regenerating from seed are minor compared to those of limes. Small-leaved limes reached the Marches about 6,500 BP, with maximum abundance during a particularly warm period from 6,000 to 5,000 BP. Temperatures then were 1.8–2.0 °C higher than those of the early 20th century. The phenomenon of a lime decline in Britain was first recognised and its cause identified as a result of analysis of pollen from peat and other organic deposits in north Shropshire.[29] Lime pollen was found to become far less common over relatively short periods, though the time of the decline varied. For example, around Boreatton Moss near Baschurch it occurred between 3,710 and 3,610 BP, but 4 km to the south at New Pool it took place between 3,600 and 3,500 BP. At Whixall Moss, 15 km to the northwest, the decline occurred still later, with dates of 3,340 to 3,020 BP. This pattern of rapid lime decline at different times on different sites is characteristic of human activity, with more and more areas being cleared for agriculture and lime trees presumably growing on the areas most suitable for growing crops. The inner bark or bass of limes may also have been attractive as a source of fibres for rope making.

Unlike other woody species, lime has not shown a recovery from its decline and both the large- and small-leaved species remain much less common in the Marches than they naturally would be. Fertile seed does not appear to be produced in most years. Seedlings are sometimes seen in large numbers, for example in 1986 in Herefordshire,[30] but often there are none. Low air temperatures following pollination can prevent pollen tube growth and therefore fertilisation.[31] Significant growth of pollen tubes occurs in the range 19–25 °C. Low temperature limits the formation of fertile seed and the regeneration of small-leaved limes at the northern limit of the distribution, but the Marches are not the northern limit. At Shrawley Wood, where there are large areas of woodland dominated by small-leaved lime, fertile seed was produced in more than half of the years between 1964 and 1979. Lack of viable seed is therefore not the sole cause of a failure to regenerate. Lime seeds and seedlings are very attractive to wood mice, bank voles and roe deer and in years when there are small crops, all will be taken.[32] In years with large crops, some seedlings can be expected to escape predation, but bank voles also kill saplings by ring-barking, so young maiden trees are still vulnerable. Although small-leaved limes are shade tolerant, their growth in shady conditions is slow, prolonging the period of vulnerability. Large amounts of seed and clearings or gaps in the canopy are needed for successful regeneration and these conditions have rarely if ever been met in recent years.

Small-leaved limes do regrow vigorously from coppiced stools and the size of some stools shows that this can happen repeatedly, perhaps for thousands of years. Coppicing has prolonged the life of many lime trees, but it prevents rather than promotes seed production. We should perhaps regard existing small-leaved limes in the Marches as a relict population that will not naturally be replaced when the trees die. Nevertheless, there are strong arguments for resisting the temptation to resort to artificial planting. Local tree nurseries have currently been importing seed from Hungary in order to raise seedlings, breaking the general principle that native plants should only be raised using seed of local provenance. It is not even certain that all of the seed is true small-leaved lime and some may be hybrid. We should redouble attempts to collect local seed for raising stock used in re-establishing small-leaved limes in woodland where they are naturally present.

The problems that oaks and limes have in regenerating are in marked contrast to the success of some non-native species that have been introduced for timber production. Sycamore germinates and grows vigorously in most areas of woodland where there are seed sources. Scots pine establishes very successfully on both the mosses and the sandstone hills of north Shropshire and Cheshire. European larch sometimes reproduces by seeding and western hemlock does so prolifically in some areas of woodland, including the Mortimer Forest with 30,000 or more stems per ha in the most severely affected areas.

CONIFER PLANTATIONS AND THE
FORESTRY COMMISSION

One of the most significant changes to the landscape and natural history of the Marches has been coniferisation. It was a politically instigated programme carried out by the Forestry Commission during 50 or so years of the 20th century. There have been hostile public reactions, particularly to the impact on the landscape. It is clear with hindsight that some schemes were carried out in an over-zealous way, including one example on the Croft Castle estate that is considered in the next chapter. However, it is also obvious that some forms of wildlife have benefited, especially after 1947 when conservation became an obligation together with the provision of a source of home-grown timber and profitable commercial forestry.

The Forestry Commission was founded in the aftermath of the First World War, when much woodland in the Marches had been felled. The decision was made to establish a strategic reserve of timber for future times of need, conifers especially being needed to provide pit props for coal mines, pulp for paper production and timber for construction of buildings.

Parts of the Marches were soon identified as suitable in terms of climate, soils and land availability. *West Siluria*, the area of Silurian marine sediments in northwest Herefordshire, proved to be a particularly fine conifer-growing area. The rock is slightly acidic but in many places is enriched by calcareous bands. It is porous and weathers rapidly to form deep brown earths that retain moisture well. The climate is relatively mild and the rainfall usually sufficient for rapid growth, but not so great that soils become leached. The leases for Bringewood Chase on the Herefordshire-Shropshire border and Wigmore Rolls in northwest Herefordshire had been signed by 1924 – some of the earliest Forestry Commission acquisitions in Britain. Three more leases were taken out on holdings adjacent to Bringewood to build up the large tract of land that is now known as the Mortimer Forest. Land values in the 1920s were low, profits from ownership of broadleaved woodland in the Marches were negligible and 999-year leases cost as little as one penny per acre. Land acquisitions continued in fits and starts through the 1930s in the hill country of northwest Herefordshire and south Shropshire. Most were either areas of former broadleaved woodland on sloping land or sheep walks on hilltops. Areas of oak coppice in Wyre were acquired.

There was another period of timber shortage and deforestation during the Second World War. The plantings from the 1920s and 1930s were not by then mature and the need for home produced timber became an even greater imperative. Land acquisition and planting therefore continued. In valleys and on well-drained sloping land Douglas fir *Pseudotsuga menziesii* and European larch *Larix decidua* were planted. Western hemlock *Tsuga heterophylla* was used on higher ground, with some Sitka spruce *Picea sitchensis* on the coldest and dampest sites, for example the summit plateau of the Long Mynd. Douglas fir has grown extremely well on most of the sites where it was planted and only in Devon are growth rates greater. Some of the original 1926 plantings are still growing in the Mortimer Forest, repeated thinnings allowing the remaining trees to grow on and form majestic groves of giants (Fig. 144). Recently, some of these trees were harvested and, in a remarkable example of coals to Newcastle, were sold at record prices to Norway for use as electricity transmission poles. Larch has also grown well in the Marches, usually with a dense ground flora, partly due to its deciduous habit but also because foresters maintain the open conditions that this genus prefers by thinning early and thinning often. Japanese larch *Larix kaempferi* grows more vigorously than the European species, but the hybrid between them grows more vigorously than either parent, so is preferred when seed is available. Grand fir *Abies grandis* has also grown very rapidly in the Marches, reaching large diameters extremely quickly, but the timber is too soft to have much value and the trunks are vulnerable to being snapped at about 3 m from their base during high winds. Some species of pine have been successfully grown in parts of Wyre where conditions are drier than further west in the Marches. Other conifer species have been tried on a small scale, including Japanese red cedar and western red cedar. Southern beeches were planted for a short period, despite not being conifers, so arguably outside the brief of the Forestry Commission, but were found to be vulnerable to frost damage.

The effect of coniferisation on wildlife has been marked. Plant species have in general fared badly. This is not surprising given the vigorous growth of the conifers with which native plants must compete. Some animal species have fared very well. The demise of a population of dormice at Huglith in south Shropshire illustrates the ability of this species to exploit conifer plantations. A particularly high density of five dormice was found in 1 ha of deciduous woodland. When an adjacent area of conifers was clear felled, the dormice disappeared, presumably because they had been reliant on the conifers for food. Elsewhere it has been found that thinned conifer plantations are not suitable habitat, as the dormice cannot move from the branches of one tree to another. To conserve dormice, there must always be areas available where the trees form a continuous canopy though which the dormice can move to feed. Invertebrates are one of the main food sources and it has become clear that large quantities are available in the canopy of plantations. Although fewer species of invertebrate inhabit alien species of conifer than native broadleaves, population densities can be very high.

FIG 144. Douglas firs
at Pitch Coppice in
Mortimer Forest.

A study of the distribution of wood-ant nests and foraging behaviour in an area of mixed woodland in Wyre did not reveal any preference for particular tree species. As long as there were enough aphids in a tree it would be targeted whatever its species. Where there is a choice of nest building material the needles of conifers are preferred. *Formica rufa* thrives in some plantations, but not others. For example, there are hundreds of nests in Bucknell Wood, but few in Hopton Wood a small distance away, for reasons that are not clear.

Of course there are some species that foresters would never wish to conserve, because they are pests of trees. Relatively few have proved really troublesome in the Marches. The most damaging is *Hylobius abietis*, a species of weevil that can multiply on stumps and brash after clear felling to form very large populations. It can then move to newly planted trees and kill them by ring-barking. To avoid catastrophic losses, replanting is delayed for two years after which the weevil numbers are usually much smaller. This adds to the area of open land within plantations, with benefits for some wild species. Bank vole populations tend to rise, for example, attracting barn owls and tawny owls that hunt them.

There are other species of bird that have fared well in conifer plantations. Goldcrests *Regulus regulus* and coal tits *Periparus ater* are obvious examples. Both are now ubiquitous in Marches plantations at much higher densities than in broadleaved woodland. Crossbills *Loxia curvirostra* are known to nest in some plantations. Given the earliness of their breeding season and difficulty of finding nest sites, they may be under-recorded. However, the crossbill's beak is adapted to extract seeds from spruce and pine cones, whereas Douglas fir and larch predominate in the Marches, so the populations may be smaller than elsewhere.

Larger areas of forestry can provide excellent undisturbed habitat for goshawks *Accipiter gentilis*; there is now a strong population of 20–30 breeding pairs in the Marches. They were already rare by the middle of the 19th century and were entirely absent from the area by the start of the 20th century, but were re-introduced to Wigmore Rolls using birds from Scandinavia that are distinctively large in size. In addition, there were probably some incidents of captive birds escaping into the wild. The current population is therefore descended from both deliberate and accidental releases. Goshawks hunt in the tree canopy and so avoid the densest woodland. Conifer plantations after first thinning suit them very well. They benefit from the abundant food sources in many plantations, including pheasants and other birds of prey. The Marches population almost always nests in conifers, usually larch or Douglas fir, using branches immediately below the leafy canopy. Woodland where there is least disturbance is usually chosen, preferably in large areas but some areas as small as 3 ha have had nests. The danger of persecution is still there and nest sites are monitored carefully. The exact locations of nests are not disclosed, but they are spread through conifer plantations from Presteigne in northwest Herefordshire to Pontesbury in Shropshire and as far eastwards as Wyre. Eastwards expansion of the range beyond the Marches has faltered, probably due to illegal persecution. Honey buzzards *Pernis apivorus* are another species of raptor that could re-establish a population as, after a long absence, a pair appeared in a conifer plantation in the Clun area, returning each year from the 1998 until 2004, with successful breeding in the early years. When ravens became restricted to upland and coastal districts of Britain in the 19th century, they used cliffs and crags for their nest sites. As their population increased in the Marches they re-established the habit, which they undoubtedly had formerly, of nesting in trees. Conifers are preferred, especially Scots pine, but in contrast to goshawks, trees close to the woodland edge are usually chosen and the nest is placed near the top of the tree rather than below the canopy. The cronk of ravens is now a familiar sound in conifer plantations, along with the mewing call of buzzards.

Woodcock *Scolopax rusticola* was known as an over-wintering species in the Marches in the 19th century, with occasional records of breeding (Fig. 145). It now breeds regularly in some conifer plantations, including Wigmore Rolls, where roding males are seen each year. Areas with young trees between 5 and 15 years old are preferred over areas with a closed canopy, so larger plantations where there are always some areas at this stage are particularly suitable. Nightjars have declined considerably in recent years. The sandy heaths that they formerly inhabited have mostly gone, but newly felled areas of conifer plantation can offer a similar habitat and they can also thrive in young plantations of up to about

FIG 145. Woodcock camouflaged on its nest in Shelfheld Coppice, Wyre. (John Robinson)

12–15 years as long as there are open areas nearby. After some years of absence from the Marches, a pair of nightjars was discovered breeding in a plantation near Clun in 2006, by Alan Reid, a Forestry Commission ranger. Two males were recorded churring in separate territories in 2007, indicating that there were probably two breeding pairs and raising hopes that a new population was establishing. The Forestry Commission will ensure that suitable open habitat continues to be available in the plantation that the nightjars have chosen, by frequent clear felling of small areas. Nightjars have also recently been reported from conifer plantations at the southern end of the Long Mynd.

DECONIFERISATION AND NEW WOODLANDS

In the 1960s, with diminishing demand for softwood for uses such as pit props and increasingly hostile public opinion, coniferisation started to fall out of favour. In Wyre the replacement of oak with conifers ended. A broadleaves policy was introduced nationally in 1985, stopping the planting of conifers on sites where there had been broadleaved woodland and encouraging the use of natural regeneration rather than planting of woodland. Policy initiatives since then have moved increasingly towards wildlife conservation and recreational uses alongside commercial forestry. For example, the Keepers of Time policy has the aim of restoring broadleaved woodland with native species in all plantations on ancient woodland sites, usually abbreviated to PAWS. Two-thirds of the Forestry Commission holding of 13,000 ha in the Marches consists of PAWS. The area is so great that it may take about 50 years to achieve.

The foresters who have been given this task are not yet sure which techniques will work best, especially given the patchy distribution of mature trees needed to act as seed sources. Three techniques are being tested in Stoke Wood, south of Craven Arms: clear felling of large areas, felling of groups of trees to create smaller cleared areas, and thinning of extensive areas. Given that the aim is to re-establish oak or mixed oak-ash woodland, the early results from all three methods look unpromising, with some rowan and ash in the cleared areas, large amounts of birch and much bracken. Very little oak has appeared. Where oak trees are not present to act as seed sources it is necessary to bring in acorns, but merely broadcasting them is unlikely to be successful. Trials using mechanical scarification to bury broadcast acorns gave a low success rate and individual planting of acorns is too labour-intensive. On other sites in the Marches, two to three-year-old oak trees have been planted, usually with tubes to guard the trees against damage by rabbits, voles and deer. Mesh tubes are preferred to solid ones as there is less infection with mildew. The costs of this method of establishing oaks amount to several pounds per planted tree, precluding its widespread use. Planting without tubes to reduce costs has been tried with mixed success. There was little damage of the young trees in Bucknell Wood, but much more in Mary Knoll Valley in Mortimer Forest. Ash usually establishes on suitable sites without difficulties, but even once young trees are growing away strongly there are still potential problems to be faced. Foresters have justifiable concerns that grey squirrels, which prefer broadleaved woodland to coniferous, will cause severe damage once trees are 20 or more years old and at the moment there is no prospect of effective control of grey squirrel numbers.

Given the difficulty of re-establishing oak on PAWS, creating woodland on new sites might be seen as an attractive alternative, but the biodiversity benefits are often less and in some cases are outweighed by losses. The Forestry Commission has prepared a Woodland Opportunity Map showing which areas are suitable, based on conservation, landscape and historical considerations. In Shropshire, axiophytes have been used to help. These are indicator species that are confined to particular habitats and therefore allow these habitats to be identified using distribution maps. A map of Shropshire has been produced according to number of axiophytes of good quality woodland and of good quality open habitats. The map shows preferred areas for woodland planting, where there are high numbers of woodland axiophytes but few open species axiophytes. It also shows sensitive areas where the opposite situation prevails and woodland planting should be discouraged. Some areas are complex because there are high numbers of both woodland and open habitat axiophytes. Wenlock Edge is an example, as there are areas of high quality woodland that should be conserved but also species-rich grassland, which should certainly not be planted with trees. Clearly, new woodland needs to be sited very carefully if it is to increase biodiversity.

THE FOREST OF WYRE

This chapter concludes with a description of the greatest forest in the Marches. Wyre is the third largest surviving area of ancient woodland in England, extending to about 2,800 ha. Its conservation importance has only gradually been recognised, despite the popular success of Norman Hickin's books describing the area.[33] By the mid-1960s only a small central area had SSSI status. Economic Forestry had bought a large holding and planned to coniferise it. At the instigation of John Thompson, then Regional Officer for the Nature Conservancy Council, this holding was purchased and became a National Nature

Reserve, now extending to 562 ha. The area of the SSSI was increased hugely in a series of steps, to 1,762 ha.

Wyre occupies an area of Upper Carboniferous rocks, with a very varied and complicated sequence of clays, shales, coal seams, sandstones and grits. Because the rock strata are mostly very thin, only a few centimetres in some cases, there is a complicated mosaic of rock types at the surface and an unmappably complex distribution of soil types derived from the rocks. The soils are very varied, but are typically poorly drained, acid, stony and deficient in nutrients, especially phosphate. Agriculture was no doubt repeatedly attempted on these soils but found to be unrewarding, apart from areas of pasture and orchards, so woodland has survived through history to the modern day.

Wyre became a royal forest stocked with fallow deer after the Norman Conquest. As with other royal forests, it fell into decline in the second half of the 16th century and the deer population was exterminated. Timber extraction, which had been controlled to an extent before, became much more intensive. Between 1550 and 1650, thousands of large oaks were felled each year, leaving the whole area almost entirely deforested – an early example of unsustainable exploitation. Gradually an improved system of coppice management was adopted, the woodland being divided into blocks and subdivided into coupes. Much of the wood was used to produce charcoal for the many iron furnaces in the area. There was also a demand for timber, so some larger standard oaks were spared from coppicing and were encouraged to grow to an even greater size. By the 19th century, a system of selective coppicing was being widely used. At the end of a cycle, 1 ha in a typical stand contained 25–30 mature trees 120 to 150 years old, 90–150 smaller single trees typically 25, 50 and 75 years old and 70–1,000 coppiced stools, up to 18 years old. To achieve this mix of ages, selective felling took place in each coupe about every 18 years, taking out most of the small wood from the coppiced oaks and a few of the larger trees. A proportion of each age of tree was left to grow on, with the straightest and best being selected and marked for this purpose. Charcoal burners, basket makers and barkers took out the small wood in the spring. In the following autumn, timber merchants felled the larger trunks, 25–50-year-old trees mostly going for pit props in coal mines and 70–150-year-old trees being sawn to produce timber. Saplings that had grown from acorns were left to grow on as they produced better timber than spared trunks from coppiced oak. Birch was tolerated as it could be cut when young to produce material for making besoms and whisks, and also brushes for use during carpet manufacture in Kidderminster. Other tree species were usually eliminated.

By the end of the 19th century, the demand for the products of coppicing was much diminished and increasingly coupes were converted to high forest.

A process called storing was used to do this, where all but one of the stems in each stool were removed. Sometimes two or three stems per stool were left, producing what is called semi-stored coppice. In other coupes coppicing simply ended with many trees growing from the neglected old stools. Coppicing was scarcely practised anywhere after 1946, though it continued in part of Far Forest until the 1960s, to provide materials for making rustic garden furniture. During both the First and Second World Wars, much of the mature timber was removed from Wyre. Some sites were clear felled during the Second World War and as active management did not follow, natural regeneration gave rise to a different type of woodland with far more silver birch and very large numbers of individual trees per hectare.

The other major change to Wyre was coniferisation. The Forestry Commission bought more than 500 ha of oak woodland and oak coppice in 1925 and by the 1950s had acquired over 1,000 ha. The policy initially was to replace the oak coppice with plantations of larch, Douglas fir and Corsican pine *Pinus nigra*. As early as the mid-1930s it became obvious that the plantations were growing more poorly than expected. Douglas fir in particular, which grows very well elsewhere in the Marches, did not perform well. Experiments with the addition of phosphate fertiliser showed that lack of this nutrient was not the limiting factor to growth. In the 1940s the Commission's policy changed to converting remaining areas of oak coppice to high forest by singling the coppiced stools and underplanting with beech.

As both the conifer plantations and the areas of oak and beech grew up, much of the diverse forest mosaic was lost. Species of open woodland that had been abundant became rarer and some were lost, for example the Kentish glory moth *Endromis versicolora* and high brown fritillary butterfly. By the 1980s the absence of open areas formerly provided by coppicing was having obvious effects. The pearl-bordered fritillaries of Wyre can be used as a paradigm. The larvae rely on violets as their food plant. Violets germinate and grow in areas with bare soil as long as they are not too shady, but cannot compete with taller plants. There are usually many suitable sites in a coupe immediately after it has been coppiced and so these areas, often having many violets, form good habitat for larvae. Brambles and other plants soon become established during the early years of regrowth, shading out the violets but used as nectar sources by adult fritillaries. Eventually the brambles and other species of ground flora are shaded out again by coppice regrowth and growth of sapling oaks, with areas of bare soil developing. This prepares the conditions needed for violets after the next coppicing has taken place. All parts of the coppicing cycle are needed for the continued survival of the fritillaries.

The Forestry Commission reintroduced coppicing on some of its holdings in the 1990s. Coppicing has also been restarted in the NNR, where senior reserve manager Tim Dixon has overseen it. Six blocks were chosen, with about 20 coupes of half a hectare in each. One coupe in every block is coppiced each winter, so there will always be some at each stage of development. As far as possible, the coppiced coupe is adjacent to a previously coppiced one, to allow easy migration of emerged adult fritillaries to areas suitable for egg laying. Wide rides have been opened up to link the blocks that are being coppiced, so that migration between these areas is encouraged. This is an example of large-scale woodland management, which is possible in Wyre because the area is so huge. As a result of the woodland-scale and coupe-scale management initiatives, the numbers of pearl-bordered fritillaries have increased, though of course this is overlain by annual fluctuations due to variation in weather and other factors.

In addition to its important pearl-bordered fritillary population, Wyre is probably now the best site in Britain for silver-washed fritillary, and it is also an important woodland site for the small pearl-bordered fritillary (Fig. 146). The value of these populations was recognised by a project called 'Back to Orange', begun in 2007, which focused conservation efforts on fritillary butterflies in Wyre. It involved monitoring of Lepidoptera populations by means of transects, timed counts and moth trapping. Use of a mobile platform allowed species to be looked at in a new way, particularly those that fly and feed in the tree canopy. Plans for the project involved research into the effects of converting areas of conifers back to broadleaves and the effects of management policies on plants needed by target species.

The fritillaries of Wyre are emblematic species and they can also be used as indicator species, but there are other species with different needs whose

FIG 146. Silver-washed fritillaries nectaring on bramble. (Patrick Clement, left; Danny Beath, right)

conservation also needs to be considered. For example, larvae of the nationally scarce common fan-foot *Pechipogo strigilata* moth require closed canopy pedunculate oak woodland, which is found along damp side valleys in Wyre. Adults use plants growing in open areas as nectar sources. Wyre has an important population of common fan-foots, which are being conserved by leaving oak woodland in the damp side valleys uncut, when adjacent areas are coppiced. The argent and sable is another nationally scarce moth with a significant population in Wyre. It uses birch as its larval food plant, so coppiced areas where birch has colonised rather than oak should not be regarded as failures from a conservation point of view. On the contrary, the aim in the NNR is to encourage invertebrate biodiversity by increasing tree species diversity. Mature specimens of scarcer native species are now left uncut during coppicing so that they can act as seed sources. This is reversing centuries of selection in Wyre against ash, rowan, small- and large-leaved lime, wild service-tree, aspen *Populus tremula* and yew. One species that is an unexpected member of the community in some coupes is false-acacia *Robinia pseudacacia*, which was encouraged because its wood was found to be ideal for the rungs of ladders used for cherry picking in Wyre orchards.

Another group of species that has been the target of specific conservation measures are invertebrates that feed on dead wood. Wyre has a significant legacy of these species, many of which are extremely scarce elsewhere (Fig. 147). Three examples will be given here. *Schiffermuelleriana grandis* is a micro-moth with RDB status, whose larvae live in dead limbs on live oaks. The type specimen is almost certainly from Wyre, where it was discovered in the 19th century. In the past it has been recorded in south Devon and Somerset, but its stronghold is still in Wyre and in Ribbesford Woods to the south. *Oecophora bractella* is a beautiful black and yellow micro-moth with blue flashes. It is another RDB species but is quite common in Wyre and some other areas of woodland in Herefordshire and Worcestershire. It only has one other centre of population in Britain, in the New Forest and some other parts of Hampshire. Its larvae live under the bark of dead tree limbs on the ground. *Synanthedon vespiformis* is a nationally notable macro-moth that is also known as the yellow-legged clearwing. It flies rapidly during the day and as its specific name suggests it avoids predation by mimicking wasps. The larvae of this species feed on oak stumps. Each of the three moth species described here has a different habitat in dead oak wood. To encourage each of them and other species that use these habitats, dead limbs on oaks are no longer trimmed off, oak stumps are left after tree felling and some wood is left on the ground after felling and coppicing, rather than all being removed or burned. There are species that exploit dead wood of other trees, for example clearwing moths are found in Wyre that favour alder and birch stumps. Dead wood of species other than oak therefore

FIG 147. Saproxylic moths of Wyre: (a) *Schiffermuelleriana grandis* (Dave Grundy); (b) *Oecophora bractella* (Patrick Clement); (c) *Synanthedon vespiformis* (Dave Grundy); and (d) *Synanthedon spheciformis* (Rosemary Winnall).

helps to promote invertebrate diversity. The area of Wyre is so great that there is room for many different tree species, as components of coppices, closed canopy high forest and, if current plans are acted on, also semi-open habitats that are discussed in the next chapter, called wood pasture.

The careful management of Wyre will help to conserve the huge diversity of species that currently inhabit the forest. There will continue to be new arrivals, so the diversity of the forest may even increase. In 2008 specimens of the little thorn moth *Cepphis advenaria* were found in Wyre for the first time and as the bilberries that it uses as its larval food plant are thriving with current management, it is likely to establish a population. Wyre is a hugely important wildlife area. It is one of the jewels of the Marches and because of the turnaround in attitudes and the remarkable changes in management policies, its future looks brighter than for many years.

CHAPTER 9

Trees

THE WOODLANDS OF THE MARCHES CONTAIN about 10 million mature trees, but whereas the focus in the previous chapter was on woodland as a whole community, the deliberate aim of this chapter is to see the trees, not the wood. There are about 5 million trees outside woodland, if we include those in linear features such as streamsides, roadsides and hedges, in-field trees that have survived the grubbing of hedges and also trees in gardens, parkland and wood pasture. Some are non-natives and many have been planted, so their presence is to a greater or lesser extent unnatural, but they are nonetheless prominent features in the landscape and form a significant part of the natural history of the Marches. In the absence of competition from other trees, isolated specimens often achieve greater growth rates and larger sizes than in woodland. There are many very large specimens, including British records for some species. This can be attributed partly to the longevity of trees here, helped by wind speeds being mostly moderate and lightning strikes infrequent, but also to the good growing conditions. Rainfall and humidity are both quite high, and soils, though variable, are in places deep and fertile.

VETERAN YEWS AND OAKS

The first trees to be considered are perhaps the most remarkable – veteran yews and oaks. A veteran tree can be defined as one that has lived long enough to experience cycles of dieback and regrowth. Trees that are grown to produce timber in woodland are harvested when they reach target yield classes. Even in unmanaged woodland, trees usually succumb to windthrow before they become veterans. Veterans become more and more valuable with age, not merely because of the 'air of respectable antiquity' that they lend, but because of the habitats that they offer for other organisms in their deeply fissured bark, dead branches, tree holes and hollow trunks. They support ivy and other climbing plants, epiphytes, lichens, invertebrates in great diversity, roosting bats and nesting birds such as little owls. Many of the species that find a habitat here have high conservation status, not just in the Marches but also at a European level. Until one understands the scarcity of veteran trees across Europe, the fact that Britain is relatively well endowed with them cannot be appreciated.

A significant proportion of Britain's veteran trees are in the Marches. The reasons are partly historical. Following the turbulent years before and after the conquest, the Marches have been a stable area. Many pieces of land including large parks and gardens have remained in the ownership of families for hundreds of years. The Brampton Bryan estate with its ancient parkland has been in the same family since 1309 for example. Trees at Brampton and elsewhere have been able to grow to a great age, in some cases over 1,000 years. They have attracted interest since the 19th century or before. A notable example is the yew tree in the churchyard at Church Preen that now has a girth of just over 7 m. The Swiss botanist Augustin De Candolle visited it in 1831 and estimated the age then to be about 1,400 years.[1] During a five-year project, over 900 veteran trees were recorded in the Shropshire Hills AONB and a similar scheme in north Shropshire logged large numbers of specimens, most of the largest specimens found close to the Welsh border. It is not possible to give an accurate total for the number of veterans in the Marches, but these surveys suggest that it is at least several thousand.

The oldest trees in the Marches are yews. They are almost always hollow, so it is impossible to count tree rings, or to radiocarbon date the oldest wood. An ancient yew with a girth of over 10 m stands near a chapel in the village of Loughton, below Brown Clee. A sample of wood was taken in 1986 from the inner surface of the hollow trunk. Radiocarbon dating, the first for a yew tree, indicated an age of 550 years, but 400 years of growth may well have preceded the laying down of the dated wood, suggesting an age of about 1,000 years. Age based on girth may in some cases be an overestimate, because soil level has risen over the centuries above the single bole of a tree, to the point where branches are splaying out more widely. It is unlikely that accurate ages will ever be obtained for veteran yews and some estimates are almost certainly exaggerated, including De Candolle's, for the Church Preen yew. However, there are specimens that are almost certainly more than 1,000 years old and so have existed in the Marches since before the Norman Conquest (see Table 3; Fig. 148).

The yews so far mentioned are just the very largest, but there are many with a girth greater than 5 m that are certainly hundreds of years old. Some specimens

FIG 148. Norbury Yew – a huge veteran in the churchyard of All Saints, Norbury, with a metre rule for scale. (David James)

TABLE 3. The largest veteran yews of the Marches

LOCATION	GRID REFERENCE	GIRTH (m)
Clun	SO 300 806	10.42
Norbury	SO 364 928	10.06
Loughton	SO 616 831	10.06
Middleton Scriven	SO 681 875	8.99
Uppington	SJ 597 094	8.64
Kenley	SJ 562 008	8.54
Ashford Carbonel	SO 525 710	8.20

were used as boundary markers. There are examples in the area around Easthope in Hopedale and on Acton Burnell Hill, but most veteran yews are located in churchyards. Shropshire has more of these than any other single county and Herefordshire also has large numbers.

According to Alan Mitchell,[2] the great measurer and recorder of trees, veteran oaks were also more frequent in Shropshire and Herefordshire than in any other counties. In contrast to yews, the majority of veteran oaks are pollards. It is well known that pollarding increase the longevity of some tree species. This is partly due to restricted height and thus a reduced chance of windthrow and lightning strikes, but also to the mechanical strength of short but stout trunks, even when hollow. As long as pollards are regularly cut, their strength to weight ratio is much greater than that of an unpruned tree, called a maiden. Pollarding is a traditional method used in open habitats where young growth that is within reach of livestock would be destroyed by browsing. Some veteran oak pollards are in hedgerows where their longevity allows them to be used to mark boundaries between estates. Many others are in wood pasture and parkland, which are described later in this chapter.

Veteran oaks often develop a distinctive appearance, partly because growth is from lateral rather than terminal buds, so branches have many knees and elbows rather than long straight limbs. Many prominent veteran oaks are named and some are famous. The Croft Oak, in the grounds of Croft Castle, north of Leominster, is one of the largest sessile oaks in Britain. At nearly 12.8 m, its girth may well be the largest of any sessile oak with an undivided bole. The Marton Oak in Cheshire, another sessile oak, stands just outside the area covered by this book. When measured in the 19th century it was larger than the Croft Oak, but its bole is now divided into four large pieces. The Lydham Manor Oak in Shropshire is one of Britain's largest pedunculate oaks. There are two slightly larger specimens in Britain: the famous Bowthorpe Oak in Lincolnshire, and a much less well known specimen that grows at an undisclosed site to the south of Leominster in Herefordshire. Some of the largest oaks in the area covered by this book are shown in Table 4 opposite (Fig. 149).

It should in theory be possible to deduce ages for these veteran oaks. Alan Mitchell used a simple method of allowing one year for every inch of girth. John White devised an improved scale by correlating girths of oaks at Windsor Great Park with ages deduced from tree ring counts.[3] Where the ages of oaks in the Marches are known from planting or other records, their girths have been found to be greater than the Windsor scale would lead us to expect. Growth rates are faster, probably due to higher humidity. Another complication is the past treatment of oaks. Trees that are pollarded have reduced growth rates

TABLE 4. The largest veteran oaks of the Marches

NAME	GIRTH	DESCRIPTION	GRID REFERENCE
Croft Oak	12.80 m	In the grounds of Croft Castle at Croft Ambrey north of Leominster – possibly England's largest sessile oak	SO 447 653
Lydham Manor Oak	Nearly 12 m in 1984	A huge tree that grew in girth by 1.8 metres between 1946 and 1984; both holly and elder trees grow upon it	SO 331 900
Crowleasowes Oak	Over 11 m	A large oak that has been pollarded more recently than most veterans	SO 547 783
Powis Oak	10.36 m	Near a stream and wood close to Underhill Hall between Picklescott and Pulverbatch	SJ 430 010
Easthampton Oak	Over 10 m in 1994	One of the largest sessile oaks in Britain	SO 408 630
Moor Park Oak	9.52 m in 2010	An enormous pedunculate oak in the Pinetum of the former Moor Park estate	SO 505 712
Acton Round Oak	8.8 m	A huge pollarded sessile oak used as a boundary tree	SO 637 955
Holt Preen Oak	Over 8.8 m in 1983	Water emerges from a spring beneath the tree	SO 534 965
Dryton Oak	8.43 m in 1983	On the lane leading from B4380 to Eyton on Severn racecourse	SJ 585 064
Aston Oak	8.25 m	Southeast of Oswestry at Aston Hall	SJ 318 273

FIG 149. Moor Park Oak – Baron Inchiquin set up a protective covenant to prevent the felling of this tree when he sold the estate on which it stands in 1951.

and narrower annual rings in the years after cutting of the canopy, but growth gradually increases as the canopy re-establishes. Almost all of the Marches veterans are pollards, whereas most of the Windsor trees are maidens. Altitude and waterlogging also have an effect on growth rates and these are much more variable than at Windsor. A revised scale could be devised specifically for the Marches, but even then we would only be able to give cautious estimates of age.

LIMES

Some of the lime trees of the Marches may be as old as the yews and oaks, but as they have mostly been coppiced, they are even harder to age than pollards. Both small- and large-leaved limes are native to the Marches and grow within and without woodland. Large-leaved lime has native populations in several parts of England but its stronghold is an area covering Herefordshire and parts of Shropshire and Worcestershire. Small-leaved lime is more widely distributed in Britain, but the Marches are again an area where woodlands with native populations are commoner than in most other areas. The Marches is one of the few regions in Britain where the natural ranges of the small-leaved and large-leaved limes overlap and the two species co-exist in some areas of woodland, for example Downton Gorge NNR. According to the *New Atlas of the British and Irish Flora*,[4] natural hybrids are found in north Herefordshire and Derbyshire, but nowhere else in Britain. Large-leaved limes usually flower 10–12 days earlier than small-leaved, preventing cross-pollination, but this breaks down if the weather is first cold and then hot, thus delaying the flowering of the large-leaved limes and accelerating that of the small-leaved limes. If large-leaved limes grow on north-facing slopes of river gorges and small-leaved on south facing, the reproductive isolation can also break down.[5]

Despite the occurrence of natural hybrids, almost all hybrids growing in the Marches are of non-native origin and have been planted. Most are members of clones imported from the Netherlands.[6] Genetically uniform stock can easily be propagated by layering, giving trees with even growth when planted in groups or avenues. The planted clones are closer in character to the large-leaved than small-leaved lime but are more tolerant of poor or dry soils. They can grow to a greater height than either parent, perhaps as a result of hybrid vigour. When in flower they have a wonderfully sweet scent: 'at dewy eve distilling odours' according to Leighton's *Flora*,[7] and produce nectar profusely enough to gladden the beekeepers heart. Thomas Wright planted avenues of hybrid limes in Shrewsbury's Quarry Park in 1719. They had reached heights of 40 m or more

by the early 1950s, but were felled on the orders of Percy Thrower, then parks
superintendent of Shrewsbury.[8] A falling branch had killed a young girl and so
the trees were considered to be unsafe, a theme that we shall return to when
considering roadside trees. The felled trees were found to contain bee and wasp
nests, large amounts of mistletoe and much dead wood. They were replaced with
hybrid limes at a wider spacing, which are now reaching maturity. The clone
that was planted produces large numbers of epicormic sprouts, which have to be
pruned off annually and native large-leaved limes would almost certainly have
been a better choice.

The two native species are well adapted to conditions here, as is demonstrated
by the large size to which specimens outside woodland can still grow. The biggest
large-leaved lime in Britain is in the grounds of Pitchford Hall near Shrewsbury,
with a girth of 7.41 m. This is a famous specimen, with a tree house in its
branches that Queen Victoria climbed up to in 1832. Estate maps of 1692 show
'the tree with the house in it' so the Pitchford lime must be at least 400 years
old (Fig. 150). The small-leaved lime with the greatest girth in the Marches is in
Brampton Bryan Park. At 5.84 m, it is the third largest in Britain.

FIG 150. Pitchford Lime, with mistletoe and the historic tree house, now with supports to
protect the tree.

BLACK POPLARS

Although black poplars *Populus nigra* subsp. *betulifolia* rapidly take on the look of veterans with burrs and bosses on the trunk, they are fast growing and do not usually live to a great age – only about 200 years. The two tallest specimens in Britain are both 38 m, one in the grounds of Longnor Hall to the south of Shrewsbury and the other at Leighton Hall near Welshpool. Perhaps the most famous black poplar of all is the Arbor Tree at Aston-on-Clun. When the original tree fell in 1995, it was replaced from a cutting and the tradition of dressing it with flags each year on Oak Apple Day continues. This custom dates back to 1786, by which time the original tree was already well established, so its total lifespan was at least 275 years. The exceptional longevity of this poplar may have been the result of regular pruning to encourage large numbers of lateral branches to grow on a trunk of about 6 m height. The technique is called shredding and is distinct from pollarding, which has rarely been practised on black poplars in the Marches.

It is very likely that black poplars are native. Poplar pollen is delicate and does not persist for long in peat or soil, so no conclusion can be drawn from its absence in the pollen record. There are likely to have been populations on flood plains, for example beside the Severn and its tributaries, but the timber would have been useful and the flood plains were soon converted by human inhabitants to grazing. Black poplar was widely planted in the past in hedgerows and on pond margins, but its numbers dropped from about 1800 onwards when the hybrid black Italian poplar was introduced and planted in preference. It was estimated that by the early 21st century there were only about 7,500 black poplars in the whole of Britain, with 4,500 of these in the Vale of Aylesbury. There are probably about 500 in the Marches, so the population here is a small but significant part of the total. The distribution is uneven, with the highest density in Corvedale.

Planting is essential to maintain the Marches population, as natural regeneration is almost impossible. The seeds have a short period of viability and must germinate on a bare substrate and need to grow without competition. Suitable sites are sometimes formed where sand and gravel build up on the inside of meanders on the Severn and other rivers, but there is unlikely to be pure-bred black poplar seed available to establish natural stands on these sites. The female trees that bear seed are rarely planted because they produce large quantities of fluffy fruits, which are a nuisance to humans in various ways. There are reports of hay crops being ruined by a blanket of the fruits for example. A survey carried out by the 'Blue Remembered Hills' project located 263 black poplars in south Shropshire, all but two of them males. Even the seed produced by the small numbers of females is suspect, as the promiscuity of poplars means that pollen from any local male will be used in fertilisation, resulting in hybridisation. Planting of purebred black poplars will continue to be necessary to conserve the species. The survey in south Shropshire was followed up by the planting of 600 young trees from a variety of provenances, giving the largest boost to the population for many years. Establishment of a naturally regenerating population of black poplars would require some strong proactive conservation measures. An area would have to be found where natural processes of erosion and building of riverbanks could be allowed, despite loss of agricultural land. Males and females would have to be planted initially, with all non-native seed and pollen sources eliminated in the surrounding area. This would be a fascinating ecological experiment. There is sometimes a presumption that reintroductions are to be avoided, but there are strong arguments for this policy within the former natural range of a species. Successful examples with both plant and bird species are well known.

DOUBTFULLY NATIVE BROADLEAVES

The species described so far in this chapter arrived and spread without human assistance. There are some other species that have inhabited the Marches for a long period and regenerate naturally, but may well have originally been introduced. Beech was a late colonist of Britain after the last glaciation. In the Marches it has been widely planted for commercial forestry, but also as an ornamental in parks and gardens, both as specimen trees and in avenues. The most remarkable avenue marches up the exposed slopes of Linley Hill, where windswept conditions have moulded the trees into extraordinary shapes, especially towards the upper end of the avenue (Fig. 151). A specimen that fell in 1996 was found to date from the early 19th century, so the remaining trees are now over 200 years old. Beech can clearly survive much harsher conditions than it would usually encounter in its natural range to the south and east of the Marches. It also regenerates from seed prolifically where conditions suit it. Therefore it seems likely that beech would have arrived naturally given time, and its planting merely pre-empted this.

Hornbeam has also usually been regarded as introduced, but may have spread naturally to the Ironbridge Gorge. In both Lydebrook Dingle and Lloyds Coppice there are groups of trees that may be outliers of the native population in southeast and central England.[9] Sweet chestnut by contrast is also almost certainly non-native, but has been grown in the Marches for hundreds of years. It was widely planted in parks, to provide shelter for deer and nuts to fatten pigs. There is a magnificently characterful row of huge sweet chestnuts in the park at Brampton

FIG 151. Linley beeches – the avenue marches up a windswept hill and is over 200 years old. (Ben Osborne)

FIG 152. Brampton Bryan sweet chestnuts – the avenue is probably over 350 years old and is located within the deer park established in the early 14th century.

Bryan that was probably planted in the 1650s[10] (Fig. 152). (As with other privately owned estates, visits are only possible with the permission of the owners.) There are also large specimens at Grinshill, Kinlet and Ferney Hall near Clungunford. Perhaps the most remarkable sweet chestnuts are in an avenue at Croft Castle. They have huge, gnarled trunks and look ancient, but Alan Mitchell estimated their planting date to have been about 1750. By then sweet chestnut had largely fallen out of favour for the planting of avenues because of its irregular growth and tendency to drop limbs. Post-restoration, after 1660, elm, lime or horse chestnut were usually chosen, with redwoods from the 19th century onwards.

Sycamore is the species whose status has been most keenly debated and consensus has not yet been achieved among dendrologists. Some regard it as an undesirable alien and others as the native Celtic maple. Sycamore is certainly well adapted to conditions in the Marches and self-sows prolifically in woodland and hedgerows, but it is often deformed due to the stripping of bark in summer by the indubitably non-native grey squirrel. Like beech, sycamore is a resilient tree, often growing to a large size in apparently uncongenial conditions, including windswept upland farmsteads. There are huge specimens at Loton Park and on glebeland near Malpas there is a well-known group called The Disciples.

NON-NATIVE AND FORMERLY NATIVE CONIFERS

Many species of conifer grow well in the Marches, with cedars of Lebanon *Cedrus libani*, coastal redwoods *Sequoia sempervirens*, giant sequoia *Sequoiadendron giganteum*, silver firs *Abies* spp., western yellow pines *Pinus ponderosa*, Douglas firs, grand firs and Caucasian firs *Abies nordmanniana* all recorded with heights above 40 m in parks or gardens. Grand firs and Douglas firs in excess of 55 m have been recorded. The Charles Ackers Grove, adjacent to Offa's Dyke at Leighton Hall near Welshpool, is a remarkable example of the vigour of conifers in the Marches. A group of about 30 coastal redwoods was brought back in pots from the USA and planted in 1858. They are now the tallest redwoods in Europe and, having an estimated 19,000 cubic feet of timber to the acre, this is probably the most heavily timbered area in Britain. In days when carbon sinks are needed, here is an important demonstration of what can be achieved. Unlike most conifers, coastal redwoods are able to regenerate after coppicing and propagate by layering. Charles Ackers Grove contains an extraordinary example of this – from a large fallen redwood a series of now very substantial offspring has become established, ranged along the horizontal trunk (Fig. 153). The Royal Forestry Society owns the grove and an adjacent arboretum, which can both be visited by permission.

FIG 153. Self-layered coastal redwood in Charles Ackers Grove near Welshpool – the parent tree fell in 1936 and a series of clones has developed from it.

The vigorous growth of conifers in the Marches should not be a surprise to us. Absence from the native flora is not necessarily due to them being ill adapted. As with beeches, it could also be due to a failure to spread north rapidly enough after the ending of the last ice age. There is evidence from macrofossil remains and preserved pollen that several conifer species did previously grow in these parts, including hemlocks, firs and spruces. The most recent British record for Norway spruce *Picea abies* was from Chelford in Cheshire 60,000 years ago. Scots pine did return after the last ice age, but disappeared again in the late Bronze to Iron Age, possibly due to human activity. A layer of stumps found in parts of the Fenn's–Whixall complex of mosses has become known as the Hardy Pine Stump Layer, after E. H. Hardy. He described it in the 1930s[11] and also found pollen of pine trees in peat deposits from the early post-glacial period onwards. So, some conifers are reintroductions to the Marches, rather than new introductions.

An argument could even be made for Leyland cypress being native to the Marches. In 1888, seed from a clone of Nootka cypress *Chamaecyparis nootkatensis* at Leighton Hall near Welshpool was sown and some of the seedlings were found to differ from typical Nootka seedlings. They were the result of hybridisation with a Monterey cypress *Cupressus macrocarpa* also growing on this estate, so are named × *Cuppressocyparis leylandii*. As the ranges of the two trees do not overlap in North America, we can assume that these hybrids were the first Leyland cypresses to occur anywhere, though other clones raised subsequently are the much-despised ones that are so widely and inappropriately used for hedging.

WOOD PASTURE AND PARKLAND

In some parts of the world there are natural communities consisting of trees scattered through grassland. Where this type of community currently occurs in the Marches it is either called wood pasture if domesticated livestock are present, or parkland if there are deer. Predators are of course controlled and there are densities of herbivores high enough to preclude the survival of tree seedlings and prevent the development of scrub or closed-canopy woodland. What is far from clear is whether relative population densities of predators would have allowed similar communities to exist before the advent of human pastoralists. There may have been enough deer and other grazers in some areas to limit the establishment of trees, so there would have been areas resembling the wood-pasture and parkland that exists today. What is unquestionable is that many species are adapted to this type of habitat, some of which are not currently found elsewhere.

There are fine examples of both wood pasture and parkland in the Marches but also tantalisingly recent losses. An example of loss in progress can be seen to the south of Downton Gorge where there is an area scattered with huge old pollard oaks and limes. Large numbers of other oaks were felled here in the 1950s. The pasture that surrounded them has been ploughed almost to the trunks of remaining trees, which are being progressively lost as a result of damage to the roots from agrochemicals and machinery. The damage to this area of wood pasture is considered to be too severe for conservation initiatives to be worthwhile. Croft Castle has surviving wood pasture, but until the 1930s there was a much more extensive area that succumbed to the perceived need to protect the national interest by planting conifers. Ancient oaks and chestnuts were poisoned, ring barked and pushed over to make way for spruce and western hemlock. About 10 per cent of the veterans survived this onslaught. Efforts are being made to preserve them and restore the wood pasture.

Over 200 species of epiphytic lichen have been recorded at Croft, which is more than at the nationally important wood pasture in Brampton Bryan Park. However, when these sites are compared using the Revised Index of Ecological Continuity, calculated from the numbers of lichen species that are indicative of ancient woodland, Croft is eclipsed. The index for Brampton Bryan Park is 65, whereas that for Croft it is 50. Brampton Bryan is located on a ridge to the south of the Teme, between Leintwardine and Knighton. The veteran trees in the wood pasture support very rare lichens such as *Lobaria pulmonaria* and *L. amplissima*. There is also a wide diversity of invertebrates, including rare species dependent on dead wood, for example the Welsh oak longhorn beetle and another beetle, *Lymexylon navale*. Not only are the trees of ecological importance, the pasture contains herbs whose flowers are valuable nectar sources for many butterflies, including one of Britain's most threatened species, the high brown fritillary.

There is another fascinating area of wood pasture at Walcot, to the southwest of Bishop's Castle, that is now in the ownership of the National Trust. It lies in a small sheltered valley below the hill fort of Bury Ditches and is a remnant of an Elizabethan deer park, most of which was cleared after the Second World War. There are about 40 veteran oaks, but also a cohort of smaller oaks indicating a gap in grazing in the middle of the 20th century. When the National Trust acquired the site in 1994 there was a dense shrub layer, especially of hawthorn, as a result of more recent interruptions in grazing. The veteran oaks are about 400 years old and many have grown to a huge size, their girths being over 4 m and even over 6 m in a few cases. They are magnificently varied in form. Some have very unusual shapes, including long, low-lying branches that are within easy reach of browsing livestock. This suggests either that the site was used for pigs rather than sheep or cattle, or that grazing was restricted to the period from autumn to spring.

In a survey conducted in 1997, a total of 140 tree-growing lichen species were found, including 18 species that are characteristic of old woodland. These lichens vary in their requirements, in terms of light, moisture, pH and nutrient concentrations. The most obvious species is the very common *Lepraria incana*, consisting of powdery grey-green thalluses on drier exposed parts of the trunks. Scarcer species inhabit deep crevices, underhangs and dead wood. Several RDB species were found: *Caloplaca lucifuga*, *Protoparmelia oleagina* on dead wood that is well-illuminated and *Lecidea nylanderi* at its first British site. Beetles were surveyed at Walcot in 1991 and 87 species were recorded. Dead and decomposing wood were found to hold the greatest number of species, but there were also grassland specialists present. Again, individual beetle species have distinct requirements. Many nationally scarce species have been found at Walcot, for example *Dorcatoma serra*, which breeds in hard bracket fungi on trees with dead wood, *Platypus cylindrus*, on newly fallen oak, and *Ctesias serra*, which feeds on the remains of insects caught in cobwebs under the bark of old trees. The crab spider *Philodromus praedatus* has been recorded. It is a nationally scarce species that is typical of mature oaks in wood pasture. Many more invertebrate species will no doubt be found.

Walcot poses some interesting management questions. Grazing is needed to prevent invasion by sycamore, ash and a variety of shrubs, but with oak branches below the browse line, careful monitoring is needed to avoid tree damage.

Lichens need light, so clearance of shrubs from around the veteran oaks to create more typical wood pasture conditions seems an obvious step, but humidity is also required and veteran oaks on nearby land where there is more exposure have a far less rich lichen flora. The bryophyte flora emphasises the need to maintain humidity levels as species are present that are more typical of damp climates to the west. The policy adopted by the National Trust involves tagging of individual veteran trees and matching management of the 25 to 30-m diameter area around each to its lichen flora. Selected young oaks are being retained and in 150–200 years will form valuable new habitat for old woodland species. Where shrubs and trees are being cleared, a gradual approach is being adopted, which allows species to adjust to changes in conditions.

There are also some fascinating areas of wood pasture on the Stiperstones ridge. One of these is Brook Vessons, where there is a mixture of trees, but most notably some very large specimens of rowan. A core taken from the trunk of one of them gave an age of about 100 years, which is considerable, given that members of the rose family usually succumb to infection or some other fate long before this. One of the rowans is among the largest in Britain and six others are also very large. Adjacent to Brook Vessons is The Hollies, which is unusual enough to merit separate description.

THE HOLLIES

The novelist Mary Webb referred to this area as 'God's little mountain'.[12] The Hollies is located on the northeast side of the Stiperstones at an altitude of about 330 m. There are more than 200 holly trees dotted across 37 ha of acid grassland and bracken (Fig. 154). Some of the trees are estimated to be 300–400 years old, so they are probably the oldest members of their species in Europe. Hollies do not

FIG 154. The Hollies, a remarkable wood pasture on the north end of the Stiperstones, here photographed in the 1960s. (George Peterken)

naturally live to such a great age and, as with oaks, pollarding is the reason for the exceptional longevity. It is clear from the form of these ancient trees that they have been repeatedly cut. Far from damaging the trees, it has rejuvenated them by stimulating regrowth. Local records dating back to the 18th century refer to the right to cut branches for use as winter fodder for livestock. It is thought that wood pastures dominated by hollies were once found quite widely in Britain, particularly in the Marches and the Pennines, where there are many examples of places named Hollies or Hollins. George Peterken[13] has suggested that these sites would have originally resembled holly orchards or groves, with parallels to the olive groves of the Mediterranean.

Holly leaves are nutritious and palatable to cattle, so lower leaves and branches of trees in hedgerows and pastures are usually browsed off, despite their defensive spines. Leaves on branches above browsing height do not have spines, making them particularly useful as forage, but as they are out of reach they must be cut and fed to cattle. This was traditionally done in the hungry winter months, when the meagre stores of forage had run out. Many of these areas of holly were grubbed out when agricultural methods changed in the 18th century and livestock farmers started to produce some hay and grow turnips as winter fodder. However, tithe records show that stocking rates were low in the upland area around the Hollies, with typical farms only able to make enough hay to feed about ten cattle through the winter. There was therefore little impetus to clear trees and resow the hill pastures used for summer grazing.

After the Second World War, when agricultural intensification caused the loss of many interesting sites, The Hollies was bought by the Home Office and used as a prison farm, so was spared the usual commercial pressures. The significance of the area was recognised in the 1960s when Charles Sinker, George Peterken and John Thompson visited and when the Home Office sold it, the Dudlestone family who bought it were sympathetic owners and co-operated when conservation initiatives were proposed. SSSI status was granted in 1989 and since then there has been some active conservation work.

Pollarding had long ceased, though there has been some cutting of branches from female trees to provide foliage and berries for making Christmas wreaths, a traditional local industry. Many trees had grown to a size where wind damage was increasingly likely. From 1990 onwards, small numbers of hollies have been pollarded, on an experimental basis. This has been done in April, partly because it was probably the hungriest time for livestock and so replicates traditional management, but also because subsequent holly regrowth should be safe from frost damage. Encouragingly, none of the pollarded trees have died and most have regrown strongly.

A longstanding conservation concern is the lack of young holly trees. The existing trees are probably relicts of former woodland, so the method by which they became established is not now possible. Prodigious amounts of seed are set particularly in the year following a warm summer, but seedlings fail to survive. Three factors contributory to this failure are grazing, competition with grassland plants and the harsh climate, including exposure to wind and dry summer periods. Recently planted young trees have almost all failed to survive. Fenced exclosure areas were created in the 1990s, in an attempt to encourage natural regeneration, but rowan trees, rather than holly have become established in these. Rowan seedlings are even more attractive to grazing animals than holly, explaining a distinctive feature of the Hollies. There are almost no free-standing rowans, but significant numbers of rowan growing either inside or immediately adjacent to holly trees (Fig. 155). The sequence of events is probably this: repeated pollarding of the holly trees creates a stout bole with a height of about 2 m and eventually the core of this rots. Fieldfares and other berry-eating birds perch in the tree and defecate. Rowan seeds in the faeces can germinate and grow in the rotting core of the tree. Rowan can therefore become established inside the holly, protected from browsing by the spiny holly foliage. All other rowans are destroyed as seedlings by grazing. The rowan's growth rate is typically greater than that of the holly, so it

FIG 155. Holly trees at the Hollies (left) in fruit, with Lawn Hill to the right and the Wrekin beyond in the far distance (Ben Osborne) and (right) in snow with a rowan growing from the centre.

splits out of the holly trunk, sometimes knocking it over, leading to its destruction. However, the holly often survives and a bizarre holly-rowan chimera develops.

The tenacity of holly trees is remarkable and the survival of the Hollies can be attributed to this, along with several strokes of good fortune and recent conservation initiatives. In 2008 Philip Dudlestone sold the site to the Shropshire Wildlife Trust. Conservation has therefore become the main aim, but decisions have to be made about the type of management that will be most successful in achieving this aim. Grazing must be continued, or the site will rapidly change from wood pasture to scrub. Grazing by cattle in addition to sheep is recommended, as it will help to prevent bracken encroachment. Holly bark is sometimes stripped off and eaten by livestock, killing or severely damaging the tree, but as this occurs mostly in winter, it can be avoided by moving the livestock elsewhere at this time. Pollarding can be continued on a selective basis, with the confidence that it should rejuvenate rather than kill the trees. A more intractable problem is finding a method of establishing young holly trees to replace the inevitable losses of older trees. It would not be unreasonable to aim to establish 1,000 young trees, scattered across the site rather than concentrated in groups to maintain the character of a wood pasture. The rarity of the Hollies not only makes its conservation very important, but also explains why it is not yet known what management techniques will be successful. When the Shropshire Wildlife Trust was bidding for this site it was suggested that the Hollies had been saved, and the trust's magazine stated that 'we need every bit of support we can get to save this precious relic of holly forest'.[14] Statements like these are often made when a conservation agency acquires a site, but the ownership of land is never enough. What is needed over the short, medium and long-term is genuine stewardship through effective management.

It should be emphasised that the Hollies is not a natural community and that natural regeneration will not occur here. It is nonetheless a landscape of great beauty and a site of significant value to wildlife. For example, the berries are significant food source for resident mistle thrushes *Turdus viscivorus* and blackbirds *Turdus merula*, as well as visiting flocks of fieldfares *Turdus pilaris* and redwings *Turdus iliacus*. Terminal leaves and flower buds are a larval food source for the caterpillars of the spring generation of holly blue butterflies *Celastrina argiolus*, the adults of which fly in large numbers during April. The roots are parasitised by toothworts, whose flowers also appear in April. A theme that has run through this chapter is that many species and communities in the Marches may not be truly native. Where levels of biodiversity are high, it is likely that the species are indeed native and the communities are at least to an extent natural. Even if they are not, it should probably not over-concern us, and we should be content that wild species have found a habitat in which they can thrive.

CHAPTER 10

Rivers

FEW PLACES IN THE MARCHES ARE FAR FROM the sight or sound of flowing water. There are dry valleys in a few areas created by the torrents from melting ice sheets, where water now percolates into the porous sand and gravel deposits, rather than flowing over the surface. Elsewhere, with little limestone and no chalk for water to sink into, almost every small valley has a stream flowing through it. These streams merge to form rivers of increasing size and power. Flow rates in the Severn and other major rivers in the Marches can be very high, with frequent floods in winter. This is because their catchment areas include large parts of Mid-Wales.

Many fine rivers rise in the Welsh hills to the west of the Marches. From north to south, they are the Alun, Clywedog, Dee, Ceiriog, Tanat, Vyrnwy, Severn, Clun, Teme and Lugg. Those that only flow a short distance into England before reaching their confluence with a larger river mostly have only Welsh names, but those that flow further into England tend also to have an anglicised version of the original name. Afon Llugwy is the River Lugg once it is in England for example, Afon Tefeidiad becomes the Teme and Afon Hafren the Severn.[1] Whatever names we use, the upper parts of these rivers are beautiful and eminently worth exploring. As the orientation of their valleys is mostly west to east, access is much easier from England than from North or South Wales. Nevertheless, the landscape, the pattern of settlement and most of the population are Welsh and some argue that on both historical and geographical grounds mid-Wales should be regarded as the heartland of the principality.[2]

The Camlad is unusual in that it rises to the east of Offa's Dyke, but flows westwards to its confluence with Afon Hafren in Wales. Other rivers have their sources and entire catchment within the Marches. The Onny and Corve rise in the hills of south Shropshire, with contributions from many fast-flowing streams. The streams and rivers that drain the North Shropshire–Cheshire Plain are of a very different type, flowing slowly along gentle gradients and often having to follow tortuous routes around glacial deposits. The Tern falls less than 30 m in 40 km. Perhaps surprisingly for such a low-lying area, watersheds cross the plain. The rivers Perry, Roden and Tern drain the southern parts and discharge into the Severn. The rivers Dee, Gowy and Weaver drain the northern parts and discharge into the Irish Sea. Tributaries of the Trent, which discharges into the North Sea, drain part of the east of the plain. There is therefore a point to the northeast of Market Drayton where three watersheds meet and depending on precisely where rainwater falls, it can flow to the Irish Sea, the North Sea or the Severn Estuary (Fig. 156).

The rivers that flow through the Marches are rich in wildlife. The whole of the Dee and the Teme have SSSI status. The Dee and several of its tributaries are SACs, as is the Clun. One of the primary reasons for the Dee's SAC designation is the transition that it makes, in a relatively short distance, from a mountain area to a low-lying plain. Other Marches rivers show this feature at least as strongly and change in character hugely over a short distance. This is another example

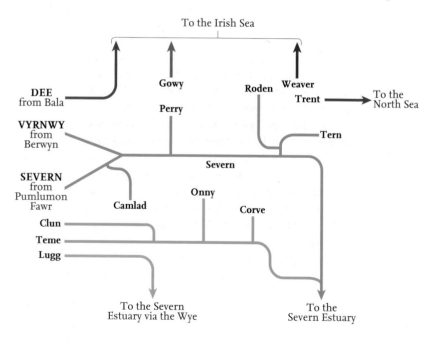

FIG 156. Stylised map of Marches drainage.

of the transitions that characterise the natural history of the Marches. It would be impossible in the space available for this chapter to describe in detail all of the rivers. The rivers that discharge into the Irish Sea and the North Sea flow for the majority of their distance outside the Marches, so they are, with apologies, only occasionally mentioned. It is the Severn and its tributaries that are the main focus of this chapter.

STREAMS OF THE UPLANDS

Few upland streams begin with anything as definite as a spring. Instead, water that is usually acidic and oligotrophic oozes through the many flushes near of the heads of valleys and emerges as tiny runnels, often hidden in the vegetation. These runnels merge to form small streams that flow rapidly because of the steep gradients. Streams on the Long Mynd descend more than 100 m in a kilometre, with waterfalls where resistant bands of rock outcrop. The fast flow rates cause fine particles of silt and sand to be carried away, leaving a gravelly substratum with large stones and bare rock in places. Wilson's filmy-fern *Hymenophyllum wilsonii* has been found in the splash zone at Light Spout Hollow and other smaller waterfalls – an eastern outpost of this species' westerly oceanic distribution. Where the material on the streambed is unstable, few plants are able to colonise and instead the rock fragments have a covering of unicellular or filamentous algae. If the substratum is stable then various species can colonise. The red alga *Lemanea mammilosa*, the aquatic lichens *Verrucaria aethiobola* and *Staurothele fissa*, the mosses *Hygroamblystegium fluviatale*, *Eurynchium platyhypnoides*, *Racomitrium aciculare*, and *Brachythecium rivulare* and the liverwort *Scapania undulata* are all found in Long Mynd streams. Flowering plants and ferns are confined to the banks, with lemon-scented fern *Oreopteris limbosperma* characteristic of this habitat. Monkeyflower *Mimulus guttatus* is a rather exotic sight along these upland streams, both in the sense that its flowers are showier than those of its neighbours and because it is an alien, introduced as a garden plant and colonising the Marches uplands from the 19th century onwards.

Upland streams in open country are typically well oxygenated and unpolluted, so they can support a diverse range of invertebrates. Most of these are concealed under stones or in gravel, so are only revealed by kick sampling or some other active method. A detailed study of one stream on the Long Mynd was carried in the 1960s.[3] In the upper sections of the stream the most abundant invertebrates were freshwater shrimps, caddisfly and stonefly larvae, helodid beetle larvae and riffle beetles. Two species of flatworm were found, one of which only occurred in spring water at the head of the stream where temperatures were lowest. This was *Crenobia alpina*, sometimes called the alpine flatworm. It breeds at temperatures up to 14 °C and most rapidly at 10 °C. It can only survive for a few days at temperatures above 25 °C. A wider range of invertebrates was found in the middle and lower reaches of this hill stream, including the larvae of 15 species of stonefly, 18 species of caddisfly and nine species of mayfly. Water beetles, black-fly larvae and non-biting midge larvae were also present in abundance. Freshwater limpets, cockles and pea mussels were also found. In addition to the species found during this study, many others have been discovered on the Long Mynd. These include some of national importance, for example *Hydroporus ferrugineus*, a diving beetle found in springs and flushes, and *Laccobius atrocephalus*, which inhabits small streams and flushes. Many upland streams have not yet been investigated and there will no doubt be more discoveries in the future, especially among the less charismatic groups.

Several species of Odonata breed here. The golden-ringed dragonfly *Cordulegaster boltonii* is scarce to the east of the Marches, but its larvae are abundant in shallow streams on the Long Mynd, the Clee hills and occasionally elsewhere in south Shropshire (Fig. 157). Larvae of the beautiful demoiselle *Calopteryx virgo* occur both in hill streams and further downstream as long as there is still fast-flowing water. They favour reaches where the substratum is gravelly and there is moderate shading by bankside trees or shrubs. The keeled skimmer *Orthetrum coerulescens* is a scarcer species with a patchy distribution through southern and western Britain. It favours acidic peaty streams and bog pools where there is at least some flow of water. There are isolated populations in streams and flushes at Cramer Gutter, east of Titterston Clee, and at Wild Moor on the Long Mynd.

Spring-fed streams in the hills have a relatively narrow and cool temperature range during the year, suiting brown trout, which occur very widely. They spawn in gravelly sections and use some reaches as nursery areas, growing to modest sizes, up to 300 mm. Bullheads are also commonly present in the hill streams. They are bottom dwellers and well camouflaged, emerging to feed at dusk. Some streams have unusually high densities, for example in Ashes Hollow on the Long Mynd. Brook lampreys *Lampetra planeri* are also sometimes found, but they are more common downstream where there is more organic matter in the water.

Grey wagtails *Motacilla cinerea* and dippers *Cinclus cinclus* are the birds that are most characteristic of these hill streams. Dippers require fast-flowing shallow water with gravel beds in which to feed on invertebrate larvae, so they are largely an upland species (Fig. 158). They are on the eastern edge of their range in the Marches, but are present on many streams and rivers in the south Shropshire and north Herefordshire hills. As found elsewhere, nesting and winter roosting

FIG 157. Golden-ringed dragonfly on the Long Mynd. (David Williams)

FIG 158. Dippers – three fledglings on the Teme in Ludlow. (Gareth Thomas)

sites are often located under bridges. Some modern bridges lack suitable ledges or holes and where nest boxes are installed dippers or grey wagtails often occupy them. Dry summers cause a reduction in the dipper population, but numbers can rise quickly in following years. The range of grey wagtails includes many streams in the hill country but also rivers in the Marches where there are riffles or rapids. Weirs and confluences of streams can also cause enough water disturbance to suit them. High banks with crevices are needed for the nest site, which can be several hundred metres from the river.

So far in this account of hill streams the assumption has been made that the adjacent land is open, but many of the narrow upland valleys are dingles with

FIG 159. Beechfield Dingle, near Worthen, with alder, ash and ramsons in flower. (Mark Duffell)

steep wooded sides (Fig. 159). Streams in dingles are different in many ways from those in open hill country. Humidity is typically high and rocks protruding from the water and stream banks are usually covered with mosses and liverworts. Both opposite-leaved and alternate-leaved golden-saxifrage *Chrysosplenium oppositifolium* and *Chrysoplenium alternifolium* are also often present, sometimes in extensive patches. Light intensities are low and fallen leaves and twigs contribute large amounts of organic matter to the water, so decomposers rather than photosynthesisers are therefore at the start of many food chains. Oxygen is consumed when decomposition is occurring in the water, but steep gradients and frequent small waterfalls or cascades over rock shelves can keep oxygen levels up and this is reflected in the types of invertebrate that are found.

Fallen wood and logjams are often present, which may look untidy but should not routinely be cleared out because they form an important habitat for invertebrates such as craneflies (Fig. 160). The larvae of *Lipsothrix nervosa* feed on waterlogged wood near streams or seepages; those of *Lipsothrix errans*, which is nationally scarce, feed on coarse woody debris in streams; *Lipsothrix nobilis*, a cranefly with RDB1 status, has larvae that feed on dead wood in logjams in streams.[4] The dingles are one of the specialities of the Marches, so it is not surprising that rare invertebrates have been discovered here. Other RDB species of dingle streams include the hoverfly *Chalcosyrphus eunotus* on semi-submerged logs in dappled shade and the dolichopodid fly *Syntormon macula* on coarse woody debris.[5] There are many dingles, but most are difficult of access and rarely visited. A habitat action plan has been proposed specifically for dingle streams to promote their conservation, though they do not appear to be particularly threatened at present.

FIG 160. Insects of the dingles: *Lipsothrix remota* newly emerged (Pete Boardman) and *Chalcosyrphus eunotus*. (Bob Kemp)

UPLAND RIVERS

The hill streams merge to form larger rivers that flow through upland valleys. There are many fine examples, especially the West and East Onny in *Ordovicia* and the Unk, Clun, Redlake and Teme in *West Siluria*. They meander though land that is typically pasture and meadow, though there is some arable farming. The meanders are of a relatively small radius compared with those downstream on the flood plains. The valleys in which these rivers flow usually have porous glacial deposits of sand and gravel. These are often compacted enough to resist erosion and form cliff like vertical faces on the outer side of meanders, with a visible sequence of layers of varying particle size as a result of cycles of deposition. The materials, which range from microscopic clay particles up to large rocks, are eventually dislodged by the flow of water. Flow rates are mostly rapid, except in dry summers, so small particles of clay and silt are carried away, leaving sand and gravel in the riverbed. Common sandpipers sometimes nest where these coarse materials become exposed, especially on the inside of meanders or on shingle bars. There are breeding records from the Teme, Clun and Onny. Sandpipers are at the eastern extreme of their breeding range in the Marches and are more characteristic of upland rivers. Much more common on these rivers are the dippers and grey wagtails, whose habitat extends down from the hill streams. They are absent where there is too much silt deposition, as on parts of the Teme and the Clun.

In dry summers the water level in some rivers can drop below the surface of the sand and gravel; the river appears to have gone dry, but groundwater will still be flowing in the riverbed. A section of the Teme between Knighton and Leintwardine does this for example, even when visible flow continues in the river above Knighton and below Leintwardine. There are parallels here with winterbournes of chalk country that only flow when the water table is higher than the riverbed. The Environment Agency has carried out analyses to find whether very low or no flow in rivers such as the Teme is caused by water abstraction, but it appears to be a natural phenomenon. Despite this, the agency sometimes mounts rescues of stranded fish. There are anecdotal reports that the Clun has still not recovered from losses sustained during the severe drought of 1976.

As with hill streams, there are still relatively few plants in these rivers. Areas of exposed bedrock and large boulders of glacial origin form a secure anchorage for mosses such as *Rynchostegium riparioides*, but flowering plants cannot root into them and areas with smaller stones or sand are too unstable. Further downstream there is much greater diversity, as shown by a survey of the Lugg[6] (Fig. 161).

The fish that dominate the rivers of upland valleys are salmonids. Brown trout are almost always the predominant species, especially in side streams such

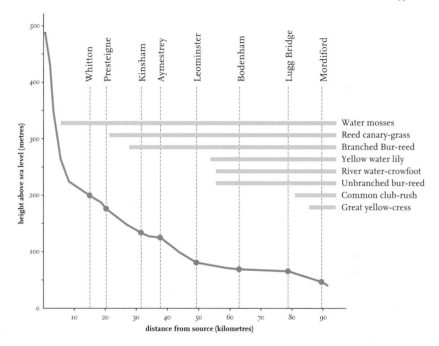

FIG 161. The number of plant species in the Lugg increases from the steeply descending and fast-flowing headwaters to the gentle gradients below Leominster and confluence with the Wye.

as the tributaries of the Teme above Bromfield and the Onny. Spawning takes place wherever there are gravelly sections with riffle pools. Atlantic salmon *Salmo salar* are present as far upstream as natural and manmade obstructions allow. They can overcome most of the many weirs that survive from the days of water power if flow rates are reasonable. Other obstructions are insurmountable, most notably the huge dam on the Clywedog river in Wales, which denies salmon access to 30 km of ideal habitat. At least some individuals get past all obstacles on the Severn in the Marches, swimming into Wales to reach spawning sites. Some of these sites are as far up the river as the weir at Felindre just above Llanidloes or further still up the Dulas, one of Afon Hafren's tributaries. The Teme as far upstream as Knighton is one of the best salmon spawning rivers in England. Fish passes have been constructed to help upward migration on some but not all weirs. Buckton and Brampton weirs located a few kilometres upstream of Leintwardine both now have passes but Lingen further upstream does not, nor does a weir downstream of Leintwardine in Downton Gorge. Passes have been constructed on the Onny at Stokesay weir and Halford Mill near Craven Arms.

Another severe problem is silt deposition in the gravel beds used for spawning. A 300 mm depth of clean gravel is needed for salmon to spawn. This is still available on upper reaches of the upland rivers, but a study of the Lugg, from where the river crosses Offa's Dyke downstream to Leominster, has shown increasing levels of siltation and no suitable spawning grounds below Leominster.[7] Changes in agricultural practice have made matters worse, especially production of maize silage, which leaves fields bare for long periods and does not even stabilise soils much during crop growth.

There are also coarse fish that favour the relatively cool water and fast flow rates of rivers in upland valleys, especially grayling *Thymallus thymallus*, but also brook lamprey, bullhead and stone loach *Barbatula barbatula*. Bullheads and stone loaches are adapted to life in fast flowing water by their streamlined shape. Brook lamprey larvae burrow into the riverbed where it is silty and feed on particles of organic matter in the water. They metamorphose into adult form after about six years and swim upstream to spawn. Like the other two lamprey species in Britain, they cannot scale waterfalls or artificial obstacles but as they do not migrate to and from the sea during their adult life, populations can exist above these barriers to migration. Brook lampreys are therefore found in higher reaches of Marches rivers than the other two species, river lamprey *Lampetra fluviatilis* and sea lamprey *Petromyzon marinus*.

The white-clawed crayfish *Austropotamobius pallipes* is another species of conservation interest found in these rivers (Fig. 162). There are populations in tributaries of the Clun, but also in rivers that are more lowland in character – the Rea Brook, Ledwyche Brook and even in the Meese. The conventional view is that white-clawed crayfish prefer sites where the water is clear, without the turbidity caused by silt from arable land, or from riverbanks poached by

FIG 162. White-clawed crayfish being measured during research into populations in Shropshire. (Neal Haddaway)

livestock. However, there is a population in the Cound Brook near Condover – a small river that flows through agricultural land and is affected by siltation. There is a huge population in Trench Pool in Telford, formerly a canal feeder reservoir for the Shrewsbury Canal, but now an angling lake, where high levels of sulphate and other minerals indicate significant pollution. Another population thrives in Simpson's Pool at Horsehay, near Coalbrookdale on the south side of Telford. Ostensibly less surprising is the strong population in the River Redlake, a headstream of the Teme with a cobbly riverbed that provides crayfish with the shelter that they need. Even here the habitat might not seem totally suitable, as the upper reaches of the river flow through an area of livestock farming at Purlogue, but as the Telford pool populations show, mesotrophic water seems to be acceptable. From Purlogue down to Bucknell the Redlake sometimes stops flowing completely in dry summers, but the crayfish seem able to cling on in pools along the riverbed, even though the water quality including oxygen concentration must be low. A population of 650 white-clawed crayfish was recently found in the Redlake at Bucknell, using holes in the stone revetment of a road that was due to be rebuilt. The crayfish were kept in tanks while the building work was done. Holes were deliberately left in the new revetment and the crayfish were then returned to the river.

We might expect all other rivers of the upland valleys to have native crayfish populations and indeed the SSSI citation for the Teme published in 1996[8] reports a good population on that river. The Clun had a healthy population in the past, but this has been damaged by two devastating events. In 1991 many individuals were killed by crayfish plague in the Clun at Clungunford, and then in 1996 pollution of the river with sheep dip insecticide killed all invertebrates over a considerable length of the river. A survey in 2002 found 75 individuals in the upper reaches of the Clun above the site of the pollution, but none below it. By 2009 white-clawed crayfish had returned in small numbers to some parts of the Clun, but the recovery was far from complete, despite good populations in side streams. The Camlad had a thriving population until an outbreak of crayfish plague in 1990 and a survey in 2002 found no crayfish. The Environment Agency has since carried out a release programme with the aim of re-establishing the population, but so far this has not been successful. The source of crayfish plague is the non-native signal crayfish *Pacifastacus leniusculus*, which has spread or been introduced to some rivers in the Marches. Direct contact between the two species may not be necessary for infection, both salmonid fish and anglers' nets having been suggested as plague vectors. Signal crayfish are abundant in some lowland rivers, including the Tern at Wollerton. There are scattered populations in upland streams, including Darnford Brook, a tributary of the Onny and Lakehouse Brook under Wenlock Edge. There are also populations in some artificial fishing lakes. There is a huge population in Bayliss Pools behind the service station on the M54 at Telford. Some individuals in this population are 10–15 years old and an impressive 300 mm in length.

The habitat in Bayliss Pools is not dissimilar to that of the Telford pools where white-clawed crayfish have been found. It seems that introduction by humans rather than differences in habitat preference determine where each species currently occurs. Sceptics have suggested that the white-clawed crayfish may itself be an introduced species in the Marches, as there are no records from before 1500. We may never be certain about the origins of local populations, but the original species distribution is from Italy to Ireland, so the Marches are certainly within the natural range and it is not unreasonable to consider this a native species. It has in any case the status of a species of European importance in legislation stemming from the EU habitats directive, with BAP priority status both locally and nationally. White-clawed crayfish populations have declined significantly throughout Europe since the 1960s, with many populations disappearing entirely and many others dropping in density by 90 per cent. The declines have been much less drastic in Ireland and this suggests that the Marches populations, also at the western edge of the current species range, could continue to fare better. Some of the populations here are now important strongholds for the species, but they are fragmented. Given the continued presence of crayfish plague, they face an uncertain future. We must therefore continue to do everything possible to conserve them.

Another invertebrate species that is both fascinating and seriously threatened is the freshwater pearl mussel *Margaritifera margaritifera*. There are small populations in several Marches rivers, but much the most significant is in the Clun. A survey in 2008 revealed several thousand individuals to be present in one stretch of the river. Although it is impossible to be certain, only two other rivers in England and Wales are thought to have larger populations. The pearl mussel's life cycle is similar in length to our own. They become capable of reproduction when 15–20 years old and can survive to an age of 100 or more, making them one of the longest lived of invertebrates. Mature female pearl mussels release larvae in huge numbers during late summer. The survival of these larvae, called glochidia, depends on their being inhaled by young brown trout or Atlantic salmon and becoming attached to their gills. There they encyst and feed parasitically until the following spring when they drop off and burrow into sandy or gravelly areas of riverbed. If there is too much silt in the riverbed, it is highly unlikely that any released individuals will survive.[9] Water quality also needs to be high at this stage, so that oxygen penetrates to where the young pearl mussels are living. They feed and grow there for several years until large enough to move to the gravel surface, where they live for the remainder of their lives.

All of the individuals in the Clun population are 40 years old or more. This is because no recruitment has taken place for several decades. Although this population could persist for many more years, a return to successful reproduction is vital for its long-term survival. There are almost certainly sufficient young salmon and brown trout in the Clun for the reproduction of pearl mussels, with both species of fish spawning naturally and supplementary releases of salmon parr from hatcheries adding to the population. However, it is possible that glochidia are failing to get though the parasitic stage in their life cycle. The Environment Agency has therefore been collecting pearl mussels and rearing the glochidia that they produce at a salmon hatchery at Clywedog (Fig. 163). The survival rates of glochidia in the hatchery have not been great, but nonetheless sufficient young pearl mussels should soon be reared for them to be released in significant numbers when they are between five and eight years old. Captive rearing and release of young pearl mussels will only be successful if the Clun provides the conditions needed for continued survival. Much more needs to be done to improve conditions sufficiently for natural reproduction to

FIG 163. Pearl mussels removed from the Clun, for captive rearing of young at a salmon hatchery. (James Griffiths)

recommence. Ironically, the establishment of a larger population of adults would help to maintain high water quality, as pearl mussels, being filter feeders, remove suspended organic matter from the water.

It would be a tragedy if the Clun population were not to survive. It has probably remained genetically distinct from other populations since the last ice age, as the only significant dispersal stage is while the young are attached to the gills of young salmon or trout, which are hardly likely to migrate between river systems during the autumn or winter. Tests indicate that it is more similar to populations in Ireland that others in England, perhaps because of the way in which ice sheets melted. The freshwater pearl mussels of the River Clun should be a real conservation priority for the Marches. The key to improvements in water quality is change to agricultural practices and this is being encouraged through agri-environment schemes. These involve catchment sensitive methods, such as prevention of clean storm water flowing into the Clun from becoming mixed with water draining off farmyards contaminated with animal wastes. They also involve changes to the management of riverbanks.

Trees grow along substantial lengths of the Clun and other upland rivers. Alders are overwhelmingly dominant and account for 80 per cent or so of bankside trees, with some willows and a few oaks and ashes. Most of the approximately 2,000 km of flowing water in south Shropshire and north Herefordshire is alder lined. Leighton[10] describes the tree as being of 'agreeable verdure and dense shade'. Alder leaves provide nutrition for many associated invertebrates – this is a field where more research could be done, as less has been published than for oaks and other trees.

Alders have traditionally been coppiced and some have therefore lived to a great age, with huge stools developing. The largest are more than 2 m in diameter. The wood had a variety of uses, including fuel for furnaces and limekilns, production of charcoal for gunpowder manufacture and the construction of the timber frames of cruck houses. It was also sold to Lancashire clog makers. Coppicing ceased during the 20th century and there are now many magnificent specimens with increasing girth and height. One disadvantage of coppicing has been that trunks never reach a large size or reach an age where they are starting to senesce and develop tree holes. Pied flycatchers and other birds are therefore denied natural nesting sites.

A long-running nest box project has been carried out in the Clun valley since the late 1980s. About 1,000 nest boxes have been maintained on 10 km of the Clun and one of its tributaries, Folly Brook. The boxes are visited on about ten occasions in the year to monitor occupancy and breeding success. All adult pied flycatchers and their young are ringed when possible. Records of ringed individuals show that most return to breed within 20 km of the upper Clun valley and also that average life expectancy is short, but some individuals live for seven years and maybe more. Other bird species use these riverside nest boxes, including blue tits *Cyanistes caeruleus* and great tits in large and increasing numbers, also tree sparrows *Passer montanus*, nuthatches *Sitta europaea*, marsh tits and coal tits occasionally, and redstarts very occasionally. Even with these unintended occupants, the number of young flycatchers reared in nest boxes put up by the Clun Valley Pied Flycatcher Project is approaching 20,000 and a huge amount of data has been collected.[11] At the start of the project about 250 of the boxes were occupied by pied flycatchers, declining during the 1990s to stabilise at about 150. It is not clear what the reasons are for this decline. It could be due to problems during migration or at the overwintering sites in Africa. It could also be due to local factors such as insecticides killing aquatic larvae that would otherwise emerge as adults and act as a food; however, the average brood size has remained close to six, making it less likely that a problem of food supply is the cause. An interesting trend, persisting throughout the period of the project, is that more young have been reared to pullus stage on the upper reaches of both the Clun and the Folly Brook, than on lower reaches. This is not unexpected as pied flycatchers are at the edge of their range in the Marches with their heartland to the west in Wales. The trend raises the possibility that the decline in pied flycatcher nests is due to warmer springs and summers, forcing a retreat up valleys to high, cooler sites.

A recent threat to alders and the species dependent on them is dieback due to *Phytopthora alni*. This strain of fungal pathogen was identified relatively recently as the cause of increasing numbers of deaths, especially in the Marches. The epidemiology of this apparently new disease is still being studied, but trials in the Clun valley suggest that it is not confined to certain strains of alder and instead that there is broad susceptibility. Newly coppiced alders appear to show increased resistance and even signs of recovery from infection. Landowners in the Shropshire Hills AONB have been encouraged to restart a programme of coppicing as a part of improved riparian management. Infection rates are very variable. They are particularly high on the Kemp below Brockton and become higher and higher going downstream from Duffryn on the Clun. They are high on lower reaches of the Onny, but are much lower on the Corve.

High infection rates seem to be linked with pollution of water with manure or sewage, as on the Byne Brook for example, which joins the Onny near Craven Arms. Exclusion of livestock from a strip of land along watercourses reduces this pollution, with the additional benefit of preventing the overgrazing and poaching that tends to cause soil erosion and diffuse pollution of rivers

FIG 164. Cattle, with access to the Camlad in the Vale of Montgomery, are a source of diffuse pollution, exacerbated by a lack of bankside vegetation.

(Fig. 164). Improved riparian management also involves conservation of bankside trees, as they reduce diffuse pollution by stabilising riverbanks and have favourable effects on water flow within rivers. A study of the Upper Severn and other rivers in Mid-Wales showed that the bank-to-bank width was nearly 20 per cent less for a given flow rate where banks were tree-lined, compared with sections where there was grass or negligible bankside vegetation.[12] Water flow rates are therefore greater in tree-lined sections, cleaning out silt from redds where fish spawn and from sites where freshwater pearl mussels formerly bred. Of course, the bankside ribbons of alder are remnants of much larger areas of alder carr and ideally wider areas of this riverine woodland would be allowed to develop on flood plains of upland rivers.

SMALL LOWLAND RIVERS

The rivers that flow through the upland valleys eventually emerge into broad lowland valleys or onto flood plains. In some cases they then enter a gorge where their character reverts to that of an upland river, for example the Teme in Downton Gorge and the Severn in Ironbridge Gorge, but they resume the character of lowland rivers below these gorges. The rivers of the North Shropshire–Cheshire Plain either rise in low hills or on the plain itself, so are lowland in character for all or most of their length. Although the lowland rivers share some common features, there are also disparities resulting from differences in geology, topography and human influences. Each river is therefore worthy of study and comparison is often instructive, but only a partial account is possible here, which might encourage the reader to enquire or research further.

The Perry is typical in some respects of lowland rivers in the Marches. It rises in low hills to the west of Gobowen, descends 150 m rapidly in its first 6 km stony-bottomed stretch and then takes another 30 km to fall 40 m.[13] The Perry drains a largely agricultural catchment of 200 km² and has a mean flow rate of 200 million litres per day. Permian and Triassic sandstones underlie almost all of the catchment and act as an aquifer, maintaining flow rates in dry seasons. There is a six- to seven-fold difference between the low and high flow rates during the year, which is comparable with chalk streams and much lower than ratios for streams on lowland clay or hard upland rocks, where the difference is typically more than ten-fold.

Students from Preston Montford Field Studies Centre recorded invertebrates and aquatic plants in the Perry in the early 1980s.[14] Over 100 species in more than 50 families were found. The distributions of both invertebrates and water plants were used to assess water quality. Discharge of sewage, septic tank overflows and creamery effluent were found to be having measurable impacts. The poorest water quality, downstream of Ellesmere, was due to a combination of all of these types of pollution, with the effects apparent for more than 15 km. Environment Agency data for 2008 show a marked improvement in water quality, with biotic indices for upper and lower reaches of the Perry indicating no significant pollution and intermediate sections only mildly contaminated. As elsewhere in Britain, investment in sewage treatment work and in the treatment of effluent from creameries and other industries has had clear benefits. However, in other respects there has been no improvement in recent decades. Nitrate levels are now in the range of 25–35 mg per litre and phosphates 50–250 μg per litre. These are higher than in the 1980s, largely as a result of leaching from the intensively farmed catchment area. The 1980s surveys revealed considerable differences in invertebrate populations between slow-flowing silt-bottomed sections of the Perry and stony riffle-dominated stretches. As an example, freshwater mussels *Anodonta* spp. were confined to the siltiest sections where the Perry flows across Baggy Moor, whereas river limpets *Ancylus fluviatilis* were only found in stony-bottomed sections of the upper reaches and downstream of Ruyton XI Towns. The silty sections are largely the product of agriculture. Tillage, land drainage and poaching by livestock all cause silt to enter streams and rivers. In the past, water boards and landowners were legally obliged to carry out maintenance work on ditches and other watercourses to ensure efficient drainage of agricultural land.

During the 20th century, the Perry was repeatedly dredged, widened and straightened, in works collectively known as canalisation or channelisation (Fig. 165). The most recent scheme was carried out in the 1980s. In 1984 biotic indices for the Perry at Fitz and at Rednal Mill were similar. After canalisation the index fell significantly at Rednal in the winter of 1986/7, whereas at Fitz no canalisation work took place and the index was unchanged. Canalisation destroys the natural riffle-pool system of rivers, evening out flow rates and allowing deposition of silt. Experiments were carried out in the Perry at Ruyton XI Towns in the late 1970s to test three possible methods of remediation.[15] Small dams were constructed creating deeper pools above each dam and faster flowing water with turbulent riffles below. Current deflectors were constructed, consisting of

FIG 165. The Perry has been canalised where it crosses Baggy Moor (left), but still follows a natural meandering course downstream near Fitz (right).

dams extending halfway across the river, angled downstream at a 45° angle to the bank. These increased flow rates in the narrowed channel and created pools of quiet water below the deflector. The third method involved artificial shading of water near the riverbank using floating sheets of plywood. The numbers, biomass and distribution of fish were investigated by electro-fishing, before and after the installations. Large numbers of dace *Leuciscus leuciscus* and chub *Squalius cephalus* congregated above the dams. Gudgeon *Gobio gobio*, stone-loach and other bottom-dwelling species were concentrated in the water below the dams, where the fast flow rates aerated the water and scoured silt out of the gravel, encouraging the invertebrates on which these fish feed. The fry of chub, dace and roach sheltered in the quiet water below the deflectors, with accumulated floating debris providing overhead cover. Dace favoured the fast-flowing water below the tips of the deflectors. Dace, chub and roach were found in large numbers beneath the artificial shading, which provided the low light conditions that would naturally be created by overhanging trees and submerged tree roots. Numbers and biomass of fish increased overall in the section of the Perry where these structures were installed, and the distribution of fish showed that to some extent a natural riffle-pool system had been re-established.

It is unlikely that structures such as these will ever be installed in the Perry on a basis widespread enough fully to repair the damage done by canalisation. It is even less likely that comprehensive river rehabilitation will be carried out, as was done experimentally by the Environment Agency on Padgate Brook in Cheshire in the 1990s.[16] This trial showed that wildlife habitat could be transformed without increased flooding. Despite these results it seems the trend is still to canalise, as seen recently on the Lugg to the north of Leominster.

The problem of silt deposition in the Perry continues to be severe in some parts. It has hampered recent attempts to establish a trout fishery on a 3.5 km section of the lower reaches near Yeaton. It is probably natural for the Perry to be dominated by non-salmonid species, yet salmon parr are sometimes recorded and there is a small breeding trout population. Trout excavate redds in gravelly sections of the river and lay their eggs there in winter, but the river runs brown with silt from the start of autumn rains until April and during the four to five month incubation the trout eggs are usually killed by the lack of oxygen that results from deposition of silt. The projected income from the trout fishery has encouraged remedial work, including installation of flow constrictors and soft revetments on the outside of eroded meanders, and fencing to exclude livestock from riverbanks in pastures. Reed-canary grass and purple loosestrife have established and spread along the riverbanks and should eventually narrow the channel causing scallops to develop in faster flows, providing suitable sites for trout redds. These measures have helped, but they cannot prevent silt being washed down from the large catchment area upstream.

Other measures that have been carried out to develop the trout fishery on the Perry are more controversial. There has been some pollarding and coppicing where trees lining both banks were thought to be creating excessively shaded tunnel-like sections of the river. The stated aim was to create unshaded water, allowing herbs to colonise the banks and stabilise them more effectively than tree roots. However, evidence quoted earlier suggests that trees stabilise the bank more successfully than herbs, and the real motive for removal of trees may have been to allow unimpeded access for fly-fishing. River water-crowfoot *Ranunculus fluitans*, known to anglers simply as 'weed', grows as vigorously in the Perry as in chalk streams. The dense beds of long trailing leaves provide cover for trout and increase the potential number of territories, but make it harder to catch fish (Fig. 166). There has been some weed cutting in the section of the Perry where the trout fishery is being developed. The Environment Agency operates a programme of cutting on other parts of the Perry to promote free flow, but from an ecological point of view the moderate flow restriction caused by water-crowfoot and the consequent raising of water levels in summer might be seen as desirable. Another controversial measure is the artificial stocking with thousands of young trout from a hatchery. This has been done legally, with permission from

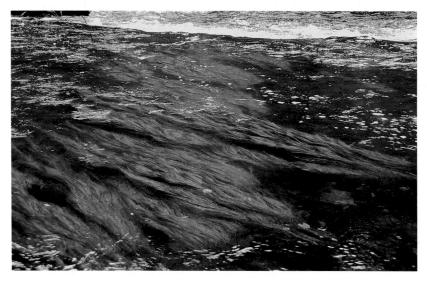

FIG 166. River water-crowfoot in the clear waters of the Teme as it flows through Downton Gorge.

the Environment Agency. Studies elsewhere have shown that introduced trout compete poorly with the wild fish, do not cope well with periodic spates and have poor winter survival rates. However, they interbreed with the wild trout and so alter the gene pool. From 2015 onwards, all artificially released trout must be triploid and therefore infertile: this prevents further interbreeding, but the other deleterious effects of artificially introduced fish remain.

The Roden drains an area to the east of the Perry, including the group of meres and mosses to the south and east of Ellesmere, with water in the upper reaches stained brown with peat. It flows on through an area of intensive arable farming to the small towns of Wem and Shawbury and then to its confluence with the Tern east of Shrewsbury. There are no large urban or industrial sources of pollution in its catchment. Despite this, the Roden is in relatively poor state, canalised in many parts with little protection of its banks and with few of the trout, grayling and dace for which it was once known.

Further to the east again, the Tern rises northeast of Market Drayton and flows through one of the most intensively farmed regions in the Marches, dominated by dairy farming in the upper reaches and arable in the lower parts. The Tern has been extensively canalised, with frequent channel maintenance operations. The river receives effluent from the Müller Dairies creamery at Market Drayton, the Dairy Crest creamery at Crudgington and treated effluent from various sewage works, the largest being at Market Drayton and Rushmoor to the west of Telford. The Tern also receives the run-off from the northern half of the Telford conurbation. Until its recent closure, the sugarbeet factory at Allscott contributed effluent; weirs and sluice gates associated with this factory prevented upstream colonisation and temporary migration of fish seeking refuge during flood events. This long list of factors has inevitably had physical, chemical and biological impacts on the Tern. There is a lack of marginal habitat and bankside cover. Most of the natural riffle-pool sequence has been lost and silt deposition is considerable, with consequent damage to fish spawning and nursery areas. The water is fairly eutrophic and there is extensive growth of macrophytes, especially river water-crowfoot. The Environment Agency monitors biological water quality on the Tern and other rivers by identification of macro-invertebrates in kick samples. The data is used to calculate the Biological Monitoring Working Party index, from which the Average Score Per Taxon index is derived. These biotic indices are usually abbreviated to BMWP and ASPT; ten is the highest possible ASPT score, indicating pristine water quality; the BMWP index has no maximum.

At the Longdon on Tern sampling point, near Rushmoor, water quality is still rated good, with ASPT scores of 5–6, BMWP scores of 105–150, and a good range of mayfly and caddisfly larvae. However, there are no stoneflies, which are more demanding in terms of water quality, many of the invertebrate species present are characteristic of the sluggish flow conditions of a drainage ditch rather than of natural lowland rivers and the two biotic indices have shown a trend of declining water quality. Surveys carried out in the 1970s recorded 18 fish species in the Tern, with dace and gudgeon dominating.[17] The Environment Agency now monitors fish populations by electro-fishing. No fish at all were caught at Rushmoor in 2002, whilst small and very variable numbers of a few species of coarse fish were recorded in subsequent years. Clearly, human activities are having a very detrimental effect on the ecology of the Tern.

The Rea Brook is a small lowland river in a much better state than previous examples. Its source is Marton Pool in the broad valley between the Long Mountain and *Ordovicia*. It runs northeast through the villages of Minsterley, Pontesbury and Hanwood, joining the Severn at the English Bridge in Shrewsbury. The upper reaches flow through an area of intensive farming and the Uniq creamery at Minsterley discharges its effluent into the river. Nevertheless, monitoring of macro-invertebrates a few kilometres downstream at Lea Cross shows that water quality is good, with stonefly, mayfly and caddisfly larvae, as well as the molluscs, beetles and leeches typical of a healthy lowland river. There has been some canalisation of the Rea Brook near Shrewsbury, however, a natural riffle-pool sequence persists over most of its 25 km and gives a variety of habitat. There is less growth of river water-crowfoot and other macrophytes than in the Tern or the Perry, which may be related to differences in geology of the catchment areas and associated differences in water chemistry. Monitoring of the lower reaches at Cruckmeole shows that there is a diverse and healthy fishery. Anglers regard the Rea Brook as a chub-dace river and these two species form a continuous element of the community, but grayling, with the same habitat requirements as dace, are also a constant presence. There are no significant barriers to fish migration, so species such as brown trout and salmon can use the Rea Brook as a refuge during times of flood in the Severn. Although this is not primarily a salmonid river, both of these species spawn in places. In conclusion, the Rea Brook is an example of a lowland river in excellent overall condition, in contrast to the previous examples. It is affected by agriculture and other human disturbance but to an extent limited enough for a diverse community of plants and animals to find a habitat.

The last river to be considered in this section is the Teme. It is initially upland in character but qualifies as a small lowland river as it flows through a broad and fertile valley from Ludlow down to Tenbury Wells. Sandstone and other easily weathered sedimentary rocks underlie the Teme here, as they do most of the lowland rivers of the Marches. This is of course not coincidental – lowlands occur where rocks have been easy to erode. Sandstone shelves and ledges in the bed of the river indicate outcrops of resistant strata, and provide a solid surface on which various species of aquatic moss can gain anchorage. The Teme is the only river in Britain where *Cinclidotus riparius* has been recorded, with a range from Downton Gorge to Little Hereford and beyond. It grows on rocks that are submerged for much of the year and was first recorded in Britain at Ludlow in 1891, where it can still be found in abundance on flagstones in the river by Ludford Bridge. It does not appear to produce spores in Britain and so presumably spreads by vegetative means, thus limiting it to downstream dispersal.

Mixed farming characterises these reaches of the Teme, with both nutrient enrichment and siltation affecting water quality. Nevertheless, biological indices of water quality based on macro-invertebrates are relatively high, the mayfly, stonefly and caddisfly larvae present being intolerant of organic pollution. Monitoring of water quality showed a dip in the summer of 2007, but this was probably due to heavy rainfall and flood conditions in the river and it was reversed in following years. Both salmon and trout spawn wherever they can find fast-flowing water and clean gravel, but as with the other small lowland examples this is more of a coarse fish than a salmonid river. There is a good assemblage of species, with dace, chub, roach and bleak *Alburnus alburnus* predominating and eels *Anguilla anguilla*, common bream, barbel *Barbus barbus* and gudgeon also recorded (Fig. 167). A few river lampreys migrate up the Teme but brook lamprey are more abundant. In their larval stage these two lamprey species are very similar in appearance, behaviour and detritivorous diet, but instead of ceasing to feed after metamorphosis, river lampreys migrate downstream to the estuary. There they feed parasitically on other larger fish, growing in size considerably before ceasing to feed and swimming back upstream to spawn. At the end of the 19th century they were reported to be common in Shropshire streams 'where bunches of eighteen or twenty may often be seen in the gravelly bottoms, which it prefers for spawning'.[18] Numbers are now much smaller.

FIG 167 a & b. Plates from British Freshwater Fishes (1879), by the Rev. W. Houghton, who was rector of Preston upon the Weald Moors: (a) chub; (b) roach.

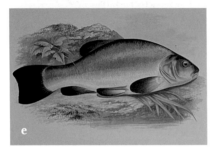

FIG 167 c–f. Plates from British Freshwater Fishes (1879), by the Rev. W. Houghton: (c) twaite shad, with allis shad behind; (d) gudgeon, with barbel behind; (e) tench; and (f) bream.

LARGER RIVERS OF THE LOWLANDS – THE SEVERN AND THE DEE

In its lower reaches, as it nears its confluence with the Severn below Worcester, the Teme becomes a large rather than a small lowland river, and aspects of its natural history are therefore different. This can by illustrated by considering twaite shad *Alosa fallax*. They are relatives of herring and spend their adult life in coastal waters, but migrate into rivers to spawn between May and July. This now happens in very few places in Britain. On the lower Teme males and females gather in pools during the day and then move to shallow riffles to spawn at night into sand and gravel. This occurs where the river is about 20 m wide – the narrowest recorded site for twaite shad, with wider rivers such as the Severn being more typical. Although twaite shad does not currently reach any further on the Severn than Diglis weir in Worcester, in the past it migrated much further upstream, reaching as far as Shrewsbury and even Welshpool in the 19th century. The greater penetration of the Marches by twaite shad in the Severn was possible because it is a substantially larger river than the Teme, with a markedly different nature.

The greatest lowland rivers of the Marches are the Severn and the Dee. The Severn attains the character of a lowland river at its confluence with the Vyrnwy. It then flows across flood plains and in shallow valleys to the Ironbridge Gorge. Below the gorge it flows through the broad, terraced Severn Valley to Bewdley and then Stourport. The Dee becomes a lowland river when it emerges from the Vale of Llangollen and it then flows northwards across flood plains and areas of gentle river terraces to Chester. Where these rivers flow through thick deposits of easily eroded sediment, large meanders can develop. Probably the finest series of meanders in Britain is on the Dee, from Worthenbury to Holt (Fig. 168). A variety of features is seen, from simple to double-headed meanders, gravel and sand bars in the existing river channel, abandoned channels and old meander loops, actively eroding cliffs of sediment on the outside of existing meanders and the remains of these cliffs along the former channels. Sand martins excavate nest burrows in actively eroding cliffs both on the Dee and on the Severn between

FIG 168. Meanders on the Dee between Worthenbury and Holt.

Shrewsbury and Buildwas. Kingfishers *Alcedo atthis* also build their nest tunnels in vertical banks of these rivers and their tributaries. Common sandpipers sometimes attempt to nest on banks of gravel or shingle on the inner side of meanders, but they are rarely successful. Nests on the Severn are vulnerable to flash floods, trampling by cattle and disturbance by anglers.

A select group of plants is able to grow in these large rivers when levels drop in spring and summer. River water-crowfoot is found on stony riffles with shallow turbulent water, especially on the Severn and the lower Teme, where it can form large pure patches with prominent white flowers. Spiked water-milfoil roots into stony sections of riverbed but reaches the surface to flower. Perfoliate pondweed *Potamogeton perfoliatus* also roots firmly in stony sections of riverbed and can tolerate swiftly flowing water, so it is very resistant to damage from spates. It is locally frequent in the Severn from Welshpool down to Ironbridge and is abundant below Bridgnorth. Fennel pondweed roots in muddy sections of riverbed, usually in moderately fast-flowing water, either shallow or deep. Its main range starts further downstream in the Severn than perfoliate pondweed and it is only common below Arley. Shallow areas of slowly flowing water with a muddy substratum are called slacks and they usually occur along the river margins, particularly on the inside of meanders. Flowering rush *Butomus umbellatus*, branched bur-reed *Sparganium erectum*, arrowhead *Sagittaria sagittifolia* and slender tufted-sedge *Carex acuta* are emergent plants that can grow here, overwintering as tubers or rhizomes in the mud. Floating plants such as fat duckweed *Lemna gibba* can also be found where flow rates are slowest. Where water levels drop sufficiently for the muddy riverbed to be exposed, a group of ephemeral plants can be found such as celery-leaved buttercup *Ranunculus sceleratus*, marsh cudweed *Gnaphalium uliginosum* and toad rush *Juncus bufonius*. There are relatively few exposures of solid rock in the riverbed but a nationally scarce species of moss, *Fissidens fontanus*, is found on submerged boulders and the stonework or concrete of bridge footings. It was first recorded in Britain in the Severn at Bewdley in 1901. It thrives in nutrient-rich water and is now more often found in canals than rivers.

The larger rivers contain a greater diversity of fish than other Marches rivers because they offer a range of habitats and act as a natural route for migrants. Thomas Pennant described the Vyrnwy just above its confluence with the Severn as *piscosus amnis* – a river teeming with fish. He listed 20 types that were present: 'salmon, trout, samlet, grayling, minnow, perch, rough or pope, carp, tench, roach, dace, gudgeon, bleak, chub, loche, bullhead or miller's thumb, shad, eel, lamprey and flounder'.[19] Although trout are present in the Severn and salmon do spawn from the Vyrnwy confluence as far downstream as a clean gravel bed near the discharge of the Dowles Brook above Bewdley, these are not primarily salmonid waters. Coarse fish dominate the middle reaches of the Severn and other larger rivers. At Shrewsbury, anglers consider the Severn be a barbel river, though it should be remembered that this species had to be reintroduced to Marches rivers in 1956 and again in the 1970s, so arguably should not be regarded as native. Bream is considered to be the dominant coarse fish further downstream at Stourport.

Catches of sea trout are not infrequently reported, but almost always prove to be brown trout with atypical coloration and size. There is a local term for these fish – slob trout. It seems that if brown trout move into deep and turbid water, a brown back is not needed for camouflage, so the whole fish turns silvery. Slob trout adopt a cannibalistic diet, which allows rapid growth to a large size – a 4.3 kg specimen was caught on the Severn at Newtown recently, for example. There is only one reliable record of a sea trout in rivers in the Marches in the last 20 years. This was an individual caught at the Severn–Vyrnwy confluence whose scales were examined to confirm the identification. The middle and upper Severn probably never had many sea trout for the simple reason that the river is too long. Either very few young trout manage to migrate out to sea, or very few find their way back upstream as far as the Marches. Even rarer than sea trout in the Severn are white sturgeon *Acipenser transmontanus*. A specimen weighing nearly 90 kg and 2.4 m long was caught in 1802 at the weir in Shrewsbury – one of the largest fish ever caught in a river in Britain. Sturgeon should be classed as a vagrant species – the true migrants are sea lamprey, river lamprey, eels, salmon and twaite shad. They are all either rare or rarer than they once were, for reasons that we must consider.

River lampreys were discussed earlier. Sea lampreys have a similar life cycle but migrate further out to sea and reach a larger size. The Severn was at one time celebrated for its sea lampreys, migrating up the river through the Marches and into Wales. There was extensive exploitation by fisheries in the estuary and upstream, and over 100 years ago numbers had dropped so much that there were predictions that the species would become extinct in the Marches. Catches of single individuals in the Severn at Shrewsbury and the Teme at Tenbury became sufficiently rare to be worthy of special mention.[20] The reason for the decline again seemed to be the construction of obstacles that prevented migration upstream from the sea. Despite the gloomy prognostication, some sea lampreys still migrate up the Severn at least as far as the Severn–Vyrnwy confluence and up the Teme as far as a weir at Ashford Carbonell, just south of Ludlow. Spawning can be observed each year below the weir in Shrewsbury in mid-June. Nevertheless, numbers are still lower than historically they once were. Many of the passes that have been constructed at weirs for salmon are not suitable for lampreys, or indeed for twaite shad. Vertical slot passes that allow all migrating fish to get beyond an obstacle have been constructed at a few weirs, but many more are needed.

Eels migrate in the opposite direction to the other species – downstream to spawn in the Sargasso Sea and then upstream as young eels, known as elvers or glass eels. Eels have a remarkable capacity for migration over damp ground to reach ponds and lakes, but they have nevertheless been severely affected by obstructions to their passage. Numbers of migrating adults, known as silver eels, used to be large enough to justify the construction of traps for catching them, known as fish weirs. These consisted of wattle funnels with the entrance facing upstream, and a bag-like net at the downstream end to trap the eels as they migrate downstream in the autumn. Domesday Book in 1086 records the presence of at least eight fish weirs on the Severn in Shropshire[21] and 28 were recorded in Shropshire in a document of 1575, but in 1634, exceptional floods 'broke all wares on the Severn'. Some at least were rebuilt but the number declined, largely because eels were less important as a food. The last fish weir on the middle or upper Severn was at Preston just downstream of Shrewsbury, which fell into disuse and decay by 1910, after continuous use since Domesday and before. Soon after this, the Salmon and Inland Fisheries Act of 1923 banned the construction and use of all types of traps on rivers. Eels could still be caught with rod and line and 2 kg specimens were often caught in the Severn at Shrewsbury, but there now seem to be very few. Obstructions to migration are an obvious reason, but the netting and export of large numbers of elvers in the lower Severn is also blamed. Parliament prohibited taking of elvers for any reason from 1553 until 1778, when catches for human consumption but not for sale became legal. The Salmon Act of 1873 introduced a close season, which initially made it almost impossible to catch elvers, but the dates were soon changed to allow catches in most of March and April. The close season was abandoned in 1935 and since then elver catches have been legal throughout the year, though in practice the season ends in May. An eel management plan has recently been prepared for the Severn, but it does not recommend severe restrictions on the elver catch unless more of the obstructions to migration are removed or bypassed and habitat is improved and increased.[22] Unless the amount of available habitat is increased, greater numbers of elvers migrating upstream will not necessarily result in a larger eel population. It would probably result in dense populations accumulating below obstructions, with a consequent increase in elver mortality.

In the past, large numbers of Atlantic salmon have migrated up-river to reach their spawning grounds in the Severn and its tributaries. Reduction in salmon numbers as a result of over-exploitation has been a longstanding concern.[23] Acts of Parliament in 1667 and 1778 imposed restrictions on the seasons, types of net and methods of catching salmon that could be used, in particular banning the use of poisonous berries to stun the fish and make them float to the surface. A traditional method for catching involved nets stretched between pairs of coracles. Salmon are much more capable of overcoming obstacles than lampreys, but nevertheless salmon runs became much smaller after 1847 when locks were constructed without adequate fish passes on the Severn at Stourport in Worcestershire. By the end of the 19th century, few fish were passing up as far as Shrewsbury. Excessive netting in the lower reaches, pollution of the river, changes in the river channel and construction of weirs or other obstacles were all cited as causes.[24] It was also reported by anglers that poachers were taking large numbers of young salmon, known locally as samlets, by sweeping shallow water with small-meshed nets. A 60–70 per cent decline in salmon numbers was reported during the second half of the 20th century.

In addition to the previous causes given, acidification due to conifer plantations, silt deposition, compaction of gravel in spawning grounds, unauthorised river works including gravel extraction, increases in water temperatures and low summer flow rates have all been suggested as contributory factors. Acidification is not a widespread problem in the Marches, though 50 km of stream and river in the Hafren forest in Wales are fishless. Increases in water temperature do not yet seem to have had significant effects, but the impending extinction of salmon from rivers in the south of England shows that this may change. Anglers still claim that too many fish are taken by netting, particularly in the Severn Estuary.

There have been efforts over many years by the National Rivers Authority and its successor the Environment Agency to improve the fortunes of the Atlantic salmon on the Severn. Water has been discharged from the Vyrnwy and Clywedog reservoirs to prevent flow rates falling too low for juvenile survival and migration. Crushed limestone has been used to reduce the acidity of the upper reaches of some rivers. Byelaws have been introduced to ban salmon being killed before 16 June,[25] thus sparing the larger salmon that have spent more than one year at sea. The ratio of these salmon to those that have only spent one winter at sea was amongst the highest for any river in England or Wales, but has been getting lower. Now most large salmon are grilse – individuals that only spent one year at sea. Surveys in 1998–2001 showed that there were large numbers of redds in suitable sections of the river, but spawning rates were not as high as conservation targets. In the light of this, a salmon action plan was produced for the Severn, which was carried out over a five-year period from 2003–8. More fish passes have been constructed and obstacles to migration have been removed, raising the percentage of the Severn catchment that is accessible to adult salmon from 15 per cent to about 20 per cent. However, a further 30 per cent that would naturally be accessible is still blocked by artificial obstructions. Initiatives have been taken to prevent the removal of gravels needed for spawning from rivers, whilst compacted or silted up gravels have in places been restored to a suitable condition. Temporary traps are installed each autumn in fish passes at Ashford-on-the-Teme and elsewhere to catch salmon migrating upstream. These fish are held at Clywedog hatchery until they are mature, when eggs are stripped from the hen salmon and then fertilised. The resulting offspring are reared until the fry stage and are then released, especially in areas opened up by new fish passes, as on the Teme. Annual surveys at 15 sites on the Severn have been carried out to monitor the population and 171 other sites are monitored on a five-yearly cycle. Electronic fish counters have been installed at several locations. Sadly, numbers have not yet increased and a total of 300 anglers with rod licences now catch an average of one salmon each per year despite spending a hundred or so hours each in the attempt. Those fish that are caught are reported to be 'skinnier' than in the past and hatcheries find that they are less fecund. The inescapable conclusion is that the feeding grounds at sea are not as good as they were, the krill and sand eels on which salmon gorge now driven further north to escape warming seawater.

FLOODS, FLOOD PLAINS AND FLOOD PREVENTION

The larger rivers of the Marches are characterised by very variable water levels and flow rates, because of their large catchment areas and uneven distribution of rainfall. Flood plains have developed where the larger rivers burst their banks. A thick deposit of silt is often left at the end of winter on riverbanks and adjacent flood plains. Evidence that this is a consequence of soil erosion caused by deforestation and agriculture was discussed in Chapter 8.[26] More silt is deposited close to the river than further away on the plain, so a deep river channel tends to develop, with steep banks. As Ogier Ward wrote of the Severn in 1841,[27] 'The noble river rarely forms a feature in the prospect, as, from the rapidity of its current, it has hollowed out for itself too deep a channel to be visible except from eminences on its banks.' The amplitude between typical winter and summer river levels is as much as 6 m on the Severn. Small islands called eyots can be formed by silt deposition, aided by the stabilisation that plant roots provide. They are favoured by mute swans for nesting, because the steep riverbanks with their sudden changes of water level and fast flow rates during floods are too treacherous.

The riverbank flood-zone habitat is a distinctive one that relatively few native species of plant tolerate – as we might expect if it is the relatively recent product of human activity. Plants that survive tend to grow very vigorously as there is an abundance of nutrients in the thick deposits of silt. Broad-leaved dock *Rumex obtusifolius* is found in other habitats but produces particularly large leaves on these riverbanks. Common nettles are another generalist species that grows vigorously on riverbanks, benefiting from the damp, phosphate-rich soils. An obvious strategy for coping with winter floods and silt deposition is to germinate in the new deposits, and set seed before the next floods. Black mustard *Brassica nigra* is such an annual and is common on the riverbanks. Indian balsam *Impatiens glandulifera* is native to the Himalayas but has now become a well-known member of the tall herb community of flood-plain riverbanks. It is Britain's tallest annual and establishes itself each year in huge numbers in bare silt, growing rapidly to overtop even nettles. The seeds can be dispersed a few metres by their explosive release but are also carried by floodwater. The sweet scent of Indian balsam wafts over long stretches of the Severn from August until the first frosts and honeybees benefit from its copious production of late-season nectar and pollen. Other members of this tall herb community are tansy *Tanacetum vulgare*, purple-loosestrife *Lythrum salicaria*, mugwort *Artemisia vulgaris* and marsh woundwort *Stachys palustris*.

Various species of willow can establish and grow vigorously, especially on eyots (Fig. 169). Crack-willow *Salix fragilis* is able to spread by self-struck

FIG 169. The Severn in its deep-river channel downstream of Welshpool, with low, summer flow rates, an eyot and crack-willows. (Chris Walker)

cuttings carried in floodwater, but desirable clones have also been deliberately planted and pollarded. Osier *Salix viminalis* is a non-native that was originally planted to produce material for basket making but has spread freely by seed and suckers, to become common in the Marches. Purple willow *Salix purpurea* and almond willow *Salix triandra* are much scarcer. They have also been planted for basket making but it has been suggested that both may be native along parts of the Severn between Welshpool and Ironbridge. Alder also grows vigorously in the flood-zone and would naturally form large areas of woodland on flood plains, as described earlier. The trunks, branches and exposed roots of trees growing in the flood-zone provide a habitat for a specialised group of mosses and liverworts. *Syntrichia latifolia* and *Leskea polycarpa* are characteristic species (Fig. 170). *Myrinia pulvinata* is a scarce species that occurs on the Severn near Shrewsbury, usually growing on alder trees.

There are also invertebrate species that are characteristic of the flood-zones. The club-tailed dragonfly *Gomphus vulgatissimus* has a restricted distribution in Britain but is common on slow-flowing sections of both the Severn and the Dee (Fig. 170). The larvae burrow into silt in the riverbed and grow for between three and five years before metamorphosing, usually in May. Hundreds of adults may emerge at this time on the riverbanks. The banded demoiselle *Calopteryx splendens* is a more widely distributed species that is also common in lowland rivers in the Marches. The white-legged damselfly *Platycnemis pennipes* is at the northwestern edge of its range in slow-flowing rivers in the Marches.

Summer water levels in the Severn, the Vyrnwy and the Dee used to drop much lower, with parts of the riverbed becoming a series of pools and little or

FIG 170. Flood zone bryophytes on a willow beside the Severn on the Loton estate, including *Syntrichia latifolia* and *Leskea polycarpa* (left). Club-tailed dragonfly (right). (Emma Broad)

no flow of water between them. Artificial release of water from reservoirs is now used to maintain minimum flow rates, allowing abstraction for irrigation and to supply drinking water. When particularly high tides are due to flow upstream from the Severn estuary, the flow rate is increased to prevent saline water from reaching the point at which drinking water for Gloucester is abstracted. To maintain flow in the Severn, water is released from the Clywedog and Vyrnwy reservoirs and is also sometimes pumped from boreholes that have been drilled into the Permian and Triassic sandstones underlying the north Shropshire plain. A minimum flow rate of 850 megalitres per day is currently maintained at Bewdley. This may be increased in the future, as higher rates in the Upper Severn might be beneficial for salmon swimming upriver to their spawning grounds. Release of water down Afon Tryweryn from Llyn Celyn maintains a minimum flow rate in the Dee, to maintain the supply of water to Chester and other settlements.

Discharges are often made during the autumn from Clywedog reservoir, to ensure that it is not full at the start of winter and can therefore intercept any subsequent surges of water and reduce flow rates downstream. However, water only flows into this reservoir from a small part of the overall catchment of the Severn, so this policy can only reduce flooding, not prevent it. There is a common perception that floods on the Severn have recently become more frequent and more severe. The highest level ever reached was in the Great Flood of 1795, which damaged or destroyed every bridge on the Severn, apart from the Ironbridge which had been opened in 1781. The four next highest flood levels recorded, in decreasing order, were in 1770, 1672, 1946 and 1869. Recent floods are therefore not the highest on record and it is unclear whether floods have become more frequent either, as we lack reliable records for smaller floods in the past (Fig. 171). What is undeniable is that human activities have almost certainly increased flooding. If the catchment of the Severn was still predominantly wooded, and if land drainage did not carry rainwater so quickly and effectively into rivers, the peaks and troughs in flow rates would not be so extreme. There is increasing realisation that construction of physical barriers along rivers cannot prevent flooding, but merely displaces the problem. Ironically the reverse policy is more likely to succeed – encouraging water to escape from the river channel and flood adjacent land. This already sometimes happens in the area around the confluence of the Severn and the Vyrnwy. The land here is low-lying and flat, with large areas between 58 and 60 m above sea level. It has traditionally been protected from flooding during most spates using earth flood banks, known locally as argaes. Plymley wrote in 1803:

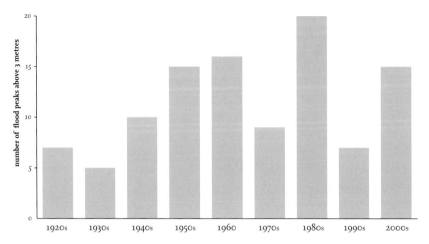

FIG 171. The water level in the Severn is monitored at the Welsh Bridge in Shrewsbury. The bar chart shows the number of floods where the river rose more than 3 m above datum level in each decade from the 1920s onwards. No clear trend is visible.

'inconveniences arising from irregularities of the water ... have been increased by the embankments which have lately been raised to protect the lowlands of Montgomeryshire and the upper parts of the county of Salop. Formerly the river which had arrived at a moderate height overflowed these lands to a great extent, which thereby operated as a side reservoir, and took off the waters of high floods; and these waters returning to the bed by slow degrees ... but now being confined to a narrow channel they rise suddenly to a great height, and flow with more rapidity than formerly.'

Perhaps flood banks should be removed, to allow an estimated 3.5 million m³ of water to be temporarily stored in the Severn–Vyrnwy confluence area (Fig. 172).

Seasonal flooding of the Severn–Vyrnwy confluence area has created fertile alluvial soils but prevented certain forms of agriculture. There have traditionally been large areas of unimproved damp grassland dominated by tussock grass and soft-rush, with areas of marsh and pools. On freer draining soils there were hay meadows and arable crops were sown late in spring. This has therefore been ideal breeding habitat for waders, including lapwing, curlew, redshank *Tringa tetanus* and snipe. In the latter part of the 20th century, flood defences were increased and field perimeter drains were deepened, reducing the extent and duration of floods. The area of rough grassland and late-sown spring crops fell and there was a considerable increase in intensive leys cut

FIG 172. Floods at the Severn–Vyrnwy confluence in July 2007, looking west towards Wales, with the Breidden hills in the middle distance. (Shropshire Council)

repeatedly from April or May onwards for silage. Not surprisingly, the numbers of breeding waders fell considerably as a result of the loss of suitable habitat, both redshank and snipe disappearing completely. *Wetland Vision*, a report published in 2008 by the Environment Agency and a group of conservation organisations,[28] identified areas including the Severn–Vyrnwy confluence that are suitable for re-establishment of grazing marsh. Shropshire Wildlife Trust has already bought Holly Bank, a small farm in this area. The conservation priorities for this new reserve are to increase the numbers of breeding curlew and lapwing and, if possible, to re-establish populations of redshank and snipe. Floating water-plantain, a BAP species that is rare and threatened over the whole of its European range, was found in 2003 growing in a damp hollow on cattle pasture close to Holly Bank, so there are also opportunities on this reserve for assisting the conservation of endangered plants. There is a large population of black poplar in hedgerows in the Severn–Vyrnwy confluence. It would be fascinating to try to re-establish black poplar woodland on a flood plain, and this would be an ideal area.

RIVER MAMMALS

Three native species of mammal are semi-aquatic: otters, water voles and water shrews. They have not so far been mentioned because they are not confined to a particular type of river. Otters are one of the great success stories of conservation. They were regarded as plentiful in the 19th century despite the activities of otter hunts in Cheshire and Shropshire and trapping by angling associations. They remained widespread in the Marches until the 'Silent Spring' years of the 1950s and 1960s, when dieldrin, aldrin and heptachlor were in use in agricultural seed dressings and sheep dips. The banning of the most harmful insecticides has allowed a gradual return to most but not all streams and rivers. This was helped by the survival of a small population of otters on the upper reaches of the Severn in Wales, saved by a voluntary ban on organochlorine pesticides that land managers had instigated locally, prior to the national ban.

Surveys of the Severn catchment show an encouraging rate of return to the Upper Severn and the Teme[29] (see Table 5). The recovery has been less complete in the tributaries of the middle Severn on the north Shropshire plain – rivers that have in places been canalised, destroying habitat for otters and other riparian

TABLE 5. Otter recovery in the Severn catchment

AREA	PERCENTAGE OF SITES OCCUPIED BY OTTERS			
	1977–9	1984–6	1991–4	2000–2
Upper Severn, excluding sections in Wales	20	60	100	100
Middle Severn, including the Tern, Roden and Worfe	0	1	45	62
Teme, including the Clun Onny and Corve	22	33	73	80
Lower Severn including the Avon and other tributaries	0	0	14	17

species. Nevertheless, nearly two-thirds of the sites on these rivers that were examined in the study showed signs of otter activity, so there must still be areas of good habitat. Recovery has been much slower on the Severn below Stourport and tributaries that join it there. This is east of the Marches and is characterised by intensive agriculture with few areas of wetland left undrained. There is little emergent or bankside vegetation to provide the undisturbed areas that are needed, especially by female otters and their cubs. It also carries large amounts of recreational boat traffic, with weirs and locks to maintain water levels. The river therefore lacks riffles, bars and backwaters with obvious consequences for the species of fish on which otters mostly feed. By contrast, it is the presence of these features that is probably significant in the success of otters on rivers in the Marches and it is important that they are maintained. At the time of writing, there were plans for making a limited section of the Severn in Shrewsbury more easily navigable, which would have a limited impact, but extensive schemes should be resisted.

Otters are now rarely persecuted and seem to be getting bolder, with increasing numbers of sightings. Although usually regarded as a crepuscular species they have probably always been active during the day when they feel secure. Some of the main rivers of the Marches probably now have as many occupied territories as they can hold, but where there is over-grazing, with exposed and eroded riverbanks, there is still the potential for habitat improvement and an increase in the population. Road kills show that otters are moving between rivers and ponds to feed, including hill ponds that are far from the nearest river. They use a variety of sites such as reed-beds and fallen trees as couches and hovers and also sometimes build their natal dens away from rivers. Spraint indicates the diet and, along with the remains of fish, there are often parts of the exoskeletons of dragonflies and crayfish. Otters visit the pools at Brown Moss near Whitchurch to feed on frogs, leaving gruesome remains with the skin of the hind legs pulled inside out. Mink scat in contrast contains less fish remains and more fur, but mink and otter act as competitors despite their dietary differences, with ecological consequences that are mentioned later.

Water voles are the second semi-aquatic mammal species that is native to the rivers here, building burrows in riverbanks and feeding mostly during daytime on riparian and emergent vegetation. There is evidence from semi-fossils of mammals at various sites that water voles were largely terrestrial until about 5,000 years ago. There are occasional reports from the 19th century of individuals or families living away from water.[30] The change to semi-aquatic habits and a huge reduction in the population density of water voles seems to coincide with the introduction of sheep, which competed for grass and other food plants.

Water voles were still regarded as numerous in the 19th century. Numbers declined in the second half of the 20th century, with catastrophic losses from the 1980s onwards. The Vincent Trust surveyed the distribution of water voles in 1990 and again in 1997–8.[31] The same 10 km grid squares were studied in each survey and 21 of these grid squares were within the Marches area. Fifteen had signs of water voles in 1990 but only five in 1997–8. There was a complete disappearance from much of the Marches except for the Whitchurch area in northeast Shropshire and parts of Cheshire. Habitat loss was not the cause as large sections of the Severn, Teme, Clun and Onny are still suitable. Intensive grazing up to riverbanks may have been a factor as it causes competition for food and also poaching of riverbank sites that might be used for burrows. However, intensive farming practices are not solely responsible and there is strong evidence that predation by mink had a major impact through the 1980s and 1990s.[32] Mink were introduced for fur production in the 1920s and by the 1960s there were about 700 mink farms in Britain. Some animals inevitably escaped and established feral populations. The Ministry of Agriculture attempted an eradication programme, encouraged by the eradication of another alien species.

Muskrats *Ondatra zibethicus* were also brought to Britain to be bred for their fur and escaped into the Severn in the 1920s. Their numbers reached a peak in 1934 with one of the two main populations on the Severn in Shropshire. There were widespread concerns about damage that muskrat burrows were doing to riverbanks. An eradication campaign was mounted and was completed by 1937.

In contrast, attempts to eradicate mink in the 1960s and early 1970s proved to be ineffectual and were abandoned. Mink were by then widespread on rivers in the Marches, numbers continuing to rise until the 1990s. Ironically, despite the failure of eradication attempts, mink numbers have fallen since then. The Vincent Trust recorded mink distribution during the surveys on water voles. Of the 21 Marches grid squares, 14 had signs of mink in 1990, but by 1997–8 there was evidence of their presence in only seven and the range has continued to contract since then. Attempts to control mink have continued locally, especially where there are fisheries. For example, on the section of the Perry where a trout fishery is being developed, mink rafts are used to monitor numbers. Nine individuals were trapped and killed in 2007. Nevertheless, the contraction in mink numbers is probably due largely to the return of the otter, with competition between the two species and even attacks on mink by otters causing their elimination from some rivers. With falling numbers of mink we might expect to see a return of water voles, but by 1997–8 they had not returned to any of the Marches grid squares from which mink had disappeared. In fact, three of the five grid squares still occupied by water voles contained evidence of mink, indicating co-existence. Four squares from which water vole disappeared had no evidence of mink in either 1990 or 1997–8, so predation by mink cannot be blamed for all of the water vole's problems. Competition with grazing livestock, especially sheep, remains a potent factor, as indicated by persistence of water voles in parts of the Marches where there is arable farming but not where sheep farming predominates.

The best-known water vole population in the Marches is centred on the town of Whitchurch (Fig. 173). There have been frequent sightings in a variety of water bodies including the Shropshire Union Canal, Stag's Brook, fishing pools at Bronington and beyond to water-filled ditches on Fenn's and Whixall Mosses. In 2006 many shoppers were able to watch two breeding female water voles in a ditch that runs alongside a town-centre car park. Brown rats displaced the water voles in 2007, but the rats were trapped and water voles returned to the ditch in 2008, with continuous activity seen from spring onwards. The strength of the Whitchurch water vole population has been attributed to the town's position close to the headwaters of three rivers – the Dee, Weaver and Roden. Youngsters migrate along watercourses to find breeding territories, moving 1.5 km from their parents' territory on average. The profusion of waterways around Whitchurch therefore allows recolonisation, if predation or other factors cause losses in some areas.

FIG 173. Water vole at Whitchurch. (Kate Long)

Water shrews are the third of the semi-aquatic mammals. They are mostly nocturnal so rarely seen unless caught by a domestic cat and even then are unlikely to be recognised. Males are about 150 mm long including the tail, and females are slightly smaller. They build extensive burrow systems in riverbanks and can walk underwater on the bottom of streams in a manner reminiscent of dippers. John Dovaston published an account of a colony of water shrews that he had found close to his house at West Felton in Shropshire in 1825.[33] They were thought to be common in Shropshire in the 19th century,[34] but it was not until the 21st century that a national survey gave us more than mere anecdotal evidence. About 25 sites in the Marches were surveyed and evidence of water shrews was found at six of these.[35] The survey sites were not evenly distributed and there were very few in south Shropshire or north Herefordshire, so more work is needed in these areas to establish the distribution. It appears that the population density is higher to the east and south in England and that the Marches are on the edge of the distribution range. Whereas the water vole has been studied widely, the water shrew has so far been relatively neglected and unlike water voles, otters and polecats, it is not a BAP priority species. Perhaps we would now know more about them and give their conservation a higher priority, if Kenneth Grahame had included a water shrew when writing *Wind in the Willows*.

Polecats *Mustela putorius* are regarded as a principally riparian species over much of Europe, but the abundance of rabbits in Britain has tempted them away from riverbanks and they are now considered to be generalists. Because of their former predilection for streams and rivers, they will be discussed here. Like otters, polecats are an example of a species that has recovered successfully after having been very scarce. They were extirpated from most of the Marches during the 19th century, being viewed as 'wantonly destructive of life', both gamekeepers and farmers despatching them whenever possible by trapping, shooting or hunting with dogs.[36]

Mid-Wales became the polecat's stronghold despite a preference for lowland rather than upland habitats. Occasional sightings showed that a small and scattered population always remained in Herefordshire and Shropshire. By the 1920s there were already suggestions that numbers had started to increase. This continued and probably accelerated during the 1960s, partly because of successful breeding in the Marches but also thanks to reinforcements from Wales. Various factors aided the recovery – trapping by gamekeepers had largely ceased during the First World War and conifer plantations provided new habitat. Another boost came when myxomatosis was introduced in the 1950s, putting an end to rabbit trapping, which had inadvertently caught polecats too. As the rabbit population grew again, it provided an abundant source of prey. Studies in the second half of the 20th century showed a slow expansion of both numbers and range. A survey carried out by the Vincent Trust in 2004–6[37] showed that the Marches and Wales were the current core of the British polecat range, with a winter population density of about 100 individuals per 10 km square. There were lower population densities in other counties of the Midlands, as well as in northwest and central southern England, but polecats were still mostly absent from eastern England and the southwest. Surprisingly, there were no records from a large part of south Shropshire, where polecats had previously been present. This was attributed not to their disappearance, but to the scarcity of road kills because of a lack of busy roads, and few photographs taken because this species is no longer a remarkable sight. Polecats are able to hybridise with domesticated ferrets, but this seems rare among Marches polecats, with a purity of population rated at over 95 per cent.

WATER QUALITY AND POLLUTION

Rivers are particularly vulnerable to pollution. Monitoring of living organisms within them can reveal both medium- to long-term changes in a catchment area, but can also give an early alarm when there has been a pollution incident. Freshwater biologists and chemists working for the Environment Agency collect a huge amount of both chemical and biological data on water quality, and then reduce this to numerical indices with brief descriptions for publication on their website. The detailed information is difficult and expensive to obtain, and there are strong arguments for more of it being published. Nevertheless, the Environment Agency does valuable work both in monitoring water in streams and rivers, and in ensuring that remedial action is taken where necessary. This involves work with landowners to prevent future pollution, and legal action against repeat offenders. Action has been taken to reduce problems caused by discharge of untreated sewage effluent, but storm water still sometimes overloads the capacity of sewers and sewage treatment plants, leading to discharge of this material. The pollutants that have most frequently caused acute pollution incidents in the Marches are: silage liquor, slurry from cattle and pigs, insecticide from sheep dips, and creamery wastes. Examples of accidental discharges that caused acute pollution incidents will be given here.

In 2006, the owner of Oaks Hall Farm was fined £8,000 for the discharge of cow slurry and silage liquor into a tributary of the Rea Brook. Ammonia levels in the stream reached 60 ppm, which is about ten times higher than normal levels. In 2006, more than at least 800 fish in Minsterley brook were killed, including many brown trout, after accidental discharge of water containing high concentrations of sodium hypochlorite from the Uniq Foods creamery in Minsterley. The creamery on this site had previously caused fish deaths in the Rea Brook by discharging whey washings. In June 1996, routine monitoring of invertebrate populations in the River Clun at Clun showed that there had been severe declines. The river was sampled both upstream and downstream of the village and a 30 km length of the river was found to be affected, from a farm at Hall of the Forest, upstream of Newcastle on Clun, down to the confluence with the Teme at Leintwardine. A sheep-dipping bath at the farm was located very near to the river and investigations showed that insecticide from the bath had overflowed into the river. An area where the sheep stood after dipping also drained into the watercourse. The pollution of the Clun with insecticide had been happening for many years but the farmer had changed from using an organophosphorus compound to a synthetic pyrethroid. This proved to have a far more harmful effect on aquatic invertebrates. As a result of this and other similar incidents, synthetic pyrethroids are not now permitted for use in sheep dips. It took approximately a year for invertebrates to spread back from unaffected tributaries of the Clun and for fish populations, which had also suffered due to loss of their food sources, to rebuild. There were many incidents of pollution with sheep dip chemicals in the 1990s, but an extensive programme of education for sheep farmers has greatly reduced their frequency.

Because far more land here is agricultural than urban or industrial, the health of the Marches rivers is primarily dependent on farming practices. Many farmers have worked very hard to reduce the impacts of their activities and they have been given much better advice recently about how to do this.[38] The policies of government agencies have become more enlightened and agri-environment schemes have started to reverse the damaging effects of previous grant regimes. However, there is still much more to be done in getting water quality up to a high enough standard to ensure the long-term survival of the rare and valuable species that are still found in the Clun, the Teme and other rivers.

CHAPTER 11

Distributions

N ATURALISTS HAVE BEEN MAKING LISTS OF Species for sites in the
Marches for over two centuries. The organisation of records in the
various counties has been strongly influenced by the skills, interests
and personalities of those involved, so has developed in different ways. In
Herefordshire a local records centre was established in a County Council office,
with the running costs shared between the council and the Herefordshire Nature
Trust. Local recorders are encouraged to send records to the centre, to be added
to the database by paid staff. Other Marches counties have followed a similar
approach but a different system has developed in Shropshire, with deliberate
avoidance of the establishment of a physical office that might imply ownership
of data by one body. A distributed and partly web-based records centre has been
set up instead called Shropshire Ecological Data Network. The county recorder
for each taxonomic group collects and validates both new and old records
and sends an updated dataset to the virtual records centre once a year, using a
common software package. The data can be brought together at hubs and is then
easy to access. Conservation organisations, planners, ecological consultants and
members of recording groups can use the data held by the virtual records centre.

Computer databases allow distribution maps for individual species to be
produced very easily. If maps are produced in which the dates of records can be
distinguished, changes in distribution can be revealed, allowing environmental
changes and human impacts to be studied. Distribution changes can also
pinpoint species that deserve increased conservation efforts. It is relatively easy
to produce coincidence maps, showing grid squares in which species are found
together. Pioneering examples of this type of map will be mentioned later in this
chapter, but a more recent application is seen in local opportunity maps that
have been prepared to help with planning policy in Shropshire. They indicate

the grid squares that hold the greatest number of axiophytes for woodland, grassland and other communities, thus suggesting habitat protection priorities in different parts of the county. Axiozoans, which are animal indicator species for habitats, are also being selected so the sites most worthy of conservation can be selected more appropriately.

MAPPING DISTRIBUTIONS

Ten-kilometre grid-square distribution maps of Britain are now available for plants, breeding birds, wintering birds, mammals, amphibians, reptiles, dragonflies, butterflies, bees, spiders and other invertebrate groups. They have been produced for single counties for some groups that are under-recorded elsewhere. These county maps can give us glimpses into the status and ecology of previously obscure species, for example craneflies in Shropshire.[1] Two-kilometre grid-square county maps have been produced for some groups. This size of grid square is known as a tetrad, and as there are 25 of them within one 10 km grid square, tetrad maps require huge amounts of data. The *Ecological*

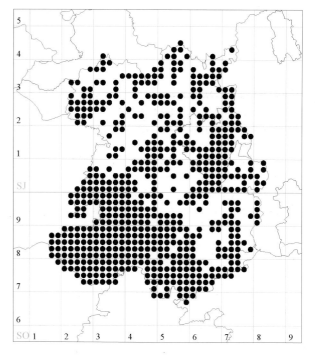

FIG 174. A 10 km grid square distribution map for the small tortoiseshell butterfly in Shropshire. (Shropshire Wildlife Trust on behalf of Shropshire Ecological Data Network)

Flora of Shropshire is a model of how to collect enough data for trustworthy tetrad maps, and also how to interpret them tellingly.[2] Its authors took a suitably liberal view of county boundaries, to establish an almost rectangular survey area stretching up the Marches for about 70 km, covering the area with the most complex geology and topography. Much can be learned from the 731 distribution maps published in the Flora. Tetrad maps have been produced for butterflies in Shropshire. These contain more records in the southwest of the county than elsewhere. This is due to the dedicated efforts of one lepidopterist, Bill Davidson, who in retirement systematically recorded butterflies throughout this area (Fig. 174). Until Bill's efforts are replicated throughout Shropshire, gaps in the butterfly distribution maps should not be taken to mean that a species is definitely absent from a tetrad. This is a well-known problem – if recording efforts are unevenly distributed, maps show the distribution of recorders rather than that of the species. Spiders in Shropshire and Herefordshire are an example. Provisional distribution maps for many of the 650 or so British species of spider suggest that they are absent or scarce in the Marches, but before we accept this inference we must remember that there were 10 km grid squares where few or even no spider records existed when these maps were prepared.[3] When work on this book is finished, the author aims to fill in some of these gaps.

BORDER COUNTRY

As the Marches straddle the border between the lowland southeast of Britain and the upland northwest, it is not surprising that many species are on the edges of their range. An example is oak fern (Fig. 175) with a range that extends from Wales into north Herefordshire, with scattered sites in south Shropshire including Wyre, but none further southeast. Beech fern is even scarcer in the Marches, being much more a plant of Wales, northern England and Scotland. It occurs in a few cool sheltered sites in south Shropshire and north Herefordshire, either in rocky woods and or on stable screes. Other examples of species at the south-eastern edge of their upland ranges are crowberries, dippers, common sandpipers and bilberry bumblebees. White bryony *Bryonia dioica*, pepper-saxifrage *Silaum silaus*, hobbies, white-letter hairstreaks (Fig. 176) and the spider *Theridion tinctum* are on the northwestern edge of their lowland ranges.

Not all species follow the northwest–southeast pattern precisely. Wood spurge *Euphorbia amygdaloides* (Fig. 177) is on the northern edge of its range, with a stronghold in Wyre but also some isolated populations in Shropshire. Some oceanic species that cannot survive winter cold or excessive summer drought

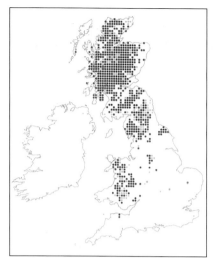

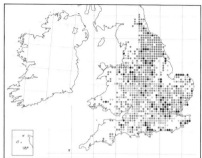

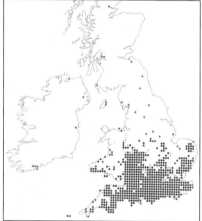

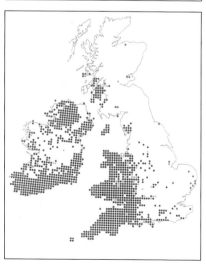

FIG 175. Above
Oak fern is at the southeastern edge of its upland range in this region. Red spots on plant distribution maps indicate grid squares where a species is regarded as non-native.

FIG 176. Above right
White-letter hairstreak butterfly is at the northwestern edge of its lowland range. Red spots indicate larger numbers of sightings than orange spots. (Butterflies for the New Millennium Recording Scheme, courtesy of Butterfly Conservation)

FIG 177. Centre right
Wood spurge is at the northern end of its southerly distribution.

FIG 178. Below right
Navelwort is at the eastern edge of its westerly distribution.

FIG 179. Navelwort facing west in a sheltered oak crevice on Offa's Dyke near Whitton.

spread up from the south and west into the Marches. An example is navelwort *Umbilicus rupestris* (Figs 178 and 179), which is locally abundant on rocks and walls, but on sites such as Grinshill it is only found on south- and west-facing slopes, indicating that the climate is only just warm enough[4]. Some species spread into the Marches from the east but do not extend further west into Wales. Yellow star-of-Bethlehem *Gagea lutea* is at the western edge of its range in the Oswestry uplands. It grows here in dry woodland and limestone pavements, whereas further east in Britain it inhabits moist base-rich woodland. There are also examples of species extending as far west as the Marches among epiphytic lichens, including *Anaptychia ciliaris*. These lichens are adapted to dryish bark and inhabit one of four British woodland types defined by lichenologists – sub-oceanic temperate woodlands, which occur in central and eastern England and eastern Scotland (Figs 180 and 181).

FIG 180. Oak fern at Clunton Coppice in the Clun valley – an upland plant that extends into the Marches. (Fiona Gomersall)

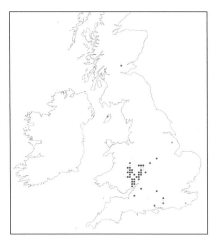 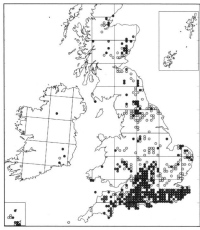

FIG 181. Spreading bellflower is found in the catchment of the Severn and its tributaries (left). The epiphytic lichen *Anaptychia ciliaris* is at the western edge of its easterly distribution (right). Yellow dots are pre-1960 records, blue dots 1960–99 and red dots are records from 2000–10. (British Lichen Society)

There are also species with enigmatic distributions that include all or part of the Marches as their stronghold. The British range of spreading bellflower, *Campanula patula*, is almost entirely restricted to the catchment of the Severn and its tributaries. It extends up from the Wye Valley as far as south Shropshire.[5] Cowbane *Cicuta virosa* is a handsome umbellifer that has its British stronghold in the northern Marches. The salticid spider *Sitticus floricola* is also characteristic of the northern Marches, with just a few other sites in Galloway. Touch-me-not balsam *Impatiens noli-tangere* has native populations in west Wales and Cumbria, but also in damp woodland in Marrington Dingle, near Montgomery, the first site in Britain where this species was discovered. Fine-leaved water dropwort is found widely from Somerset northwards up through the Marches. It is mostly absent from a central belt of England but is then widespread again in the east. Greater chickweed *Stellaria neglecta* is an annual or short-lived perennial herb of damp shady places. Its main range stretches from the West Country up through the Marches, but it also occurs in lowland parts of Wales and eastern Norfolk. Yellow-necked mice are widespread in southern England from Kent westwards to Dorset and on northwards up through the Marches. The hoverfly *Chalcosyrphus eunotus* is a rarity across Europe, but Shropshire is a stronghold for this enigmatic species, perhaps because the dingles offer suitable habitat. *Rhingia rostrata* is another scarce hoverfly that especially favours the Marches. It may be

FIG 182. *Rhingia rostrata* was formerly found only in southern England but has now established a stronghold in the Marches. (Nigel Jones)

associated with badger latrines, but this is mere conjecture at present (Fig. 182). *Pyrrhidium sanguineum*, the Welsh oak longhorn beetle, is another species with a curious distribution, mostly in central Wales but extending into the Marches, and only scattered records elsewhere, most if not all of which may be due to inadvertent introduction of beetle larvae in timber. All of these distributions merit further research.

If species whose ranges overlap in the Marches are closely related, there is the possibility of hybridisation. In Britain, the large house spider *Tegenaria gigantea* occurs in the southeast and its close relative *T. saeva* in the west and north. Both species occur in the Marches, as do individuals with intermediate morphologies, which are the result of interspecific hybridisation (Fig. 183). Where closely related species co-exist they often develop reproductive barriers to prevent hybridisation, so the presence of these hybrids suggest that the overlap between the ranges of the

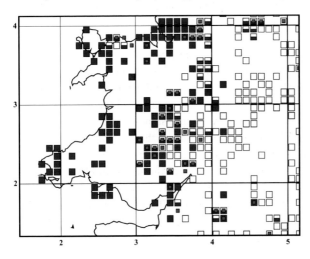

FIG 183. Hybrids (inner red squares) between *Tegenaria saeva* (grey squares) and *T. gigantea* (white squares) are found in the Marches where the distribution ranges of these species overlap. (Geoff Oxford)

two species is relatively recent. There is evidence that it is the spread of *Tegenaria saeva* westwards that has caused the overlap.[6] Upland enchanter's nightshade *Circaea* × *intermedia* persists in some areas of woodland in the Marches. It is a hybrid of the lowland and alpine species of enchanter's nightshade *Circaea lutetiana* and *C. alpina*, whose ranges must at some stage have overlapped, though the alpine parent is now found only far to the west in Wales. One of this hybrid's sites is Oaks Wood at Habberley, below the Stiperstones, where alpine enchanter's nightshade might well have grown in colder times after the last ice age.

INCREASES, DECLINES AND EXTINCTIONS

The distributions of species are not fixed. Plant, bird, butterfly and dragonfly examples will be the main focus here, as the recording efforts have been intense enough to give robust evidence of change. Population increases, decreases and extinctions occur naturally, but the rate at which they have occurred over the last few hundred years has been far from natural and there are clear anthropogenic causes in many cases.

Land drainage has caused many species of damp habitats or open water to decline in numbers. Convincing evidence of this is provided in the *Ecological Flora of Shropshire*.[7] Groups of uncommon species that are typical of particular kinds of damp habitat were chosen, and coincidence maps showing the numbers of species per tetrad were then produced. This was done for both pre-1913 and post-1969 records, to allow changes to be highlighted. Species of calcareous fens and mires showed decreases in almost all tetrads where these uncommon species were present before 1913. Losses of species typical of acid bogs and wet heaths were more severe, and those for species of oligotrophic ponds and lakes were more severe still. The most recent study, for the years 1987–2004,[8] indicates that there have been some further losses due to drainage, but at a much lower rate than before, and at a lower rate than in parts of England to the east and south of the Marches. Species that have declined markedly elsewhere such as marsh ragwort *Senecio aquaticus*, marsh pennywort and lesser spearwort *Ranunculus flammula* are still widespread. Species adapted to eutrophic conditions have tended to increase, for example bulrush and common reed.

Many arable weeds declined severely in the Marches in the second half of the 20th century, including large-flowered hemp-nettle *Galeopsis speciosa*, corn mint *Mentha arvensis* and pale persicaria *Persicaria lapathifolia*. Some disappeared entirely, such as corncockle *Agrostemma githago*, corn buttercup *Ranunculus arvensis* and shepherd's needle *Scandix pectin-veneris*. Most of these species are archaeophytes that were brought involuntarily by early farmers with their crop seeds, so perhaps we should not be concerned. Other species have defied the depredations of intensive agriculture and have remained widespread or even increased, including redshank *Persicaria maculosa* and cleavers *Galium aparine*. Species that thrive in nutrient-poor grassland have mostly declined because of the use of fertilisers. One example is the harebell, but there are many others.

Some species have been affected by changes in woodland management and in particular the cessation of coppicing. Examples are common cow-wheat and goldenrod *Solidago virgaurea*, both of which have declined. Remaining populations of woodland plants seem reasonably secure as there has been little or no recent clearance of ancient woodland and coniferisation has been put into reverse. Among animals of woodland, fallow, roe and muntjac deer have widened their ranges in the Marches, but so far the effects on ground flora have not been as severe as in southeastern Britain.

Heathland species have suffered severe declines, as heathland habitat, formerly widespread in north Shropshire, has almost all been lost. These losses occurred many years ago in most cases. Shawbury Heath is an example. It was floristically rich when Leighton published his *Flora of Shropshire* in the 19th century, but during the Second World War much of it was converted into an airfield and the rest was drained and enclosed as farmland. Examples of heathland species that have declined are heath cudweed *Gnaphalium sylvaticum*, pill sedge *Carex pilulifera* and smooth cat's-ear *Hypochaeris glabra*. The heath-like communities that have developed on pit mounds in coalfields of the Marches give an extra twist to the tale of lost heathland. Heather and other plants of heaths colonised these sites, allowing birds and butterflies to find a habitat that otherwise would have been very scarce. An example is the dingy skipper butterfly, which became common across the former Coalbrookdale coalfield. Clearance of brownfield sites for building is now causing rapid declines in these species.

Industry can of course create other types of new habitat, which allow population increases. Shelduck and gadwall have both increased as breeding species in the Marches, probably because there are more gravel pits and other areas of artificially created open water. Air pollution from industry had major effects on lichen species in parts of the Marches in the 19th century and first half of the 20th century, with only the species most tolerant of sulphur dioxide surviving in some areas. Legislation from 1956 onwards has resulted in much cleaner air in industrial areas, which has allowed lichens to recolonise. This process was studied in particular detail in willow carr in Cheshire by amateur lichenologist Brian Fox. He discovered, among many other fascinating details, that the sequence of return of lichen species as air quality improved was not simply the reverse of the sequence of loss, and some less tolerant species returned sooner than more tolerant ones, presumably because of differences in dispersal rates.[9]

A variety of other factors are implicated in the decreases of some species. Excessive collection of plant specimens for cultivation by gardeners or for herbaria by botanists had a significant impact on some rare species in the 19th century, for example oak fern and beech fern, which have not since recovered. Reports of the visit of Woolhope Naturalists' Field Club to Downton Gorge in 1869 tell of many roots of oak fern being carried off. The demise of certain raptors and birds of prey in the 19th century was caused initially by gamekeepers and then as they became increasing scarce, by trigger-happy landowner-taxidermists and by egg collectors. Ravens were not breeding in the Marches at the start of the 20th century, but there has since been a spectacular recovery throughout the hill country. The Shropshire Raven Study Group has been monitoring the county population since 1994. There were about 50 breeding pairs in 1990, rising to 175 in 1999 and 250 in 2003. The hill country still has the highest densities, but there are also now breeding pairs in the lowlands. The resurgence in the Marches is in contrast to many other upland areas of Britain, where there are grouse moors with gamekeepers.[10] The raven's return preceded that of birds of prey, probably because of differences in susceptibility to DDT and other organochlorine pesticides. Apart from specific poisoning incidents, ravens did not seem to accumulate high enough pesticide levels to cause deaths or failure to breed. At the start of the 20th century, buzzards were not breeding in the Marches, but by the 1950s they had spread back from Wales through the hill country of south Shropshire and northwest Herefordshire. This return was checked by the effects of myxomatosis on rabbit populations and then by pesticides that had been used in sheep-dips. Withdrawal of the most toxic pesticides and greatly reduced persecution has allowed buzzards to spread back throughout the Marches and beyond to eastern England. The use of organochlorine pesticides explains much of the decline of otters in the Marches from the 1950s onwards, as was described in the previous chapter, and the withdrawal of these toxic agrochemicals allowed their subsequent return.

Introductions of alien species have had very significant impacts on distributions of some native species. Grey squirrels, mink, red signal crayfish and Indian balsam were mentioned in previous chapters. New Zealand pigmyweed, Japanese knotweed *Fallopia japonica* and water fern *Azolla filiculoides* all spread widely in the Marches in the second half of the 20th century. The spread of alien species is sometimes initially quite slow. An example is the alpine newt *Icthyosaura alpestris*, which was introduced from the Netherlands to a village pond near Market Drayton in 1970 and from there to a rural pond 3.2 km away in 1974.[11] In 1993, when the latest survey was done, there were alpine newts in both of the release ponds and in eight other ponds, but the furthest of these from a release pond was only 70 m away – a rate of spread of 3 m per year. All in all, the effects of alien species have not been as serious as in other parts of the world.

While alien species have been added to the flora and fauna of the Marches, some native species have disappeared. Fifty plant species are known to have become extinct in Shropshire during the period for which records exist.[12] Loss of heathland and the collecting of specimens both caused the extirpation of some species. Clearance of woodland or cessation of coppicing had a greater effect, whilst construction of roads, houses and industry were yet more significant. Even more extinctions were caused by changes in farming methods and more still by land drainage. However, the greatest number of species extinctions by far was caused by a factor that has not so far been mentioned here – climate change.

CLIMATE CHANGE AND DISTRIBUTIONS IN THE MARCHES

Because the Marches are on the edge of the distributions of many species, changes in range should be particularly noticeable. There is plenty of anecdotal evidence of species spreading to the Marches from the south, as might be expected with global warming. The orange footman moth *Eilema sororcula* has a southerly distribution in Britain but has been spreading north with a first record in Shropshire in 2004. *Volucella zonaria*, a large hornet-sized hoverfly, became established in southeastern Britain in the 1940s and has since spread north, reaching Shropshire in 2006. The tree bumblebee *Bombus hypnorum* was first recorded in Britain in 2001 and reached Bridgnorth in the Marches seven years later in 2008. The two spiders *Argiope bruennichi* and *Steatoda grossa* have been spreading northwards for some years and are expected to arrive soon. Many other examples could be given, as there are new arrivals in the Marches from the south every year. However, rather than accumulating a long list of species we should test the evidence by looking more systematically at changes in distribution. Climate warming would cause these distribution changes:

- Arrivals of species that were previously restricted to warmer areas to the south.
- Departures of species whose main range is in the colder north and west.
- Movement of species to higher altitudes on hills.
- Little or no movement of species southwards or to lower altitudes.

The most intensively recorded groups can best be used to test these predictions. The mobility of birds and the huge number of records makes them an obvious focus, but we need to distinguish between genuine changes of range and sporadic records of vagrants, escapes and releases. We must also remember that changes in the populations of winter and summer visitors in the Marches could be due to factors at the other end of the migration route, not here. Notwithstanding these considerations, changes in bird ranges have occurred that would be expected with warming conditions.

Little ringed plovers arrived in Britain in the 1930s and were recorded in the Marches from the 1950s onwards, with breeding here since the 1970s. The next bird atlas to be published is likely to show a further northwards spread. Little egrets were once regarded as rare visitors to Britain, but the substantial influxes from northern France in the late 1980s and early 1990s showed that an expansion of their range was under way. One little egret was recorded at Venus Pool near Shrewsbury in 1992 and another further north on the Dee in the same year. There have been increasing numbers of records in the Marches since then, and there are now breeding colonies in northwest Cheshire. Dartford warblers *Sylvia undata* have been spreading northwards in Britain and are established on Cannock Chase, so may be one of the next arrivals. Woodlarks *Lullula arborea* have also been moving north and may also soon establish a breeding population in the Marches. A pair of cranes *Grus grus* has summered in Shropshire in recent years and may have attempted to breed. Winter populations of blackcaps *Sylvia atricapilla* are also on the increase: some blackcaps now migrate here for the winter, rather than to Spain, and others are year-round residents that have started to breed here rather than in Eastern Europe. These changes are partly the result of blackcaps learning to exploit bird-feeding stations in gardens, but it was warmer winters that attracted them in the first place. Chiffchaffs *Phylloscopus collybita* are wintering in small but increasing numbers in the Marches, rather than returning to Africa. There are increasing numbers of records of a variety of other species wintering in the Marches that used to fly south, but it is not yet clear whether the trends are significant.

Whitethroats *Sylvia communis* have been associated with lowlands in the Marches, but in the last ten years or so they have become much more widespread on upland sites, especially on the summit plateau of the Long Mynd. Whereas in the past a few stonechats overwintered in sheltered parts of the Marches, increasing numbers now remain through winter, both in lowland sites and on hills such as Titterstone Clee, Long Mynd and Stiperstones. The argument for climatic influence here is strengthened by the massive decline in stonechat numbers on the Long Mynd following the severe winter of 2009/10. Whinchats have decreased markedly in lowland Britain and in the Marches are now largely restricted to the hills. Ring ouzels breed in the northern and western uplands of Britain. They bred on the Long Mynd in the 19th and 20th centuries but declined rapidly towards the end of this period and last attempted to breed in 2003. Egg predation dealt the *coup de grâce* to this population but research in Scotland has shown that reduced worm populations due to drier summers is another factor contributing to range contraction northwards, or in this case westwards into Wales. The three classic birds of upland oakwoods, wood warbler, redstart and pied flycatcher, seemed to be spreading eastwards at times during the 20th century, but the next national atlas is expected to show range contractions westwards. Research with pied flycatchers shows a likely cause – arrival time in the spring has not changed, but the availability of insects for feeding to nestlings peaks about two weeks earlier. Greater breeding success and population increases can therefore be expected where spring arrives later.

There are a few species whose ranges have moved southwards or eastwards, but factors other than climate can be seen to be the cause in each case. Nightingales *Luscinia megarhynchos*, for example, were at the extreme northwest of their range in the Marches and bred in Ironbridge Gorge as recently as the 1980s, but they have retreated southwards and eastwards. This is almost certainly due not to factors in Britain but instead to changes in their Moroccan wintering grounds. The smaller numbers arriving in Britain each spring are able to remain in prime habitat in the southeast rather than having to spread out. Red-backed shrike *Lanius collurio* retreated southeastwards in Britain in the 19th century and last bred in the Marches in the 1950s. Habitat loss is the most likely cause, combined with severe decreases in the large insects used as a food supply. Changes in range of birds are therefore predominantly northwards, westwards and upwards and where they are in other directions, factors other than climate seem to be the cause.

Changes in butterfly distribution also fit predictions based on climate warming. No species of butterfly have spread south into the Marches but a number of species have spread north. In the cases of small skippers *Thymelicus sylvestris*, brimstones, purple hairstreaks, holly blues, speckled woods and ringlets *Aphantopus hyperantus*, there are longstanding records from sites in the Marches but these were on the fringes of the ranges. There are now many more sites where these species are recorded and the ranges have extended on northwards or westwards. The reasons why the distributions of these species are limited by temperature are well understood but are beyond the scope of this book. The white admiral's distribution stretches northwestwards as far as Wyre, but although there has been some evidence of northward expansion in Britain, the Marches have yet to be colonised. If summer temperatures become consistently warmer by another degree or two, then this will probably happen. The Essex skipper *Thymelicus lineola* has shown a more unequivocal northwestwards spread in Britain, reaching Wyre in 2005, and has probably now expanded its range further into the Marches. At the time of writing, brown hairstreaks *Thecla betulae* had reached Grafton Wood in Warwickshire, so may well turn out to be the next arrival. Silver-washed fritillaries have a distinctive range in Britain, with few sites north of a line from Porthmadog in North Wales to Folkestone in Kent. This line passes through the Marches, so silver-washed fritillaries are on the edge of their range here. New sites have recently been found in north Herefordshire and Shropshire, so the range appears to be extending northwards towards Cheshire. None of the butterflies found in the Marches are at the southern end of their distribution range so we cannot expect any to have retreated northwards. There is insufficient data on altitude to be able to assess trends.

Among the dragonflies and damselflies there are some clear examples of expansions of range into the Marches and in every case the spread is from the south and east, not from the north and west. The black-tailed skimmer *Orthetrum cancellatum* was absent from the Marches, apart from an isolated record from Whixall Moss, until the second half of the 20th century. It reached Worcestershire in the 1950s, Shropshire in the early 1980s and Cheshire in the late 1980s. The migrant hawker *Aeshna mixta* has spread from southeast England, arriving in Worcestershire in the 1970s, Herefordshire and Shropshire in the 1980s and Cheshire in the early 1990s. There have been similar patterns of spread with the emperor dragonfly *Anax imperator*, ruddy darter *Sympetrum sanguineum* and white-legged damselfly (Fig. 184). The yellow-winged darter *Sympetrum flaveolum* is a migrant from Europe that has so far failed to establish stable breeding populations in Britain, but there have been increasing numbers of sightings in the Marches and it may be one of the next species to become established. The evidence indicating northwards spread of dragonflies and damselflies into the Marches is clearly very strong. There is also a little evidence of spread to higher altitudes. The southern hawker *Aeshna cyanea*, despite its English name, has been abundant in lowland ponds in the Marches since recording began. From the 1980s onwards it has been recorded at ponds high up on Brown Clee and the Long Mynd. When we look for contrary movements southwards or to lower altitudes, we find none. A possible candidate would be the common hawker *Aeshna juncea*, whose main range in northern and western Britain extends into parts of the Marches, but there is no evidence of it increasing here or expanding its range into southern or eastern England.

We cannot expect such rapid movements in the more sedate world of plants. Even so, there is evidence of similar trends. Round-leaved crane's-bill *Geranium rotundifolium* and grass vetchling *Lathyrus nissolia* have recently arrived in the Marches from the south and east whilst spotted medick *Medicago arabica*, having

FIG 184. Species that are spreading from the southeast as the climate warms: (a) ruddy darter (John Balcombe); (b) white-legged damselfly (John Balcombe); and (c) violet helleborine in deep shade on Wenlock Edge (Peter Carty).

reached Wolverhampton, will no doubt soon be here. Bee orchids *Ophrys apifera*, whose main range is to the east and south, are becoming more widespread. Violet helleborine also seems to be spreading very gradually from the south and east (Fig. 184). Globeflower, cranberry and hare's-tail cottongrass, each at the edge of its northerly and westerly range, are all becoming less widespread in the Marches. Dioecious sedge has mostly been lost from lowland parts of the Marches, but is still present in the hill country. Another species that seems to be retreating uphill is shoreweed. It has disappeared from most of its lowland sites in the Marches but was recorded on the Long Mynd for the first time in the 1970s and is now widespread there in flushes and pools. It is notable how many plant species have their highest recorded site in the Marches and therefore a higher altitudinal limit here than they do elsewhere. There are several linked reasons: there is no higher ground to the southeast, sites at a certain altitude on the hills of the Marches are warmer than sites to the north and west and also many plants are at the edge of their northern and western ranges.

Some losses of northern species from the Marches occurred many years ago, when it is incorrectly thought by some that there could not have been human influences on climate. Rannoch-rush was recorded at several sites in Shropshire in the 19th century, but the last was in the 1880s. In Britain it is now only found far to the north on Rannoch Moor. Least water-lily still clings on at Colemere – its only site south of Scotland. Awlwort was recorded from one site in the Marches at Hencott Pool, but the last record was in 1805 and the nearest sites are now in the far west of Wales. These species are considered to be glacial relics. Their survival into the 19th century indicates that over the thousands of years since the last glaciation, the climate was never warm enough to kill them off. The anthropogenic rise in carbon dioxide concentrations began towards the end of the 18th century, so as early as this there could have been effects on climate. However, it is in the second half of the 20th century that the pace of change quickened markedly. The increase in annual average daily mean temperature in the Marches between 1961 and 2006 was 1.4–1.8 °C. The amount of warming over this period was not consistent across the year: daily mean temperatures rose in winter by 1.8–2.2 °C, in spring and summer by 1.4–1.8 °C and in autumn by 1.0–1.4 °C. Widely differing predictions have been made for the rate of warming during the remainder of the 21st century, but it seems very likely that there will be a rise of at least another 2 °C.[13] We can expect this rise to cause further very significant changes in distributions, but the changes would be huge if a tipping point was reached and much larger rises in temperature occurred.

CHAPTER 12

Agriculture

THE LANDSCAPE AND NATURAL HISTORY OF the Marches have been influenced more by agriculture than any other human activity. More than four-fifths of the land area is currently farmed, so the consequences of farmers' actions remain a dominant influence. The history of agriculture in the Marches has been described very fully elsewhere,[1] so a brief summary only is needed here. The remainder of this chapter will focus on the distinctive habitats created by agriculture in the Marches: walls and hedges, ponds, grassland and arable land.

AGRICULTURE AND LANDSCAPE DEVELOPMENT

There is evidence of farming activity from Neolithic times onwards, but it seems to have been very restricted during the early to mid-Neolithic period. In the late Neolithic and early Bronze Age periods from 4,400 to 3,800 BP, the rate of forest clearance increased and the cultivated area expanded considerably. Some upland areas that were in arable cultivation between 4,000 and 3,000 BP would not now be considered suitable. There is archaeological evidence for this on the Long Mynd and the sides of Caer Caradoc. Crops ceased to be grown from the late Bronze Age in these upland areas, probably a result of both soil degradation and a change to a colder and wetter climate. Pollen records show that woodland clearance accelerated in lowland areas of the Marches from the start of the Iron Age in the Marches – about 2,650 BP onwards. Iron tools allowed wetter soils in flood plains to be cultivated, after clearance of alder, willow and poplar. Upland areas were by now used for grazing, with a consequent need to safeguard livestock at times in hill forts.

The original fields created by clearance of woodland from Neolithic times onwards were mostly small and irregular. Farmers lived in isolated farmsteads or hamlets consisting of small groups of farmsteads, as in much of Wales, though the tradition of winter and summer homes, *hendref* and *hafod*, never existed here, as the hills are not high enough to necessitate migration to higher pastures in summer. A landscape of small irregular fields dating from the early days of agriculture is known as ancient countryside. It tends to have survived where livestock farming prevails, especially in the hill country of south Shropshire and northwest Herefordshire, because the size and shape of fields is unimportant. Elsewhere there was a trend in the centuries after the Roman period for hedge clearance and the replacement of the pre-existing patchwork of small fields with large open-field systems. This was accompanied by the formation of the rural settlements that we call villages, with houses clustered around a church. The trend for ancient countryside to be replaced by open-field systems continued after the Norman Conquest, though less land was ultimately converted than in southern and eastern England. The concentration of habitation into villages is usually regarded as an Anglo-Saxon or English settlement pattern and it survives in parts of the Marches, though the open fields have all now gone (Fig. 185). A pattern of

FIG 185. Ridge and furrow in fields near Maesbrook, to the east of Llanymynech. (Clwyd-Powys Archaeological Trust)

ridge and furrow is sometimes still visible in fields, showing where open-field
systems once existed. There are examples on both sides of the English–Welsh
border, including fields around Chirbury and others in the Vale of Montgomery.
As usual, the natural transitions in the Marches are between lowland and upland
rather than between England and Wales.

The relatively small proportion of the Marches converted to open-field systems
was enclosed again earlier than in other areas. Informal agreement rather than Act
of Parliament was the usual method. Only 0.3 per cent of the area of Shropshire
was subject to Parliamentary Enclosure for example. Some villages were
abandoned or shrank in size, with a return to isolated farmsteads and migration
of villagers to the growing towns. The landscape created by the enclosure of open
fields is called planned countryside. Whereas it has mostly been superseded in
other parts of Britain, planned countryside survives almost unchanged in parts of
the Marches. The western part of Maelor Saesneg is an excellent example, with its
many traditional dairy farms. Almost 2,000 ha of ridge and furrow remain in this
area, giving ample evidence of the open fields that once were farmed. Both Maelor
Saesneg and the Vale of Montgomery have been designated Historic Landscapes in
Wales, largely for the importance of their agricultural heritage.

There was yet another reversal of agricultural trends during the 20th century,
with hedgerow removal to facilitate mechanised arable farming. This happened
in much of the planned countryside in the east and northeast of Shropshire and
in other lowland parts of the Marches where arable farming dominates, but it has
not been as prevalent as in some parts of Britain. Also, it should not be presumed
that large regular fields have always originated in this way. Some were the result
of another trend – drainage of wetlands and their conversion to arable farming
in the 18th and 19th centuries. An example is Baggy Moor, drained under powers
granted by Act of Parliament in 1777, and enclosed in large fields. Plymley noted:[2]

> 'About twenty years ago there were large tracts of lands (Baggymoor and the
> other moors from Boreatton to St Martin's) in the Winter usually covered with
> water, but which are now in consequence of enclosures and drainage … rendered
> of considerable value. Hither, winter wild fowl of all sorts usually resorting in
> astonishing quantities and were annually taken at the decoy…'.

The Weald Moors to the north of Wellington were drained and enclosed at a
similar time.

The description of the development of agriculture that has been given here is
of course an oversimplification, and part of the richness of the landscape of the
Marches is its variety, with many parishes having distinctive features that do not

conform to an overall pattern. The pattern of fields, hedges and settlements form an intricate and fascinating record of the history of human activity, which in most parishes has not yet fully been investigated.

FIELD BOUNDARIES: WALLS AND HEDGES

Stone has rarely been abundant enough in fields of the Marches for the construction of field boundaries, and quarried stone is usually too expensive to use, except where walls around parks are built to impress. Sawn Triassic sandstone has been used in a few parts of north Shropshire, and in the Stiperstones area some walls have been built using Ordovician quartzite, though this is so unsuitable that most examples are tumbling down. Walls near Norbury were constructed of shelly Pentamerus Sandstone of the Silurian period and have recently been repaired as a part of a Local Heritage Initiative project. Glacial erratics have occasionally been picked off fields in sufficient numbers for wall construction, with examples around the village of Eaton Constantine. Nevertheless, these examples of walls are scarce and the traditional field boundary in most of the Marches is the hedge. There are approximately 50 km of hedges in the 8 km² area of the parish of Weston Lullingfields for example.[3] The parish of Highley has about the same length of hedges in an area of 6 km². If we extrapolate from these figures, the total length of hedges in the Marches area of this book would be 30–40,000 km. The actual figure is not known and would be difficult to determine. What we do know is that these hedges are of considerable importance to wildlife, many animals depending on the wide variety of woody species present. Fifty-six species of tree and shrub were found in a survey of roadside hedges in Shropshire.[4]

Thirty-metre lengths of over 200 hedges were surveyed in the parish of Highley in 1996 to find the relative abundance of trees and shrubs, of which over 30 different species were found. Older hedges tended to have more species, but not invariably so (Fig. 186).[5] An earlier study of hedges in three lowland areas of the Marches gave similar results, with considerable variation in the diversity of trees and shrubs, but only a weak relationship between the age of hedge and numbers of species[6] (Table 6).

Because of this, the number of species in hedges in the Marches cannot be used to estimate the age of the hedge as has been done in areas to the east in the Midlands. The mode of origin and the subsequent management of a hedge are the determinants of diversity, not the age. The most diverse hedges in lowland parts of the Marches are around fields formed by woodland clearance. Both the shrubs in the hedge and the ground flora beneath and beside can be related to

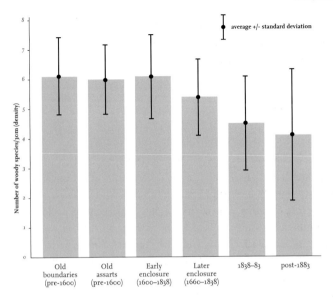

FIG 186. Mean number of tree and shrub species in hedges of different origin in Highley parish. There is a considerable overlap in the numbers of species between the six categories. (Data from Poyner & Mountford, 2005)

TABLE 6. Percentage frequency of shrubs and trees in lowland Marches hedges, classified by origin (data from Cameron & Pannett, 1980)

	WOODLAND RELIC HEDGES	OPEN FIELD ENCLOSURES	COMMONS ENCLOSURES	SMALL-HOLDERS' HEDGES
Ash	18	10	18	50
Blackthorn	92	49	32	78
Elder	33	46	25	33
Elm	15	13	10	33
Field maple	52	3	3	11
Hawthorn	97	100	100	100
Hazel	87	14	8	39
Holly	51	14	33	67
Oaks	50	17	51	11
Roses	79	51	93	78
Willows	20	0	5	0
Mean number of species	6.12	3.31	4.2	5.83

the pre-existing woodland type in the area. Hazel and field maple are far more common in these woodland relic hedges than in other types of hedge as they are not normally planted and rarely colonise after hedges have been established. Dogwood is another indicator of this type of hedge, though it is less frequent. The woodland herb dog's mercury is strongly associated with hazel in hedges. It often persists despite adjacent woodland having been cleared hundreds of years ago.

Hedges planted when common land was enclosed are poorer in species than those of woodland origin, and those planted when open fields were enclosed are poorer still. Even so, the local tradition at least until the 19th century was to plant several species, usually raised from suckers, rather than a single type of hedging shrub. Blackthorn was usually used to establish the hedge, often with elm to provide a future source of timber. Both of these species continue to spread by suckering after planting. Oak was also planted as a source of timber, but does not sucker, so does not increase after a hedge has been established. Hawthorn raised from seed was used from the 19th century onwards but by then most hedges had already been established with a wider variety of species. Even when pure hawthorn hedges are planted, vigorous colonisers can rapidly invade, helping to explain the weak correlation between age and diversity. Holly, elder, dog-rose *Rosa canina* and field-rose *Rosa arvensis* are spread by birds. Ash and sycamore are spread as winged fruits by wind. Smallholders and squatters enclosed heaths and wastes by planting hedges that often now hold surprises, as species composition reflects individual preferences, needs and opportunities, rather than any common pattern. Holly was planted to provide winter fodder, willows for basket making, plums and crab-apples as sources of fruit and damsons *Prunus domestica* for sale to dye and ink manufacturers. There are some distinctive local traditions, an example being the planting of laburnum *Laburnum anagyroides* in squatters' hedges around Shelve and Pennerley to the west of the Stiperstones, giving an unexpected splash of yellow in spring. This must have had some advantage to outweigh the disadvantage of the toxicity to livestock of the seeds. Perhaps the wood was useful for lead miners' pick handles or for a cottage industry of turnery or box making.

Studies of hedges in upland areas of the Marches have shown the relationship between the age of a hedge and its species diversity to be even weaker than in lowland hedges. There were some additional species that could tolerate conditions in upland areas: alder, birches, gorse and rowan. Though still the most frequent species, hawthorn was sometimes absent from upland hedges, in contrast to those of the lowlands where it was almost ubiquitous. The correlation between species diversity and origin of Marches hedges extends to animal species. Thirty-metre lengths of woodland relic hedges were found to have more than nine species of snail on average, including four rarely found in other hedges, whereas those of open-field enclosure between the 16th and 19th centuries had fewer than seven, and hedges planted in the 20th century had only two species on average.[7]

The condition of hedges ranges from excellent to extremely poor. In some parts of the Marches hedgelaying is still carried out in the traditional way. Shrubs respond to the cutting of stems near ground level by growth of vigorous new shoots from the old wood at the base. Mechanical flails are now more commonly used to cut hedges back, shrubs responding by forming new branches using axillary buds on aerial shoots as they do after ungulates have browsed on branches. We may expect a change in the composition of hedges as a result of the change from hedgelaying to flailing, as shrub species will differ in their adaptedness. The hedges in the poorest condition are those in arable areas that are cut too frequently and too hard, making them weak and gappy. The prevalence of hedgerow trees is also variable. In some areas they are plentiful, with landscape and wildlife benefits; in others there are now few, wood fuel merchants tempting some landowners to allow felling of remaining trees. There are severe threats to roadside trees as a result of excessive concerns over road safety. There are noticeable differences between counties in the extent of losses and in some areas the roads are increasingly treeless. Nevertheless, there are some gains, and recent road construction schemes have included the planting of large numbers of native trees and shrubs grown from local provenance seed. A good example of this is the Hodnet bypass.

PONDS

Although parts of the Marches have few farm ponds there are also areas with huge numbers. Maelor Saesneg and southwest Cheshire have 20 or more per square kilometre – probably more than anywhere else in Europe. This is the southern end of a great belt of ponds extending up through the Mersey basin into northern Lancashire. Almost all of these ponds are old pits, resulting from the digging of marl between the 12th and 19th centuries for spreading on fields to enrich the topsoil. Marl occurs in the subsoil in patches throughout this belt. It consists of a mixture of sand and clay, usually with significant amounts of lime, which made it particularly beneficial for acid sandy soils. In the 19th century digging of marl pits ended because nitrogen-fixing crops and a variety of fertilisers including bone dust and stable manure were used instead.[8] Agricultural lime had also become available, produced at limekilns such as those at Llanymynech and transported by canal.

All sides of ponds derived from a marl pit were initially steep except for the one that was used as a ramp to give access for carts used to haul the marl. Where

FIG 187. Ponds derived from marl pits in every field, in a typical area of Maelor Saesneg.

sides are still steep there is only a narrow fringe of marginal plants or trees, but trampling by livestock has sometimes created gentler inclines and a wider zone for marginal or emergent plants. The normal size of ponds is 5–20 m in diameter and 1–2 m deep. By the time a pit of this size had been dug, it was usually filling with groundwater so was abandoned and another pit was begun. Over 2,200 pits were dug in Maelor Saesneg alone (Fig. 187). Not all of these are still water-filled but many are. Pits were normally sited in the middle of fields, so the average distance to each part of the field was minimised. Occasionally they were placed in the hedge line, to give access to two or more fields.

There is a tendency for gradual silting up to occur and there has also been some deliberate infilling, but many fine examples of ponds survive. They are surprisingly diverse in both plant and animal communities (Fig. 188). Fifty-two species of aquatic plants were recorded in a survey of 145 ponds in southwest Cheshire, but only four species were found in more than half of these and many species were only found in a few ponds.[9] In a survey of 60 ponds in Maelor Saesneg, 167 different invertebrate species were recorded, including ten molluscs, 15 dragonflies and damselflies and 83 water beetles.[10] The average number of invertebrate species per pond was 30, but in the least biodiverse example where domestic ducks and geese lived, the muddy water supported only one. Water scorpions *Nepa cinerea* were found in many ponds and water stick insects *Ranutra linearis* in a few. Farm ponds are almost always stagnant, so species of highly oxygenated flowing water are absent. The only mayfly species

FIG 188. A pond in southwest Cheshire with a population of the lesser silver water beetle. (Andy Harmer)

commonly recorded for example was *Cloeon dipterum*, which is typical of ponds and canals. Some notable species were found, the rarest being the lesser silver water beetle, *Hydrochara caraboides*, an RDB 1 species that until the 1990s was only known from sites in the Somerset Levels. It has since been found in ponds in both Maelor and Cheshire. Adults breed in shallow clear water within a metre or two of the pond margin. Females lay their eggs in a floating silk chamber, constructed in a folded pondweed leaf, with a silken mast at the top of the fold (Fig. 189). The larvae that emerge are known as water tigers as they are voracious carnivores, but after pupation, about which little is known, adults emerge in the form of herbivorous silver beetles. Great crested newts *Triturus cristatus* were found in 13 per cent of ponds in the Maelor survey. Eggs or larvae of smooth or palmate newts, *Lissotriton vulgaris* and *L. helveticus* were found in about 30 per cent of the survey ponds. The results of a survey of Cheshire ponds were

FIG 189. Lesser silver water beetles: the egg chamber made from a leaf (left) and an adult beetle with an attached air bubble (right). (Andy Harmer)

different – great crested newts in 35 per cent and smooth or palmate newts in only 18 per cent of ponds.[11]

Some conclusions can be been drawn about the factors influencing species composition of marl pit pond communities. Lesser silver beetles, for example, cannot co-exist with fish. This partly explains their scarcity, although the Maelor survey found that fish, mostly stickleback, were present in only a minority of farm ponds. Most of these were on the flood plain of the Dee, allowing access at times of high floods, especially in winter. Great crested newts also struggle to co-exist with fish. Another significant factor is whether there are alders, willows or other trees fringing a pond. Where there are, the water is shallower, often with accumulations of dead leaves in the base of the pond. The water then has raised concentrations of dissolved minerals and tends to be stained brown, with a blackish sheen on the surface. The numbers of aquatic plants are reduced and there are often only water-starworts *Callitriche* spp. in the most shaded ponds. Animal communities in shaded ponds are almost entirely different, with exogenous dead organic matter, rather than aquatic plants and phytoplankton, at the base of food webs. Given the large number and varied characteristics of ponds, which can be regarded as semi-natural mesocosms, there are many opportunities for further ecological research. Computer analysis of the type that has been used for ordination of plant communities might throw up interesting results, which could help in understanding how the marl pit ponds and the rare species that they contain should best be conserved, and Environmental Stewardship now provides the means to encourage this.

GRASSLAND

The area of grassland in the Marches is greater than any other vegetation type. Unenclosed grassland in the uplands was described in Chapter 4, so the focus here will be on enclosed grassland. As elsewhere in Britain, much of this is now short-term ley, frequently resown with a few cultivars of high-yielding grasses and legumes and either grazed or cut several times each year for silage. Permanent grassland is more species-rich, but is now the exception. A survey of farms in Shropshire in the late 1970s[12] identified 466 permanent grassland sites with wildlife interest that were designated Prime Sites. Only 299 of these remained in 1989 and 250 in 1991. Extrapolation from this decline suggested that there would be none left by the late 1990s, but in fact by 2010 there were 249 sites where the main habitat was grassland on the list of wildlife sites and reserves. The loss of species-rich grasslands had not however been halted, as a few sites were lost between 1991 and 2010, but were compensated for in the total by newly discovered sites. The pattern of continued but slower depletion was repeated in other parts of the Marches, so we may hope that the losses can be ended or even reversed in the coming decades.

The most biodiverse examples of permanent grassland are scattered across all parts of the Marches, other than areas where arable farming is dominant. Some of the best sites are managed as pastures and grazed throughout the season. Others are meadows and left ungrazed during spring and early summer, so they can be cut for hay. The plant communities that develop in pastures and meadows are different, but in contrast to usual expectations, both can be species-rich in the Marches.

The local name for pasture is leasow, pronounced *lezzow*. Permanent pasture is still widespread on parts of lowland farms that would be difficult to plough or mow, especially steeply sloping banks. Anthills built by the yellow meadow ant *Lasius flavus* are frequently present, confirming long periods without disturbance. Just occasionally larger areas of permanent pasture survive on sites that could easily have been ploughed and resown. An excellent example is Fordhall Farm in the Tern valley near Market Drayton, where Arthur Hollins developed a system that he called foggage to graze pasture throughout the year with cattle and sheep.[13] He used no pesticides or artificial fertilisers from the 1940s onwards. His aim was to develop productive grassland communities by management rather than by ploughing and resowing. The result is pastures with more than ten grass species and many dicotyledonous herbs. There are no great rarities among these plants, but they help to support an unusually high diversity of animal species including large numbers of insects. Fifty-seven bird species were recorded in just three visits to the farm during a survey in 2007. Arthur Hollins' youngest children Charlotte and Ben now run the farm, the land being owned by the many members of the local population who have bought shares as a Community Land Initiative. Fordhall is a delight for naturalists and a reminder of how hospitable farms can be to wildlife.

Another example of relatively species-rich pasture is at Melverley near Whitchurch. When the fields here came on the market in the 1990s they were an island of traditionally farmed land surrounded by intensive arable fields and leys. Twenty-four hectares of pasture contained 150 plant species, with many animals and fungi that are typical of permanent grassland. Melverley was given SSSI designation in 1996 and most of it became a Shropshire Wildlife Trust reserve soon after. Since then species diversity has increased, with plants such as pignut *Conopodium majus*, common spotted- and heath spotted-orchids spreading in drier areas and ragged-robin, marsh marigold, lesser spearwort, common valerian and meadowsweet in patches that become wet in winter. These are widespread plants, but they have disappeared from most grassland on farms. Insect species also appear to be increasing, including the huge numbers of meadow brown *Maniola jurtina* and ringlet butterflies that are now recorded on annual counts in July. The increase of plant and animal diversity at Melverley is probably due to a change in management; most of the pasture is now converted to hay meadow and only lightly grazed in winter.

Permanent pasture has also survived where the water table is frequently close to or above the soil surface. Indeed, apart from on the freest draining sandy soils, permanent pasture is the most widespread type of land use in the Marches where soils hold their full capacity of water for 200 or more days per year.[14] Many low-lying fields in river valleys are substantially wetter than this and remain unploughed for long periods. Jointed rush is often present on sites of highest conservation value, whereas abundant soft-rush suggests that there has been nutrient enrichment or too few periods of hard grazing. Hard rush *Juncus inflexus* picks out more base-rich ground. When grazing is prevented by wet conditions in spring, flowers such as marsh-marigold and cuckooflower *Cardamine pratensis* colour the pasture, ragged-robin and meadowsweet appearing later. The Shropshire Wildlife Trust reserve at Ruewood on the banks of the Roden, near Wem is a good example of wet riverside pasture, common meadow rue, a scarce plant in the Marches despite its name, having the title role. Ditches at Ruewood may have been used in the past to flood the pastures in spring, a practice known as floating pastures.

The aim of floating pastures was to warm the soil and thereby encourage grass to grow faster and earlier in the year. This was achieved by repeatedly flooding the pastures with moving water in winter and early spring to a very shallow depth for short periods of time. Weirs, hatches, leats and embankments were needed. Fields where this is done deliberately are true water meadows, in contrast to areas such as the Severn–Vyrnwy confluence or the Lugg Meadows near Hereford where flooding occurs to a variable depth when a river is in spate and bursts its banks. Parts of an extensive system at Staunton on Arrow, whose construction began in 1660, can still be seen. There are also records of floating pastures at Wigmore in 1653.[15] The system was impossible where rivers were deeply entrenched, as on the Severn. The use of clover and then artificial fertilisers superseded it as a means of promoting growth of pasture in time for lambing.

Traditional hay meadows have become very scarce in the Marches for two reasons. Mowable land can usually also be ploughed up for arable cropping or leys instead. Even where meadows remain, silaging has generally replaced haymaking; the earlier mowing then prevents the flowering and setting of seed, thus precluding the development of a diverse community of plants. The change to silage also has consequences for ground-nesting birds, with significant falls in lapwing, curlew and skylark numbers. Some traditional hay meadows do still survive, usually where the farmer or landowner is enough of an individualist to persist with traditional farming practices, or where conservation has been a priority. Green-winged orchid *Anacamptis morio* is a characteristic species, both in the uplands and lowlands. Leighton[16] described it as one of the four common orchid species of Shropshire, 'as abundant and as widely distributed as orchids can be expected to be'. By the time of surveys done for the *Ecological Flora of Shropshire*,[17] it was 'now only known from a few localities'. Other plants that are found in some of the best surviving hay meadows are yellow-rattle, meadow saffron *Colchicum autumnale*, pepper-saxifrage, dyer's greenweed *Genista tinctoria*, fairy flax *Linum catharticum*, betony *Stachys officinalis*, meadow saxifrage *Saxifraga granulata*, adder's-tongue *Ophioglossum vulgatum* and moonwort *Botrychium lunaria*. On wetter sites pale sedge *Carex pallescens*, saw-wort *Serratula tinctoria* and burnet-saxifrage *Pimpinella saxifraga* are sometimes found, and on limestone, frog orchid *Coeloglossum viride*, pyramidal orchid, bee orchid and greater butterfly-orchids *Platanthera chlorantha*.

Higher Level Stewardship can now provide effective support for farmers who manage these precious hay meadows and other species-rich semi-natural grasslands, so their future seems more secure than for decades. Another possible measure is the re-establishment of species-rich meadows. Shropshire Ornithological Society recently did this with notable success in fields around Venus Pool by strewing hay from species-rich meadows elsewhere over the land after a seedbed had been prepared on it. Many species established quickly, including large numbers of green-winged orchid (Fig. 190). By February 2010,

FIG 190. Green-winged orchid in newly established meadow at Venus Pool, to the south of Shrewsbury.

over 1,000 ha of farmland in Shropshire was in Higher Level Stewardship for maintenance, restoration or creation of species-rich semi-natural grassland and over 700 ha for maintenance, restoration or creation of wet grassland for wintering waders and wildfowl or for breeding waders.

ARABLE LAND

Arable crops are grown on less than half of the agricultural land in the Marches. This is the predominant type of farming in lowland areas where there are freely draining sandy or loamy soils that hold their full capacity of water for less than 175 days per year, but there are far fewer exclusively arable farms than in areas to the east. The main area extends from central to eastern and northeastern Shropshire. Some of the broad river valleys are also suitable, such as Corvedale and parts of the valleys of the lower Teme and Lugg. Fields under the plough are more scattered elsewhere in the Marches. About half of the arable land is sown with barley, a quarter with wheat and the remainder with potatoes, oilseed rape and other break crops. Not surprisingly, arable farming is largely absent from the hill country, where the soils, topography and climate are more suited to grass, and the crops grown are mostly fed to livestock. More surprisingly there is little arable farming in Maelor and much of south Cheshire, even though some of the soils here are not dissimilar to those used for arable farming in Shropshire. Partly for reasons of tradition, these lowland areas are cattle country, especially dairying. Tradition is perhaps also the reason for the growing of hops and fruit in the valley of the Teme around Tenbury Wells, but not where there are similar fine silty soils in the valleys of the Lugg and Corve.

For obvious ecological reasons we cannot expect productive arable farmland to be rich in wildlife. The aim is for the cultivated plants to convert as much of the energy in sunlight into harvestable crops. Competition from other plants, which are regarded as weeds, must be minimised. This is done so effectively in the cultivation of some crops that there are scarcely any weeds, for example maize, now widely grown for silage where cattle are farmed in the Marches. Other crops usually have some weeds present. In a survey of the whole of the parish of Weston Lullingfields, about 25 species of arable weeds were recorded. There was remarkably little overlap between the species present with different types of crop, because of differences in the timing and method of cultivation.[18] An enlightened approach to weed control can be seen on increasing numbers of farms. Weedy stubbles with spilled grain are left unploughed for as long as possible and conservation headlands around the margins of fields are not sprayed with herbicides or other agrochemicals. These and other measures were part of the Arable Stewardship scheme, piloted in a large area of east Shropshire from 1998 to 2001.

Even these sites where the biodiversity of weed species is being maintained, the biomass of plants other than the intended crop in most arable fields is negligible. The next priority for the farmer is to defend the crop against herbivores and pathogens until it is harvested. Rabbits, brown hares *Lepus europaeus* and fallow deer move into crops to feed, which is ironic as these species were all introduced to Britain. The introduction of insecticides in the second half of the 20th century allowed such effective control of insects feeding on crops that their natural invertebrate predators and also insectivorous mammals and birds were inevitably affected. Yellow wagtails *Motacilla flava*, corn buntings *Milaria calandra*, skylarks and lapwings favour open sites with low-growing plants whereas yellowhammers *Emberiza citrinella* and grey partridge *Perdix perdix* are associated with shelter provided by hedges at field margins.

Yellow wagtail numbers declined markedly in the Marches during the latter part of the 20th century but may now have stabilised. Their distribution closely matches the main area of arable cultivation in north and east Shropshire and, although distribution maps do not show this correspondence in Cheshire, observations show that it is arable fields within livestock farming areas that are being used for breeding. Autumn-sown cereals are usually chosen as nest sites for first broods but are too tall by the time that replacement or second broods are being reared. Second broods are needed to maintain the population and success rates vary with the crop type chosen for the nest site. There is most breeding success in potato crops, helping to explain the current yellow wagtail distribution. Corn buntings also breed mostly where agricultural crops provide the preferred open habitat, so their distribution closely matches that of arable farming. They have probably never been widespread or common in the Marches;[19] their stronghold has for many years been in eastern Shropshire between Telford and Market Drayton. Recent surveys suggest that there has been little if any contraction in range or population size in Shropshire since the 1980s and that there may have been a small expansion in southeast Cheshire. This is perhaps surprising as there was an overall national decline in corn buntings during the 20th century and an almost complete disappearance from Wales. The expectation might have been that this process would have continued eastwards through the Marches, but the decrease seems to have halted in northwest Shropshire.

Skylarks have bred very widely in arable crops in the past, but changes in agricultural practice have caused a considerable decline. Cereal crops are now mostly sown in autumn rather than spring and the lack of stubbles has reduced food availability in winter. In spring the cereals grow too tall to provide the open conditions that skylarks prefer for their nests. Grassland is sometimes used instead, but the change in grass conservation method, from hay to silage, means earlier and more frequent cutting, so nests are very likely to be destroyed. Skylarks are now absent from many lowland farms, but there are still strong populations on the hills of the Marches.

Surveys of breeding lapwing in Shropshire showed a huge overall decline from 90 in 1987 to 24 in 1998, followed by a stabilisation, with 30 pairs found in 2003.[20] The decline was not consistent over the whole of Shropshire, the steepest falls being in the southern half of the county. The surveys showed how important arable land has become to lapwings – 73 per cent of pairs nested on it in 1987 increasing to 90 per cent in 2003. Almost all of these pairs were in spring-sown rather than autumn-sown crops. Lapwings transfer their young soon after hatching to feed in short grassland; pasture where cattle are feeding is particularly favoured because of the greater number of insects.

Yellowhammers have also declined, but not as much, and they do still breed in hedges throughout the Marches, even in areas of intensive arable farming. If grass strips are deliberately left alongside hedges they form a useful feeding ground, whilst winter stubbles or set-aside land also increase population densities. Grey partridge have declined from very common at the end of the 19th century[21] to being fairly common in some parts in the Marches and very scarce to the west in Wales. Increases in predation of eggs, chicks and adult birds by foxes, badgers and hawks were probably part of the cause, but partridge can hardly be expected to survive on intensively farmed land with few weeds or associated insects and no sheltered hedge bottoms for nest sites. Where farmers are willing to leave conservation headlands unsprayed with herbicides or pesticides, along with unploughed field margins adjacent to dense hedges, grey partridge can still thrive.

WILDLIFE CONSERVATION ON FARMS

The account given so far shows that many types of farmland can provide habitat for species that are scarce elsewhere, but only if it is managed in an appropriate way. The system of payments for production discouraged this in the past, but there is cautious optimism among conservationists that things are now turning in the right direction, albeit rather slowly. The latest agri-environment schemes are having some impact but they need to be reinforced. There are many farms where valuable conservation work is already being done. Just one example will be given here.

Great Wollaston Farm is located to the southeast of the Breidden Hills. It is a mixed commercial farm that succeeds in supporting a wealth of wildlife without compromising profitability. Both arable crops and grassland provide habitat for the increasingly scarce farmland birds and other species. Lapwings and curlews breed on the farm, whilst yellowhammers, tree sparrows and other traditional birds of farmland are much commoner than on other farms in the area. The management of the farm has been carefully thought out in order to achieve this. Crop rotation has been reintroduced at Great Wollaston, reducing the need for insecticide sprays and bought-in fertiliser. In a typical year insecticide spray is used only in autumn, to control aphids that might transmit virus diseases to cereal crops. Herbicide use in autumn-sown cereals has been reduced and the stubbles are left after harvest to provide feed for overwintering birds until the following March. Peas and spring barley are then sown, with an undersowing of grass and clover. Skylarks and lapwings often choose open areas of this crop away from hedgerow trees for their nest sites. The skylark chicks have fledged and the lapwing nestlings have been moved to adjacent pasture long before this spring-sown crop is cut for silage in July. The undersown grass and clover is then grazed for the next few years before being returned to arable cropping. There is also some permanent pasture on the farm, including a large field where a narrow ridge and furrow pattern created by steam ploughing shows that it has remained unploughed since before the 1920s. Its underlying heavy clay is unsuited to tillage, but cattle like the species-rich pasture that has developed and milk well off it. Meadow barley *Hordeum secalinum* has been recorded here, a very rare plant in the Marches, and part of this field has been converted to hay meadow. Chemical fertilisers and slurry are not used on the permanent grassland, but farmyard manure containing straw is spread annually.

Great Wollaston is not registered as organic, because the farmer Robert Kynaston believes that greater benefits can be obtained if he keeps up productivity on most of the farmland with some non-organic techniques, allowing smaller areas to be taken out of production and put into agri-environment schemes. Six-metre wide fertiliser-free grass margins, known as conservation headlands, are left next to hedges in arable fields. About half is mown and the rest is allowed to become rank, providing habitat for voles and feeding ground for owls. Yellowhammers, grey partridges, resting hares and many other species also benefit from these strips. They may cause a small reduction in harvestable crops, but hedges can be allowed to grow larger and only need trimming every third year. Shrubs in hedges then produce more berries and nuts in winter, and more flowers with nectar and pollen in summer. Hedgerow trees are encouraged but are pollarded rather than being allowed to grow to a size where they shade out the hedge shrubs. Permanent grassland with pollen- and nectar-rich herbs has been established in awkward corners of some arable fields, parts being mowed in June and the remainder later to encourage a succession of flowers. Other corners of arable fields are sown with wild birdseed mix on a rotational basis. These are left for two to three years to provide seeds and nectar in summer, and cover in winter. The wettest area of the farm is mixed alder and oak woodland; this is being coppiced in rotation, with some of the timber used to produce charcoal. There are eight ponds on the farm, mostly clay pits left from small-scale brick making in the 19th century. These are cleaned out when they start to silt up. A reed-bed has recently been created to treat run-off from the yard outside the milking parlour, before it flows on into a nearby stream.

Great Wollaston has won awards from English Nature and RSPB. It is a demonstration farm for an organisation called Linking Environment and Farming, usually abbreviated to LEAF. Its economic viability depends on agri-environment subsidies, but these are quite modest compared with the absurdly large amounts used in the past to drive intensification, leading to surpluses and consequent damage to agriculture elsewhere in the world by dumping food at prices lower than the cost of production. In the Marches, as elsewhere in Britain, subsidies are only justifiable if they allow production of food without harm to wildlife or the rural landscape. Farming should be evaluated as a process rather than solely for its products. This policy will only clearly be seen to be working when species that have been harmed by agriculture start to thrive again. Perhaps we should choose some indicator species for the Marches:

1. Freshwater pearl mussels regenerating again in the Clun and other rivers.
2. Lapwing breeding in substantial numbers in the uplands, on arable land and on flood plains.
3. Silver-studded blue butterflies spreading out across a network of heathland.
4. Green-winged orchids growing widely in meadows.

It will be interesting to see how these and any other indicator species that we might choose fare in the coming decades and what this will tell us about the impact of agriculture in the Marches.

CHAPTER 13

Recovering from Industry

I T IS STILL POSSIBLE TO STAND ON THE WORLD'S first iron bridge and look down on the steep-sided valley that was renamed the Ironbridge Gorge. The sides of the valley are densely wooded, belying the fact that that the gorge and surrounding areas were once at the forefront of the Industrial Revolution. In the side valley of Coalbrookdale, Quaker ironmaster Abraham Darby took the hugely significant step of using coke rather than charcoal to smelt iron in about 1710. The bridge was built in the late 1770s to span the flood-prone river Severn (Fig. 191). Carboniferous rocks of the Coalbrookdale coalfield provided the materials not only for making iron, but also for bricks, tiles, pottery and porcelain. Early industrial development and innovation also took place nearby in the Denbighshire coalfield, from Oswestry northwards. Elsewhere in the Marches there has also been scattered industry, but like that of the Coalbrookdale and Denbighshire coalfields, much of it ended years ago. Wildlife has had a chance to reclaim many of these post-industrial sites. Recovery from industry is the theme of this chapter. Local knowledge is invaluable in disentangling cause and effect and was used whenever possible in writing this chapter, but published descriptions of many sites are not available. Oral histories are often fascinating but hard to track down and there are great opportunities for more case studies to be published. There are thousands of individual post-industrial sites in the Marches. Only a small selection can be mentioned in this chapter, together with an overview of the main types of industry. Several overarching questions should be borne in mind. Does industry increase or decrease the biodiversity of a site? Should sites of former industry be tidied up or abandoned? Is conservation on post-industrial sites best achieved by active management or by letting nature take its course?

FIG 191. Ironbridge Gorge, with the bridge visible on the left. The sides of the gorge were entirely deforested during the Industrial Revolution but mixed deciduous woodland has re-established. (Severn Gorge Countryside Trust)

QUARRYING

This is perhaps the simplest of industries and one of the most widespread. A great variety of different rocks have been quarried for building stone. Particular types of stone are in some cases used in a very small area, even in just a single village. English Heritage recently commissioned a survey of types and sources of building stone in the Marches, thus trying to ensure that supplies are conserved for repair work in the future. The many small quarries from which stone was worked by hand were almost all abandoned a long time ago. Mechanisation has allowed much larger quarries to be worked. Planning permission has been given for quarrying on about 50 km² of the Marches since the current system began in 1947 and more than half of this area has been worked. Some of these large quarries are still active, but more are disused with either artificial reclamation or natural regeneration effecting changes in them.

Where hard rock has been quarried there are often steep cliff-like faces and flat quarry floors, sometimes with pools filling deeper parts of the quarry void. Frequently there are heaps of waste stone, either on the quarry floor or forming scree slopes against the faces. One species that benefits from rock faces is the peregrine falcon. Although breeding is reputed to have occurred in the past at a site 'in the uplands of western Shropshire',[1] there are no confirmed records from the Marches until the 1980s. The number of breeding pairs has since risen to more than 20. This would probably not have been possible without quarrying, as the ideal site for an eyrie is a ledge at least 5 m from both the bottom and top of a cliff. Natural rock faces in the Marches do not provide this. The sites occupied first by nesting peregrine falcons were all quarries, often with the eyrie above a pool in the quarry floor. By the mid-1990s, all suitable quarry sites were occupied and some pairs resorted to less than ideal sites. A pair nested on the church tower in Wrecsam, but after complaints from the vicar about the numbers of dead animals, a ledge was constructed on the police communications tower and the peregrines obligingly moved there. More unusually, in 2002 one pair raised young in an old carrion crow's nest in a mature oak tree near where the Severn crosses the Shropshire–Montgomeryshire border. The same pair returned in 2003 but the nest collapsed before the three eggs had hatched and though they were seen in the area again in 2004, they did not continue with their arboreal experiments.

Quarries provide a habitat for many other species. Surveys of 38 Shropshire quarries in 2006–7 gave species totals of 566 plants, 701 invertebrates, 270 bryophytes and 201 lichens.[2] Up to 100 species of bryophytes were found in a single quarry.[3] There are large areas of exposed rock and undisturbed bare soil in active quarries and, at least initially, in abandoned quarries. These are scarce habitats in the Marches, so species occur that are rarely found elsewhere. An example is the aptly named scarce blue-tailed damselfly *Ischnura pumilio* that breeds in shallow, sparsely vegetated runnels in the abandoned quarries below the summit of Titterstone Clee. Small cudweed *Filago minima*, buck's-horn plantain *Plantago coronopus* and moonwort grow nearby on unprepossessing waste heaps. The floors of many quarries are the parts to be colonised slowest by plants and ground remains bare, with some lichens and hummocks of moss. Even in quarries where neutral or acidic rocks were quarried, species associated with chalk grassland tend to colonise these flat open areas, including yellow-wort *Blackstonia perfoliata* and common centaury *Centaurium erythraea*. Autumn gentians *Gentianella amarella* are also sometimes present on quarry floors in limestone areas. Lilleshall quarry, near Much Wenlock, has a strong population.

Diversity tends to decrease and the scarcest species disappear if there is a succession to denser vegetation. Continued working of the quarry can prevent this, as can grazing or scrub clearance. Most abandoned quarries have receded into the landscape as woodland has reclaimed them, with tree species and ground flora corresponding to the rock type, drainage and other physical features. A disused quartzite quarry at Poles Coppice on the north end of Stiperstones provides an instructive example: there are three distinct woodland types within a distance of about 50 m. On steeply sloping ground at the edge of the quarry there is upland sessile oak woodland. Mixed deciduous woodland dominated by ash occurs on heaps of waste rock and on the badly drained quarry floor there is birch-alder carr. Once woodland is established, species of conservation interest often colonise. Dormice are now present in wooded sections around the margins of Lea and Lilleshall quarries on Wenlock Edge, where crevices in the quarry walls have been used as sites for hibernation.

Biodiversity is particularly high in limestone quarries, so they deserve special consideration. Limestone has been quarried or mined wherever it outcrops in the Marches. In a horseshoe-shaped area of Carboniferous limestone to the south of Titterstone Clee that was worked in the past, woodland has now returned, with ash dominating as expected, but with some self-sown Norway maple *Acer platanoides* in places. The diverse ground flora includes common twayblades *Listera ovata* and other orchids. Part of this area is Knowle Wood, a Shropshire Wildlife Trust reserve.

Silurian limestone has been quarried in many places along Wenlock Edge and to the east of Ironbridge Gorge. Small abandoned quarries are mostly now woodland, but there are also some open areas featuring plants that would previously have been widespread in unimproved limestone grassland. Despite having been abandoned in the 1930s, Patten's Rock quarry in Benthall Edge Wood

has retained areas of grassland, due to grazing by fallow deer and also periodic
clearance of scrub and birch saplings by volunteers. In the grassland are bee,
greater butterfly and other orchids, as well as the food plants needed to sustain
populations of green hairstreak and dingy skipper *Erynnis tages* butterflies. There
has been limestone quarrying on a large scale near Much Wenlock. Activity
continued until relatively recently at Farley, Shadwell and Lea quarries, but they
are all now abandoned and for the moment at least there is no quarrying on
Wenlock Edge. These large quarries are currently scars on the landscape but
given time they could become very biodiverse. In an interesting new initiative,
Lea North quarry and Lilleshall quarry are due to be acquired by the National
Trust with the aims of promoting both conservation and education. Exposures of
limestone stretch for over a kilometre around the edge of Lea quarry, revealing
the structure of Silurian patch reefs. Large numbers of abandoned limestone
blocks on the quarry floor offer an almost inexhaustible supply of fossils for
geology students. Plants more typical of southern or southeastern Britain
including small-flowered buttercup *Ranunculus parviflorus*, common gromwell
Lithospermum officinale and basil thyme *Clinopodium acinos* have been recorded
on dry sunny banks in the quarry. These are ideal sites for the development of
limestone grassland and insects, such as solitary bees, wasps and butterflies,
including dingy skippers. Part of the quarry has flooded with water, coloured
blue by suspended lime and bentonite clay (Fig. 192). This lake is likely to become

FIG 192. Lea Quarry on Wenlock Edge, with a large pool that appeared after pumping ended.
The National Trust is in the process of acquiring the quarry because of its conservation and
educational potential.

larger and deeper due to rebound of groundwater. It is hard to predict what species will colonise its alkaline waters once the suspended solids settle and the water clears, but there is already a colony of several hundred great crested newts.

There is another group of limestone quarries to the south and west of Oswestry, including Llanymynech Rocks, Llynclys Common and Dolgoch quarry, all Shropshire Wildlife Trust reserves. The most recently abandoned sections of quarry, where there is little soil and much bare rock, often have the most interesting natural history. They provide habitat for some increasingly scarce invertebrates such as small pearl-bordered fritillaries and grizzled skippers *Pyrgus malvae*. These quarries, like those previously described, tend to develop into woodland unless there is regular grazing or repeated and heroic efforts at scrub clearance by conservation volunteers. Hebridean sheep are used to prevent the spread of brambles and scrub at Llanymynech, but the quarries on Llynclys Common and at Dolgoch have not recently been grazed. Instead they are given an annual strimming, and unauthorised motorbike use at Dolgoch helps to maintain open habitats. Llanymynech was abandoned longer ago than other quarries and the amount of suitable habitat for grizzled skippers and species of open areas is reduced. There is rubbly made-up ground below the quarries that was planted up with conifers in the past. These were felled in the 1980s, since when natural regeneration has taken place, to give species-rich woodland including ash, sycamore, maple, yew, hawthorn, elder, dogwood and wych elm, with pedunculate oaks starting to establish. Both ivy and traveller's joy *Clematis vitalba* grow prolifically as lianas, sometimes bringing trees down with their weight. Llanymynech quarry also has historical interest. There are inclined planes used to take rock down to limekilns below the hill. A huge Hoffman kiln built in 1899 has been preserved and is used by roosting lesser horseshoe bats *Rhinolophus hipposideros*. There are pools of clear water at both Llynclys Common and Dolgoch that contain a rich variety of invertebrates and all three species of newt.

One very large quarry remains active in this limestone area: Llynclys Quarry, located to the north of Llynclys Common. This site is an undoubted scar on the landscape, but as at many other sites, the overall effect of quarrying is likely to be an increase in biodiversity rather than a decrease. There have been initiatives over many years to provide habitat for target species and communities, both during the working phase in sections of quarry and afterwards. Rather than leaving vertical faces at the sides of the quarry, a series of wide graded shelves are being created on which grassland can develop and be grazed. Seven orchid species have been recorded, among them autumn lady's-tresses *Spiranthes spiralis*, which soon appears when new areas of grassland establish, and also both lesser *Platanthera bifolia* and greater butterfly-orchids (Fig. 193). Other grassland herbs establish,

FIG 193. Common spotted-orchids at Llanymynech Quarry. (Keith Little)

some acting as food sources for the 12 butterfly species that have been recorded in recent years. There is a strong population of grizzled skippers, at the western edge of their range. There is another well-known population of this species on Wrecsam industrial estate, where rough grassland and disturbed ground provide suitable habitat. An existing lagoon at the centre of Llynclys Quarry currently used for washing quarried stone, will be deepened to create a permanent pool. Unlike many quarry pools, there will be shallow sloping margins rather than steep drops to deep water, which should improve habitat for both marginal and submerged plants as well as amphibians.

There have also been some gains for biodiversity from sand and gravel quarries. The deposits that are worked in the Marches are in almost all cases glacial in origin, so they tend to be in areas of natural meres in kettle holes. The voids created during quarrying resemble these kettle holes. They must usually be kept dry by pumping during excavation, but flood to form what we can regard as artificial meres when pumping ceases. This is due either to groundwater rebounding to its natural level, or to a layer of silt and clay creating a perched water table. There is an example of an active sand and gravel quarry at Condover. This site, famous for the discovery of mammoth bones, is located a few hundred metres from the Bomere–Shomere group of natural meres. There is currently a silt lagoon and a clean water lagoon, which already attract some water birds. The owners Hanson Aggregates have undertaken 'to enhance ecological interest and biodiversity in this area adjacent to the Bomere Pool SSSI and Ramsar site' when quarrying ends, with four meres on the underlying clay in the base of the quarry, agricultural land around and woodland up the sloping sides. Ideally these plans would become part of a more ambitious scheme to establish a new national nature reserve encompassing both the former quarry and the adjacent natural complex of meres. The costs could easily be borne from the Aggregates Levy.

There is an active sand and gravel quarry at Bromfield, to the north of Ludlow. This quarry is unusual in two respects: the deposits are partly alluvial, rather than being entirely glacial and more curiously, water does not have to be pumped out of the active pits, even though the nearby Onny flows at a higher level. This is presumably because alluvial or glacial deposits underlying the river form a barrier. It will be interesting to see whether water levels do eventually rise when the quarry ceases to be worked or whether it remains largely dry. Some species have already found a habitat, for example sand martins nesting in cliffs of sand and gravel (*see* Fig. 71).

Wood Lane to the south of Ellesmere is another active sand and gravel quarry, but here pits quickly became flooded when they were worked out and attracted large numbers of waders and other birds. The owner Bill Griffiths and naturalist John Hawkins began habitat creation measures to encourage this, including control of water levels in a shallow scrape created to provide a muddy waterlogged area – a habitat that is now very scarce because of land drainage. Lapwings, little ringed plovers *Charadrius dubius* and shelduck breed around the margins of the scrape. There are roosts of about 150 curlews in early autumn, 100 snipe in winter and 1,400 lapwings in February. Five hundred sand martins breed in sand banks at Wood Lane – probably the largest colony in the Marches. Wood Lane is now managed as a Shropshire Wildlife Trust reserve. Over 150 species of birds have been recorded in total and over 1,000 children visit each year in school parties (Fig. 194). Venus Pool to the southeast of Shrewsbury is another site with open water. It is a Shropshire Ornithological Society reserve in the former settling lagoon of an adjacent sand quarry. There is now a shallow

FIG 194. Wood Lane sand and gravel quarry, near Ellesmere, showing active quarrying, land fill waste disposal and the ponds, lagoons and scrapes that have been created in worked-out areas (above). There is a large colony of sand martins (left). (John Hawkins)

pool, with muddy margins and reed-beds. It has become one of the best sites for observing birds in the Marches with over 200 species recorded, including bittern and osprey.

Some abandoned sand and gravel quarries remain dry and attract heathland species that may well be the original natives. Morville sand pit between Much Wenlock and Bridgnorth is one of the best sites in the Marches for bees and wasps, with three RDB species. Alyn Waters Country Park was established from a group of quarries on either side of Afon Alun, to the north of Wrecsam. Despite human disturbance there are strong breeding populations of skylarks, song thrushes *Turdus philomelos* and linnets *Carduelis cannabina*, and also large numbers of orchids including twayblades by the thousand and bee orchids, which are scarce in much of the Marches. Marford quarry to the north of Wrecsam has SSSI status principally because of its insect populations. It was opened in 1927 to provide the sand and gravel for the construction of the Mersey Tunnel and closed in 1971. Sixteen hectares of the quarry have been allowed to regenerate naturally, with limited control of gorse and small trees. There is some emergent woodland, but more valuable are the areas of open grassland on the coarse sands and gravels. Wild liquorice *Astragalus glycyphyllos* grows here, at the northwesterly limit of its range. The non-native white mullein *Verbascum lychnitis* is also here and in many quarries around Wrecsam.

Marford Quarry is probably now the best inland site for bees, wasps and ants in the whole of Wales, with 104 species recorded since 1990 including three RDB species.[4] The quarry is at the northern edge of the Wrecsam delta plateau, a huge area of glacial deposits. Also on the delta plateau but further south is Borras, which at over 170 ha is one of the largest sand and gravel quarries in Britain. Its seemingly relentless expansion was described in Chapter 5. While still an active quarry, 94 species of bees, wasps and ants were recorded here, 31 of which were not also recorded at Marford. There were four nationally scarce and one RDB species. These insects thrive in open habitats with sandy or gravelly subsoils, so they are only likely to survive at Borras if bare ground, grassland or heathland persists after quarrying has ended. About 10 ha of woodland has already been planted on a worked out area and a 20-ha lagoon has been planned for another part of the quarry. It is important that substantial other areas are allowed to remain as natural open communities, rather than planted with trees or 'greened over' with 'amenity grassland'.

Despite the successes achieved at Llynclys, Marford and other sites, it cannot be claimed that quarries always increase biodiversity. Criggion Quarry near Welshpool had already taken a huge bite of dolerite out of Breiddon Hill when William Condry wrote of it in his New Naturalist on Wales.[5] The removal of rock has continued ever since then and another 20 million t are due to be taken in

FIG 195. The Breiddens with Criggion Quarry scarring the west face, viewed across the flood plain of the Severn from Llandrinio.

the next 30 years (Fig. 195). The scar created extends from the valley floor to the hilltop, is visible for many kilometres to the west and even more prominent when viewed in profile from north or south. The unique grassland community that has developed on Breidden Hill was described in Chapter 4. Of the rare plants in this community, there was only one small patch of rock cinquefoil by the 1980s and small amounts of spiked speedwell and sticky catchfly, though all of these plants have clung on since then. The moss *Bartramia stricta* was recorded at Breidden in the 1960s on rock that has been quarried away and it is probably now lost. Its only remaining population in England or Wales is at Stanner Rocks in Radnorshire. Quarrying has undoubtedly reduced the area of unique grassland, but there are other factors that may have had a greater impact on some of the rarities of Breidden. The population of rock cinquefoil was reported to be plentiful in the 1859 but nearly extinct by 1879, probably as a result of collecting by botanists. Between 1830 and 1931 over 100 specimens are known to have been taken and the true total was probably much more. Conifers have been planted on parts of the west crags and scrub invasion has also reduced the area of open habitat, with gorse and broom a particular problem on the south crags. Greater efforts to clear scrub are needed whilst all conifers and other non-native trees should be removed. No project is more deserving of support from the Aggregates Levy. We should also bear in mind evidence that quarrying has created open habitats that some rare plants can utilise. Narrow-leaved bitter-cress *Cardamine impatiens*, a biennial that is more typical of limestone woodland and is rare in most of the Marches, seeds itself around on disturbed ground in the quarry and travels out with lorry loads of chippings to spring up elsewhere. Rock stonecrop has spread along quarry tracks and clustered clover *Trifolium glomeratum* was recently found beside such a track. It is a winter annual, but even so is an unexpected find in Breidden's U1 grassland communities as it is rarely found outside its southern coastal range. Another recent find is small-flowered sweet-briar *Rosa micrantha*, which is very scarce on inland sites as far north as this. A recent survey found that of the 4,000 or so plants of shaggy mouse-ear hawkweed on Breidden, more than half were beside tracks, or on bunds, road cuttings and spoil heaps.[6] Quarrying has therefore increased the habitat available for this critically endangered Breidden endemic (Fig. 196).

Rock cinquefoil plants can be artificially raised from seed quite easily and plants from Breidden seed have been translocated to sloping rock benches in worked out parts of the quarry with promising results. There have also been experimental translocations of sticky catchfly and spiked speedwell, but further trials are needed. At present it has not been decided how remediation work at Criggion will ensure that as valuable a community of plants and animals are left as was present before quarrying, but this would seem a very reasonable obligation for Hanson Aggregates and Powys County Council.

FIG 196. Rock cinquefoil with bloody crane's-bill at Criggion Quarry. (Alastair Hotchkiss)

BRICKYARDS AND CLAYHOLES

Clay is quarried for making bricks, tiles and ceramic products. Although bricks had been made on a small scale in many parts of the Marches for hundreds of years, the development of large brickyards began in 1850 when the Brick Tax was abolished. The two materials required in bulk are clay and coal. These occur together in the Coal Measures, so brickyards therefore became concentrated in the Coalbrookdale and Denbighshire coalfields. Some of the best bricks were those that were made in the area around Ruabon, south of Wrecsam. They are smooth surfaced, very durable and have a distinctive bright red colour. This is due to iron content of the clay from which they were made – the Ruabon Marl occurring at the base of the Upper Coal Measures.

Clay was either extracted from open-cast quarries called clayholes, or from mines that are properly called claypits, though these terms are often incorrectly used. The oldest clayholes tend to be small and in groups. There is an intriguing example in Benthall to the west of the road leading down to the Iron Bridge, with small clayholes, spoil heaps and old roads. There is another example on the site of Gallimore's saggar works, to the south of Caughley quarries. In both cases the complex topography has precluded ploughing and so permanent grassland has developed with many ant hills (Fig. 197).

FIG 197. Caughley clayhole, south of Ironbridge Gorge, which will flood with water once pumping ends.

Deeper clayholes usually fill with water, forming pools that are often steep-sided. Suspended clay particles tend to make the water a cloudy blue or white colour. There may be emergent plants at the margins but usually few submerged plants, especially where introduced carp disturb sediments and prevent the water from gradually clearing. Ducks, coots and grebes are commonly present. A large alder-lined pool to the north of Ruabon was the clayhole for Monk and Newell Brickworks. It now resembles a mere in a kettle hole, but like many natural meres, the wildlife interest is limited by its use as a fishing lake. Blue Pool in Telford Town Park was the clayhole for Randlay Brickworks. Great crested grebes, tufted duck and common sandpiper all breed around this pool.

Other clayholes have not fared as well as the examples so far described. Many have now been used as landfill sites, for example that of Hafod brickworks, to the east of Johnstown, which is being filled with waste from Merseyside. Excavation continues in the extensive Blockleys clayholes at Hadley, in Telford. Parts of this site now have SSSI and Regionally Important Geodiversity Site (RIGS) designations, because of the interest of the sequences of Upper Carboniferous rock exposed in the former working faces, but nonetheless current plans are to infill and build on the site. Ironically, it is likely that the main material used to fill the holes will be old bricks. Fenn's Bank Brick and Tile Company created three clayholes to the east of Fenn's Moss between 1860 and 1935 that became water-filled soon after being excavated. One of these was used to dump over half

FIG 198. Clayholes at Fenn's Bank: the upper left hole was filled with aluminium oxide waste, which contaminated the water-filled right hole. (Clwyd-Powys Archaeological Trust)

a million tonnes of aluminium oxide waste from a smelting plant that operated in the second half of the 20th century on the site of the brickworks. The other two remained as lakes and were stocked with fish, but a clay bank was accidentally breached in 1995 allowing contaminated water containing ammonium and chloride ions from the oxide dump to leak into one of them. All fish were killed, and though levels of ammonium are now much lower, the Environment Agency has estimated that it will take 50 years for chloride levels to fall to a low enough level for restocking with fish (Fig. 198).

CANALS

The development of the canal network added about 130 ha of open water and more than 250 km of banksides to the amounts already existing in the Marches (Fig. 199). For comparison, Aqualate Mere, which is the largest natural open-water body, has an area of 80 ha and 4 km of banks. Soon after their opening in the late 18th century and early 19th century, plants appeared in the Shropshire Union, Shrewsbury and Llangollen canals that were at the time uncommon in the Marches, such as fennel and horned pondweeds.[7] They were adapted to eutrophic conditions, which did not then prevail in open-water habitats. The mainline Shropshire Union Canal and other heavily used parts of the network ceased to provide habitats for many aquatic plants when diesel engines and propellers replaced horse traction. This is because the wash makes the water too turbid for submerged species as well as destroying floating plants and all but the toughest of emergents. Fish, including perch, roach, pike, tench, carp, rudd and bream, thrive in moderate to heavily used canals, with herons, mink and otters predating them. Kingfishers have also adapted well and are frequently seen in sections of the Llangollen Canal, such as that between Blake Mere and Colemere. Water voles remain in some busy parts of the canal system, especially near Whitchurch. The Shropshire Union Canal remained busy, but traffic on other Marches canals declined considerably during the 20th century, allowing plant and animal species to return. Edward Wilson, a biology master at Ellesmere College, reported that only one other boat was passed during a week's cruising on the Llangollen Canal in 1951. The water was crystal clear and the bottom of the canal was visible where it was not covered with submerged plants. There was extensive fringing vegetation, which almost met in the middle in places. Ellesmere College Field Club surveyed the canal and found many species, including freshwater sponges.[8] Groups from Preston Montford field studies centre carried out an ecological survey of three reaches of canals near Ellesmere at the end of the 1950s, ranging

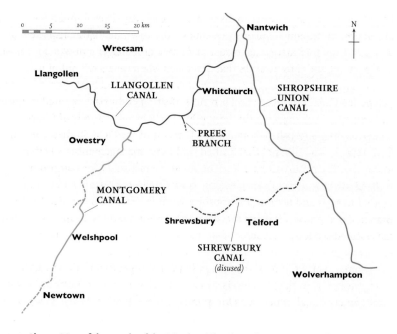

FIG 199. Above: Map of the canals of the Marches. The Shropshire Union Canal runs north to the Mersey, at Ellesmere Port, named after Ellesmere in Shropshire to which it is linked via the Llangollen Canal. Below: Chirk Aqueduct on the Llangollen Canal. Designed by Thomas Telford and built between 1796 and 1801, the aqueduct carries water from the Dee across the Ceiriog at a height of 21 m.

from lightly used in summer to disused and nearly dry. They found huge differences in the aquatic plants present and the associated animal species.[9] It was clear from this survey that disuse and a lack of management was not a means of conserving the communities that developed when canals fell out of use.

Attempts to conserve rare aquatic plants on the disused Edstaston Arm of the Llangollen Canal produced similar results. Boating enthusiasts wanted to restore and reopen it in the 1970s, with the support perhaps surprisingly of Charles Sinker, leading Shropshire botanist and Director of the Field Studies Council from 1973–83, who thought that limited traffic and management was better than none. The Nature Conservancy opposed the plans and the compromise reached was that 2 km of canal leading to a marina were restored, but 1 km beyond was not and became a Shropshire Wildlife Trust reserve called the Prees Branch Canal. Sadly, all plants that were conservation targets disappeared from the restored section as a result of disturbance and from the reserve because ecological succession led to the loss of open water (Fig. 200).

Although the wildlife of the Llangollen Canal is greatly diminished, that of another canal in the Marches is still amongst the richest in Britain. This is Montgomery Canal, which runs for 56 km from Newtown in Powys to a junction with the Llangollen Canal at Frankton. It is fed by oligotrophic upland water from the Severn near Newtown, the Tanat near Llanymynech and also from the Dee, via the Llangollen Canal. The first two of these sources are particularly clean. Traffic on the canal was never heavy and declined further in the 20th century. Scarce plants, molluscs and other species had already been recorded

FIG 200. The Prees Branch is a non-navigated section of canal near Whixall that has been colonised by emergent plants and open water has been lost. (Andrew Jenkinson)

by the time of closure in 1944. Fourteen species of dragonfly were found when a survey was done in 1947.[10] The water in many parts was crystal clear, allowing submerged plants to thrive, including autumnal water-starwort, water-violet, frogbit and an impressive group of pondweeds: red *Potamogeton alpinus*, long-stalked *Potamogeton praelongus*, flat-stalked *Potamogeton friesii* and glass-wrack *Potamogeton compressus*. Distribution maps show the importance of these populations, but it is another species that has achieved iconic status: floating water-plantain. This is a fascinating plant with a complex life cycle that involves changes of growth form and several different reproductive strategies.[11] It has declined or disappeared from most of its range in Europe, but has been recorded from the whole of the Welsh section of the Montgomery Canal and parts of the English section. It is found in a few other parts of the canal system in the West Midlands and northwest.

The initial threat after closure was infilling and conversion of the land to other uses. Efforts by the Nature Conservancy Council and local conservationists prevented this, but by the late 1960s the lack of boat traffic had allowed emergent plants to become dominant in some sections and other sections were drying out because water supplies had not been maintained. During the 1960s boat users had begun campaigning for restoration. This helped to prevent the building of a road along the line of the canal in Welshpool. Two hundred volunteers cleared out 2 km of the canal at Welshpool over one weekend in 1969 in a project now referred to as the 'Big Dig'. However, restoration of the canal and the resumption of boat traffic were prospects that alarmed some conservationists, given the known consequences in the Llangollen Canal. Through the 1970s and early 1980s the open-water habitats of the canal continued to decline and there was increasing acceptance that some form of restoration was essential.

A comprehensive ecological survey began in 1985.[12] This confirmed that SSSI status of the canal was justified, not only because floating water-plantain was present along most of the length of the canal, but also because of the other scarce water plants. Species of slow-flowing mesotrophic lowland waters were present in the main channel, but in byweirs at locks there were also species of fast-flowing oligotrophic upland streams. Nineteen species of fish were recorded and 150 species of aquatic invertebrate, including white-clawed crayfish and freshwater sponges. Records have continued to accumulate, including a variety of charophytes that are all very scarce in the Marches: fragile stonewort *Chara globularis*, delicate stonewort *Chara virgata*, smooth stonewort *Nitella flexilis* and slender stonewort *Nitella gracilis* (Fig. 201). Experiments were carried out in an attempt to marry the aims of conservation with those of boat users. Nature reserves were established in offline areas such as disused side-arms and basins.

FIG 201. The Montgomery canal with broad-leaved pondweed – at the time of the photo this section was not navigated. (Chris Walker)

Open water was re-established in the experimental areas by dredging, and communities of selected plants were introduced by transplantation. Initial results were promising and eventually the Nature Conservancy Council agreed that restoration of the whole of the Montgomery Canal could proceed if these nature reserves were maintained and 14 additional ones were established. This decision was enshrined in the British Waterways Act of 1987.

In the 20 years that followed, two large sections of the canal were restored and reopened but sections at the Newtown end and in the middle between Berriew and Guilsfield remained closed and in places dry. Boat traffic was therefore much lighter than if the whole canal were open, but even so the resultant turbidity caused the extinction of submerged plants. These included flat-stalked and grass-wrack pondweeds in their last Shropshire sites. In 2004 the Welsh part of the Montgomery Canal was given SAC status for its rare aquatic plants, particularly floating water-plantain and grass-wrack pondweed. These are both BAP species, with British Waterways as the lead partner in the plans to conserve them. To take account of the enhanced status, a new conservation management strategy was produced.[13] This recommended restoration of the whole canal and its eventual reopening to boat traffic, with an acceptance that populations of submerged aquatics would inevitably be damaged. Compensatory habitat must therefore be established in off-line nature reserves, with the canal only reopening to boat traffic when these are shown to support the target species of aquatic plant. Three off-line reserves have already been established on the English section on the Weston Arm, in the Rednal Basin and at Aston Locks, with additional areas created at the latter site in 2008. Another three reserves have been established in the Welsh section, at Wern claypits, Brithdir locks and Whitehouse bridge.

Initial results indicate varied success in establishing populations of submerged aquatics and British Waterways accepts that stronger evidence is needed before full reopening. Five years after the publication of the management strategy, only small parts of it had been implemented, because the necessary £40 million was not available. This was not necessarily good news for the aquatic plants. The Montgomery Canal presents the challenge of an ecological Catch 22: don't restore and lose significant species as open water disappears, or restore and lose species as a result of boat traffic. The challenge to ecologists of British Waterways is immense. If the management plan is successfully implemented and sustainable populations of the rare aquatic plants are established, it will be seen as an exemplar of good conservation practice. There must be some uncertainty about the future though, and it seems only prudent to back up efforts in the Montgomery Canal with others elsewhere.

Studies of floating water-plantain suggest that its natural strongholds are oligotrophic lakes.[14] Floating water-plantain spread into canals in the Marches after 1850, either from Welsh lakes or Shropshire meres. To conserve genetic diversity there should be populations in both of these types of location. The populations in Welsh lakes seem reasonably secure, but not those in the meres. This species was recorded at Hencott Pool, Blake Mere, White Mere and several other oligotrophic or mesotrophic sites in the Marches in the late 18th century. Although it became increasingly scarce in the 19th and 20th centuries because of eutrophication, it was recorded at additional sites including Bomere, and pools at Brown Moss. A real conservation priority for the Marches is the restoration of meres to their former oligotrophic or mesotrophic status so that they can support floating water-plantain and other scarce aquatic species. The Bomere complex of meres would be ideal for this, especially if expanded to include former sand and gravel quarries to the west. National Nature Reserve status would help to drive this project forward. Hencott Pool would be a much more challenging site, but restoration here is still worth attempting.

LEAD MINING

Metal ores have been mined at sites scattered across the Marches. Mines on Llanymynech Hill were worked from pre-Roman times onwards for copper, lead and zinc ores. A strange variant of red campion *Silene dioica* with hemispherical leafy cushions and almost stemless flowers has been found on spoil from copper mines in this area.[15] Green malachite was found in Triassic sandstone in the hills of north Shropshire and there were several attempts at mining it. The largest and most successful was near the village of Clive, where it is estimated that 20,000 t of rock yielded 200 t of copper metal.[16] Much the largest area of lead mining in the Marches was in the South West Shropshire Orefield,[17] in the country previously referred to as *Ordovicia*. Within 5 km of the village of Shelve there are the remains of 20 mines, worked during various periods from Roman times onward. As many as 1,000 workers produced more than a tenth of Britain's supplies of lead and up to a quarter of its barytes at the operating peak in the 1870s. There has been no mining since the middle of the 20th century but there is considerable interest in the industrial archaeology of the area[18] and some of the most important mine buildings have been conserved.

The rocks in which the lead ores occur are hard, so many of the adits and other underground mine workings are still open. One of the lead mines was called Batholes and bats still use old mines as hibernacula. The species most often found is the lesser horseshoe bat, but brown long-eared bats are also sometimes recorded, as are four members of the genus *Myotis*: Natterer's, Daubenton's, whiskered and Brandt's bats (Fig. 202). The lesser horseshoe bat is at the edge of its southwesterly range and is classed as endangered. Numbers of them vary considerably between mine workings. A recent study found that adits with air flowing through them were not used and that although a range of temperatures was tolerated, larger numbers of individuals were found in warmer adits and away from the entrances where cooler air penetrates.[19] In contrast, members of the genus *Myotis* occupied workings both with and without through flow of air. This may be because they tend to hibernate in crevices rather than in open positions. Grids through which bats can easily fly have been fitted across adit entrances to protect these hibernacula. Greater horseshoe bats have recently

FIG 202. Lesser horseshoe bat roosting in a mine. (Mike Castle)

been found in mines at Crickheath near Llanymynech, suggesting a possible extension of their southwesterly range.

Of the material removed from the mines, only a small proportion was extractable lead or other useful materials and large spoil mounds were therefore created. The main minerals within these are calcite and quartz, giving the mounds a whitish colour. The largest spoil mounds were at Snailbeach, but these have been smoothed out and covered with soil. Similar mounds remain as prominent features of the landscape; these ideally should be left as they are because of their historical interest and as a long-term ecological experiment. There are good examples at Roman Gravels, The Bog, Pennerley and Tankerville (Fig. 203). The most distinctive feature of these spoil mounds is the slow rate at which plants have colonised and the large areas of bare surface, decades after dumping of spoil ended. Possible contributory factors are the lack of moisture-retaining capacity in the deposits of rock fragments, the lack of phosphate and other mineral nutrients required for plant growth and the toxic levels of lead and other metals.

Where plants have colonised, the sequence resembles a classic primary succession. Algae, lichens and bryophytes spread first over the bare surfaces, followed by sheep's fescue with some common bent and a few ephemerals such as thyme-leaved sandwort *Arenaria serpyllifolia*, hairy bitter-cress *Cardamine hirsuta* and fairy flax. Sites with sheep's fescue are potential habitats for

FIG 203. Lead mine spoil, with sparse vegetation, at Pennerley Mine to the west of the Stiperstones. The contrast with uncontaminated pasture beyond is very marked. (William Allott)

FIG 204. Grayling butterfly on Cow Ridge, on the Long Mynd. There are also strong populations on areas of lead mine spoil. (Danny Beath)

grayling butterflies and huge numbers are sometimes seen where conditions are suitable: a mixture of tufty open turf and bare areas on parched, sunny ground where there is warmth and shelter in summer (Fig. 204). This habitat can persist for long periods after the mines have been abandoned, unless the scruffy appearance and fear of lead toxicity encourage misguided tidying up, as at Snailbeach. Graylings occur on some other sites in southwest Shropshire; perhaps surprisingly, this is usually where there has been human disturbance, such as the construction of Iron Age hill forts. Graylings have become scarce enough to be given BAP priority status. The nearest other populations in England are on the Malvern Hills, so it is important that those of the lead mines and hills of southwest Shropshire are conserved.

Colonisation by woody species does eventually occur on much lead mine spoil, the first species usually being gorse and broom, heathy birch or goat willow scrub coming later. On some spoil mounds where a deeper soil has developed oaks eventually replace the birch. The plants found on these lead spoil heaps are ones that cope with a wide range of habitats, rather than the distinctive metal-tolerant species of similar sites elsewhere in Britain, such as spring sandwort *Minuarta verna* and alpine penny-cress *Thlaspi caerulescens*. This suggests that toxicity may not be the principal problem, though experimental sowings at Roman Gravels and the Bog, in the 1980s, showed much greater root growth with lead/zinc tolerant varieties of sheep's fescue than with non-tolerant varieties.[20] It should also be added that colonisation by plants has hardly occurred at all in places, bare white areas of calcite seeming to persist indefinitely. Variation in the content of toxic metals may explain this. The total metal content of mine spoil from the large bare heap at Snailbeach was found to be 20,500 ppm of zinc and 20,900 ppm of lead.[21] Spoil from bare areas at Tankerville mine also had very elevated total metal contents: 2,590 ppm zinc and 5,790 ppm of lead. Other areas where woodland has developed would no doubt have lower concentrations. Much of the water that percolates through the former lead mines of southwest Shropshire and their spoil heaps drains into Hope Brook. The zinc content of the water is elevated downstream of these inputs and the percentage of aquatic invertebrates that are zinc-tolerant rises considerably, reaching nearly 100 per cent where the stream flows through the village of Minsterley. Below this, Hope Brook discharges into the much larger Rea Brook and because of the dilution of the zinc content, the percentage of zinc-tolerant aquatic invertebrates falls to less than 50 per cent.[22]

IRON SMELTING

Although archaeologists can find traces of smelting in the Marches from the Iron Age onwards, the earliest significant impacts date from the 16th century, when small-scale bloomeries were superseded by blast furnaces. These needed to be located close to the source of iron ore, as well as to limestone for use as a flux, waterpower from a stream or river and charcoal for use as a fuel in the furnace. Two bands of iron ore in the Coal Measures of the Marches were used: pennystone and crawstone.[23] Pennystone consists of ironstone nodules embedded in mudstone. After being mined it was left to weather on the surface until the mudstone softened to clay and the nodules could be removed. Large amounts of waste clay were left, which was said to be 'injurious to vegetation' due to its high sulphite content. The flat-topped mound to the north of the Free Bridge in the Ironbridge Gorge is an example of a waste heap of this type of clay. Old pennystone mines can be recognised by the water leaking from them, as it is stained bright orange with ochre (Fig. 205). Crawstone is sandstone impregnated in bands with iron carbonate. Much less waste resulted from its use, but it had the disadvantage of lying deeper in the sequence of strata and having a higher phosphorus content that remained as a deleterious impurity in iron smelted from it.

Charcoal for iron smelting was made using cordwood from woodland coppiced on an 18-year cycle. Sites of production were called charcoal hearths. Many examples can still be found in coppices in Wyre, consisting of a circular platform about 5 m across. Because charcoal is very resistant to decay, hearths that have not been used for a hundred or more years can still be recognised by the black soil and small charcoal lumps. The naturally acidic soil of the forest is enriched with bases, encouraging the growth of plants such as primrose

FIG 205. Stream water stained red with ochre at Upper Furnace Pool, Coalbrookdale.

Primula vulgaris, wood spurge, false brome and also lily-of-the-valley. A recent Light Detection and Ranging (LIDAR) aerial survey of Wyre has shown many hundreds of hearths. A similar survey of Benthall Edge also revealed traces of charcoal hearths but these were in the form of elliptical depressions, on platforms cut into the steep slope of the woodland. The surrounding soils here are already base-rich so no special flora seems to be associated.

Large areas of coppice were needed to produce the prodigious quantities of charcoal used by blast furnaces. Small furnaces that could be supplied by surrounding areas of coppice were therefore scattered through rural areas of the Marches. On the north side of the Clee Hills there were furnaces at Abdon, Bouldon and Charlcotte for example. One of the most productive furnaces was built during the late 16th century in Downton Gorge and supplied with charcoal from Bringewood Chase and other coppices in north Herefordshire and south Shropshire. It was one of the last charcoal ironworks to close, in about 1810. Coppices in Wyre supplied many furnaces, including those on the Dowles Brook in the forest itself, nearby in Mawley and Cleobury Mortimer, as well as those further afield in the Black Country. Charcoal from Wyre was also used for glass blowing in Stourbridge and Bromsgrove, hop drying in the Teme valley, brine boiling to produce salt around Droitwich and brass making in Bewdley.

Cast iron from furnaces was converted into wrought iron by forges. These also had to be sited on a watercourse to supply power and required large supplies of charcoal. There are records of a forge at Cleobury Mortimer requiring 400 wainloads of charcoal per year in the 17th century for example. Local supplies were therefore needed, but it was also worth transporting cast iron considerable distances from different sources to a forge, as quality was improved by using a mixture. There were forges in rural areas to the south of Shrewsbury and also in the valley of the Tern, including a very productive forge beside the weir on the Tern in what is now Attingham Park.

Even with the scattered distribution of furnaces and forges, and an increase in the area of coppice, there were shortages of charcoal during the 16th and 17th centuries. This did not lead to widespread deforestation as has been suggested. Most coppices used to produce charcoal for furnaces were carefully managed to ensure a continuity of supply and an expansion of agriculture is much more likely to have caused forest clearance. Nevertheless, the impetus is obvious for the experiments conducted by Abraham Darby that led to the first successful smelting of iron using coke. His original blast furnace in Coalbrookdale has been preserved and is part of Ironbridge Gorge Museum. We might now question whether the change from the use of charcoal to a fossil fuel was something to be celebrated. Charcoal making was carbon neutral and sustainable; its use also placed a limit on the production and use of iron. Underground reserves of coal that could be mined and charked to coke were finite and non-renewable. However, they were so abundant that it became possible for individual furnaces to smelt larger quantities of iron than before and for furnaces to be located close to each other in small areas, so that concentrated areas of industry could develop. The production of iron and its use in the industrial revolution could now increase greatly.

Industrial areas developed in the Coalbrookdale coalfield, where there were 232 furnaces and 11 forges by 1873.[24] In the Denbighshire coalfield, Bersham to the west of Wrecsam is another historically important site. A blast furnace was opened there in 1718 and started smelting iron using coke soon afterwards. John Wilkinson took over the works in 1763 and developed a machine for boring cannons from solid metal. This was modified in 1775 to bore cylinders for James Watt's steam engines and, for the 20 years that followed, most of the cylinders for Boulton and Watt engines were from Bersham. These engines were used to provide more powerful pumping of air into blast furnaces than waterpower could, leading to the exponential rise in iron production and industrialisation. It is from the 1770s onwards that anthropogenic rises in atmospheric carbon dioxide concentrations are detectable. The remains of the ironworks at Bersham are now a museum. Wilkinson opened furnaces on a new site at Brymbo to the northwest of Wrecsam and transferred iron production there in the late 18th century. The Brymbo works made iron through the 19th century until the 1880s when local supplies of coal and iron ore were running out. Instead of closing, the works converted to steel production. They were the first steelworks in Britain to use the open-hearth method and the last steelworks to close in the Marches in 1990.

The waste material produced when limestone reacts with impurities in iron ore and charcoal or coke during smelting is called furnace slag. Charcoal contains less sulphur than coke, so less lime was needed during smelting. There are therefore differences in chemical composition between charcoal and coke slag. Mounds of base rich charcoal slag are found at some former furnaces, where it was dumped more than 200 years ago. These undisturbed sites are now tree-covered, as at Charlcotte, to the east of Burwarton; dating from 1670 it now has ash, alder, hazel and hawthorn on steep-sided heaps around the well preserved stone-built furnace (Fig. 206). At the site of Cornbrook Furnace, southeast of Cleehill, there is ash and willow on the stream-side heaps, on which pieces of hard brittle black glass-like charcoal slag are visible. Lumps of coke slag sometimes have an intense blue colour hence the name bluestone. They can also have beautiful green, blue and grey banding – colours due to silicates derived from clay impurities and fine quartz silt or sand in the pennystone ore. Far greater quantities of coke slag were produced than charcoal slag and there are heaps on many furnace sites in both the Coalbrookdale and Denbighshire coalfields. Where these have been undisturbed they are now mostly covered in

FIG 206. Charlcotte Furnace on the right, with heaps of charcoal slag to the left, colonised by ash and hawthorn.

dense hawthorn scrub or woodland dominated by goat willow, birch and ash. Ivy often forms a complete ground cover and grows vigorously into the trees. Hart's-tongue fern is often abundant on moist banks. Where there is ancient woodland nearby, scarce plants can colonise, for example common wintergreen has colonised a slag heap in Lydebrook Dingle, near Coalbrookdale. There are good examples of regeneration on coke slag heaps at the former Old Park Iron Works, now part of Telford Town Park. There is a flat-topped heap of coke slag in the lower part of Lloyds Coppice in the Ironbridge Gorge with lianas of travellers' joy ascending to the tops of ash and goat willow (Fig. 207).

Coke slag is not as abundant on blast furnace sites as might be expected. This is because it proved to be a useful material, especially as ballast on 19th-century railways throughout the Marches and in the 20th century for road surfacing. Between the two world wars, two firms crushed and sold the slag from Blists Hill for roads. Most disused railways in the Marches are now visible in the landscape as narrow linear woodland corridors, often in areas that are not otherwise heavily wooded. The material from which embankments were built determines the tree species that grow on them, ash and goat willow usually dominating on coke slag. In cuttings the underlying rock type is more significant. The presence of coke slag on railway embankments allows plants to thrive that otherwise would not. An example is the disused Tenbury and Bewdley railway in Wyre, where embankments of slag support a diversity of species, including long-stalked crane's-bill *Geranium columbinum*, wild basil *Clinopodium acinos*, soft-leaved sedge *Carex montana*, columbine *Aquilegia vulgaris*, fly honeysuckle *Lonicera xylosteum*, Turkey oak *Quercus cerris*, common wintergreen and deadly nightshade *Atropa belladonna*. Ground flora from any adjacent woodland can rapidly colonise undisturbed track beds. For example, dog's mercury has spread extensively along the former Severn Valley line in woodland near Sheinton (Fig. 208).

COAL MINING

There are five coalfields within the Marches. The Coalbrookdale coalfield has been the most intensively worked and productive. It underlies the area that is now the town of Telford. In addition to coal, mines here produced red clays, ironstone, fireclay, limestone and even bitumen. Part of the Denbighshire coalfield extends from Wrecsam southwards to Oswestry. The three other coalfields, Shrewsbury, Wyre Forest and Clee Hills were worked less intensively in small or short-lived mines.

FIG 207. Dense growth of trees and ground flora on a coke slag heap in Telford Town Park.

FIG 208. Dog's mercury colonising coke slag used on the track bed of a disused section of the Severn Valley Railway between Sheinton and Buildwas.

Coal seams in the Marches are close to horizontal with a maximum dip of about 12 degrees. Surface outcrops were exploited first and then seams close to the surface. Initially this was on a small scale, using bell-pits. A short central shaft was dug into the ground, from which a seam was worked in each direction as far as was deemed safe. The remains of this industry have generally been destroyed by larger scale coal working or by the land being returned to agricultural use, most early miners also being farmers. Where former bell-pits survive, each now consists of a central depression, surrounded by a circular mound of spoil. There are many of them in two areas on the Clee Hills coalfield. These are at Whatsill on Clee Hill and parts of Catherton Common on the northeast slopes of Titterstone Clee. The sides of bell-pits are attractive to sheep, so closely cropped acid grassland often develops, with moonwort, sand spurrey, small cudweed and upright chickweed sometimes present. Small pools in the base of some of these pits contain great crested newts. There are also bell-pits in Workhouse Coppice in Benthall, owned by the Woodland Trust. A distinctive feature of former bell-pits in woodland is that they have mostly been colonised by dense holly thickets (Fig. 209).

By the early 17th century adits were already being excavated into hillsides to reach coal seams. These have invariably collapsed and are marked only by a linear depression, sometimes with seepage of water. Deeper seams were exploited by sinking vertical shafts. Because the labour involved in reaching coal by digging shafts or adits was much greater than with bell-pits, larger areas were worked from each pit entrance, using timber props and pillars of coal to support underground workings. This method of working made the ground

FIG 209. Bell-pit in Workhouse Coppice to the south of Ironbridge Gorge, with snow in the base and around the rim and typical dense growth of holly.

above unstable and prone to irregular subsidence when the pit props or pillars of coal failed. Local collapses create a landscape of water-filled hollows, known as flashes. There are examples in Birch Coppice and Black Hayes to the east of the Ercall. Deep hollows in woodland to the northwest of New Works and to the north of Lawley are reminiscent of kettle holes but were actually formed by mining activity; they now have water in their bases, with much organic matter from fallen leaves. Around Johnstown in the Denbighshire coalfield there are a large number of water-filled hollows, at least some of which were formed by subsidence. Three areas of these ponds at Stryt Las and Hafod have been given composite SSSI and SAC status as they have one of the largest known populations in Britain of great crested newts – more than 250 have been counted on occasions. There are also significant populations of frogs, toads and newts, both smooth and palmate. Amphibians have thrived in this area because the many ponds and habitat between them allows migration and interbreeding. Areas such as this are known as pondscapes. They are increasingly rare and their conservation can be challenging.[25] Great crested newt numbers at Stryt Las and Hafod are now below their peak, because of introduced fish, invasion by *Crassula helmsii* and other problems (Fig. 210).

FIG 210. Pit mounds with silver birch and pools colonised by great crested newts at Hafod, between Ruabon and Wrecsam.

Two to three tonnes of spoil were produced per tonne of coal. As deeper seams of coal were worked, the quantities of spoil increased, so larger pit mounds were created – those in the Coalbrookdale coalfield were typically 3–6 m in height. During the development of Telford, over 3,000 mineshafts were capped, so there were huge numbers of pit mounds covering more than 10 km². The dip in the seams of the Coalbrookdale coalfield is east to southeasterly, so in this direction increasingly deeper mines were needed to reach the coal. The deepest mines were not worked until the middle of the 19th century and these created larger mounds than had been typical, for example Paddock Mound in Dawley. Much of the coal was high in sulphur and ash, so was relatively low in value. The seams were mostly narrow, so were harder to work than in other coalfields. It was not therefore economic to sink shafts deeper than about 300 m. For these reasons and also because exploitation of the Coalbrookdale coalfield had begun early, many mines were worked out by the start of the 20th century. The National Coal Board only took over six collieries in 1948 and only one of these survived beyond the 1960s. This was Granville Colliery, which closed in 1979. Even the most recently abandoned pit mounds have therefore had more than 30 years for natural regeneration of plant and animal communities to occur.

The most interesting pit mounds are the ones on which communities have been allowed to develop naturally. According to classical ecology, the process is primary succession rather than secondary as no soil is present initially, though the pulverised nature of the rock makes plant establishment easier than on solid unweathered rock. The Carboniferous rocks that were brought to the surface and dumped during coal working varied, but shales formed the largest part. These weather to form clays that would be badly drained, were it not for the hummocky topography of the mounds. Colonisation by plants can be slow, particularly where the spoil is acidic due to high sulphur content. A heathy community usually develops after the primary colonisation period, featuring heather, wavy hair-grass, gorse, bilberry and sometimes heath milkwort *Polygala serpyllifolia*. On some of the most challenging sites this community seems to have persisted for some decades, but it may be that it is invariably a transient stage and as no more pit mounds are being created it will disappear. Alternatively, modest intervention could probably conserve areas of this heathland indefinitely. One obvious site would be the former pit mounds in Dawley that is known as Langley Fields. They were levelled for use as sports pitches, but these were too waterlogged to be of use, so heathland restoration was carried out. This started to work remarkably well after some years, with a variety of species colonising, including grass snakes, but the area is now scheduled for building. One reason

FIG 211. Butterflies at Langley Fields of Telford, a site threatened with development: left, dingy skipper and right, green hairstreak (David Williams)

for conservation of heath communities of pit mounds is that bird's-foot trefoil is often part of the community and is the larval foodplant of both dingy skippers and green hairstreaks. These butterflies were at one time common throughout the Coalbrookdale coalfield and though greatly reduced, they are still commoner than elsewhere in the Marches (Fig. 211).

On many mounds, rather than a heathy community developing, less acid conditions allow birch and oak rapidly to colonise, forming scrub and then woodland. The pit mounds that are scattered across the Shrewsbury coalfield are now all wooded, for example the mounds between the road and railway line at Hanwood and beside the road near Asterley. The Hanwood mounds have a dense and diverse covering of ground flora and also vigorous growth of birch, holly and oak; seedling and sapling oaks show that natural regeneration is occurring. At Asterley there are even larger oaks together with holly, but the site is grazed and the ground flora therefore depauperate. Other woody species are sometimes present, including hawthorn, hazel, rowan, ash, sycamore and goat willow.

The ground flora on 20 pit mounds was investigated as a part of a wider survey of woodland in Telford.[26] Soils were acidic on the more recently abandoned mounds, pH ranging from 3.5 to 5.0 with a mean of 4.2. Soil pH was slightly higher on less recently abandoned mounds but was still distinctly acidic. Wavy hair-grass was present at all stages of vegetation development. Heather was often present initially but disappeared as the woodland canopy became denser. Grasses then dominated the ground flora, including common bent and Yorkshire-fog *Holcus lanatus*. On the sites that had been allowed to develop naturally for longest, soil pH ranged from 4 to 6.5 with a mean of 4.6. Birch and oak were the dominant trees and characteristic members of the ground

FIG 212. Yellow archangel flowering on pit mounds at Lightmoor.

flora were creeping soft-grass, velvet bent *Agrostis canina*, broad buckler fern, rosebay willowherb and ivy, so both trees and ground flora start to resemble the upland oak woodland described in Chapter 8. The ground flora on wooded pit mounds typically contains few species, but on the most biodiverse there are wood anemones, yellow archangel *Lamiastrum galeobdolon* (Fig. 212) and greater stitchwort *Stellaria holostrea*. These are the mounds where the soils have the highest pH, probably because the spoil includes material from clay-ironstone containing up to 2 per cent iron carbonate, compared with less than 0.5 per cent in spoil from coal. They may also have been in areas where spoil was tipped into areas of ancient woodland, some of which survived, allowing the pit mounds to be colonised with ancient woodland indicators. Plants of ancient woodland have been deliberately introduced in a few cases, for example in woodland at Nedge Hill in Telford.

Survey work has shown that pit mounds can be valuable habitat for birds.[27] Clear correlations were found between the species present and the type of plant community. Where trees had colonised there were about 30 woodland species including chiffchaffs and blackcaps. Other species were present if there were areas of scrub, such as whitethroats, willow warblers *Phylloscopus trochilus* and garden warblers *Sylvia borin*. Diversity was also increased if there was adjacent open standing water, which is quite common because mounds were often built between furnace pools, or without concern for the natural drainage of an area. Species such as woodpeckers, nuthatches and treecreepers *Certhia familiaris* that require tree holes or dead and dying wood were not generally present on pit mounds, but if areas of woodland are left to mature they will no doubt join the community. Bird diversity was lower where conifers had been planted.

One of the survey sites, Paddock Mound in Dawley, was almost entirely covered by even-aged Scot's pine, planted in the 1920s by redundant miners. The number of species of breeding bird was the lowest of any of the survey sites, but there were still 23, and also some winter visitors such as redpoll *Acanthis flammea* and siskins *Carduelus spinus* that were scarce elsewhere. Sadly, the woodland on Paddock Mound was all clear felled by Telford Council in 2010 and the site was levelled in preparation for building a school, the former school site having been sold for house building.

There are other pit mounds where trees have been planted instead of natural processes being allowed to take their course. On a ring of five large mounds at Madeley Court a mixture of oak and sweet chestnut was planted in the 19th century. The trees have reached an impressive height, showing that growth is not limited by soil conditions. The many saplings on these mounds show that natural regeneration is now occurring. Trees have also been planted at Bonc y-Hafod north of Ruabon, but these are still relatively young and the site still has the characteristics of a plantation. Much more interesting is the large mound at Bryn Alyn, north of Wrecsam, much of which is still developing naturally, with dense colonisation by birches. There are plans for a ski slope here with some movement of spoil to create the required topography, but woodland will be allowed to continue developing on the rest of the mound.

Some pit mound sites have been reprofiled to create level or gently undulating areas of open space. An example is the former Ifton Colliery at St Martin's near Oswestry, which is now Ifton Meadows Local Nature Reserve. In the Wyre Forest coalfield, the sites of Highley and Alveley collieries on opposite sides of the Severn south of Bridgnorth have been developed into the Severn Valley Country Park with planting of trees, sowing of meadows and other examples of what is known as habitat creation. There were suggestions that the largest pit mound in the Marches should be levelled. This is at the former Bersham Colliery near Erddig, to the southwest of Wrecsam (Fig. 213). The mound is visible for many kilometres around and is viewed by some as an eyesore. Colonisation by plants here has been patchy for various reasons. The colliery was the last to close in the Denbighshire coalfield, and indeed in the whole of the Marches in 1986, so there has been less time for natural communities to develop. The mound is much higher and more exposed than most and in places disturbance from recreational use has prevented plants from sealing the surface and beginning soil formation. In 2007 Cadw decided that it should be preserved as a part of the industrial heritage of the area. The headgear, engine house and other pithead buildings have become a mining museum and natural processes of community development will continue on the strangely beautiful pit mound.

FIG 213. Pit mound at the former Bersham Colliery, south of Wrecsam, with scattered birch established, viewed from Erdigg, a country house now owned by the National Trust.

By contrast, in Telford the importance of surviving pit mounds has won scant recognition and many are threatened with clearance. The development corporation had a stated aim of retaining areas where generation of natural communities had been successful, however most areas of pit mounds have been removed to allow the building of industrial and housing estates, shopping centres and roads – all the expected components of a new town. Over 1 million m³ of spoil was removed to level the area where Telford Town Centre was to be built. The material was used to fill a small valley to the east at Hollinswood, where woodland had developed on old pit mounds – an example of 'how green was my valley', where the green had been post- rather than pre-industrial.

There is a continuing drive to use these so-called brownfield sites. A recent example of the destruction of pit mounds took place during the early years of the 21st century in a large area of Ketley to the south of the Wellington–Oakengates railway line. This was part of a government initiative to create a 'millennium village', in this case consisting of over 700 houses. Natural communities had been developing in this area for over a hundred years. Three pit mounds have been left, but as housing will surround each they are unlikely to be of much value for wildlife. Another larger area was used for attempted 'relocation' of acid grassland from pit mounds elsewhere on the site that were removed, but only because previous illegal dumping of waste would have made remediation very expensive. Central government is currently insisting that 25,000 houses have to be sited somewhere in Telford in the coming years and that the human population must be allowed to increase by 100,000. It therefore seems likely that many surviving pit mounds will be lost. Whereas belts of countryside and wild corridors now separate isolated built-up areas, in future there may instead be isolated semi-wild areas in a continuum of housing and industry.

At Lightmoor, to the northeast of Coalbrookdale, there is a fascinating group of old pit mounds and pools, with marshy areas where mining activity has interfered with the natural drainage (Fig. 214). Most of the mounds are of coal waste and are dominated by oak and birch, with wavy hair-grass and heather, but there is also one much rarer mound of waste from fireclay mining with soils that are much richer in bases. The species here are oak and birch, with sycamore, goat

FIG 214. Lightmoor, an area that epitomises the ability of wildlife to return after intense industrial activity, if it is allowed to do so.

willow, rowan, holly, aspen, guelder rose and a diverse ground flora. Lightmoor has a genuinely wild feel, but the relentless advance of housing estates is now not far away. Its future is uncertain and it is therefore imperative for a conservation agency to acquire and manage it. Two areas of very interesting pit mounds lie to the west and north of Lawley; they are mostly wooded with tall oaks, rowans and hawthorns but also have flashes and areas of grassland. These areas are currently on the outskirts of the built-up area of Telford; in many places they would be given green belt protection, but no doubt housing will probably soon spread westwards to them and beyond.

Many other examples could be given of sites worthy of conservation. As so often with distinctive but locally common features, the importance of pit mounds and other post-industrial sites has not been fully recognised. Telford and Wrekin Council's first biodiversity plan made no mention of post-industrial sites. Instead it adopted a formulaic approach with a narrow list of priority species such as great crested newts rather than recognising special features of the natural history of the area. Like other post-industrial or brownfield sites, pit mounds develop much richer wildlife than most greenfield sites, because energy flows along natural food chains rather than into agricultural production. Pit mounds in the Marches could form the subject of interesting research because there are still relatively large numbers of them and because soil pH and other abiotic and biotic factors vary. This research would be all the more revealing because they have been abandoned for varying and in some cases considerable lengths of time. Although limited management is probably advisable to conserve scarce habitats, in most cases pit mounds are best left to develop naturally.

The extraction of coal from deep mines in the Coalbrookdale coalfield has not been economic for decades, but open cast working of shallower seams in the west has continued sporadically. The geological map[28] shows how extensively this has already been done in the area between Telford and the Wrekin. Plant and animal communities have been totally obliterated, as has the geological history recorded in the rocks below, and the industrial archaeology that forms another fascinating overlay on the landscape. Nothing can reverse this damage and all open cast sites are initially at least large biodiversity cold-spots. Some have been returned to agricultural use and what is euphemistically called habitat restoration has been carried out on others. Plantations of trees have mostly failed to thrive and nothing remotely approaching a natural ground flora becomes established, the previous extirpation of vegetation having removed local seed sources. Far preferable to this, if natural habitats are the aim, is a policy of strict non-intervention. Recolonisation may be a slow process, but other post-industrial sites show that it does happen, and that the communities that develop are of

FIG 215. Fir clubmoss is one of three clubmoss species that grew in the 1980s at Stoney Hill. (John Box)

far greater integrity and ecological interest than those designed and paid for by mining companies. It might even be better if topsoil scraped off open cast sites was not returned, allowing scarce species of open infertile conditions to thrive at least for a while. There was considerable excitement among botanists in the early 1980s when three species of clubmoss were found on a site at Stoney Hill near Coalbrookdale, where there had been open cast coal and clay mining in the 1960s[29] (Fig. 215). The spoil varied considerably but parts were very acidic, with a pH as low as 3. Fir clubmoss *Huperzia selago*, alpine clubmoss *Diphasiastrum alpinum* and stag's-horn clubmoss *Lycopodium clavatum* were all recorded on these areas, together with the moss *Racomitrium lanuginosum*. Alpine clubmoss had not been recorded in Shropshire since 1726, when it was found on the Stiperstones and the two other clubmosses are rare plants in the Marches. Despite the interesting flora, most of the Stoney Hill site became a landfill waste dump, and roads were constructed on other parts of it. A small area where the clubmosses grew was left, but birch woodland developed and they were lost. The lesson is clear – open cast mining could create interesting habitats, but it rarely if ever seems to be allowed to do this.

At the time of writing it seems that open cast coal mining is to continue. In the run up to the Copenhagen climate change talks, Westminster politicians gave permission for a large new site on nearly 100 ha on the west side of Telford. The mine, called Huntington Lane, will adjoin part of the Shropshire Hills Area of Outstanding Natural Beauty (Fig. 216). The burning of the coal from the mine will release over 3 million t of carbon dioxide into an already overloaded atmosphere. The economics of coal extraction on this site are dubious, and the real profits are likely to come from building on the site. This will no doubt be justified by the need to house Britain's growing population.

FIG 216. Steam, smoke and early morning mist at Buildwas coal-burning power station in Ironbridge Gorge. (Clywd-Powys Archaeological Trust)

It is hard, given cases such as this, not to become pessimistic about the changes that lie ahead for the Marches. Increases in human population almost inevitably harm landscape and wildlife. Central government has so far failed to provide effective protection and indeed seeks to prevent local communities from resisting population increase and the associated environmental degradation. There is much wildlife to treasure, study and protect in the Marches. Readers of this book can decide whether they feel optimistic about its future. But it is the prerogative of the author to have the last word: we should not treat a description of the natural history of an area as a mere valediction; we should refuse to accept that loss of biodiversity is inevitable and should work as vigorously as possible to conserve and enhance it, in the Marches and elsewhere.

To quote the 160-year-old motto of the Woolhope Naturalists Field Club of Herefordshire: 'Hope on', and 'Hope ever.'

Endnotes

CHAPTER 1

1. Watson, 2002
2. Sylvester, 1969
3. Rowley, 1972
4. Morgan, 2008
5. Evans, 1928
6. Peterken, 2008
7. Feryok, 2001; Hill & Worthington, 2003
8. Housman, 1896

CHAPTER 2

1. Ogier Ward, 1841
2. Toghill, 2006
3. Murchison, 1839, 1854
4. Lapworth & Watts, 1894
5. Webb, 1917
6. Sinker et al., 1985
7. Scard, 1990
8. Leighton, 1841
9. D. C. Smith, unpublished communication, 2008

CHAPTER 3

1. Toghill, 2006
2. Darwin, 1859
3. Salter, 1857
4. Callow & Brasier, 2009
5. Cobbold, 1927
6. Whittard, 1955–67
7. Holland & Bassett, 1989
8. Thackray, 1977
9. Ziegler, 1965
10. Marston, 1882
11. Briggs et al., 1996
12. Rodgerson et al., 2002
13. Edwards & Richardson, 2004
14. Harding, 1998
15. Pentecost et al., 2000
16. Pentecost & Zhaohui, 2002
17. Pentecost et al., 2000
18. Benton et al., 1994

CHAPTER 4

1. Sinker et al., 1985
2. Forrest, 1899
3. Tucker, 2006
4. Tucker, 2006
5. Tucker, 2006
6. Tucker, 2006

7. I. Cheeseborough, 2003, unpublished report for the National Trust
8. Darwin, 1859
9. Darwin, 1859
10. Davis, P. in Davies et al., 2003
11. Watt, 1976
12. Sinker et al., 1985
13. Andrews, 2008
14. Deans et al., 1992
15. Sinker et al., 1985
16. Sinker et al., 1985
17. Timperley, 1947
18. Lawley, 2009a
19. Thorne, 2000
20. Rich & Proctor, 2009
21. Porley & Hodgetts, 2005
22. Pinnock, 2004
23. Smith, 2003; Smith, 2004
24. Smith et al., 2007
25. Smith, 2011

CHAPTER 5

1. Toghill, 2006
2. Darwin, 1887
3. Toghill, 2006
4. Francis, 2009
5. Lawley, 1999
6. Aikin, 1797
7. Forrest, 1899
8. Sinker, 1962

CHAPTER 6

1. Reynolds, 1979
2. Kilinc & Moss, 2002
3. Preston et al., 2002
4. Reynolds, 1979
5. Kilinc & Moss, 2002
6. James et al., 2003
7. Kilinc & Moss, 2002
8. James et al., 2003

9. Hameed et al., 1999
10. Reynolds, 1979
11. Phillips, 1884
12. Reynolds, 1971, 1973
13. Moss, personal communication
14. McGowan et al., 1999
15. Fisher & Barker, 2007; Fisher et al., 2009
16. Moss et al., 1994
17. James et al., 2003
18. Moss et al., 1994
19. Reynolds, 1979
20. Reynolds, 1979
21. Moss, 1998
22. James et al., 2005
23. Barker et al., 2008
24. James et al., 2005
25. Lockton, 2008
26. Whild, 2008
27. Forrest, 1899
28. Smith & Moss, 1994
29. C. R. Goldspink, personal communication, January 2009
30. Goldspink & Barr, 1993
31. Wickenden, 1993
32. Calvert, 2005
33. Sinker, 1962
34. Tansley, 1939
35. Ecoline, 2009
36. Fisher & Barker, 2007
37. Phillips, 1884
38. Whild, 2008
39. Davies, 1997
40. McGowan, 1996
41. Brooks et al., 2001
42. Smith & Moss, 1994

CHAPTER 7

1. Pannett, 1997
2. Hamilton, 1901–4
3. Leighton, 1841
4. Poore & Walker, 1959
5. Tallis, 1973
6. Sainter, 1878

7. Daniels, 2011
8. Gilman, 2000
9. Horton, 2009
10. Hargreaves, 2005; Cuertero Villavilla, 2006
11. Sinker, 1962
12. Sinker, 1962
13. Sinker, 1962
14. Leah et al., 1998

CHAPTER 8

1. Peterken, 1981
2. For more information on NVC, *see* www.jncc.gov.uk/page-4259
3. For more information on the BAP, *see* www.ukbap.org.uk
4. Sinker *et al.*, 1985
5. Leighton, 1841
6. Duffell, 2009
7. Brown, 1988
8. Tansley, 1939
9. Kendrick, 1982
10. Yapp, 1962
11. P. Thompson, unpublished study
12. Pryce, 1983
13. Hickin, 1971
14. Green & Westwood, 2005a, b
15. Boardman, 2007
16. Green & Westwood, 2006
17. Joy, 2006
18. Yapp, 1962
19. Marsh, 1999
20. Bright, 1996
21. Shorten, 1954
22. Richardson, 2000
23. Forrest, 1899
24. Harding, 1996
25. Bradley, 2007
26. Joy, 2006
27. Southcott, 2008
28. Peterken, 1996
29. Turner, 1962
30. Thomson, 1986

31. Pigott & Huntley, 1981
32. Pigott, 1985
33. Hickin 1965, 1971

CHAPTER 9

1. Morton, 1986
2. Mitchell, 1974
3. White, 1998
4. Preston *et al.*, 2002
5. C. D. Pigott, unpublished research
6. Pigott, 1992
7. Leighton, 1841
8. Riley 1975
9. Peterken, 2001
10. Whitehead, 2000
11. Hardy, 1939
12. Webb, 1917
13. Peterken, 1981
14. Preston, 2007

CHAPTER 10

1. Ekwall, 1928; Owen & Morgan, 2007
2. Conradi, 2009
3. Arnold & Macan, 1969
4. Boardman, 2007
5. Boardman, 2005
6. Brian, 1983
7. N. S. Burke, personal communication based on PhD thesis in progress, 2009
8. *see* www.english-nature.org.uk/citation/citation_photo/2000102.pdf (accessed 15 February 2011)
9. Skinner *et al.*, 2003
10. Leighton, 1841
11. C. Wright & C. J. Whittlesea, unpublished data, 2009
12. Scott, 1984
13. Harper, 1990
14. Harper, 1990
15. Swales & O'Hara, 1983

16. Nolan, 1998
17. Bryan *et al.*, 1980
18. Forrest, 1899
19. Pennant, 1784
20. Forrest, 1899
21. Pannett, 1987–8
22. Defra, 2010
23. Kissack, 1982
24. Forrest, 1899
25. *see* www.environment-agency.gov.uk/
    static/documents/Leisure/Midlands_
    byelaws.pdf (accessed 15 February 2011)
26. Brown, 1982
27. Ogier Ward, 1841
28. Hume, 2008
29. Crawford, 2003
30. Forrest, 1899
31. Jeffries, 2003
32. Jeffries, 2003
33. Dovaston, 1829
34. Forrest, 1899
35. Carter & Churchfield, 2006
36. Forrest, 1899
37. Birks, 2008
38. Shropshire Council, 2009

CHAPTER 11

1. Boardman, 2007
2. Sinker *et al.*, 1985
3. Harvey *et al.*, 2002
4. Trueman, 2009
5. Lockton & Whild, 2005
6. Croucher *et al.*, 2007
7. Sinker *et al.*, 1985
8. Braithwaite *et al.*, 2006
9. Fox & Guest, 2003
10. Ratcliffe, 1997
11. Bell & Bell, 1995
12. Lockton & Whild, 2005
13. Natural England, 2009

CHAPTER 12

1. Baugh, 1989
2. Plymley, 1803
3. Parker, 2001
4. Helliwell, 1975
5. Poyner & Mountford, 2005
6. Cameron & Pannett, 1980
7. Cameron *et al.*, 1980
8. Boothby & Hull, 1999
9. Newton, 1971
10. Harmer, 2004
11. Boothby & Hull, 1999
12. Kohler *et al.*, 1989
13. Hollins, 1984
14. Ragg *et al.*, 1984
15. Jones, 1961
16. Leighton, 1841
17. Sinker *et al.*, 1985
18. Parker, 2001
19. Forrest, 1899
20. Dawes & Smith, 2003
21. Forrest, 1899

CHAPTER 13

1. Ratcliffe, 1980
2. Wrench, 2007
3. Lawley, 2009b
4. Formstone, 2005
5. Condry, 1981
6. Cope, 2006
7. Lockton, 2000
8. Wilson, 2008
9. Twigg, 1959
10. Briggs, 1993
11. Lansdown & Wade, 2003
12. Briggs, 1993
13. Lees, 2005
14. Kay *et al.*, 1999
15. Sinker *et al.*, 1985
16. Pearce, 1995
17. Davies & Pearce, 1995; Brown, 2001

18. Brown, 2001
19. Thompson, 2008
20. I. Trueman, personal communication, 2010
21. Smith & Bradshaw, 1972
22. S. Townsend, personal communication, 2010
23. Alfrey & Clark, 1993

24. Trinder, 1996
25. Boothby & Hull, 1999
26. Tobin *et al.*, 1987
27. Bishton, 2003
28. British Geological Survey 'Classic Areas of British Geology', Telford sheet
29. Box & Cossens, 1988

References

Aikin, A. (1797). *Journal of a Tour Through North Wales and Part of Shropshire; with Observations in Mineralogy, and other Branches of Natural History.* J. Johnson, London.

Alfrey, J. & Clark, C. (1993). *The Landscape of Industry: patterns of change in the Ironbridge Gorge.* Routledge, London.

Andrews, E. J. (2008). The effect of sward height in the distribution of *Bolaria selene* (small pearl-bordered fritillary) in Shropshire. MSc dissertation for Birmingham University.

Arnold, F. N. & Macan, T. T. (1969). Studies on the fauna of a Shropshire hill-stream. *Field Studies* **3**, 157–84.

Barker, T., Hatton, J., O'Connor, M., Connor, L. & Moss, B. (2008). Effects of nitrate load on submerged plant biomass and species richness: results of a mesocosm experiment. *Fundamental and Applied Limnology Archiv für Hydrobiologie* **173/2**, 89–100.

Baugh, G. C. (1989). *A Victoria County History of Shropshire Volume IV: agriculture.* Oxford University Press.

Bell, B. D. & Bell, A. P. (1995). Distribution of the introduced alpine newt *Triturus alpestris* and of native *Triturus* species in north Shropshire, England. *Australian Journal of Ecology* **20**, 367–75.

Benton, M. J., Warrington, G., Newell, A. J. & Spencer, P. S. (1994). *A Review of British Middle Triassic Tetrapod Assemblages.* In: *In the Shadow of the Dinosaurs* (Eds Fraser, N. C. & Sues, H.-D.). Cambridge University Press.

Birks, J. D. S. (2008). *The Polecat Survey of Britain 2004–2006. A Report on the Polecat's Distribution, Status and Conservation.* Vincent Wildlife Trust.

Bishton, G. (2003). Breeding birds of Telford and Wrekin Woodland. *The Shropshire Bird Report* **43**, 16–30.

Boardman, P. (2005). *Red Data Book Invertebrates of Shropshire – a compilation and review of data.* Shropshire Biodiversity Partnership.

Boardman, P. (2007). *A Provisional Account and Atlas of the Craneflies of Shropshire.* Pete Boardman, Oswestry.

Boothby, J. & Hull, A. (1999). *Ponds of the Mersey Basin: habitat, status and future.* In: *Ecology and Landscape Development: A History of the Mersey Basin* (Ed. Greenwood, E. F.). Liverpool University Press.

Box, J. D. & Cossens, V. (1988). Three species of clubmoss (Lycopodiaceae) at a lowland station in Shropshire. *Watsonia* **17**, 69–71.

Bradley, C. (2007). The fallow deer of Wyre Forest. *Wyre Forest Study Group Review* **8**, 6–7.

Braithwaite, M. E., Ellis, R. W. & Preston, C. D. (2006). *Change in the British Flora 1987–2004.* BSBI, London.

Brian, A. (1983). The effect of man-made structures on the distribution of plants growing in the River Lugg. *Transactions of the Woolhope Naturalists' Field Club* **XLIV**, 147–64.

Briggs, J. (1993). Wildlife and conservation on the Montgomery Canal. *Shropshire Naturalist* **2**, part 1, 6–11.

Briggs, D. E. G., Siveter, David J. & Siveter, Derek J. (1996). Soft-bodied fossils from a Silurian volcaniclastic deposit. *Nature* **382**, no. 6588, 248–250.

Bright, P. W. (1996). Status and woodland requirements of the dormouse in England. *English Nature Research Report* no. **166**.

Brooks, S. J., Bennion, H. & Birks, H. J. B. (2001). Tracing lake trophic history with a chironomid-total phosphorus inference model. *Freshwater Biology* **46**, 513–33.

Brown, A. G. (1982). *Human Impact on the Former Floodplain Woodlands of the Severn.* In: *Archaeological Aspects of Woodland Ecology* (Eds Bell, M. & Limrey, S.). Oxford. *British Archaeological Report (British Series)* **146**.

Brown, A. G. (1988). The palaeoecology of *Alnus* (alder) and the Postglacial history of floodplain vegetation. Pollen percentages and influx data from the West Midlands, United Kingdom. *New Phytologist* **110**, 425–36.

Brown, I. J. (2001). *West Shropshire Mining Fields.* Tempus, Stroud.

Bryan, K. A., Harper, D. M. & Hellawell, J. M. (1980). Environmental aspects of river augmentation by means of groundwater. *Progress in Water Technology* **13**, 115–26.

Callow, R. H. T & Brasier, M. D. (2009). A solution to Darwin's dilemma of 1859: exceptional preservation on Salter's material from the late Ediacaran Longmyndian Supergroup, England. *Journal of the Geological Society, London* **166**, 1–4.

Calvert, M. (2005). *Reed Warblers at Rostherne Mere.* English Nature, Peterborough.

Cameron, R. A. D. & Pannett, D. J. (1980). Hedgerow shrubs and landscape history: some Shropshire examples. *Field Studies* **5**, 177–94.

Cameron, R. A. D., Down, K. & Pannett, D. J. (1980). Historical and environmental influences on hedgerow snail faunas. *Biological Journal of the Linnean Society* **13**, 75–87.

Carter, P. & Churchfield, S. (2006). *Distribution and Habitat Occurrence of Water Shrews in Great Britain.* Environment Agency, Almondsbury, Bristol.

Cobbold, E. S. (1927). Stratigraphy and geological structure of the Cambrian area of Comley, Shropshire. *Quarterly Journal of the Geological Society* **83** (4), 551–73.

Condry, W. (1981). *The Natural History of Wales.* New Naturalist **66**. Collins, London.

Conradi, P. J. (2009). *At the Bright Hem of God. Radnorshire Pastoral.* Seren Books, Poetry Wales Press Ltd, Bridgend.

Cope, S. (2006). The autecology of *Pilosella petereriana* ssp. *peleteriana* at Breidden Hill, Montgomeryshire. MSc dissertation for the University of Birmingham.

Crawford, A. (2003). *Fourth Otter Survey of England 2000-2002.* Environment Agency, Bristol.

Croucher, P. J. P., Jones, R. M., Searle, J. B. & Oxford, G. S. (2007). Contrasting patterns of hybridisation in large house spiders (*Tegenaria atrica* group, Agelenidae). *Evolution* **61**, part 7: 1622–40.

Cuartero Villavilla, A. (2006). Analysis of the regeneration of the vegetation on Bettisfield Moss National Nature Reserve. Conservation and Utilisation of Plant Genetic Resources. MSc dissertation, University of Birmingham.

Daniels, J. L. (2011). *Fenn's and Whixall Mosses Management Plan.* Natural England.

Darwin, C. D. (1859). *On the Origin of Species by Means of Natural Selection.* John Murray, London.

Darwin, C. (1887). In: *The Life and Letters of Charles Darwin, including an autobiographical chapter* (Ed. Darwin, F.). John Murray, London.

Davies, J. (1997). Using a diatom-based phosphorus transfer function and reconstructed pH as a potential tool for future lake management strategies on the Ellesmere group of meres. Unpublished MSc thesis, Wolverhampton University.

Davies, D. & Pearce, A. (1995). *South West Shropshire Orefield.* In: *Mining in Shropshire* (Ed. Pearce, A.). Shropshire Books.

Davies, P. B. , Packham, J. R. & Musgrove, N. J. (2003). *Bracken Encroachment in Belmore Ring in the Mid-1980s.* In: *The Long Mynd: its Ecology, Past, Present and Future* (Eds Musgrove, N. J., Carty, P., Packham, J. R. & Uff, C.). University of Wolverhampton and the National Trust.

Dawes, A. & Smith, L. (2003). Breeding Lapwing in Shropshire 2003. *Shropshire Bird Report* **43**, 31–6.

Deans, P., Sankey, J., Smith, L., Tucker, J., Whittles, C. & Wright, C. (1992). *An Atlas of the Breeding Birds of Shropshire.* Shropshire Ornithological Society.

Defra (2010). *Eel Management plans for the United Kingdom Severn River Basin District.* Department for Environment Food and Rural Affairs.

Dovaston, J. F. M. (1829). Some account of the water-shrew: a mouse supposed to have been lost for about a century. *Loudon's Magazine of Natural History,* 219–22.

Duffell, M. S. (2009). The distribution and native status of monk's-hood *Aconitum napellus* sens. lat. in Shropshire. MSc dissertation for Birmingham University.

Ecoline (2009). *Proposed Shrewsbury Northwest Relief Road, Hencott Pool, Ramsar and Site of Special Scientific Interest, General Habitat, Botanical and Invertebrate Survey Report.*

Edwards, D. & Richardson J. B. (2004). Silurian and Lower Devonian plant assemblages from the Anglo-Welsh Basin: a palaeobotanical and palynological synthesis. *Geological Journal* **39**, 375–402.

Ekwall, E. (1928). *English River-Names.* Clarendon Press, Oxford.

Evans, E.E. (1928). Historical Geography of the Shropshire–Montgomeryshire Borderland. *Montgomeryshire Collections* **40**, 242–70.

Feryok, M. (2001). *Offa's Dyke.* In: *Mercia the Anglo-Saxon Kingdom of Central England* (Ed. Sarah Zaluckyj). Logaston Press.

Fisher, J. & Barker, T. (2007). Current knowledge of the relative concentrations of nitrogen and phosphorus in the meres of Cheshire and Shropshire. Report for the Natural England **FST19/04/076.**

Fisher, J., Barker, T., James, C. & Clarke, S. (2009). Water quality in chronically nutrient-rich lakes: the example of the Shropshire-Cheshire Meres. *Freshwater Reviews* **2**, 79–99.

Formstone, B. (2005). Bees, wasps and ants recorded from Marford and

Borras Quarries, Wrexham (VC50 Denbighshire) between 1990 and 2005. *Journal of the Lancashire and Cheshire Entomological Society* **129**, 7–25.

Forrest, H. E. (1899). *Fauna of Shrophire*. Wilding, Shrewsbury.

Fox, B. W. & Guest, J. (2003). *The Lichen Flora of Cheshire and the Wirral*. Nepa Books.

Francis, K. (2009). New thoughts of the Origins of Downton Gorge. *Proceedings of the Shropshire Geological Society* **14**, 30–41.

Gilman, K. (2000). *Hydrological assessment of the implications of NNR management at Fenn's, Whixall & Bettisfield Mosses*. Report to English Nature & Countryside Council for Wales.

Goldspink, C. R. & Barr, A. (1903). Fishy goings on in the Meres. *Shropshire Naturalist* **2**, part 1, 12–15.

Green, G. H. & Westwood, B. (2005a). The land or terrestrial caddis (*Enoicyla pusilla*) and Wyre Forest. *Wyre Forest Study Group Review* **6**, 3–9.

Green, G. H. & Westwood, B. (2005b). In search of the land caddis. *British Wildlife* **17**, part 1, 21–6.

Green, G. H. & Westwood, B. (2006). The shining guest ant *Formicoxenus nitidulus* in Wyre Forest. *Wyre Forest Study Group Review 2006* **7**, 9–11.

Hameed, H. A., Kilinc, S., McGowan, S. & Moss, B. (1999). Physiological tests and bioassays: aids or superfluities to the diagnosis of phytoplankton nutrient limitation? A comparative study in the Broads and Meres of England. *European Journal of Phycology* **34**, 253–69.

Hamilton, W. P. (1901–4). The peat of Whixall Moss. *Transactions of the Severn Valley and Caradoc Field Club* **3**, 72–5.

Hardy, E. M. (1939). Studies of the post-glacial history of British vegetation. V. The Shropshire and Flint Maelor Mosses. *New Phytologist* **38**, 364–96.

Harding, B. (1996). Sectional report for mammals. *Transactions of the Woolhope Naturalists' Field Club Herefordshire* **XLVIII**, 617–18.

Harding, B. (1998). Tufa formation today and in the past. *Transactions of the Woolhope Naturalists Field Club Herefordshire* **XLIX**, 170–81.

Hargreaves, S. (2005). A report on the regeneration of vegetation on the Bettisfield Moss National Nature Reserve. Unpublished MSc thesis, University of Birmingham.

Harmer, A. (2004). *Wrecsam Borough Council Freshwater Invertebrate Study*.

Harper, D. M. (1990). The ecology of a lowland sandstone river: the river Perry, Shropshire. *Field Studies* **7**, 451–68.

Harvey, P. R., Nellist, R. D. & Telfer, M. G. (2002). *Provisional Atlas of British Spiders*, Volumes 1 and 2. Biological Records Centre, CEH Monks Wood.

Helliwell, D. R. (1975). The distribution of woodland plant species in some Shropshire hedgerows. *Journal of Biological Conservation* **7**, 61–72.

Hickin, N. E. (1965). *Forest Refreshed – the Autobiographical Notes of a Biologist*. Hutchinson, London.

Hickin, N. E. (1971). *The Natural History of an English Forest: The Wild Life of Wyre*. Hutchinson, London.

Hill, D. & Worthington, M. (2003). *Offa's Dyke History and Guide*. Tempus Publishing, Stroud.

Holland, C. H. & Bassett, M. G. (1989). *A Global Standard for the Silurian System*. National Museum of Wales.

Hollins, A. (1984). *Farmer, the Plough and the Devil: Story of Fordhall Farm, Pioneer of Organic Farming*. Ashgrove Press, Bath.

Horton, K. D. (2009). The effects of rehabilitation management on the vegetation of Fenn's Whixall and

Bettsifield Mosses National Nature Reserve – a cut over lowland raised mire. PhD thesis, University of Wolverhampton.

Housman, A. E. (1896). *A Shropshire Lad*. K. Paul, Trench, Treubner, London.

Hume, C. (2008). *Wetland Vision Technical Document: overview and reporting of project philosophy and technical approach*. The Wetland Vision Partnership.

James, C., Fisher, J. & Moss, B. (2003). Nitrogen driven lakes: the Shropshire and Cheshire Meres? *Archiv für Hydrobiologie* **158**, 249–66.

James, C., Fisher, J., Russell, V., Collings, S. & Moss, B. (2005). Nitrate availability and hydrophyte species richness in shallow lakes. *Freshwater Biology* **50**, 1049–63.

Jeffries, D. J. (2003). *The Water Vole and Mink Survey of Britain 1996-1998 with a History of the Long-term Changes in the Status of Both Species and Their Causes*. The Vincent Wildlife Trust, London.

Jones, E. L. (1961). Agricultural conditions and changes in Herefordshire, 1660-1815. *Transactions of the Woolhope Naturalists' Field Club Herefordshire* **XXXVII**, 32–55.

Joy, J. (2006). Butterflies of the Wyre Forest – the last five years. *Wyre Forest Study Group Review* **7**, 17–20.

Kay, Q. O. N., Jones, R. F. & Jones, R. A. (1999). Biology, genetic variation and conservation of *Luronium natans* (L) Raf. in Britain and Ireland. *Watsonia* **22**, 301–15.

Kendrick, F. M. (1982). Sectional report for botany. *Transactions of the Woolhope Naturalists' Field Club Herefordshire* **XLIV**, 124–5.

Kilinc, S. & Moss, B. (2002). Whitemere, a lake that defies some conventions about nutrients. *Freshwater Biology* **47**, 207–18.

Kissack, K. (1982). *The River Severn*. Terrence Dalton, Lavenham, Suffolk.

Kohler, T., Tucker, T. & Mileto, R. (1989). *Losing Ground in Shropshire*. Shropshire Wildlife Trust, Shrewsbury.

La Touche, J. D. (1884). *A hand-book of the Geology of Shropshire*. Stanford, London.

Lansdown, R. V. & Wade, P. M. (2003). Ecology of the floating water-plantain. *Conserving Natura 2000 Rivers Ecology Series No. 9*, English Nature, Peterborough.

Lapworth C. & Watts, W. W. (1894). The geology of south Shropshire. *Proceedings of the Geologists' Association* **13** (9), 297–355.

Lawley, M. (1999). *A Botanical Stroll Through North Herefordshire*. Herefordshire Botanical Society, Hereford.

Lawley, M. (2009a). *A Bryological Survey of Selected Areas of Wet Ground on the Long Mynd, Shropshire in 2009*. Report for the National Trust.

Lawley, M. (2009b). Bryophytes in Shropshire's quarries and pits. Unpublished report for Shropshire Bioodiversity Partnership.

Leah, M. D., Wells, C. E., Stamper, P., Huckerby, E. & Welch, C. (1998). *The Wetlands of Shropshire and Staffordshire*. Lancaster University Archaeological Unit.

Lees, S. (2005). *Conservation Management Strategy for the Montgomeryshire Canal*. British Waterways Board.

Leighton, W. A. (1841). *A Flora of Shropshire*. John van Voorst, London and John Davies, Shrewsbury.

Lockton, A. (2000). The conservation value of Shropshire's canals. *Shropshire Botanical Society Newsletter* Spring, 9–14.

Lockton, A. (2008). *Nuphar pumila* in Shropshire. *Shropshire Botanical Society Newsletter* Autumn, 8–9.

Lockton, A. J. & Whild, S. (2005). *Rare Plants of Shropshire*. Third edition. Shropshire Botanical Society, Montford Bridge, Shropshire.

Marsh, A. (1999). The national yellow-necked mouse survey. *The Mammal Society Research Report* No. 2.

Marston, A. (1882). *Guide to the Geology of Ludlow.* Privately published, Ludlow.

McGowan, S. (1996). Ancient cyanophyte blooms – studies on the palaeolimnology of White Mere and Colemere. PhD thesis, University of Liverpool.

McGowan, S., Britton, G., Haworth, E. & Moss, B. (1999). Ancient blue-green blooms. *Limnology and Oceanography* **44**, 436–9.

Mitchell, A. (1974). *A Field Guide to the Trees of Britain and Northern Europe.* Collins.

Morgan, R. (2008). *Place-names in the Northern Marches of Wales.* In: *A Commodity of Good Names: essays in honour of Margaret Gelling* (Eds Padel, O. J. and Parsons, D. Y.). Shaun Tyas, Donington, Lincolnshire.

Morton, A. (1986). *Trees of Shropshire.* Airlife Publishing, Shrewsbury.

Moss, B. (1998). *Ecology of Fresh Waters: man and medium, past to future.* Blackwell Science, Oxford.

Moss, B., McGowan, S. & Carvalho, L. (1994). Determination of phytoplankton crops by top-down and bottom-up mechanisms in a group of English lakes, the West Midland meres. *Limnology and Oceanography* **39**, 1020–9.

Murchison, R. I. (1839). *The Silurian System founded on Geological Researches in the Counties of Salop, Hereford, Radnor, Montgomery, Caermarthen, Brecon, Pembroke, Monmouth, Gloucester, Worcester, and Stafford : with descriptions of the coal-fields and overlying formations.* John Murray, Albermarle Street, London.

Murchison, R. I. (1854). *Siluria: a history of the oldest fossiliferous rocks and their foundations, with a brief sketch of the distribution of gold over the Earth.* John Murray, Albermarle Street, London.

Natural England (2009). Climate change impact assessment and response strategy: Shropshire Hills character area. *Natural England report* **E 117R**.

Newton, A. (1971). *Flora of Cheshire.* Cheshire Community Council, Chester.

Nolan, P. A. (1998). River rehabilitation in an urban environment: examples from the Mersey Basin, North West England. *Aquatic Conservation: Marine and Freshwater Ecosystems* **8**, 685–700.

Ogier Ward, T. (1841). *On the Medical Topography of Shrewsbury and its Neighbourhood Comprising a Sketch of its Climate, Geology, Natural Productions, Vital and Medical Statistics, etc.* Deighton, Worcerster.

Owen, H. W. & Morgan, R. (2007). *Dictionary of the Place Names of Wales.* Gwasg Gomer, Llandysul.

Pannett, D. J. (1987–8). Fish weirs of the River Severn. *Folk Life* **26**, 54–64.

Pannett, D. J. (1997). The origin of the old river bed at Shrewsbury. *Shropshire Flora Group Newsletter* **5**, 5–15.

Parker, P. (2001). *A Flora of Weston Lullingfields, Wild Flowers of a Shropshire Country Parish at the Turn of the Millennium.* Shropshire Wildlife Trust, Shrewsbury.

Pearce, A. (1995). *Mining in Shropshire.* Shropshire Books, Shrewsbury.

Pennant, T. (1784). *A Tour of Wales.* Benjamin White, London.

Pentecost, A. & Zhaohui, Z. (2002). Bryophytes of some travertine-depositing sites in France and the UK: relationship with climate and water chemistry. *Journal of Bryology* **24**, 233–41.

Pentecost, A., Viles, H. A., Goudie A. S. & Keen, D. H. (2000). The Travertine deposit at Shelsley Walsh, Hereford and Worcester. *Transactions of the Woolhope Naturalists' Field Club Herefordshire* **L**, 25–36.

Peterken, G. F. (1981). *Woodland Conservation*

and Management. Chapman & Hall, London & New York.

Peterken, G. F. (1996). *Natural Woodland. Ecology and Conservation in Northern Temperate Regions.* Cambridge University Press, Cambridge.

Peterken, G. F. (2001). Ecological evaluation of woodlands in the Severn Gorge Development of the Severn Gorge. Unpublished report for the Severn Gorge Countryside Trust.

Peterken, G. F. (2008). *Wye Valley. New Naturalist No. 105.* HarperCollins, London.

Phillips, W. (1884). The breaking of the Shropshire meres. *Transactions of the Shropshire Archeological and Natural History Society* 7, 1–24.

Pigott, C. D. (1985). Selective damage to tree-seedlings by bank voles (*Clethrionomys glareolus*). *Oecologia* (Berlin) 67, 367–71.

Pigott, C. D. (1992). The clones of common lime (*Tilia* x *vulgaris* Hayne) planted in England during the seventeenth and eighteenth centuries. *New Phytologist* 121, 487–93.

Pigott, C. D. & Huntley, J. O. (1981). Factors controlling the distribution of *Tilia cordata* at the northern limits of its geographical range III. Nature and causes of seed sterility. *New Phytologist* 87, 817–39.

Pinnock, A. L. (2004). An investigation of the age and growth cycle of the hawthorn trees of the Long Mynd. Unpublished thesis, University of Wolverhampton.

Plymley, J. (1803). *General View of Shropshire Agriculture.* Board of Agriculture, London.

Poore, M. E. D. & Walker, D. (1959). Wybunbury Moss, Cheshire. *Mem. and Proc. Manchester Lit. and Phil. Soc.* 101, 72–5.

Porley, R. & Hodgetts, N. (2005). *Mosses and Liverworts. New Naturalist No. 97.* HarperCollins, London.

Poyner D. R. & Mountford E. P. (2005). Long term patterns of land use, evolution of the fieldscape and hedge composition in the parish of Highley. *Transactions of the Shropshire Archaeological and Historical Society* 80, 17–51.

Preston, C. (2007). *Overview from the Director. Shropshire Wildlife.* Winter 2007. Shropshire Wildlife Trust, Shrewsbury.

Preston, C. D., Pearman, D. A. & Dines, T. D. (2002). *New Atlas of the British and Irish Flora.* Oxford University Press.

Pryce, M. W. (1983). Sectional report for entomology. *Transactions of the Woolhope Naturalists' Field Club Herefordshire* XLIV, 258–62.

Ragg, J. M., Beard, G. R., George, H., Heaven, F. W., Hollis, J. M., Jones, R. J. A., Palmer, R. C., Reeve, M. J., Robson, J. D. & Whitfield, W. A. D. (1984). Soils and their use in Midlands and Western England. *Soil Survey of England and Wales Bulletin* No. 12.

Ratcliffe, D. (1997). *The Raven.* T. and A. D. Poyser, London.

Reynolds, C. S. (1971). The ecology of the planktonic blue-green algae in the North Shropshire meres, England. *Field Studies* 3, 409–32.

Reynolds, C. S. (1973). Growth and buoyancy of *Microcystis aeruginosas* Kütz. emend. Elnkin in a shallow eutrophic lake. *Proceedings of the Royal Society, London, Series B* 184, 29–50.

Reynolds, C. S. (1979). The limnology of the eutrophic meres of the Shropshire–Cheshire Plain. *Field Studies* 5, 93–173.

Rich, T. C. G. & Proctor, M. C. F. (2009). Some new British and Irish *Sorbus* L. Taxa (Rosaceae). *Watsonia* 27, 207–16.

Richardson, P. (2000). *Distribution Atlas of Bats in Britain and Ireland 1980–1999.* Bat

Conservation Trust, London.

Riley, G. (1975). *The World's Wonder Show. The 100-year Story of the Shrewsbury Flower Show*. Shropshire Horticultural Society, Shrewsbury.

Rodgerson, E. C. W., Edwards, D., Axe, L. & Davies, K. L. (2002). A new embryophyte from the Upper Silurian of Shropshire, England. *Special Papers in Palaeontology* **67**, 233–49.

Rowley, T. (1972). *The Shropshire Landscape*. Hodder & Stoughton, London.

Sainter, J. D. (1878). *Scientific Rambles Round Macclesfield*. Swinnerton & Brown, Macclesfield.

Salter, J. W. (1857). On annelide burrows and surface markings from the Cambrian rocks of the Longmynd. *Quarterly Journal of the Geological Society of London* **13**, 199–207.

Scard, M. A. (1990). *The Building Stones of Shropshire*. Swan Hill Press, Shrewsbury.

Scott. T. A. (1984). Vegetation as a factor affecting river bank erosion on three rivers in mid-Wales. *Nature in Wales* **3**, 65–8.

Shorten, M. (1954). *Squirrels*. Collins New Naturalist Monographs.

Shropshire Council (2009). *Teme River Water Friendly Farming Good Practice Guide*.

Sinker, C. A. (1962). The North Shropshire meres and mosses, a background for ecologists. *Field Studies* **1**(4), 101–38.

Sinker, C. A., Packham, J. R., Trueman, I. C., Oswald, P. H., Perring, F. H. & Prestwood, W. V. (1985). *Ecological Flora of the Shropshire Region*. Shropshire Trust for Nature Conservation, Shrewsbury.

Skinner, A., Young, M. & Hastie, L. (2003). Ecology of the freshwater pearl mussel. *Conserving Natura 2000. Rivers Ecology Series* no. **2**. English Nature, Peterborough.

Smith, L. (2003). *Upland Birds of the Long Mynd (1994-98)*. Report of the Long Mynd Breeding Bird Project.

Smith, L. (2004). *Decline of Ground Nesting Birds on the Long Mynd 1995–2004*. Report of the Long Mynd Breeding Bird Project.

Smith, L. (2011, in preparation). *Upland Birds of the Long Mynd*. Report of the Long Mynd Breeding Bird Project.

Smith, L., Carty, P. & Uff, C. (2007). *Wild Mynd Biology and Wildlife of the Long Mynd*. Hobby Publications for the National Trust.

Smith, R. A. H. & Bradshaw, A. D. (1972). Stabilisation of toxic mine wastes by the use of tolerant plant populations. *Transactions of the Institute of Mining and Metallurgy Sector A* **81**, 230–7. Hobby Publications

Smith, P. & Moss, B. (1994). *The Role of Fish in the Management of Freshwater Sites of Special Interest*. Final Report to English Nature, Contract F72-06-38.

Southcott, A. (2008). The impact of deer browsing on coppiced vegetation at the Wyre Forest. *Wyre Forest Study Group Review* **8**, 42–6.

Swales, S. & O'Hara, K. (1983). A short-term study of the effects of a habitat improvement programme on the distribution and abundance of fish stocks in a small lowland river in Shropshire. *Fish. Mgmt* **14**, 135–44.

Sylvester, D. (1969). *The Rural Landscape of the Welsh Borderland*. Macmillan, London

Tallis, J. H. (1973). The terrestrialisation of lake basins in North Cheshire, with special reference to the development of a Schwingmoor structure. *Journal of Ecology* **61**, 537–67.

Tansley, A. G. (1939). *The British Islands and their Vegetation*. Cambridge University Press.

Thackray, J. C. (1977). T. T. Lewis and Murchison's Silurian System. *Transactions of the Woolhope Naturalists' Field Club Herefordshire* **XLII**, 186–93.

Thompson, S. (2008). What factors influence bat hibernacula in Shropshire's underground mining sites and adits? Unpublished BSc dissertation, Worcester University.

Thomson, P. (1986). Sectional Report for Botany. *Transactions of the Woolhope Naturalists' Field Club Herefordshire* **LL**, 519–29.

Thorne, A. K. (2000). Grassland survey of the Long Mynd common land. Unpublished survey for the National Trust.

Timperley, H. W. (1947). *Shropshire Hills.* J. M. Dent & Sons, London.

Tobin, R. W., Packham, J. R. & Willis, A. J. (1987). The woodlands of Telford New Town: their history, variation and conservation. *Field Studies* **6**, 589–616.

Toghill, P. (2006). *Geology of Shropshire.* Second edition. The Crowood Press.

Trinder, B. (1996). *Industrial Archaeology of Shropshire.* Phillimore.

Trueman, I. (2009). Plant distribution in Shropshire. *Shropshire Wildlife*, Winter 2009, Shropshire Wildlife Trust, Shrewsbury.

Tucker, J. (2006). *Skylarks and Meadow Pipits on the Long Mynd, Shropshire, 1996–2004. Are their population sizes changing?* Report for the National Trust. Lanius, Aston on Clun.

Turner, J. (1962). The *Tilia* decline, and anthropogenic interpretation. *New Phytologist* **61**, 328–41.

Twigg, H. M. (1959). Freshwater studies in the Shropshire Union Canal. *Field Studies* **1**, 116–42.

Watson, M. (2002). *Shropshire: An Archaeological Guide.* Shropshire Books.

Watt, A. S. (1976). The ecological status of bracken. *Botanical Journal of the Linnean Society* **73**, 217–39.

Webb, M. (1917). *Gone to Earth.* Constable, London.

Whild, S. J. (2008). Detecting change in the aquatic vegetation of the West Midlands meres of Great Britain. Unpublished PhD thesis, University of Birmingham.

White, J. (1998). Estimating the age of large and veteran trees in Britain. Forestry Commission Information Note, **12**. Forestry Commission, Edinburgh.

Whitehead, D. (2000). *Brampton Bryan Park, Herefordshire: A Documentary History.* In: *A Herefordshire Miscellany, The Sesquicentennial Woolhope Book.* (Eds Whitehead, D. & Eisel, J.). Lapridge Publications, Hereford.

Whittard, W. F. (1955–67). *The Ordovician Trilobites of the Shelve Inlier, West Shropshire.* Palaeontographical Society, London.

Wickenden, C. A. J. (1993). A summary of the results of research into the fauna, sediment characteristics and bioturbation activity on the littoral of Cole Mere, Shropshire. Unpublished BSc thesis, Wolverhampton University.

Wilson, E.A. (2008). The ramblings of a Shropshire Naturalist. Unpublished memoirs lodged with Ellesmere Library.

Wrench, D. (2007). *Shropshire Quarries: Positive Action for the Future.* Shropshire County Council, Shrewsbury.

Yapp, W. B. (1962). *Birds and Woods.* Oxford University Press.

Zielger, A. M. (1965). Silurian marine communities and their environmental significance. *Nature* **207**, 270–2.

Indexes

lichen, aquatic, *Staurothele fissa* 291
aquatic, *Verrucaria aethiobola* 291
epiphytic, *Anaptychia ciliaris* 335, **336**
Caloplaca lucifuga 284
Cetraria aculeata 121
Cladonia arbuscula 105
C. sub-cervicornis 105
Lasalia pustulata 121
Lecanora polytropa 121
Lecidea nylanderi 284
Lepraria incana 284
Lobaria amplissima 284
L. pulmonaria 284
Parmelia omphalodes 118
P. saxatilis 118
Porpidia crustulata 119
P. macrocarpa 119
Protoparmelia oleagina 284
Pseudovernia furfuracea 119
Stereocaulon vesuvianum 121
woolly (*Racomitrium lanuginosum*) **121**, 403
Xanthoparmelia conspersa 119
lily-of-the-valley (*Convallaria majalis*) 127, 238–9, 389
lime, large-leaved (*Tilia platyphyllos*) 126, **127**, 230, 269, 276, **277**
small-leaved (*Tilia cordata*) 126, **127**, 230, 257–8, 269, 276, 277
Limenitis camilla (white admiral butterfly) 245, 343
Limnephilus luridus (caddis fly) 198
limpet, river (*Ancylus fluviatilis*) 305–6
Limuloides (xiphosuran eurypterid) 60
ling (*Calluna vulgaris*) 132, 197, 201, 218, 226 *see also* heather (*Calluna vulgaris*)
Lingula lewisi (silurian brachiopod) **55**, 58
linnet (*Carduelis cannabina*) 374
Linum catharticum (fairy flax) 359, 386
Lipsothrix errans (cranefly) 295
nervosa (cranefly) 295
nobilis (cranefly) 295
remota (cranefly) **295**
liquorice, wild (*Astragalus glycyphyllos*) 374
Lissotriton helveticus (palmate newt) 203, 355, 356, 370, 395
vulgaris (smooth newt) 355, 356, 370, 395
Listera ovata (common twayblades) 368, 374
Lithospermum officinale (common gromwell) 369
Littorella uniflora (shoreweed) 143, 156

liverwort, *Jamesoniella undulifolia* **101, 102**
Odontoschisma sphagni 214
Scapania undulata 291
leafy, *Gymnomitrium obtusum* 121
leafy, *Lepidozia cupressina* 120
leafy, *Marsupella* 121
lizard, common (*Zootoca vivipera*) 203
loach, stone (*Barbatula barbatula*) 298, 307
Lobaria amplissima (lichen) 284
pulmonaria (lichen) 284
lobelia, water (*Lobelia dortmanna*) 156, 173
Lobelia dortmanna (water lobelia) 156, 173
Lochmaea suturalis (heather beetle) 90
Lonicera periclymenum (honeysuckle) 228, 245, 249
xylosteum (fly honeysuckle) 392
loosestrife, purple (*Lythrum salicaria*) 307, 319
lords-and-ladies (*Arum maculatum*) 230
Lotus corniculatus (bird's foot trefoil) 99, 132, 133, 246, 397
Loxia curvirostra (cross bill) 262
Lullula arborea (woodlark) 342
Luronium natans (floating water plantain) 126, 170, 173, 323, 382, 384
Luscinia megarhynchos (nightingale) 343
Lutra lutra (otter) 163, 233, 324–5, 326, 379
Lycaena phlaeas (small copper butterfly) 133
Lychnis flos-cuculi (ragged-robin) 180, 357, 358
viscaria (sticky catchfly) 105, 375, 376
Lycopodium clavatum (stag's-horn clubmoss) 403
Lymexylon navale (beetle) 284
Lysimachia nemorum (yellow pimpernel) 236
Lythrum salicaria (purple loosestrife) 307, 319

macroalga, red freshwater (*Lemanea mammilosa*) 291
male-fern, mountain (*Drypoteris oreades*) 122
scaly (*Dryopteris affinis*) 122
mallard (*Anas platyrhynchos*) 165, 203
Malus sylvestris (crab apple) 230, 352
mammoth, woolly (*Mammuthus primigenius*) **113**
Mammuthus primigenius (woolly mammoth) **113**
Maniola jurtina (meadow brown butterfly) 358
maple, celtic (*Acer buergerianum*) 281
field (*Acer campestre*) 230, 232, **351**, 352
Norway (*Acer platanoides*) 368

GENERAL INDEX

The New Naturalist Library